Heinrich August Wilhelm Meyer

Critical and exegetical handbook to the Gospel of Matthew tr. from the 6th ed. of the German

Vol. 2

Heinrich August Wilhelm Meyer

Critical and exegetical handbook to the Gospel of Matthew tr. from the 6th ed. of the German
Vol. 2

ISBN/EAN: 9783337714239

Printed in Europe, USA, Canada, Australia, Japan

Cover: Foto ©ninafisch / pixelio.de

More available books at **www.hansebooks.com**

CRITICAL AND EXEGETICAL

COMMENTARY

ON

THE NEW TESTAMENT.

BY

HEINRICH AUGUST WILHELM MEYER, Th.D.,

OBERCONSISTORIALRATH, HANNOVER.

From the German, with the Sanction of the Author.

THE TRANSLATION REVISED AND EDITED BY

WILLIAM P. DICKSON, D.D.,

AND

WILLIAM STEWART, D.D.

PART I.

THE GOSPEL OF ST. MATTHEW.

VOL. II.

EDINBURGH:

T. & T. CLARK, 38 GEORGE STREET.

MDCCCLXXIX.

PRINTED BY MORRISON AND GIBB,

FOR

T. & T. CLARK, EDINBURGH.

LONDON, . HAMILTON, ADAMS, AND CO.

DUBLIN, ... ROBERTSON AND CO.

NEW YORK, . . . SCRIBNER AND WELFORD.

CRITICAL AND EXEGETICAL

HANDBOOK

TO

THE GOSPEL OF MATTHEW.

BY

HEINRICH AUGUST WILHELM MEYER, Th.D.,

OBERCONSISTORIALRATH, HANNOVER.

TRANSLATED FROM THE SIXTH EDITION OF THE GERMAN BY
REV. PETER CHRISTIE.

THE TRANSLATION REVISED AND EDITED BY

WILLIAM STEWART, D.D.,

PROFESSOR OF BIBLICAL CRITICISM IN THE UNIVERSITY OF GLASGOW.

VOL. II.

EDINBURGH:
T. & T. CLARK, 38 GEORGE STREET.
MDCCCLXXIX.

PREFATORY NOTE.

A S Dr. Crombie has been prevented by other engagements from continuing his co-operation with me in the revision and editing of this series of translations, I have asked my esteemed colleague, Dr. Stewart, to take part in it. He has kindly consented to do so; and he has revised, and seen through the press, the present volume, with the exception of a few pages at the beginning which I had previously looked over. I learn from him that the translation has been executed with care and skill by Mr. Christie.

Mr. Christie desires me to mention that at the time of preparing his translation of the earlier portion of the Commentary on Matthew (from chapter vi. onward) he was not aware of the mode of rendering, which had been adopted in the previous volumes, for Dr. Meyer's references to other portions of his own Commentary (*e.g.* " comp. on Luke xvi. 7 ;" " see on Rom. viii. 5 "); and he requests that, in conformity to it, the word " note " inserted by him in such cases may be held as deleted, since the references are, in general, to the text of the commentary itself, and not to the notes or Remarks appended (except when so specified).

The following important work ought to have been included in the " Exegetical Literature " prefixed to vol. I. :—

WEISS (Bernhard): Das Matthäusevangelium und seine Lukas-Parallelen.   8°, Halle, 1876.

WILLIAM P. DICKSON.

GLASGOW COLLEGE, *February* 1879.

GOSPEL OF MATTHEW.

CHAPTER XVIII.

VER. 1. ὥρᾳ] Lachm.: ἡμέρᾳ, which Fritzsche has adopted, against decisive evidence; although ancient, since both readings are found as early as the time of Origen, ἡμέρᾳ is a gloss instead of ὥρᾳ, as there appeared to be nothing in the context to which the latter might be supposed to refer. — Ver. 4. ταπεινώσῃ] The future ταπεινώσει is, with Lachm. and Tisch., to be adopted on decisive evidence. — Ver. 6. εἰς τὸν τρ.] for εἰς Elz. has ἐπί, while Lachm. and Tisch. 8 read περί. Only εἰς and περί have anything like important testimony in their favour. But περί is taken from Mark ix. 42; Luke xvii. 2. — Ver. 7. On weighty evidence we should follow Lachm. in deleting ἐστιν after γάρ, and ἐκείνῳ in the next clause, as words that might naturally have been inserted; Tisch. 8 has deleted ἐστιν only. — Ver. 8. αὐτά] B D L ℵ, min. vss. and Fathers: αὐτόν. So Lachm. and Tisch. correctly; αὐτά is an emendation to include both.—Further on Lachm. and Tisch. 8 have κυλλὸν ἢ χωλόν, following B ℵ, Vulg. It.; a transposition to suit χείρ and πούς. — Ver. 10. The evidence is too weak to warrant us in substituting ἐν τῷ οὐρανῷ (so Lachm. in brackets) for the first ἐν οὐρανοῖς; still weaker is the evidence in favour of omitting the words, although they are omitted at an early period (as early as the time of Clem. Or. Syr. ?). — Ver. 11. This verse does not occur in B L* ℵ, 1*, 13, 33, Copt. ·Sahid. Syrjer. Aeth. (cod. 1), Eus. Or. Hil. Jer. Juv. Deleted by Lachm. and Tisch.; condemned also by Rinck. Already suspected by Griesb. to have been an interpolation from Luke xix. 10, which in fact it is, considering how much evidence there is against it, and considering, on the other hand, that, if it had been genuine, there was no obvious motive on exegetical grounds for the omission. — Ver. 12. ἀφείς . . . πορευθείς] Lachm.: ἀφήσει . . . καὶ πορευθείς, following B D L, min. Vulg. It. (of which, however, D, Vulg. have ἀφήσιν, and D, πορευόμενος). Exegetical analysis, in order to remove ambiguity as to the connection. — Ver. 14. εἷς] Lachm. and Tisch.: ἕν, following B D L M* ℵ, min. Altered to εἷς in accordance with ver. 10; while πατρός μου, which Lachm. substitutes for πατρ. ὑμῶν (following B F H J, min. vss. Or.), is to be regarded in the same light. — Ver. 15. εἰς σέ] deleted by Lachm. and Tisch. 8, after B ℵ, 1, 22, 234*, Sahid. Or. Cyr. Bas. This evidence is too weak, especially as the omission of ΕΙΣΣΕ might easily enough have happened from its following ΗΣΗ (ἁμαρτήσῃ), while it is further to be borne in mind that, in what goes before, it was sin in general, not merely an offence, that was in question. The εἰς σέ, which is here genuine, was inserted from our passage into Luke xvii. 3, Elz. — ἔλεγξον] Elz., Scholz: καὶ ἔλ., against B C ℵ and many min. vss. and Fathers. The καί was inserted as a connective particle. — Ver. 19. πάλιν ἀμήν] Elz. (so also Griesb. Scholz, Fritzsche, Rinck, Tisch. 8) has merely πάλιν, and Lachm., following min. only (B being erroneously quoted), has merely ἀμήν. But the attestation for πάλιν ἀμήν (Tisch. 7) is about equal in weight (incl. B) to that in favour of the simple πάλιν (incl. ℵ), and one of the words might easily enough have been omitted from the combination not occurring anywhere else. — συμφωνήσωσιν] Seeing that the future συμφωνήσουσιν is supported by the preponderating evidence of B D E H I L V Δ ℵ, min., and seeing, on the other hand, that it might very readily have been supplanted by the subjunctive as being the mood most in accordance with the usual construction, it is, with Tisch., to be adopted as the correct reading. — Ver. 24. προσηνέχθη] Lachm. and Tisch. 7: προσήχθη, following B D Or. Correctly; this and Luke ix. 41 are the only instances in which προσάγειν occurs in the Gospels, προσφέρειν being the form most familiar to the copyists. — Ver. 25. εἶχε] Lachm. and Tisch. 7: ἔχει, following only B, min. Or.; but it is to be preferred, since to the mechanical transcribers the present would doubtless seem to be improper. — Ver. 26.] κύριε before μακρ. is to be regarded as interpolated, being omitted by B D, min. Vulg. codd. of It. Syr^cur Or. Chrys. Lucif., and deleted by Lachm. and Tisch. — Ver. 27. ἐκείνου] omitted by Lachm., only after B, min., as is also ἐκεῖνος, ver. 28, only after B. — Ver. 28. μοι] not found in the more weighty witnesses; deleted by Lachm. and Tisch. An interpolation. — εἴ τι] Elz.: ὅ, τι, against decisive evidence. Erroneous emendation. — Ver. 29. αὐτοῦ] Elz. Fritzsche, Schulz, Scholz, Tisch. 7, insert εἰς τοὺς πόδας αὐτοῦ, which, however, is omitted by B C* D G L Δ ℵ, min. Copt. Sahid. Aeth. Syr^cur

It. (Brix. excepted) Vulg. Or. Lucif. Gloss on the simple πεσών. In regard to εἰς, comp. John xi. 32, *al.* — πάντα] Deleted by Matth., Scholz, Tisch., on preponderating evidence; bracketed by Lachm. It is a mechanical interpolation from ver. 26. — Ver. 31. For the first γενόμενα Fritzsche and Tisch. substitute γινόμενα, following only D L א**, min. Vulg. It. Chrys. Lucif., but correctly. The transcribers failed to notice the difference of meaning. — For αὐτῶν or αὐτῶν we should, with Lachm. and Tisch., read ἑαυτῶν, upon decisive evidence; the reflexive reference of the pronoun was overlooked, as was often the case. — Ver. 34. αὐτῷ] not found in B D א**, min. vss. Lachm.; but it may easily enough have been left out in conformity with ver. 30. — Ver. 35. ὑμῶν] Elz. Fritzsche, Schulz, Scholz insert τὰ παραπτώματα αὐτῶν, which is not found in B D L א, min. and several vss. and Fathers. Gloss from vi. 14, 15; Mark xi. 25, 26. — But ἐπουράνιος, for which Fritzsche, Lachm. Tisch. 8 substitute οὐράνιος (B C** D K L Π א, min. Or. Damasc.), is to be retained, all the more that the expression ὁ πατὴρ ὁ ἐπουρ. occurs nowhere else, though we frequently find ὁ π. ὁ οὐράνιος.

Ver. 1. Ἐν ἐκείνῃ τῇ ὥρᾳ] the account of Matthew, which is throughout more original in essential matters than Mark ix. 33 ff. and Luke ix. 46 ff., bears this impress no less in this definite note of time : *in that hour*, namely, when Jesus was holding the above conversation with Peter. — τίς ἄρα] *quis igitur* (see Klotz, *ad Devar.* p. 176). The question, according to Matthew (in Mark otherwise), is suggested *by the consideration of the circumstances:* Who, *as things stand*, is, etc.; for one of them had just been peculiarly honoured, and that for the second time, by the part he was called upon to take in a special miracle. Euthymius Zigabenus says well: ἀνθρώπινόν τι τότε πεπόνθασιν οἱ μαθηταί. — μείζων] *greater* than the other disciples in rank and power. — ἐστίν] they speak as though the approaching Messianic kingdom were *already present.* Comp. xx. 21.

Ver. 2. Παιδίον] According to Nicephorus, ii. 35, the child in question is alleged to have been St. Ignatius. Chrysostom correctly observes that it is a *little* child (σφόδρα παιδίον); τὸ γὰρ τοιοῦτον παιδίον καὶ ἀπονοίας καὶ δοξομανίας κ. βασκανίας κ. φιλονεικείας κ. πάντων τῶν τοιούτων ἀπήλλακται παθῶν, καὶ πολλὰς ἔχον τὰς ἀρετάς, ἀφέλειαν, ταπεινοφ-

ροσύνην, ἀπραγμοσύνην, ἐπ᾽ οὐδενὶ τούτων ἐπαίρεται. Comp.
Mark ix. 36 ; Luke ix. 47.

Ver. 3. Εἴ τις ἀπέχεται τῶν προαιρετικῶν παθῶν, γίνεται
ὡς τὰ παιδία, κτώμενος δι᾽ ἀσκήσεως, ἅπερ ἔχουσι τὰ παιδία
ἐξ ἀφελείας, Euthymius Zigabenus. — *To turn round* (στρα-
φῆτε, representing the μετάνοια under the idea of turning
round upon a road), *and to acquire a moral disposition similar
to the nature of little children*—such is the condition, without
complying with which you will assuredly not (οὐ μή) *enter*,
far less be able to obtain a high position in, the Messianic
kingdom about to be established. The *same* truth is presented
under a *kindred* figure and in a wider sense in John iii. 3,
5 ff. ; the divine agent in this moral change, in which child-
like *qualities* assume the character of manly *virtues*, is the Holy
Spirit; comp. Luke xi. 13, ix. 55.

Ver. 4. Inference from the general principle of ver. 3 to
the special child-like quality in which the disciples were
deficient, as well as to the special subject of their question.
If your entering the future Messianic kingdom at all is determined by your returning again to a child-like frame of mind,
then above all must you acquire, through humble self-abase-
ment, the *unassuming* character of this child, in order to
be *greater* than others in the Messiah's kingdom. — ὅστις]
quicunque ; " de *individuo,* de quo quaerebant, non respondet,"
Bengel.   In what follows ταπεινώσει is emphatic, and accordingly stands near the beginning of the sentence. Had the
subjunctive been critically certain, we should not have had to
borrow ἐάν from the second part of the statement (Fritzsche),
but rather to observe the distinction in the manner of presenting the idea, according to which the insertion of ἄν marks
the presupposition as conditioned. The *future* assumes the
action as *actually* occurring in the future ; while the *subjunctive* after the relative *without* ἄν keeps the future realization
still within the domain of thought, without, however, conceiving
of the realization as conditioned (ἄν).   For this usage among
Attic prose writers, see Kühner, *ad Xen. Mcm.* i. 6. 13.—
Moreover, the words of vv. 3, 4, inasmuch as they are essentially
connected with the question of the disciples, are certainly

original, not an anticipation of xix. 13 ff. (Holtzmann), and dispose us to prefer the account of Matthew to that of Mark or Luke.

Ver. 5. Comp. Mark ix. 37 ; Luke ix. 47. The question of the disciples has been answered. But His eye having lighted upon this child who happened to be present, Jesus now seizes the opportunity of inculcating upon them the duty of *taking* an affectionate *interest in* such little ones,—an exhortation, of which the jealous and ambitious spirit evinced by their question in ver. 1 must have shown they stood but too much in need. — παιδίον τοιοῦτον] *such a little child,* i.e. according to the context, not a literal *child* (Bengel, Paulus, Neander, de Wette, Arnoldi, Bleek, Hilgenfeld), which would give a turn to the discourse utterly foreign to the connection, but *a man of such a disposition as this little child represents*— one who with child-like simplicity is humble and unassuming. So Chrysostom (παιδίον γὰρ ἐνταῦθα τοὺς ἀνθρώπους τοὺς οὕτως ἀφελεῖς φησὶ καὶ ταπεινοὺς καὶ ἀπερριμμένους παρὰ τοῖς πολλοῖς), Erasmus, Beza, Calvin, Grotius, Wetstein, Kuinoel, Olshausen, Kern, Baumgarten-Crusius, Ewald, Keim. Jesus well knew how much the unassuming, child-like disposition, free from everything like self-assertion, was just that which others, animated by an opposite spirit, were in the habit of overlooking, slighting, and thrusting aside. — ἕν] *a single one.* So very *precious* are they ! — δέξηται] denotes a loving reception with a view to further care for the soul ; the opposite to this is σκανδαλίζειν, ver. 6. — ἐπὶ τῷ ὀνόματί μου] *on the ground of my name* (xxiv. 5)—i.e. *on account of* my name, which, however, is not, with de Wette, to be taken subjectively, and referred to the faith of the *one who receives* (whosoever confessing my name, on account of his faith in me, etc.), but is to be understood as referring to the παιδίον τοιοῦτον *that is to be received* (Mark ix. 41 ; Matt. x. 42), *because my name* (Jesus the Messiah) *contains the sum of his belief and confession* (" non ob causas naturales aut politicas," Bengel). — ἐμέ] comp. x. 40, xxv. 40 ; John xiii. 20.

Ver. 6. Comp. Mark ix. 42 ; Luke xvii. 2. — σκανδαλίσῃ] Opposite of δέξηται, meaning : will have been to him the

occasion of his fall, especially of his apostasy from the faith
(v. 29, xi. 6). — τῶν μικρῶν τούτων] not to be understood,
any more than παιδίον τοιοῦτο, ver. 5, of literal *children* (Holtzmann), and consequently not to be used as proof of the faith
of little children (Baur, Delitzsch), but as meaning : one of
those little ones,—a way of designating modest, simple-minded,
unassuming believers, that had just been suggested by seeing
in the child then present a model of such simplicity.   This is
not quite the same as τῶν μικρῶν τούτων, x. 42 (xxv. 40),
where the expression is not borrowed from the illustration of
a child. — συμφέρει αὐτῷ, ἵνα, κ.τ.λ.] For the construction,
comp. note on v. 29.   "But whoever will have offended one
of those little ones,"—*it is of service to him, with a view
to,* i.e. *in hunc finem ut.*   That, which such a person may
have come to deserve, is thus expressed in the form of a
divine *purpose,* which his evil deed must help him to bring
about ; comp. John xi. 50.   A *comparative* reference of
συμφέρει (Jerome : " quam aeternis servari cruciatibus ; " others :
than *again to commit* such a sin) is a pure importation. —
μύλος ὀνικός] The larger mills (in contradistinction to the
χειρομύλαι, xxiv. 41) were driven by an *ass ;* Buxtorf, *Lex.
Talm.* p. 2252.   Comp. also *Anth. Pal.* ix. 301 ; Ovid, *A. A.*
iii. 290. — The καταποντισμός (Wesseling, *ad Diod. Sic.*
xvi. 35 ; Hermann, *Privatalterth.* § 72, 26 ; Casaubon, *ad
Suet. Oct.* 67) was not a Jewish method of putting to death,
neither was it a *practice* in Galilee (Joseph. *Antt.* xiv. 15. 10),
but belonged to the Greeks, Romans, Syrians, and Phoenicians.
Consequently it here expresses in a manner all the more
vivid and awe-inspiring that punishment of *death* to which
the man in question has become liable, and which is intended
to represent the loss of *eternal* life ; comp. vv. 7–9.

Ver. 7. Οὐαί] θρηνεῖ ὡς φιλάνθρωπος τὸν κόσμον ὡς μέλ-
λοντα βλαβῆναι ἀπὸ τῶν σκανδάλων, Theophylact. — ἀπό]
indicating the *causal origin* of the woe for humanity (τῷ
κόσμῳ).   The world is not conceived of as *giving* the offence
(in answer to Jansen, Arnoldi, Bleek), but as *suffering* from it.
With regard to ἀπό, see Buttmann, *Neut. Gramm.* p. 277 [E. T.
322]. — ἀνάγκη γάρ] assigns the reason for the ἀπὸ τῶν

σκανδάλ. immediately before : on account of offences, I say, for they cannot but come. This *necessity* (necessitas *consequentiae*) has its foundation in the morally abnormal condition of mankind, yet (comp. 1 Cor. xi. 19) is to be traced back to the divine purpose (not merely permission), which, however, does away neither with the moral freedom of him who, by word or deed, gives offence (Rom. xiv. 13), nor with his liability to punishment. Hence: πλὴν (*yet*) οὐαὶ τῷ ἀνθρώπῳ, κ.τ.λ.——τὰ σκάνδαλα] temptations, as a general conception.—— τὸ σκάνδ.] the temptation as conceived of in each individual case.

Ver. 8 f. Comp. Mark ix. 43 ff. A passing direction, suggested by ver. 7, for avoiding certain specified offences, and substantially the same as in v. 29. A repetition depending here, no doubt, on Mark (Weiss), yet not to be regarded as out of place, because the proverbial saying refers to one's own temptations as coming through the senses, while here the point in question is the temptation of others (de Wette, Kuinoel, Strauss, Holtzmann, Hilgenfeld), but on the contrary as quite appropriate, inasmuch as the σκάνδαλα occasioned from without operate through the senses, and thereby seduce into evil. —— καλόν σοι ἐστὶν . . . ἤ] a mixture, by attraction, of two constructions : *It is good to enter into the life* (of the Messiah's kingdom at the second coming) *maimed (and better) than*, etc. See Fritzsche's note on this passage, and *Dissert.* II. *ad* 2 *Cor.* p. 85 ; Winer, p. 226 [E. T. 302]; Buttmann, p. 309 [E. T. 360]. For examples from classical writers, see Kypke, *Obss.* I. p. 89 ; Bos, *Ellips.*, ed. Schaefer, p. 769 ff. See besides, the note on v. 29, 30. But in the present passage the *material representation of mortification* as the condition of eternal life is somewhat more circumstantial and graphic. — χωλόν] refers to the *feet*, one of which, indeed, is supposed to be awanting (comp. Hom. *Il.* ii. 217 : χωλὸς δ' ἕτερον πόδα) ; while, according to the context, κυλλόν here (more general in xv. 30) refers to mutilation of the *arm*, from which the hand is supposed to be cut off. Hence : *limping* (χωλόν) or *maimed* (κυλλόν). But the circumstance of χωλόν being put *first* is due to the fact that the cutting off of the *foot* (αὐτόν, see critical notes) had been specified, although at the same time an identical proceeding in regard to the hand is, of course, to be understood. — μονόφθαλμ.] Herod. iii. 116, iv. 27 ; Strabo, II. p. 70.   According to the grammarians, we should have had ἑτερόφθαλμ. in contradistinction to μονόφθαλμ., which denotes the condition of one *born* with one eye.   See Lobeck, *ad Phryn.* p. 136 f. ; Becker, *Anecd.* I. p. 280.

Ver. 10. Jesus now proceeds with His cautions, which had been interrupted by the parenthetical exhortation in vv. 7–9. The belief that every *individual has a guardian angel* (see Tob. v.; comp. in general, Schmidt in Ilgen's *Denkschr.* I. p. 24 ff.) —which is a post-Babylonian development of the Old Testament view, that God exercised His care over His people through angelic instrumentality—is here confirmed by Jesus (Acts xii. 15),—a point which is to be simply admitted, but not to be explained symbolically, neither by an *" as it were "* (Bleek), as though it were intended merely to represent the great value of the little ones in the sight of God (de Wette), nor as referring to *human* guardians, who are supposed to occupy a position of pre-eminent bliss in heaven (Paulus). — ἐν οὐρ. διὰ παντὸς βλέπουσι, κ.τ.λ.] inasmuch as they are ever in immediate proximity to God's glory in heaven, and therefore belong to the *highest order* of angels.   This is not merely a *way of expressing* the great importance of the μικροί, but a *proof* which, from λέγω ὑμῖν and τοῦ πατρός μου, receives all the weight of an emphatic *testimony ;* while the *mode* of representation (comp. מלאכי פנים of the Rabbinical writers, Schoettgen's note on this passage) is borrowed from the court arrangements of Oriental kings, whose most confidential servants are called הָרֹאֵי פְּנֵי הַמֶּלֶךְ, 2 Kings xxv. 19 ; 1 Kings x. 8 ; Tob. xii. 15 ; Luke i. 19.

Ver. 11 f. Omitting ver. 11, which is not genuine (see critical notes), we come to the parable vv. 12–14, which is intended to show that it would be in direct opposition to God's desire for human salvation to lead astray one of those μικροί, and to cause him to be lost, like a strayed sheep. Luke xv. 4 ff. records the same beautiful parable, though in a different connection, and with much tenderer, truer, and more original features.   But the time-hallowed parable of the shepherd came so naturally to Jesus, that there is no reason why He should not have employed it more than once, in a shorter or more detailed form, according as it happened to be appropriate to the occasion. — τί ὑμῖν δοκεῖ] "suavis communicatio," Bengel. — ἐὰν γένηται, κ.τ.λ.] *if a hundred sheep have fallen to a man's lot*, if he has come into the possession of them (Kühner, II. 1, p. 364). The contrast to ἕν requires that we should conceive of ἑκατόν as a *large* number (not as a *small* flock, Luke xii. 32). Comp. Lightfoot. — It is preferable to connect ἐπὶ τὰ ὄρη with ἀφείς (Vulgate, Luther), because the connecting of it with πορευθείς (Stephanus, Beza, Casaubon, Er. Schmid, Bengel) would impart an unmeaning emphasis to ἐπὶ τὰ ὄρη. The man is pasturing his sheep upon the hills, observes that one of them is amissing, therefore meanwhile leaves the flock alone upon the hills (for the one that has strayed demands *immediate* attention), and, going away, searches for the one sheep that is lost. The reading of Lachmann represents the right connection. — ἐπὶ τὰ ὄρη] ἐπί is not merely *upon* (as answering the question : where ?), but expresses the idea of being *scattered over the surface of anything*, which corresponds exactly with what is seen in the case of a flock when it is grazing, and which is likewise in keeping with ἀφείς, which conveys the idea of being *let out, let loose*. Comp. notes on xiii. 2, xiv. 19, xv. 35. — ἐὰν γένηται εὑρεῖν αὐτό] *if it should happen that he finds it.* Comp. Hesiod, *Theog.* 639 ; in classical Greek, found mostly with, though also without, a dative. Xen. *Mem.* i. 9. 13 ; *Cyr.* vi. 3. 11 ; Plato, *Rep.* p. 397 B; Kühner, II. 2, p. 582. This expression is unfavourable to the notion of *irresistible* grace. — χαίρει, κ.τ.λ.] This picture, so psychologically true, of the first impression is not applied to God in ver. 14 (otherwise in Luke xv. 7), although, from the popular anthropopathic point of view, it might have been so. Luke's version of the parable is characterized by greater freshness.

Ver. 14. Accordingly, as it is not the will of that man that one of his sheep should be lost, so it is not the will of God that one of those μικροί should be lost (should fall into eternal perdition). The *point of the comparison* therefore lies in the

unwillingness to let perish ; in the parable this is represented
by the case of a *strayed* sheep, for the purpose of teaching the
disciples that if a μικρός happens to err from the faith and the
Christian life, they should not abandon him, but try to induce
him to amend.—What is said in regard to the μικροί is therefore put in the form of a climax : (1) Do not despise them,
inasmuch as you would cause them to go astray, and be the
occasion of their ruin (vv. 6–10) ; (2) On the contrary, if
one does go wrong, rescue him, just as the shepherd rescues his
wandering sheep, in order that it may not be lost (vv. 12–14).
— ἔμπροσθεν] *coram* (xi. 26 ; Luke xv. 10). *There is not
before God* (before the face of God) *any determination having
as its object that,* etc. ; consequently, no predestination to
condemnation in the divine will. On the idea involved in
θέλημα, comp. note on i. 19. For the *telic* sense of ἵνα, comp.
vii. 12 ; Mark vi. 25, x. 35, *al.*, and the ἐθέλειν ὄφρα of
Homer ; Nägelsbach's note on *Iliad,* i. 133. — ἔν] See critical
notes. The idea of the *sheep* still lingers in the mind.

Ver. 15. The connection with what precedes is as follows :
" *Despise* not one of the μικροί (vv. 10–14) ; if, however, one
offends against thee, then proceed thus." The subject changes
from that of *doing* injury to the μικροί, against which Jesus
has been warning (vv. 10–14), to that of *suffering* injury, in
view of which he prescribes the proper method of brotherly
visitation. However, in developing this contrast, the point
of view becomes so *generalized* that, instead of the μικροί,
who were contemplated in the previous warning, we now
have the Christian *brother generally,* ὁ ἀδελφός σου — therefore, the *genus* to which the μικρός as *species* belongs. —
ἁμαρτήσῃ εἰς σέ] The emphasis is not on εἰς σέ, but on
ἁμαρτήσῃ : *but if* thy brother *shall have sinned* against thee,
which he is supposed to do not merely " *scandalo* dato "
(Bengel), but by *sinful treatment* in general, by any un-
brotherly *wrong* whatsoever. Comp. ver. 21. Ch. W. Müller
in the *Stud. u. Krit.* 1857, p. 339 ff., Julius Müller, *Dogmat.
Abh.* p. 513 ff., reject the reading εἰς σέ, ver. 15, though on
internal grounds that are not conclusive, and which might
be met by stronger counter-arguments against the use of

ἁμαρτήσῃ without modification of any sort. How can it be supposed that the procedure here inculcated was intended to apply to *every sin* without any limitation whatever ? Would we not have in that case a supervision *omnium contra omnes ?* The reference can only be to private charges, to offences in which the one sins against the other (εἰς σέ), and which, as such, ought to be dealt with within the Christian church. Comp. 1 Cor. vi. 1 ff. — ὕπαγε] do not wait, then, till he himself come to thee. — μεταξὺ σοῦ κ. αὐτοῦ μόνου] so that except him no one else is to be present along with thee, so that the interview be strictly confined to *the two of you.* We must not therefore supply a μόνου after σοῦ as well. But the rebuking agency (Eph. v. 11) is regarded as intervening between the two parties. The person who reproves mediates between the two parties, of which he himself forms one. — ἐάν σου ἀκούσῃ] if he will have listened to thy admonition, will have complied with it. But Fritzsche and Olshausen connect the preceding μόνου with this clause: " *Si tibi soli aures praebuerit.*" This would imply an arrangement that is both harsh and foreign to New Testament usage. — ἐκέρδησας] usually explained : as thy friend ; πρῶτον γὰρ ἐζημιοῦ τοῦτον, διὰ τοῦ σκανδάλου ῥηγνύμενον ἀπὸ τῆς ἀδελφικῆς σου συναφείας, Euthymius Zigabenus. But what a truism would such a result imply ! Therefore it should much rather be explained thus : thou hast *gained* him *for the eternal blessedness of my kingdom,* to which, from not being brought to a state of repentance, he would otherwise have been lost (ver. 17). But the *subject* who gains is the *party that has been aggrieved* by the offence of the brother, because the successful result is understood to be brought about by his affectionate *endeavours* after an adjustment. Comp. 1 Cor. ix. 19 ; 1 Pet. iii. 1.

Ver. 16. *Second gradus admonitionis.* The one or the two who accompany him are likewise intended to take part in the ἐλέγχειν (see αὐτῶν, ver. 17). — ἵνα ἐπὶ στόματος, κ.τ.λ.] *in order that, in the mouth of two or three witnesses, every word may be duly attested ;* i.e. in order that every declaration which he makes in answer to your united ἐλέγχειν may be heard by two or three persons (according as one or two may happen to

be present besides thyself), and, on the strength of their testimony (ἐπὶ στόματος, פּי עַל), may be duly authenticated, so that
in the event of his submitting to the ἐλέγχειν the possibility
of evading or denying anything afterwards will be precluded ;
or else, should he prove so refractory that the matter must
be brought before the church, then, in the interests of this
further disciplinary process, it will be of consequence to have
the declaration made by him in the previous attempt to deal
with him in an authentic and unquestionable shape. — In
order to convey *His* idea, Jesus has used, though somewhat
freely (otherwise in 2 Cor. xiii. 1), the words of the law,
Deut. xix. 15, and made them *His own.*   Comp. 1 Tim. v. 19.

Ver. 17. *Tῇ ἐκκλησίᾳ*] is not to be understood of the
Jewish synagogue (Beza, Calvin, Fritzsche), which is never
called by this name, and any reference to which would be
contrary to the meaning of Jesus ; but it is to be taken as
referring to the *community of believers* on Jesus (comp. note on
xvi. 18), which is, as yet, regarded as one body with the
apostles included (ver. 18).   There is here no allusion to
individual congregations in different localities, since these
could come into existence only at a later period ; neither, for
this reason, can there be any allusion to *presbyters* and *bishops*
(Chrysostom), or to those whom they may have invested, as
their representatives, with spiritual jurisdiction (Catholic
writers, comp. besides, Döllinger).   There is, further, nothing
to warrant the assumption of an historical *prolepsis* (de Wette,
Julius Müller), for the truth is, the קָהָל of believers was
actually existing ; while, in the terms of this passage, there
is no direct reference to individual congregations.   But
as Jesus had already spoken elsewhere of *His* קָהָל (xvi. 18),
it was impossible for the disciples to misunderstand the
allusion.   The *warrant* for regarding the judgment of the
church as final in regard to the ἔλεγξις lies in the moral
power which belongs to the unity of the Holy Spirit, and,
consequently, to true understanding, faith, earnest effort,
prayer, etc., the existence of all which in the church is *pre-*
supposed.   It is not inconsistent with this passage to suppose
that, under the more developed circumstances of a later

period, when local congregations sprung up as offshoots from the קהל, there may have been some *representative body*, composed of individuals chosen for the purpose of maintaining discipline, but the choice would necessarily be founded on such conditions and qualifications as were in keeping, so far as it was possible for man to judge, with the original principle of entrusting such matters only to those who were actual believers and had been truly regenerated. — ἐὰν δὲ καὶ τ. ἐκκλ. παρακ.] *but if he refuses to listen even to the church;* if he will not have submitted to its advice, exhortation, injunction. — ἔστω σοι ὥσπερ, κ.τ.λ.] *let him be for thee* (ethical dative); let him be in thy estimation *as*, etc.; λοιπὸν ἀνίατα ὁ τοιοῦτος νοσεῖ, Chrysostom. What is here indicated is the breaking off of all further Christian, brotherly fellowship with one who is hopelessly obdurate, " as not being a sheep, nor caring to be sought, but willing to go right to perdition," Luther. In this passage Christ says nothing, as yet, about formal *excommunication on the part of the church* (1 Cor. v.); but the latter was such a fair and necessary *deduction* from what he did say, as the apostolic church, in the course of its development, considered itself warranted in making. " Ad eam ex hoc etiam loco non absurde *argumentum* duci posse non negaverim," Grotius. In answer to the latter, Calovius, in common with the majority of the older expositors, asserts that the *institution* of excommunication is, in the present passage, already expressly declared. — ὁ ἐθνικός] generic.

Ver. 18 f. By way of giving greater confidence in the exercise of this last stage of discipline at which the matter is finally disposed of by the church, let me assure you of two things : (1) Whatever you (in the church) declare to be unlawful on the one hand, or permissible on the other (see note on xvi. 19), will be held to be so in the sight of God ; your judgment in regard to complaints brought before the church is accordingly ratified by divine warrant. (2) If two of you agree as to anything that is to be asked in prayer, it will be given you by God ; when, therefore, your hearts are thus united in prayer, you are assured of the divine help and illumination, in order that, in every case, you may arrive at

and, in the church, give effect to decisions in accordance with the
mind of God.—Those addressed in the second person (δήσητε,
κ.τ.λ.) are the *apostles* (Hofmann, *Schriftbew.* II. 2, p. 266 f.),
but not the *disciples in the more comprehensive sense of the word*
(Weiss, *Bibl. Theol.* p. 103), nor the *church* (Bleek, Schenkel,
Keim, Ahrens), nor its *leaders* (Euthymius Zigabenus, de Wette),
nor *the parties who have been injured* (Origen, Augustine,
Theophylact, Grotius). In order to a clear understanding of
the whole discourse from ver. 3 onwards, it should be observed
generally, that wherever the address is in the second person
plural (therefore in vv. 3, 10, 12, 14, 18, 19), it is the *Twelve*
who came to Jesus, ver. 1, that are intended; but that where
Jesus uses the second person *singular* (as in vv. 8, 9, 15–17),
He addresses *every believer* individually (including also the
μικροί). But as far as the ἐκκλησία is concerned, it is to be
understood as meaning the *congregation of believers, including the
apostles.* It is the possessor and guardian of the apostolic moral
legislation, and consequently it is to it that the offender is in
duty bound to yield *obedience.* Finally, since the power of binding and loosing, which in xvi. 19 was adjudged to *Peter*, is
here ascribed to the *apostles generally*, the power conferred
upon the former is set in its proper light, and shown to be
of necessity a power of a collegiate nature, so that Peter is
not to be regarded as exclusively endowed with it either in
whole or in part, but is simply to be looked upon as *primus
inter pares.* — πάλιν ἀμὴν λ. ὑμ.] Once more a solemn
assurance! and that to the effect that, etc.   Comp. xix. 24.
For ἐάν with the *indicative* (συμφωνήσουσιν, see critical
notes), see note on Luke xix. 40, and Buttmann, *Neut.
Gramm.* p. 192 [E. T. 222]; Bremi, *ad Lys. Alc.* 13. The
construction is a case of attraction; πᾶν should have been
the subject of the principal clause of the sentence, but was
attracted to the subordinate clause and joined to πράγματος,
so that without the attraction the passage would run thus:
ἐὰν δύο ὑμ. συμφωνήσουσιν ἐπὶ τ. γῆς περὶ πράγματος,
πᾶν ὃ ἐὰν αἰτήσωνται, γινήσεται αὐτοῖς.   Comp. Kühner,
II. 2, p. 925.   For the contrast implied in ἐπὶ τ. γῆς, comp.
ix. 6.

Ver. 20. Confirmation of this promise, and that not on account of any special preference for them in their official capacity, but generally (hence the absence of ὑμῶν in connection with the δύο ἢ τρεῖς) owing to the fact of His gracious presence in the midst of His people when met together : *for where two or three are gathered together with reference to my name, there am I* (my presence being represented by the Holy Spirit, comp. Rom. viii. 9 f.; 2 Cor. xiii. 5 ; 1 Cor. v. 4 ; Gal. ii. 20 ; Eph. iii. 16 f. ; also in general, xxviii. 20) *in the midst of them ;* so that you need therefore have no doubt as to the γενήσεται just promised to you, which I, as associated with my Father (ver. 19), will bring about. The statement is put in the form of an *axiom;* hence, although referring to the future, its terms are *present.* The *higher, spiritual* object of the meeting together of the two or three lies not in συνηγμένοι, which expresses nothing more than the simple fact of being met (in answer to Grotius, de Wette), but in εἰς τὸ ἐμὸν ὄνομα, which indicates that the name of Jesus Christ (*i.c.* the confession, the honouring of it, etc.) is that which in the συνηγμένον εἶναι is contemplated as its specific motive (μὴ δι' ἑτέραν αἰτίαν, Euthymius Zigabenus). "Simile dicunt Rabbini de duobus aut tribus considentibus in judicio, quod שכניה sit in medio eorum," Lightfoot.

Ver. 21. At this point Peter steps forward from amongst the disciples (ver. 1), and going up to Jesus, νομίζων φανῆται μεγαλοψυχότατος (Euthymius Zigabenus), proposes that forgiveness should be shown more than twice the number of times which the Rabbis had declared to be requisite. *Babyl. Joma,* f. 86. 2, contains the following words : "Homini in alterum peccanti semel remittunt, secundo remittunt, tertio remittunt, quarto non remittunt."

Ver. 22. Οὐ λέγω σοι] are to be taken together (in answer to Fritzsche), and to be rendered thus : *I do not say to thee,* I do not give thee *the* prescription ; comp. John xvi. 26. — ἐβδομηκοντάκις ἑπτά] not : *till seventy times seven, i.c.* till the four hundred and ninetieth time (Jerome, Theophylact, Erasmus, Luther, Grotius, de Wette, Bleek) ; but, seeing that we have ἑπτά, and not ἑπτάκις again, the rendering should simply be: *till seventy-seven times.* No doubt, according to the classical usage of adverbial numerals, this would have been expressed by ἑπτὰ καὶ ἑβδομηκοντάκις or ἑβδομήκοντα ἑπτάκις; but the expression in the text is according to the LXX. Gen. iv. 24.[1] So, and that correctly, Origen, Augustine, Bengel, Ewald, Hilgenfeld, Keim; comp. "the Gospel of the Hebrews" in Hilgenfeld's *N. T. extra can.* IV. p. 24. — For the sense, comp. Theophylact: οὐχ ἵνα ἀριθμῷ περικλείσῃ τὴν. συγχώρησιν, ἀλλὰ τὸ ἄπειρον ἐνταῦθα σημαίνει· ὡς ἂν εἰ ἔλεγεν· ὁσάκις ἂν πταίσας μετανοῇ συγχώρει αὐτῷ.

Ver. 23. Διὰ τοῦτο] must refer to the reply to Peter's question, for a new scene was introduced at ver. 21. Therefore to be explained thus: "because I have enjoined such *unlimited* forgiveness" (not merely a conciliatory disposition generally, in answer to de Wette and Bleek). The duty of *unlimited* forgiveness proves *any shortcoming* in regard to this matter to be but the more reprehensible, and to point this out is the object of the parable which follows. — ὡμοιώθη ἡ βασ. τ. οὐρ.] See note on xiii. 24. — The δοῦλοι are the king's ministers who are indebted to him through having received money on loan (δάνειον, ver. 27), or, relatively, as treasurers, land stewards, or the like. But it is not without reason that · ἀνθρώπῳ is joined to βασιλεῖ, seeing that the *kingdom of heaven* is likened to a *human* king. Comp. the ἀνὴρ βασιλεύς of Homer. — συναίρειν λόγον] *to hold a reckoning, to settle accounts,* occurs again in xxv. 19, but nowhere else. Classical writers would say: διαλογίζεσθαι πρός τινα, Dem. 1236. 17.

Ver. 24 ff. According to Boeckh, *Staatshaush. d. Athener,* I. p. 15 ff., an (Attic) talent, or sixty minae, amounted to 1375 thalers [about £206 sterling]. Ten thousand talents, amounting to something considerably over thirteen millions of thalers, are intended to express a sum so large as to be well-nigh

---

[1] Where, indeed, שִׁבְעִים וְשִׁבְעָה cannot possibly mean anything else than seventy-seven, as is clear from the וְ, not seventy *times* seven; comp. Judg. viii. 14. This in answer to Kamphausen in the *Stud. u. Krit.* 1861, p. 121 f. The (substantive) *feminine* form שבעה cannot be considered strange (seventy and *a seven*). See Ewald, *Lehrb. d. Hebr. Spr.* § 267 c., and his *Jahrb.* XI. p. 198.

incalculable. So *great* was the debt of *one* (εἷς). — ἐκέλευσεν αὐτὸν ... ἔχει] according to the Mosaic law; Lev. xxv. 39, 47; 2 Kings iv. 1; Ex. xxii. 2. See Michaelis, *M. R.* § 148; Saalschütz, *M. R.* p. 706 f. The word αὐτόν is emphatic: that *he* should be sold, etc. On the *present indicative* ἔχει (see critical notes), which is derived from the idea of the narrative being *direct*, comp. Kühner, II. 2, p. 1058. — καὶ ἀποδοθῆναι] *and that payment be made.* This was the king's *command : it must be paid,* viz. the sum due. The fact of the proceeds of the sale not proving sufficient for this purpose did not in any way affect the order; hence ἀποδοθ. is not to be referred merely to the *proceeds* (Fritzsche). The king wants his money, and therefore does the best he can in the circumstances to get it. — πάντα σοι ἀποδώσω] in his distress and anguish he promises far more than he can hope to perform. And the king in his compassion goes far beyond what was asked (ἀφῆκεν αὐτῷ). — For δάνειον, *money lent,* comp. Deut. xxiv. 11; found frequently in classical writers since the time of Demosth. 911. 3.

Ver. 28. *A hundred denarii,* about forty Rhenish Gulden, or 23 thalers [about £3, 9s. sterling] (a denarius being not quite equal to a drachma), what a *paltry* debt compared with those *talents* of which there were *a hundred times a hundred!* — ἔπνιγε] Creditors (as the Roman law allowed them to do) often dragged their debtors before the judge, holding them by the throat. Clericus and Wetstein on this passage. — ἀπόδος, εἴ τι ὠφείλεις] εἴ τι is not to be taken, as is often done, as though it were equivalent to ὅ, τι. For where εἴ τι, like *si quid,* is used in the sense of *quicquid* (see Kühner, *ad Xen. Anab.* i. 10. 18), εἰ always has a conditional force, which would be out of place in the present instance; but, with Fritzsche and Olshausen, to trace the expression to Greek *urbanity,* would be quite incongruous here. Neither, however, are we to affirm, with Paulus and Baumgarten-Crusius, that the conditional expression is rather more severe in its tone, from representing the man as *not being even certain* in regard to the debt; for the certainty of the debt is implied in the terms of the passage, and, moreover, in the κρατήσας αὐτ. ἔπνιγε was

MATT. II.   B necessarily to be presupposed on the part of the δοῦλος. No, the εἰ is simply the expression of a pitiless logic : PAY, if thou owest anything (ἀπόδος being emphatic). From the latter the former follows as matter of necessity. If thou owest anything (and such is the case), then thou must also pay,—and therefore I arrest thee !

Ver. 29. Πεσών] *after that he had fallen down,*—that is, as one who προσεκύνει, which follows, as a matter of course, from ver. 26, without our requiring to insert such words as εἰς τοὺς πόδας αὐτοῦ (see critical notes). Chrysostom appropriately observes : οὐ τὸ σχῆμα τῆς ἱκετηρίας ἀνέμνησεν αὐτὸν τῆς τοῦ δεσπότου φιλανθρωπίας.

Ver. 31 f. Ἐλυπήθησαν] *They were grieved* at the hardheartedness and cruelty which they saw displayed in what was going on (τὰ γινόμενα, see critical notes). — διεσάφ.] not simply *narrarunt* (Vulgate), but more precisely : *declararunt* (Beza) ; Plat. *Prot.* p. 348 B ; *Legg.* v. p. 733 B ; Polyb. i. 46. 4 ; ii. 27 3 ; 2 Macc. i. 18, ii. 9. — τῷ κυρίῳ ἑαυτῶν] The *reflective* pronoun (see critical notes) indicates that, as befitted their position, the σύνδουλοι addressed themselves to *their own master.* Their *confidence* in him led them to turn to him rather than to any one else. — ἐπεὶ παρεκάλ. με] *because thou entreatedst me.* And he had not gone so far as to beg for entire remission of the debt, but only for forbearance !

Ver. 33. On the well-known double καί used *comparatively,* see Klotz, *ad Devar.* p. 635. Baeumlein, *Partik.* p. 153. — ἔδει] the *moral oportuit.* — τοῖς βασανισταῖς] *to the tormentors* (Dem. 978, 11 ; 4 Macc. vi. 11) to torture him, not merely to cast him into prison, which latter was only a part of their functions (Fritzsche). The idea involved in βασανίζειν is of essential importance, typifying as it does the future βάσανος of Gehenna. Comp. viii. 29 ; Luke xvi. 23 ; Rev. xiv. 10. Grotius well observes, though he takes the βασανιστάς as = δεσμοφύλακας (Kuinoel, de Wette), "utitur autem hic rex ille non solo creditoris jure, sed et judicis."— ἕως οὗ ἀποδῷ] as in ver. 30. *until he shall have paid.* Though not expressly asserted, it is a legitimate inference from the terms of the passage (comp. v. 26) to say: τουτέστι διηνεκῶς, οὔτε γὰρ ἀποδώσει ποτέ, Chrysostom.

Doctrine of the parable: The remission which thou hast obtained from God of thy great unpayable debt of sin, must stimulate thee heartily to forgive thy brother the far more trifling debt which he has incurred as regards thee; otherwise, when the Messianic judgment comes, the righteousness of God will again rise up against thee, and thou wilt be cast into Gehenna to be punished eternally; comp. v. 25 f., vi. 14 f.— That motive, drawn from the forgiving mercy of God, could only be exhibited in all its significance by the light shed upon it in the atoning death of Christ (Eph. iv. 32, Col. iii. 12 f.), so that Jesus had to leave to the future, which was fast approaching, what, as yet, could be but inadequately understood (so far we have here a ὕστερον πρότερον), and hence our passage is not inconsistent (*Socinian* objection) with the doctrine (also expressly contained in xx. 28, xxvi. 28) of satisfaction. — ἀπὸ τ. καρδ. ὑμ.) *from your heart*, therefore out of true, inward, heartfelt sympathy, not from a stoical indifference. Comp. ver. 33. This is the only instance in the New Testament of ἀπό being used in connection with this phrase; elsewhere it is ἐκ that is employed. But comp. the classical expressions ἀπὸ γνώμης, ἀπὸ σπουδῆς, ἀπὸ φρενός, and the like; also ἀπὸ καρδίας in Antoninus ii. 3, and ἀπὸ τῆς ψυχῆς. Dem. 580, 1.

CHAPTER XIX.

VER. 3. οἱ Φαρισ.] Lachm. has deleted οἱ, following B C L M Δ Π,
min.   Correctly; the οἱ Φαρ. would suggest itself mechanically
to the transcribers from being in current use by them; in
several manuscripts it is likewise inserted in Mark x. 2. —
After λέγοντες Elz. and Scholz insert αὐτῷ, which, owing to the
preponderance of evidence against it, is to be regarded as a
common interpolation, as are also αὐτοῖς, ver. 4, αὐτήν, ver. 7. —
ἀνθρώπῳ] is wanting in B L Γ א* min. Aug., deleted by
Lachm.   Correctly; supplement from ver. 5, and for which
Cod. 4 has ἀνδρί (Mark x. 2). — Ver. 5. προσκολληθ.] Lachm.
and Tisch., also Fritzsche: κολληθ., following very weighty
evidence.   The compound form, however, is more common,
and is taken from the LXX.—Ver. 9. ὅτι before ὅς is not,
with Lachm. and Tisch. 7, to be deleted.   It has the preponderance of evidence in its favour, and how readily
may it have been overlooked, especially before ὅς, seeing
that it is not indispensable. — Instead of μὴ ἐπὶ πορνείᾳ Lachm.
has παρεκτὸς λόγου πορνείας, following B D, min. It. Or., but
clearly borrowed from v. 32 by way of a gloss.   For μή, Elz.
and Scholz have εἰ μή, against decisive evidence; an exegetical
addition. — κ. ὁ ἀπολελυμ. γαμ. μοιχᾶται] are deleted by
Tisch. 8, following C** D L S א, vss. Or.? Chrys.   But there is
preponderating evidence in favour of the words; and the
homoeoteleuton might readily enough be the occasion of their
omission.   Moreover, there is no parallel passage verbally
identical with this. — Ver. 13. προσηνέχθη] Lachm. and Tisch.:
προσηνέχθησαν, following B C D L א, min. Or.   In presence of
such weighty evidence, the singular is to be regarded as a grammatical correction. — Ver. 16. ἀγαθέ] is justly condemned by
Griesb. and deleted by Lachm. and Tisch. (B D L א, min.
codd. of It. Or. Hilar.).   Inserted from Mark x. 17; Luke
xviii. 18. — Ver. 17. The Received text (so also Fritzsche and
Scholz) has τί με λέγεις ἀγαθόν; οὐδεὶς ἀγαθὸς εἰ μὴ εἷς ὁ θεός.
But the reading: τί με ἐρωτᾷς περὶ τοῦ ἀγαθοῦ; εἷς ἐστιν ὁ ἀγαθός,
is attested by the very weighty evidence of B D L א, Vulg.

It. Or. and other vss. and Fathers. So Griesb., Lachm., Tisch. The reading of the Received text is taken from Mark and Luke, and would be adopted all the more readily the more the original reading seemed, as it might easily seem, to be inappropriate.[1] The order: εἰς τὴν ζωὴν εἰσελθ. (Lachm., Tisch.), has decisive attestation; but τηρεῖ (Lachm., Tisch. 7) for τήρησον finds but inadequate support, being favoured merely by B D, Homil. Cl. — Ver. 20. ἐφυλαξάμην ἐκ νεότητός μου] Lachm. and Tisch.: ἐφύλαξα, following important, though not quite unanimous, witnesses (B D L ℵ* among the uncial manuscripts; but D has retained ἐκ νεότ., though omitting μου). The reading of the Received text is taken from Luke and Mark. — Ver. 23. Lachm. and Tisch., following decisive evidence, read πλούσιος δυσκόλως. — Ver. 24. Instead of the first εἰσελθεῖν, Elz. has διελθεῖν, which is defended by Fritzsche and Rinck, and also adopted again by Lachm., in opposition to Griesb., Matth., Scholz, Schulz, Tisch., who read εἰσελθεῖν. The evidence on both sides is very weighty. διελθεῖν is a correction for sake of the sense, with which εἰσελθεῖν was supposed not to agree. Comp. note on Mark x. 25; Luke xviii. 25. If the *second* εἰσελθεῖν were to be retained, the preponderance of evidence would be in favour of inserting it after πλούσιον (Lachm.); but we must, with Tisch., following L Z ℵ, 1, 33, Syr^cur Or. and other Fathers, delete it as being a supplement from the parallel passages. — Ver. 28. For καὶ ὑμεῖς read, with Tisch. 8, καὶ αὐτοί, following D L Z ℵ, 1, 124, Or. Ambr. The reading of the Received text is an exegetical gloss. — Ver. 29. ὅστις] The simple ὅς (Elz., Griesb., Fritzsche, Scholz) is opposed by preponderating evidence; τις was omitted as unnecessary (but comp. vii. 21, x. 32). — ἢ γυναῖκα] after μητ. is correctly deleted by Lachm. and Tisch., on the evidence of B D, 1, Or. Ir. Hil. vss. Taken from Mark and Luke. — For ἑκατονταπλασίονα Lachm. and Tisch. have πολλαπλασίονα, following B L, Syr^ier Sahid. Or. Cyr. Correctly; it would be much more natural to explain the indefinite πολλαπλασ. from Mark x. 30 by means of the definite expression ἑκατονταπλασ., than to explain the latter from Luke xviii. 30 by means of πολλαπλασ.

Ver. 1 f. With his usual formula, κ. ἐγέν. ὅτε ἐτέλ., κ.τ.λ. (vii. 28, xi. 1, xiii. 53), Matthew here introduces the *account of the closing stage* in Christ's ministry by mentioning His

[1] So also Rinck, *Lucubr. crit.* p. 268 f. Differently Hilgenfeld in the *Theol. Jahrb.* 1857, p. 414 f., but not on critical evidence.

departure from Galilee to Judaea. It does not follow (comp. note on xvi. 21) that there may not have been previous visits to Judaea (in answer to Baur), but, in order to give to *this* journey, above all, the prominence due to its high significance, it was necessary that the Synoptists should confine their view to the Galilaean ministry until the time came for this final visit to the capital.—The *conversation concerning divorce and marriage* is likewise given in Mark x. 1 ff., and, on the whole, in a more original shape. — μετῆρεν ἀπὸ τῆς Γαλιλ.] Comp. xvii. 22, 24. — πέραν τοῦ Ἰορδάνου] This expression cannot be intended to define the *locale* of εἰς τὰ ὅρια τῆς Ἰουδαίας, for the reader knew, as matter of course, that Peraea and Judaea (iv. 15, 25) meant *different* districts, although, according to Ptolem. v. 16. 9, several towns east of the Jordan might be reckoned as included in Judaea; neither can it belong to μετῆρεν ἀπὸ τ. Γαλ. (Fritzsche: "Movens a Galilaea transiit fluvium"), for κ. ἦλθεν εἰς τ. ὅρ. τ. Ἰουδ. is not of the nature of a parenthesis; rather is it to be regarded as indicating the *route* (Mark x. 1) which Jesus took, thus *defining* ἦλθεν (Mark vii. 31) somewhat *more precisely,* lest it should be supposed that He was on this side Jordan, and therefore approached Judaea by going through Samaria, whereas, being on the farther side of the river, He went *by Peraea,* and reached the borders of Judaea by crossing over to the west side of the Jordan (somewhere in the neighbourhood of Jericho, xx. 29). The expression is not awkward (Volkmar); nor, again, is it to be erroneously understood as showing that the Gospel was written in some district east of the Jordan. — Further, the narrative of Matthew and Mark cannot be reconciled with that of Luke, who represents Jesus as keeping to *this side* of the Jordan (ix. 51, and see note on xvii. 11); nor with the account of John, who, x. 22, says nothing about the *journey* to Jerusalem, but represents Jesus as *already* there, and in ver. 40 as setting *out from that city* to make a short sojourn in Peraea. — ἐκεῖ] that is, in Peraea, just mentioned, and through which He was travelling on His way to the borders of Judaea, ver. 1. On αὐτούς *(their sick),* see Winer, p. 139 [E. T. 183]. Instead of the healing, Mark speaks of the *teaching* that took place on this occasion.

Ver. 3. Πειράζοντες] The question was of an ensnaring nature, owing to the rivalry that existed between the school of Hillel and that of the more rigorous Sammai. See note on v. 31. There is not the slightest foundation in the text for the idea that the questioners had in view the matrimonial relations of *Antipas* (Paulus, Kuinoel, de Wette, Ewald), as though they wanted to involve Jesus, while yet in Peraea, within that prince's domains, in a fate similar to that of the Baptist. Moreover, the adoption of this view is altogether unnecessary, since the whole school of Sammai had already condemned that most unlawful state of matters just referred to, and therefore there was on this score nothing of a specially tempting character about the question. But they expected that Jesus in His reply would declare in favour of *one* of the rival schools (and that it would doubtless be that of Sammai ; for with κ. πᾶσαν αἰτίαν they suggested the answer, *No*), so that they might be able to stir up party feeling against Him. Falling back, however, upon the divine idea on which the institution of marriage is founded, He took higher ground than *either* of the schools in question, inasmuch as from this divine idea He deduces that marriage is a union which no human authority has a right to dissolve ; but as for Himself, He avoids prescribing any law of His own with reference to this matter ; comp. Harless, *Ehescheidungsfr.* p. 34 ff. — εἰ] See note on xii. 10. — τὴν γυναῖκα αὐτοῦ] Assuming ἀνθρώπῳ to be spurious, the αὐτοῦ can only refer to something in the context, and that doubtless to the logical subject, to the τίς implied in the ἔξεστι. For a similar classical usage, comp. Stallbaum, *ad Plat. Rep.* p. 503 D. — κατὰ πᾶσαν αἰτίαν] *for every cause*, which he has to allege against her,—the view maintained by the school of Hillel, and which was precisely that which gave to this question its *tempting* character, though it is not so represented in Mark. As given by the latter evangelist the question is not presented in its original form ; as it now stands it would have been too general, and so not calculated to tempt, for it would certainly have been foolish to expect from Jesus any answer contrary to the law (in answer to Weiss, Keim); but, according to Matthew's version, the persons who were tempting Jesus appear to have framed their question with a view to His splitting on the casuistical rock implied in κ. πᾶσαν αἰτίαν. After having laid down as a principle the indissoluble nature of the marriage tie, Jesus, in the course of the conversation, replies to this captious point in their query in the very decided terms of ver. 9, where He says, μὴ ἐπὶ πορνείᾳ.

Ver. 4. Αὐτούς] δηλαδὴ τοὺς ἀνθρώπους· τουτὶ μὲν οὖν τὸ ῥητὸν ἐν τῇ βίβλῳ τῆς γενέσεως (i. 27) γέγραπται, Euthymius Zigabenus. The following αὐτούς should be understood after ὁ ποιήσας, as the object of the succeeding verb has often to be supplied after the participle (Krüger's note on Xen. *Anab.* i. 8. 11). For ποιεῖν, *to create*, comp. Plat. *Tim.* p. 76 C; Hesiod, *Theog.* 110, 127 (γένος ἀνθρώπων). — ἀπ' ἀρχῆς] does not belong to ὁ ποιήσας (as *usually* explained), in which case it would be superfluous, but to what follows (Fritzsche, Bleek), where great stress is laid on the expression, " *since the very beginning* " (ver. 8). — ἄρσεν κ. θῆλυ] as *male and female*, as a *pair consisting of one of each sex*. — ἐποίησεν] after ὁ ποιήσας the same verb. See Kühner, *ad Xcn. Mem.* iv. 2. 21, and *Gramm.* II. 2, p. 656.

Ver. 5. Εἶπεν] *God.* Comp. note on 1 Cor. vi. 16. Although, no doubt, the words of Gen. ii. 24 were uttered by Adam, yet, as a rule, utterances of the Old Testament, in which God's will is declared, are looked upon as the words of God, and that altogether irrespective of the persons speaking. Comp. Euthymius Zigabenus and Fritzsche on the passage. — ἕνεκεν τούτου] refers, in Gen. ii. 24, to the formation of the woman out of the rib of the man. But this detail, which belongs to an incident assumed by Jesus to be well known, is included in the general statement of ver. 4, so that He does not hesitate to generalize, somewhat freely, the particular to which the ἕνεκεν τούτου refers. Observe, at the same time, that vv. 4 and 5 *together* constitute the scriptural basis, the *divine premisses* of what is to appear in the shape of an inference in the verse immediately following. — κατα-

λείψει] " necessitudo arctissima conjugalis, cui u‑ μοιχᾶται]
materna cedit," Bengel. — οἱ δύο] These words are with the
in the Hebrew, though they occur in the Samaritan ‑et been
they must also have done in that which was followe? this
the LXX. They are a subsequent addition by way of m an
distinctly emphasizing the claims of monogamy. See note
on 1 Cor. vi. 16. The *article* indicates the two *particular*
persons in question. — εἰς σάρκα μίαν] Ethical union may
also be represented by other ties; but this cannot be said of
bodily unity, which consists in such a union of the sexes,
that in marriage they cease to be two, and are thenceforth
constituted *one* person. Comp. Sir. xxv. 25 and Grimm's
note. The construction is not Greek (in which εἶναι εἰς
means to refer to anything, or to serve for anything, Plat.
Phil. p. 39 E; *Alc.* I. p. 126 A), but a rendering of the
Hebrew לְ הָיָה (Vorst, *Hebr.* p. 680 f.).

Ver. 6. Οὐκέτι] after this union, ver. 5. — εἰσί] *are they*,
that is, the two of ver. 5. — ὅ] *quod*, " ut non tanquam de
duobus, sed *tanquam de uno corpore* loqueretur," Maldonatus.
— ὁ θεός] through what is said in ver. 5. Observe the contrast to ἄνθρωπος. — Having regard, therefore, to the specific
nature of marriage as a divine institution, Jesus utterly condemns divorce generally as being a putting asunder on the
part of man of what, in a very special way, God has joined
together. With regard to the exception, by which, in fact,
the essential idea of marriage as a divine institution is already
practically destroyed, see ver. 9, and comp. note on v. 32.

Ver. 7. Supposed counter-evidence. — ἐνετείλατο] Deut.
xxiv. 1, in which, indeed, there is no express command,
though it may be said to contain κατὰ διάνοιαν the prescription of the bill of divorce. Mark—and in this his account is
certainly more original—represents the whole reply of Jesus
as *beginning* with the *question* as to the law of Moses on
the matter (x. 3). Moreover, the more appropriate expression
ἐπέτρεψεν, which in ver. 8 is ascribed to *Jesus* (not so in
Mark), undoubtedly betrays the influence of riper reflection.
— Comp. besides, note on v. 31.

Ver. 8. Πρός] *out of regard to*, with (wise) consideration

to expect frert greater evil. — σκληροκαρδίαν] *stubbornness* answer to Mark xvi. 14; Rom. ii. 5; Acts vii. 51; Sir. xvi. the perscut. x. 16), which will not be persuaded to self-their union, gentleness, patience, forbearance, etc.; κατὰ διαφόροcὺς αἰτίας μισούντων τὰς γαμετὰς, καὶ μὴ καταλλαττομένων ραὐταῖς. 'Ἐνομοθέτησε γὰρ ἀπολύειν ταύτας, ἵνα μὴ φονεύωνται, Euthymius Zigabenus. — οὐ γέγονεν οὕτω] *non ita factum est*, namely, that a man should have permission to put away his wife. The above primitive institution of God is accordingly not abrogated by Moses, who, on account of the moral obduracy of the people, is rather to be understood as only granting a dispensation in the form of a letter of divorce, that the woman might be protected against the rude severity of the man.

Ver. 9. See note on v. 32. — μὴ ἐπὶ πορν.] *not on account of fornication*, i.e. *adultery*. The *deleting* of those words (Hug, *de conjug. vinculo indissolub.* p. 4 f.; Maier's note on 1 Cor. vii. 11; but also Keim, who sees in them the correction of a subsequent age) is justified neither by critical evidence, which Keim himself admits, nor by the following ὁ ἀπολελ. γαμ. μοιχᾶται, which is in no way inconsistent with the exception under consideration, seeing that, as a matter of course, the ἀπολελ. refers to a woman who has been divorced arbitrarily, μὴ ἐπὶ πορν. (see note on v. 32); nor by ver. 10, where the question of the disciples can be sufficiently accounted for; nor by 1 Cor. vii. 11 (see note on this passage). We are therefore as little warranted in regarding the words as an interpolation on the part of the evangelist in accordance with a later tradition (Gratz, Weisse, Volkmar, Schenkel). The exception which they contain to the 'law against divorce is the *unica et adaequata exceptio*, because adultery destroys what, according to its original institution by God, constitutes the very essence of marriage, the *unitas carnis*; while, on this account also, it furnishes a reason not merely for separation *a toro et mensa* (Catholic expositors), but for separation *quoad vinculum*. To say, as Keim insists (according to Mark), that Jesus *breaks* with Moses, is unwarranted, not only by Matthew's narrative, but also by Mark's; and any indication of such a

breach would betray the influence of a later age. — $\mu o \iota \chi \hat{a} \tau a \iota$]
commits adultery, because, in fact, his marriage with the
woman whom he has arbitrarily dismissed has not yet been
disannulled. The *second* $\mu o \iota \chi \hat{a} \tau a \iota$ is justified: because this
$\dot{a} \pi o \lambda \epsilon \lambda \upsilon \mu \dot{\epsilon} \nu \eta$ is still the lawful wife of him who has, in an
arbitrary manner, put her away.

Ver. 10. This conversation is to be understood as having
taken place *privatim*, in a house (Mark x. 10), or elsewhere.
— $\epsilon \dot{\iota} \; o \ddot{\upsilon} \tau \omega \varsigma \; \dot{\epsilon} \sigma \tau \dot{\iota} \nu \; \dot{\eta} \; a \dot{\iota} \tau i a, \kappa.\tau.\lambda.$] $\dot{\eta} \; a \dot{\iota} \tau i a$ means *causa*, but
not in the sense of *res* or *relation* (Grotius) : "*si ita res se habet
hominis cum uxore*" (Grimm), which is at variance with the
Greek usage, and would be tantamount to a Latin idiom ; nor
is it to be understood in the sense imported by Fritzsche :
" causa, *qua aliquis cum uxore versari cogatur.*" According to
the text, $\dot{\eta} \; a \dot{\iota} \tau i a$ can only be taken as referring back to the
question concerning divorce, $\kappa a \tau \dot{a} \; \pi \hat{a} \sigma a \nu \; a \dot{\iota} \tau i a \nu$, ver. 3. The
correct interpretation, therefore, must be as follows : *If it
stands thus with regard to the reason in question, which the
man must have in relation to his wife* (in order, namely, to her
divorce). The Lord had, in fact, declared the $\pi o \rho \nu \epsilon i a$ of the
wife to be such an $a \dot{\iota} \tau i a$ as the disciples had inquired about,
and that, moreover, the sole one. This also leads me to with-
draw my former interpretation of $a \dot{\iota} \tau i a$ in the sense of *guilt*,
that, namely, which was understood to be expressed by the
$\mu o \iota \chi \hat{a} \tau a \iota$. The correct view is given by Hilgenfeld in his
Zeitschr. 1868, p. 24, and, in the main, by so early an expositor
as Euthymius Zigabenus : $\dot{\epsilon} \dot{a} \nu \; \mu i a \; \mu \acute{o} \nu \eta \; \dot{\epsilon} \sigma \tau \dot{\iota} \nu \; \dot{\eta} \; a \dot{\iota} \tau i a \; \dot{\eta} \; \mu \acute{\epsilon} \sigma o \nu$
$\tau o \hat{\upsilon} \; \dot{a} \nu \delta \rho \dot{o} \varsigma \; \kappa. \; \tau \hat{\eta} \varsigma \; \gamma \upsilon \nu a \iota \kappa \dot{o} \varsigma \; \dot{\eta} \; \delta \iota a \zeta \epsilon \upsilon \gamma \nu \acute{\upsilon} o \upsilon \sigma a. \; — \; o \dot{\upsilon} \; \sigma \upsilon \mu \phi. \; \gamma a \mu.$]
because one cannot be released again, but, with the exception of
adultery alone, must put up with all the woman's other vices.

Vv. 11, 12. The disciples have just said : $o \dot{\upsilon} \; \sigma \upsilon \mu \phi \acute{\epsilon} \rho \epsilon \iota$
$\gamma a \mu \hat{\eta} \sigma a \iota$. But *to this saying* must $\tau \dot{o} \nu \; \lambda \acute{o} \gamma o \nu \; \tau o \hat{\upsilon} \tau o \nu$ be referred, not to the *statement concerning the indissoluble nature of
marriage*, as though Jesus meant to say that this was to be
insisted on only in the case of those who had been endowed
with the *donum continentiae* (Hofmann, *Schriftbew.* II. 2, p.
410 f.) ; which would be to contradict His argument in favour
of non-dissolution taken from the objective *nature* of marriage,

no less than His absolute declaration in v. 32, as well as to render nugatory, for all practical purposes, the primitive moral law of non-dissolution, by making it dependent on a subjective condition. Besides, the illustration of the *eunuchs* is only applicable to *continence generally*, not to a mere abstaining from the sin of *adultery*. No. Jesus wishes to furnish His disciples with the necessary explanation regarding their οὐ συμφέρει γαμῆσαι, and for this end He by no means questions their λόγος, but simply observes that : *it is a proposition which all do not accept, i.e.* which all cannot see their way to adopt as a maxim, *but only such as God has endowed with special moral capabilities*. Then, in ver. 12, He explains who are meant by the οἷς δέδοται, namely, such as have become *eunuchs;* by these, however, He does not understand *literal* eunuchs, whether born such or made such by men, but those who, for the sake of the Messiah's kingdom, have made themselves such so far as their moral dispositions are concerned, *i.e.* who have suppressed all sexual desire as effectually as though they were actual eunuchs, in order that they might devote themselves entirely to the (approaching) Messianic kingdom as their highest interest and aim (to labour in promoting it, comp. 1 Cor. vii. 32, 34). Finally, He further *recommends* this ethical self-castration, this " voluntary chastity " (Luther), when He exclaims : *Whosoever is able to accept* (to adopt) *it* (that which I have just stated), *let him accept it!* Chrysostom well observes : He says this, προθυμοτέρους τε ποιῶν τῷ δεῖξαι ὑπέρογκον ὂν τὸ κατόρθωμα, καὶ οὐκ ἀφιεὶς εἰς ἀνάγκην νόμου τὸ πρᾶγμα κλεισθῆναι. Comp. 1 Cor. vii. 1 f. The χωρεῖν, ver. 11 f., means simply *to receive*, and to be understood as referring to a *spiritual* reception, a receiving in the heart (2 Cor. vii. 2) ; and those endowed with the power so to receive it have, in consequence of such endowment, not only the inclination to be continent, but at the same time the moral force of will necessary to give effect to it, while those who are not so endowed " aut nolunt, aut non implent quod volunt," Augustine. The *more common* interpretation, *praestare posse* (" negat autem Jesus, te, nisi divinitus concessis viribus tam insigni abstinentiae, qua a matrimonio abhorreas, parem esse," Fritzsche), might be traced to the rendering *capere*, but it is precluded by the fact that the object of the verb is a λόγος (*a saying*). *Others* take it in the sense of : *to under-stand*, with reference, therefore, to the power of apprehension on the part of the *intellect* (Maldonatus, Calovius, Strauss, Bretschneider, Baumgarten-Crusius, Ewald ; similarly Bengel, de Wette, Bleek, who, however, arbitrarily take τὸν λόγ. τοῦτ. as pointing forward to ver. 12). So Plut. *Cat. min.* 64 ; Ael. *V. H.* iii. 9 ; Phocyl. 86 : οὐ χωρεῖ μεγάλην διδαχὴν ἀδίδακτος ἀκούειν ; Philo, *de mundo* 1151 : ἀνθρώπινος λογισ-μὸς οὐ χωρεῖ. But the difficulty with respect to what the disciples have said, and what Jesus says in ver. 12, is not connected with the apprehension of its meaning, but with its ethical appropriation, which, moreover, Jesus does not abso-lutely *demand*, but leaves it, as is also done by Paul, 1 Cor. vii., to each man's *ability*, and that according as he happens to be endowed with the gift of continence as a *donum singulare*. Consequently, the celibate of the clerical *order*, as such, acts in direct opposition to this utterance of the Master, especially as the εὐνουχίζειν ἑαυτόν cannot be acted on by any one with the certainty of its *lasting*. Comp. *Apol. Conf. A.*, p. 240 f. : " non placet Christo *immunda continentia*." As showing how voluntary celibacy was by no means universal, and was exceptional even among the apostles themselves, see 1 Cor. ix. 5.—The metaphorical use of εὐνούχισαν ἑαυτούς to denote entire absence from sexual indulgence, likewise occurs in *Sohar Ex.* f. 37, c. 135 ; *Levit.* f. 34, c. 136 b ; Schoettgen, p. 159.—It is well known that from a misunderstanding of the meaning of this passage Origen was led to castrate himself. On the correctness of this tradition (in answer to Schnitzer and Bauer), see Engelhardt in the *Stud. u. Krit.* 1838, p. 157 ; Redepenning, *Origenes*, I. p. 444 ff.—That *Jesus* was not here contemplating any *Essenian* abstinence (Strauss, Gfrörer, *Philo*, II. p. 310 f., Hilgenfeld), is already manifest from the high estimate in which marriage is always held by Him, and from His regard for children. The celibacy which a certain class of Essenes observed was founded on the fact that they regarded marriage as *impure*.

Ver. 13. Comp. Mark x. 13. At this point (after being suspended from ix. 51–xviii. 14) the narrative of Luke again becomes parallel, xviii. 15.—*Little children* were brought to Jesus, as to a man of extraordinary sanctity, whose prayer was supposed to have peculiar efficacy (John ix. 31); as, in a similar way, children were also brought to the presidents of the synagogues in order that they might pray over them (Buxt. *Synag.* p. 138). The *laying on of the hands* (Gen. xlviii. 14) was desired, not as a mere symbol, but as *a means of communicating* the blessing prayed for (Acts vi. 6); hence, with a nearer approach to originality, Mark and Luke have simply ἅψηται and ἅπτεται (which, in fact, was understood to be of itself sufficient for the communication in question).—The *conjunctive* with ἵνα after the preterite (Kühner, II. 2, p. 897; Winer, p. 270 [E. T. 359]) serves to represent the action as immediately present. — αὐτοῖς] are those of whom the προσηνέχθη is alleged, *i.e.* those who brought the children. The disciples wished to protect Jesus from what they supposed to be an unseemly intrusion and annoyance; a *verecundia intempestiva* (Bengel), as in xx. 31.

Ver. 14. By τῶν τοιούτων we are not to understand literal *children* (Bengel, de Wette), for the Messianic kingdom cannot be said to belong to children as such (see v. 3 ff.), but men of a child-like disposition and character, xviii. 3 f. Jesus cannot consent to see the children turned away from Him; for, so far from their being too insignificant to become the objects of His blessing, He contemplates in their simplicity and innocence that *character* which those who are to share in His kingdom must acquire through being converted and *becoming* as little children. If they thus appeared to the Lord as types of the subjects of His kingdom, how could He withhold from them that prayer which was to be the means of communicating to their opening lives the blessing of early fellowship with Him! Herein lies the *warrant*, but, according to 1 Cor. vii. 14, not the *necessity*, for infant baptism; comp. in general, note on Acts xvi. 15.

Ver. 16 ff. Comp. Mark x. 17 ff.; Luke xviii. 18 ff. — Εἷς] *One*, a single individual out of the multitude. According to

Luke, the person in question was an ἄρχων, not a νεανίσκος (ver. 20), which is explicable (Holtzmann) on the ground of a different tradition, not from a misunderstanding on the part of Matthew founded on ἐκ νεότητ. μου (Mark x. 20). — τί ἀγαθὸν ποιήσω] is not to be explained, with Fritzsche, as equivalent to τί ἀγαθὸν ὂν ποιήσω, quid, quod bonum sit, faciam? for the young man had already made an effort to do what is right, but, not being satisfied with what he had done, and not feeling sure of eternal life in the Messiah's kingdom, he accordingly asks : which good thing am I to do, etc. ? He wishes to know what particular thing in the category of the eternal good must be done by him in order to his obtaining life.

Ver. 17. Thy question concerning the good thing, which is necessary to be done in order to have eternal life in the Messianic kingdom, is quite superfluous (τί με ἐρωτᾷς, κ.τ.λ.) ; the answer is self-evident, for there is but one (namely, God, the absolute ideal of moral life) who is the good one, therefore the good thing to which thy question refers can be neither more nor less than obedience to His will,—one good Being, one good thing, alterum non datur! But if thou (δέ, the continuative autem : to tell thee now more precisely what I wished to impress upon thee by this εἷς ἐστὶν ὁ ἀγαθός) desirest to enter into life, keep the commandments (which are given by this One ἀγαθός). Neander explains incorrectly thus: " Why askest thou me concerning that which is good ? One is the good one, and to Him thou must address thyself; He has, in fact, revealed it to thee also ; but since you have asked me, then let me inform you," etc. This view is already precluded by the enclitic με (as otherwise we should necessarily have had ἐμέ).—For the explanation of the Received text, see note on Mark x. 18 ; the claim to originality must be decided in favour not of Matthew (in answer to Keim), but of Mark, on whom Luke has also drawn. The tradition followed by Matthew seems to have already omitted the circumstance of our Lord's declining the epithet ἀγαθός. The claims of Mark and Luke are likewise favoured by Weisse, Bleek, Weiss, Schenkel, Volkmar, Holtzmann, Hilgenfeld, the last of whom, however, gives the

palm in the matter of originality to the narrative of the Gospel
of the Hebrews (*N. T. extra can.* IV. p. 16 f.).—For οὐδεὶς
ἀγαθὸς, κ.τ.λ., comp. Plat. *Rep.* p. 379 A : ἀγαθὸς ὅ γε θεὸς
τῷ ὄντι τε καὶ λεκτέον οὕτως.—On the dogmatic importance
of the proposition that God alone is good, see Köster in the
Stud. u. Krit. 1856, p. 420 ff. ; and on the fundamental
principle of the divine retribution : εἰ θέλεις . . . τήρησον τὰς
ἐντολάς, which impels the sinner to repentance, to a renuncia-
tion of his own righteousness, and to faith ; comp. notes on
Rom. ii. 13 ; Gal. iii. 10 ff.   Bengel well remarks : "Jesus
securos ad legem remittit, contritos evangelice consolatur."
Comp. *Apol. Conf. A.*, p. 83.

Ver. 18 f. Agreeably to the meaning of his question, ver.
16, the young man expected to be referred to commandments
of a *particular* kind, and therefore calls for further information respecting the ἐντολάς to which Jesus referred ; hence
ποίας, which is not equivalent to τίνας, but is to be understood as requesting a *qualitative* statement.—For the purpose
of indicating the kind of commandments he had in view,
Jesus simply mentions, by way of example, one or two
belonging to the second table of the decalogue, but also at
the same time the fundamental one (Rom. xiii. 9) respecting
the love of our neighbour (Lev. xix. 18), because it was
through *it* (for which also see note on xxii. 39) He wished
the young man to be tested.   This latter commandment,
introduced with skilful tact, Origen incorrectly regards as an
interpolation ; de Wette likewise takes exception to it ; comp.
Bleek, who considers Luke's text to be rather more original.

Ver. 20. *In what respect do I still come short ?* what further
attainment have I yet to make ?   Comp. Ps. xxxix. 4 : ἵνα γνῶ
τί ὑστερῶ ἐγώ ; 1 Cor. xii. 24 ; 2 Cor. xi. 5, xii. 11.   This
reply (Plat. *Rep.* p. 484 D : μηδ' ἐν ἄλλῳ μηδενὶ μέρει ἀρετῆς
ὑστεροῦντας) serves to show that his moral striving after the
Messianic life is confined within the narrow limits of a decent
outward behaviour, without his having felt and understood
the *spirit* of the commandments, and especially the boundless
nature of the duties implied in the commandment of love,
though, at the same time, he has a secret consciousness that

there must be some higher moral task for man, and feels impelled towards its fulfilment, only the legal tendencies of his character prevent him from seeing where it lies.

Ver. 21. *Τέλειος*] *perfect*, one, who for the obtaining of eternal life, *οὐδὲν ἔτι ὑστερεῖ. In accordance with the moral tendencies and disposition which He discerned in the young man*, Jesus demands from him that moral perfection to which, from not finding satisfaction in legalism, he was striving to attain. The following requirement, then, is a *special* test for a *special* case,[1] though it is founded upon the universal duty of absolute self-denial and devotion to Christ; nor is it to be regarded merely in the light of *a recommendation*, but as a *command*. Observe that the Lord does not prescribe this to him as his sole duty, but only in connection with *ἀκολούθει μοι*. It was intended, by pressing this requirement upon him, that the young man should be led to realize his own shortcomings, and so be enabled to see the necessity of putting forth far higher efforts than any he had hitherto made. It was meant that he should feel himself weak, with a view to his being made morally strong; accordingly it is precisely upon the weak side of the young man's character that Jesus imposes so heavy a task, for with all his inward dissatisfaction he was not aware of his actual weakness in that direction. — *πτωχοῖς*] *the poor. — ἐν οὐρανῷ*] thou wilt have (instead of thy *earthly* goods) a treasure *in heaven*, i.e. *in the hands of God*, where it will be securely kept till it comes to be bestowed at the setting up of the Messiah's kingdom. Comp. v. 12, vi. 20. For the whole saying, comp. *Avoda Sara* f. 64, 1: "Vendite omnia, quae habetis, et porro oportet, ut fiatis proselyti."

Ver. 22 f. *Λυπούμενος*] because he could not see his way to compliance with that first requirement, and saw himself thereby compelled to relinquish his hope of inheriting eternal life. "Aurum enervatio virtutum est," Augustine. — *δυσκόλως*] because his heart usually clings too tenaciously to his possessions (vi. 19—21) to admit of his resigning them at

---

[1] The Catholics found upon this passage the *consilium evangelicum* of *poverty*, as well as the *opera supererogativa* in general. See, on the other hand, Müller, *von d. Sünde*, I. p. 69 ff., ed. 5.

such times and in such ways as the interests of the kingdom may demand. For analogous passages from the Greek classics bearing on the antagonism between wealth and virtue, see Spiess, *Logos spermat.* p. 44.

Ver. 24. " Difficultatem exaggerat," Melanchthon. For πάλιν, comp. xviii. 19. The point of the comparison is simply the fact of the impossibility. A similar way of proverbially expressing the utmost difficulty occurs in the Talmud with reference to an *elephant.*[1] See Buxtorf, *Lex. Talm.* p. 1722, and Wetstein. To understand the expression in the text, not in the sense of a camel, but of a *cable* (Castalio, Calvin, Huet, Drusius, Ewald), and, in order to this, either supposing κάμιλον to be the correct reading (as in several cursive manuscripts), or ascribing this meaning to κάμηλος (τινές in Theophylact and Euthymius Zigabenus), is all the more inadmissible that κάμηλος never has any other meaning than that of a *camel*, while the form κάμιλος can only be found in Suidas and the Scholiast on Arist. *Vesp.* 1030, and is to be regarded as proceeding from a misunderstanding of the present passage. Further, the proverbial expression regarding the camel likewise occurs in xxiii. 24, and the Rabbinical similitude of the elephant is quite analogous. — εἰσελθεῖν after ῥαφ. is universally interpreted : *to enter in* (to any place). On the question as to whether ῥαφίς is to be recognised as classical, see Lobeck, *ad Phryn.* p. 90. To render this word by a *narrow gate*, a narrow *mountain-pass* (so Furer in Schenkel's *Lex.* III. p. 476), or anything but a *needle*, is simply inadmissible.—The danger to salvation connected with the possession of riches does not lie in these considered *in themselves,* but in the difficulty experienced by sinful man in subordinating them to the will of God. So Clemens Alexandrinus : τίς ὁ σωζόμενος πλούσιος. Hermas, *Pastor,* i. 3. 6.

Ver. 25. Τίς ἄρα] *who therefore,* if the difficulty is so great in the case of the *rich,* who have the means of doing much good. The inference of the disciples is *a majoribus ad minores.*

[1] The passage in the Koran, *Sur.* vii. 38 : "Non ingredientur paradisum, donec transeat camelus foramen acus," is to be traced to an acquaintance with our present saying ; but for an analogous proverb concerning the camel which " *saltat in cabo,*" see *Jevamoth* f. 45, 1.

The general expression τίς cannot be intended to mean *what* *rich man* (Euthymius Zigabenus, Weiss), as is further evident from what is said by Jesus in vv. 23, 24.

Ver. 26. Ἐμβλέψας] This circumstance is also noticed by Mark. The look which, during a momentary pause, preceded the following utterance was doubtless one of a telling and significant character, and calculated to impress the startled disciples (Chrysostom, Euthymius Zigabenus: ἡμέρῳ βλέμματι). Comp. Luke xx. 17 ; John i. 43. — παρὰ ἀνθρώποις] *so far as men are concerned*, *i.e.* not *hominum judicio* (Fritzsche, Ewald), but serving to indicate that the impossibility is *on the part of man*, is owing to human inability, Luke i. 37. — τοῦτο] namely, the σωθῆναι, not : that the *rich* should be saved. See ver. 25 (in answer to Fritzsche, de Wette). Jesus invites the disciples to turn from the thought of man's own inability to obtain salvation, to the omnipotence of God's converting and saving grace.

Ver. 27. Peter's question is suggested by the behaviour of that young man (hence ἀποκρ., see note on xi. 25), who left Jesus rather than part with his wealth. The *apostles* had done quite the contrary (ἡμεῖς placed emphatically at the beginning, in contrast to the young man).—ἀφήκαμεν πάντα] employment, the custom-house, worldly things generally. It is therefore a mistake to suppose that the disciples were still pursuing their former avocations while labouring in the service of Jesus (not to be proved from John xxi. 3 ff.). See Fritzsche, *ad Mark.* p. 441. — τί ἄρα ἔσται ἡμῖν] ἄρα: *in consequence of this*. The question has reference to some special compensation or other by way of reward ; but as to the *form* in which it is to be given, it leaves that to be explained by Jesus in His reply. In spite of the terms of the passage and the answer of Jesus, Paulus incorrectly explains thus : *what, therefore, will there be for us still to do ?* Similarly Olshausen : *what is awaiting us ? Are we, too, to be called upon yet to undergo such a test* (as the young man had just been subjected to) ? In Mark x. 28 and Luke xviii. 28 it is not expressly asked, τί ἄρα ἔσται ἡμῖν; but the question is *tacitly* implied in the words of Peter (in answer to Neander, Bleek), as reported by those evangelists, while Matthew appears to have gleaned it from Mark.

Ver. 28. This part of the promise is omitted in Mark, but comp. Luke xxii. 30. — In answer to the *question* concerning the reward, Jesus, in the first place, *promises* a *special* recompense to His disciples, namely, that they should have the honour of being associated with Him in judging the nation at the second coming; then, in ver. 29 (comp. Mark x. 29; Luke xviii. 29), He adds the *general* promise of a reward to be given to those who for His sake have sacrificed their worldly interests; and finally, in ver. 30, He makes a statement calculated *to rebuke* everything in the shape of *false pretensions*, and which is further illustrated by the parable in xx. 1 ff.— There is no touch of *irony* throughout this reply of Jesus (in answer to Liebe in Winer's *exeget. Stud.* I. p. 73). Comp. Fleck, *de regno div.* p. 436 ff. — ἐν τῇ παλιγγενεσίᾳ] *in the regeneration*, does not belong to ἀκολουθήσαντές μοι (Hilary, explaining the words by baptismal regeneration (Titus iii. 5); also Calvin, who understands by παλιγγενεσία the renovation of the world begun in Christ's earthly ministry), for the disciples could only have conceived of the renovation of the world as something that was to take place contemporaneously with the actual setting up of the kingdom; the ἀποκατά-στασις, Acts iii. 21, does not represent quite the same idea as the one at present in question. Neither are we, with Paulus, to insert a point after παλιγγεν., and supply ἐστε ("you are already in the position of those who have been regenerated," spiritually transformed), which would have the effect of introducing a somewhat feeble and irrelevant idea, besides being incompatible with the abruptness that would thus be imparted to the ὅταν (otherwise one should have expected ὅταν δέ). The words belong to καθίσεσθε, and signify that *change by which the whole world is to be restored to that original state of perfection in which it existed before the fall*, which renewal, *restitutio in integrum*, is to be brought about by the coming Messiah (חדוש העולם). See Buxtorf, *Lex Talm.* p. 712; Bertholdt, *Christol.* p. 214 f.; Gfrörer, *Jahrh. d. Heils*, II. p. 272 ff. Comp. Rom. viii. 19 ff; 2 Pet. iii. 13. When the resurrection is over, and the last judgment is going on (and it is to this part of the scene that the Lord is here

referring), this renovation will have already begun, and will be
in the course of development, so that Jesus can say with all
propriety : ἐν τῇ παλιγγ. "Nova erit genesis, cui præerit
Adamus secundus," Bengel. Comp. παλιγγενεσία τῆς πατρίδος
in Joseph. *Antt.* xi. 3. 9 ; παλιγγεν. τῶν ὅλων in Anton. xi. 1.
Philo, *de mund.* p. 1165 C.; *leg. ad Caj.* p. 1037 B. Augustine, Theophylact, Euthymius Zigabenus, Fritzsche, interpret
the expression of the *resurrection,* in favour of which such
passages might be quoted as Long. iii. 4 ; Lucian, *Musc.
enc.* 7 ; but this would be to understand it in too restricted a
sense, besides being contrary to regular New Testament usage
(ἀνάστασις). — ὅταν καθίσῃ, κ.τ.λ.] as *judge.* — δόξης
αὐτοῦ] the throne, that is, on which the Messiah shows
Himself in His glory, xxv. 31.—καὶ αὐτοί (see critical notes) :
likewise, just as the *Messiah* will sit on His throne. —
καθίσεσθε] *you will take your seats upon.* Christ, then, is
to be understood as already *sitting.* Moreover, though the
promise applies, in a general way, to the twelve disciples, it
does not preclude the possibility of one of them failing,
through his apostasy, to participate in the fulfilment of the
promise ; " thronum Judae *sumsit alius,* Acts i. 20," Bengel. —
κρίνοντες] not: *ruling over* (Grotius, Kuinoel, Neander,
Bleek), but, as the word *means* and the context requires:
judging. As believers generally are to be partakers of the
glory and sovereignty of Christ (Rom. viii. 17 ; 2 Tim. ii. 12),
and are to be associated with Him in judging the non-
Christian κόσμος (1 Cor. vi. 2), so here it is specially promised to the disciples as such that they shall have the
peculiar privilege of taking part with Him in judging the
people of Israel. But it is evident from 1 Cor. vi. 2 that the
people of Israel is conceived of as still forming part of the
κόσμος, therefore it will be so far still *unconverted,* which
coincides with the view that the second coming is *near at hand,*
x. 23. It is a mistake, therefore, to take the people of Israel
as intended to represent the people of God in the *Christian*
sense (de Wette, Bleek) ; but it is no less so to suppose that
the judging in question is merely of an *indirect* character,
such as that which in xii. 41 is ascribed to the queen of the

south and the Ninevites (Chrysostom, Euthymius Zigabenus,
Erasmus, Maldonatus),—a view which does not at all correspond with the picture of the judgment given in the text,
although those expositors correctly saw that it is the *unbeliev-
ing* Israel that is meant.   This *sitting upon twelve thrones*
belongs to the accidental, Apocalyptic *form* in which the
promise is embodied, though it is not so with regard either to
the *judging itself* or its special reference to the δωδεκάφυλον
of Israel (Acts xxvi. 7), to which latter the number of the
apostles expressly corresponds; for the second coming, instead
of subverting the order of things here indicated, will only
have the effect of exhibiting it in its perfection, and for the
apostles themselves in its glory.   It is therefore too rash
to infer, as has been done by Hilgenfeld, that this passage
bears traces of having been based upon an original document
of a strictly Judaeo-Christian character.   Even the Pauline
Luke (xxii. 30) does not omit this promise, although he
gives it in connection with a different occasion,—a circumstance which by Schneckenburger, without sufficient reason,
and by Volkmar, in the most arbitrary way possible, is
interpreted to the disadvantage of Matthew.   It is not the
case that ver. 28 interferes with the connection (Holtzmann),
although Weizsäcker also is disposed to regard it as " a manifest interpolation."

Ver. 29. The promise that has hitherto been restricted to
the apostles now becomes general in its application : *and*
(in general) *every one who*, etc. — ἀφῆκεν] has *left*, completely abandoned.   Comp. ver. 27. — ἕνεκεν τ. ὀν. μ.] *i.e.*
because my name represents the contents of his belief and
confession.   Comp. Luke xxi. 12.   This leaving of all for the
sake of Jesus may take place *without* persecution, simply by
one's choosing to follow Him as a disciple; but it may also
be forced upon one *through* persecution, as for instance by
such a state of matters as we find in x. 35 ff. — πολλαπλασίονα (see critical notes) λήψεται, according to the context
(see καθίσεσθε, ver. 28 ; κληρονομήσει, ver. 29 ; ἔσονται,
ver. 30), can certainly have no other reference but to the
recompense *in the future kingdom of the Messiah*, in which a

manifold compensation will be given for all that may have
been forsaken. Here the view of Matthew diverges from
that of Mark x. 38, Luke xviii. 30, both of whom represent
this manifold compensation as being given during the period
preceding the second advent. This divergence is founded
upon a difference of conception, existing from the very first,
regarding the promise of Jesus, so that the distinction between
the καιρὸς οὗτος and the αἰὼν ἐρχόμενος in Mark and Luke
may be regarded as the result of exegetical reflection on the
meaning of the expressions in the original Hebrew. The
words are likewise correctly referred to the reward of the
future world by de Wette, Bleek, Keim, Hilgenfeld, while
Fritzsche is at a loss to decide. In opposition to the context,
the *usual* interpretation in the case of Matthew as well, is to
refer the promise of a manifold compensation to the αἰὼν
οὗτος, some supposing it to point to the happiness arising
from Christian ties and relationships, as Jerome, Theophylact,
Euthymius Zigabenus, Erasmus, Grotius, Wetstein ; others, to
the receiving of all things in return for the few (1 Cor.
iii. 21 ; Olshausen); others, again, to inward peace, hope, the
fellowship of love (Kuinoel, Calvin), or generally, the *spiritual
blessings* of believers (Bengel) ; and others still, to *Christ
Himself*, as being (xii. 49 f.) infinitely more to us than father,
mother, brother, etc. (Maldonatus, Calovius). *Julian mocked
at* the promise. — κ. ζωὴν αἰ. κληρ.] the crown of the whole,
which perfects all by rendering it an eternal possession.
Observe, further, how what is promised is represented as a
recompense, no doubt, yet not for meritorious works, but for
self-denying, trustful obedience to Christ, and to His invitation and will. Comp. *Apol. Conf. A.*, p. 285 f.

Ver. 30. However, the measure of rewards in the Messianic
kingdom is not to be determined by the time, sooner or later,
at which any one may have entered into fellowship with me.
No, it is not *seniority* of discipleship that is to be the standard
of reward at the setting up of the approaching kingdom :
*Many who were the first to enter will receive just the same treat-
ment as those who were the last to become my followers, and* vice
versâ. The correct construction and translation are not those

of Fritzsche, who interprets: *Many will be first though last* (ἔσχατοι ὄντες, namely, before the second coming), *and last though first* (πρῶτοι ὄντες), but those usually adopted, according to which πρῶτοι is the subject of the first, and ἔσχατοι that of the second part of the sentence. This is not forbidden by xx. 16, where, on the other hand, the order seems to have been inverted to suit the context. Observe, further, that the arrangement by which πολλοὶ . . . πρῶτοι stand so far apart serves to render πολλοί very emphatic: *In multitudes, however, will the first be last,* and *vice versâ*. The second clause is to be supplemented thus: καὶ πολλοὶ ἔσονται ἔσχατοι πρῶτοι. But to understand πρῶτοι and ἔσχατοι as referring, not to *time*, but to *rank*, regarded from the divine and human point of view, as though the idea were that " when the rewards come to be dispensed, many a one who considers himself among the highest will be reckoned among the lowest" (Hilgenfeld, following Euthymius Zigabenus, Erasmus, Jansen, Wetstein, de Wette, Bleek),—is forbidden by the subsequent parable, the connection of which with the present passage is indicated by γάρ. However, there is a little warrant in the text for taking the words as referring specially to the *Jews* on the one hand, and the *Gentiles* (who were later in being called) on the other (Theophylact, Grotius).

CHAPTER XX.

VER. 6. ὥραν] is, with Lachm. and Tisch., to be deleted as a supplement, following B D L א, vss. Or. — ἑστῶτας] Elz., Fritzsche, Scholz insert ἀργούς, which is not found in B C** D L א, vss. and Fathers.   Interpolation taken from vv. 3 and 7. — Ver. 7. x. ὅ ἐὰν ᾖ δίκαιον, λήψεσθε] is wanting in important codd. (B D L Z א), vss. and Fathers.   Deleted by Lachm. and Tisch.   For λήψεσθε, several vss. have *dabo vobis*.   The words are a very ancient interpolation, in conformity with ver. 4. — Ver. 8. Delete αὐτοῖς, with Tisch. 8, following C L Z א, Or.   A supplement. — Ver. 10. πλείονα] Fritzsche, Lachm. and Tisch. 7 : πλεῖον, following B C* N Z Δ, min. vss. Or.   The reading of the Received text is of the nature of an explanation (a greater number of denarii). — For ἀνά read τὸ ἀνά, with Tisch., following C L N Z א, 33.   The article was omitted in conformity with ver. 9. — Ver. 12. ὅτι] does not occur, it is true, in B C** D א, 1, Vulg. It. Syr., and is deleted by Lachm. and Tisch.; but how readily may it have been overlooked before οὗτοι! — Ver. 15. The first ἤ is deleted by Lachm., following B D L Z, Syr.^cur Arm. (in accordance with which evidence, as well as that of א, the arrangement ὅ θέλω ποιῆσαι should be restored).   Correctly ; an old interpolation for the purpose of marking the question.   There would be no motive whatever for omitting the ἤ.   For the second ἤ (in Elz.) we should, with Tisch. 7, read εἰ, following B** H S Γ, Chrys. Did. and many min.   From not being understood, εἰ was all the more readily replaced by ἤ, owing to the pronunciation being much the same. — Ver. 16. πολλοὶ γάρ εἰσι κλητοί, ὀλίγοι δὲ ἐκλεκτοί] omitted in B L Z א, 36, Copt. Sahid., and deleted by Tisch. 8, with whom Keim concurs.   But it is not at all likely that the words would be interpolated from xxii. 14 ; for, so far from there having been any occasion for so doing, they have here more the appearance of being out of place than otherwise.   This apparent irrelevancy may have led to the omission of the saying, which is supported by testimony so old as that of C D, It. Syr., unless we suppose it to have been due rather to the simple homoeoteleuton ἰσχα-

ΤΟΙ... ἐκλεκΤΟΙ.— Ver. 17. ἐν τῇ ὁδῷ καὶ] read with Lachm. and Tisch.: καὶ ἐν τῇ ὁδῷ, following B L Z ℵ, min. Copt. Sahid. Arm. Pers[p]. Or. (twice).   At a very early period (Vulg. It. Hil.), ἐν τῇ ὁδῷ was omitted either accidentally, or because it is likewise awanting in the parallel passages in the other Synoptists.   But, in restoring it, it would most naturally occur to those who did so to insert it after κατ᾽ ἰδίαν. — Ver. 19. ἀνασ- τήσεται] Tisch.: ἐγερθήσεται, following C* L N Z ℵ, Or. Chrys. The reading of the Received text is taken from the parallel passages. — Ver. 22. πίνειν;] Elz., Scholz insert: καὶ (Scholz: ἢ) τὸ βάπτισμα, ὃ ἐγὼ βαπτίζομαι, βαπτισθῆναι, against B D L Z ℵ, 1, 22, the majority of vss. and Or. Epiph. Hilar. Jer. Ambr. Juv.   Taken from Mark x. 38. — Ver. 23. πίεσθε] Elz., Scholz, in opposition to the same witnesses, insert: καὶ (Scholz: ἢ) τὸ βάπτισμα ὃ ἐγὼ βαπτίζομαι, βαπτισθήσεσθε. — Ver. 26. ἔσται ἐν ὑμῖν] for ἔσται, Lachm. has ἐστίν, following B D Z, Cant. Sahid.   Correctly; the reading of the Received text is an alteration to suit what follows in this and the 27th verse, where, with Fritzsche, Lachm. Tisch. 8, we ought to read ἔσται instead of ἔστω, in accordance with preponderating evidence; ἔστω (like- wise derived from Mark x. 43) is a gloss.   But Fritzsche was scarcely warranted in restoring δὲ after οὕτως, ver. 26, for it is condemned by decisive evidence, and is a connecting particle borrowed from Mark. — Ver. 31. ἔκραζον] Lachm. Tisch. 8: ἔκραξαν, following B D L Z Π ℵ, min. Copt. Sahid.   A repetition from ver. 30. — Ver. 33. ἀνοιχθῶσιν ἡμ. οἱ ὀφθ.] Lachm. Tisch. 8: ἀνοιγῶσιν οἱ ὀφθ. ἡμ., following B D L Z ℵ, min. Or. Chrys.   To be adopted, inasmuch as the first aorist was the more common tense, comp. ix. 30, John ix. 10. — Ver. 34. ὀφθαλμῶν] B D L Z, min. Or. have ὀμμάτων.   So Lachm., Rinck, Tisch. 8. Correctly; the more usual term has been adopted from the context. — Lachm. and Tisch. 8 delete αὐτῶν οἱ ὀφθαλμοί after ἀνέβλεψαν.   The words are not found in B D L Z ℵ, min. vss. (also Vulg. It.) and a few Fathers, but they were left out as being superfluous and cumbersome.   There was no motive whatever for inserting them.

REMARK.—After ver. 28 there occurs in D (and in codd. of It. with many variations in detail) the following interpolation, apocryphal, no doubt, but akin to Luke xiv. 8 ff.: ὑμεῖς δὲ ζητεῖτε ἐκ μικροῦ αὐξῆσαι κ. ἐκ μείζονος ἔλαττον εἶναι. Εἰσερχόμενοι δὲ καὶ παρα- κληθέντες δειπνῆσαι μὴ ἀνακλίνεσθε εἰς τοὺς ἐξέχοντας τόπους, μή ποτε ἐν- δοξότερός σου ἐπέλθῃ, καὶ προσελθὼν ὁ δειπνοκλήτωρ εἴπῃ σοι· ἔτι κάτω χώρει, καὶ καταισχυνθήσῃ. Ἐὰν δὲ ἀναπέσῃς εἰς τὸν ἥττονα τόπον καὶ ἐπέλθῃ σου ἥττων, ἐρεῖ σοι ὁ δειπνοκλήτωρ· σύναγε ἔτι ἄνω, καὶ ἔσται σοι τοῦτο χρήσιμον. Comp. Hilar., also Syr^{cur}.

Ver. 1. The parable is peculiar to Matthew. — γάρ] explaining and confirming what has been said in xix. 30. — ἀνθρ. οἰκοδ.] See notes on xiii. 24, xviii. 23. — ἅμα πρωΐ] Comp. notes on xiii. 29, Acts xxviii. 23 : ἀπὸ πρωΐ. Classical writers would say : ἅμα ἕῳ, ἅμα τῇ ἡμέρᾳ, ἅμα ὄρθρῳ, and such like. — εἰς τὸν ἀμπελ. αὐτοῦ] into his vineyard, into which he wished to send them, ver. 2. Comp. Acts vii. 9 ; and see, in general, Wilke, Rhetor. p. 47 f. — On the whole parable, see Rupprecht in the Stud. u. Krit. 1847, p. 396 ff. ; Steffensen, ibid. 1848, p. 686 ff. ; Besser in the Luther. Zeitschr. 1851, p. 122 ; Rudel, ibid. p. 511 ; Münchmeyer, ibid. p. 728. For proof that it is not to be regarded as furnishing directions for the regulation of offices, see Köstlin, d. Wesen d. Kirche, 1854, p. 52 ff.

Ver. 2. Ἐκ δηναρίου τὴν ἡμέραν] After he had agreed with the labourers, on the condition that he was to pay them a denarius per day. ἐκ does not denote the payment itself (which would have been expressed by the genitive, ver. 13), although ἐκ δηναρ. is that payment (xxvii. 7 ; Acts i. 18); but it is intended to indicate that this payment was the thing, on the strength of which, as terms, the agreement was come to; comp. Kühner, II. 1, p. 399 f. τὴν ἡμέραν is the accusative, as further defining the terms of the agreement : in consideration of the day, so that a denarius was to be the wages for the (current) day during which they might work. As an accusative of time (which it is usually supposed to be), it would not correspond with συμφων. to which it belongs. — A denarius was the usual wages for a day's work (Tob. v. 14). See Wetstein.

Ver. 3. The third hour: somewhere about nine o'clock in the morning. In ordinal numbers the article is unnecessary. See note on 2 Cor. xii. 2. — ἐν τῇ ἀγορᾷ] where they were waiting in expectation of getting employment. The men in question belonged to the class of free labourers ; Poll. iii. 82 : ἐλεύθεροι μὲν, διὰ πενίαν δὲ ἐπ' ἀργυρίῳ δουλεύοντες.

Ver. 4. Κἀκείνοις] to those also he spoke. The point

of assimilation (*also*) lies in the circumstance that, as he had invited the first, so he now invites these also to go into the vineyard. — ὃ ἐὰν ᾖ δίκαιον] so that, as part of the day had already elapsed, he did not make with them any definite agreement as to wages *for the day*, and therefore acted *differently* in this case from what he had done in the former.

Ver. 5 ff. Ἐποίησεν ὡσαύτως] the same thing, namely, as he had done in the preceding case, ver. 4, sending them away, and promising them also only *what was equitable*. Comp. ver. 7. — ὅτι] because.

Ver. 8. Ὀψίας δὲ γεν.] *i.e.* at the close of the twelfth hour (six o'clock in the evening). — τῷ ἐπιτρόπῳ αὐτοῦ] the chief of the servants (οἰκονόμος), to whom was entrusted the management of the household, Luke viii. 3. — τὸν μισθόν] the wages in question. The οἰκονόμος had instructions from his master to give the same amount of wages to all, although all had not wrought the same number of hours. — ἕως τῶν πρώτων] is connected with ἀπόδος αὐτ. τ. μισθ., without anything requiring to be understood (*and continuing*, and such like), as is evident from those passages in which the *terminus ad quem* is placed *first;* for example, Plat. *Legg.* vi. p. 771 C: πάσας τὰς διανομὰς ἔχει μέχρι τῶν δώδεκα ἀπὸ μιᾶς ἀρξάμενος. Comp. Luke xxiii. 5; Acts i. 21; John viii. 9.

Ver. 9 ff. Οἱ περὶ τὴν ἐνδεκ. ὥραν] that is, *those* who, according to ver. 6, were sent into the vineyard *about the eleventh hour.* — πλεῖον] *more* than a denarius, plainly not more *denarii.* — ἀνά] used distributively; Winer, p. 372 [E. T. 496]. The article τό before ἀνὰ δην., ver. 10 (see critical notes), denotes: *the sum amounting in each case to a denarius,* so that in analyzing ὅν would require to be supplied. — According to ver. 10 f., they do not contemptuously decline to lift the denarius (Steffensen), but begin to murmur *after* receiving it (Münchmeyer).

Ver. 12. Ὅτι] *recitative,* not *because* (γογγύζομεν, ὅτι), inasmuch as the words λέγοντες· ὅτι κ.τ.λ. express the *contents* of the γογγύζειν. — οὗτοι] spoken disdainfully. — ἐποίησαν] they have *spent* one hour (Acts xv. 33, xviii. 23; 2 Cor. xi.

25; Eccles. vi. 12; Wetstein on this passage; Schaeffer, *ad Bos.* p. 313; Jacobs, in *Anthol.* IX. p. 449, X. p. 44). The *ordinary* interpretation: they have *wrought, laboured,* one hour, is in opposition to the terms of the passage (as little is it to be confirmed by an appeal to Ruth ii. 19, where ποῦ ἐποίησας means: where hast thou been *occupying* thyself ?); there would have been more reason to interpret thus: they have been *doing* it (that is, the work) for one hour, if the specifying of the time in connection with ἐποίησαν had not suggested our explanation as · the most obvious and most natural. — τ. καύσωνα] Those others had not entered till the evening.

Vv. 13-15. Ἑνί] *One,* as representing the whole. — ἑταῖρε] *Comrade,* a mild way of introducing a rebuke, similar to "*good friend*" among ourselves. Comp. xxii. 12, xxvi. 50. So also ἀγαθέ, βέλτιστε. See Herm. *ad Vig.* p. 722. Comp. Wetstein. — οὐκ ἀδικῶ σε] From the standpoint of *justice.* — δηναρίου] genitive of price. Somewhat different from the idea of ver. 2. — θέλω δέ] "Summa hujus vocis potestas," Bengel. — ἐν τοῖς ἐμοῖς] not to be taken in the general sense of: *in my affairs* (Fritzsche, de Wette), but, according to the context, to be understood in the more definite sense of: *in disposing of my own property.* Comp. τὸ σόν, and Plato, *Legg.* ii. p. 969 C. — εἰ ὁ ὀφθαλμός σου, κ.τ.λ.] see critical notes. The εἰ is not *interrogative,* as in xii. 10, xix. 3 (for, according to the connection, the *doubt* implied in such a question would be entirely out of place), but the speaker is to be regarded as saying that, though such and such be the case, his right to do what he pleases with his own is by no means impaired, so that εἰ may be taken as almost equivalent to εἰ καί (Jacobs, *Del. Epigr.* p. 405; Hartung, *Partikell.* II. p. 212; Kühner, II. 2, p. 991): if thine eye is evil (*i.e.* envious, comp. Mark vii. 22, and רע, Prov. xxviii. 22; Ecclus. xiv. 10), because I (I, on my part, hence ἐγώ) am good ! The mark of interrogation after ἐμοῖς is therefore to be deleted.

Ver. 16. The teaching of the parable: *So,* — just, as in the case here supposed, those who were the last to be sent into the

vineyard received the same amount of wages as the first; *so
in the Messiah's kingdom*, the *last will be on the same footing
as the first, and the first as the last*, without a longer period
of service giving an advantage, or a shorter putting to a disadvantage.   Comp. xix. 30. — ἔσονται] that is, practically,
as far as the *reward* they are to receive is concerned.   The
first will be *last*, inasmuch as the former receive *no more*
than the latter (in answer to de Wette's objection, as though,
from the expression here used, we would require to suppose
that they will receive less than a denarius).   There is nothing
whatever in the text about the *exclusion* of the πρῶτοι from
the kingdom, and the *admission* of the ἔσχατοι (Krehl in the
Sächs. Stud. 1843); and as little to favour the view, adopted
by Steffensen: *those who esteem themselves last shall be first,
and those who esteem themselves first shall be last*, for the
labourers in the parable *were in reality* ἔσχατοι and πρῶτοι.
The proposition: "that, in dispensing the blessings of the
kingdom of heaven, God takes no account of human merit,
but that all is the result of His own free grace" (Rupprecht,
Bleek, Holtzmann, Keim), does not constitute the *leading
thought* set forth in the parable, though, no doubt, it may be
supposed to *underlie* it. — πολλοὶ γὰρ, κ.τ.λ.] Confirmation of
what has just been said about the ἔσχατοι being put upon an
equality with the πρῶτοι : "for although many are called to
share in the future recompense for services rendered to the
Messiah's kingdom, yet those chosen to receive rewards of a
pre-eminent and peculiarly distinguished character in that
kingdom are but few."   These ἐκλεκτοί are not the ἔσχατοι
(those, as Olshausen fancies, whose attitude toward the kingdom is of a more spontaneous nature, and who render their
services from hearty inclination and love), but those who are
selected from the multitude of the κλητοί.   We are taught in
the parable *what* it is that God chooses them *for*, namely, to
be rewarded in an extraordinary degree (to receive more than
the denarius).   The train of thought, then, is simply this: It
is not without reason that I say : καὶ οἱ πρῶτοι ἔσχατοι, for,
from this equalizing of the first with the last, only a few will
be excepted, — namely, those whom God has selected for

this from among the mass of the called. Thus the parable concludes, and that very appropriately, with language which, no doubt, allows the Apostles to contemplate the *prospect* of receiving rewards of a peculiarly distinguished character (xix. 28), but does not warrant the *certainty* of it, nor does it recognise the existence of anything like so-called *valid claims ;* for, according to the idea running through the parable, the ἐκλογή is to be ascribed simply to the purpose of God (Rom. ix. 11, 15 f.). See ver. 15. Comp. also note on xxii. 14.

REMARK.—The simple application of ver. 16 ought to warn against arbitrary attempts to trace a meaning in all the little details of the parable, many of which belong to the mere drapery of the story. The *householder* is God; the *vineyard* is the Christian theocracy, in which work is to be done in the interests of the approaching kingdom of the Messiah; the οἰκονόμος is Christ; the *twelfth hour*, at which the wages are paid, is the time of the second coming; the *other hours* mark the different periods at which believers begin to devote themselves to the service of God's kingdom; the *denarius* denotes the blessings of the Messianic kingdom in themselves, at the distribution of which the circumstance of an earlier entrance into the service furnishes no claim to a fuller measure of reward, however little this may accord with human ideas of justice; hence the πρῶτοι are represented as *murmuring*, whereupon they are dismissed from the master's presence. Calvin appropriately observes: "hoc murmur asserere noluit ultimo die *futurum*, sed tantum *negare causam fore* murmurandi." But there is nothing to warrant the view that, inasmuch as they consented to be hired only for definite wages, the πρῶτοι betrayed an *unworthy* disposition, while those who came later exhibited a more *commendable* spirit in being satisfied simply with the promise of ὅ ἐὰν ᾖ δίκαιον. It can only be of service in the way of edifying *application*, but it is not reconcilable with the historical sense of the passage, to explain the different hours as referring to the different stages of life, childhood, youth, manhood, and old age (Chrysostom, Theophylact, Euthymius Zigabenus), inasmuch as they are meant to represent various periods between the time of Christ and the close of the αἰὼν οὗτος, at which the second coming is to take place, and are therefore to be regarded as exhibiting the time embraced by the generation then existing (xvi. 28) under the figure of a day with its various divisions. Origen supposed that the allusion was to

the leading epochs of history from the *beginning of the world*
(1) till the flood; (2) till Abraham; (3) till Moses; (4) till
Christ; (5) till the end of the world. This view is decidedly
forbidden by xix. 29 f. Yet similar explanations, based upon
the history of the world, are likewise given by Theophylact
and others. No less foreign is the reference to the *Jews and
Gentiles*, which Grotius, but especially Hilgenfeld, following
Jerome, has elaborated, so that the first of the labourers are taken
to represent the Jews, whose terms of service, so to speak, are
distinctly laid down in the law, and subsequently re-affirmed,
at least, in an indefinite form; while those who come last are
supposed to represent the Gentiles, who, in accordance with
the new covenant of grace, receive, and that before all the
others, precisely the same reward as those who were the first
to be called. Scholten is disposed to think that the parable
was also intended to expose the pretensions of the Jews to
precedence and distinction in the kingdom.

Vv. 17–19. According to the Synoptists, Jesus now takes
occasion, as He approaches Jerusalem (ἀναβ. εἰς Ἱεροσ. is the
continuation of the journey mentioned in xix. 1), to intimate
to His disciples more plainly and distinctly than before (xvi.
21, xvii. 22) His impending fate. Comp. Mark x. 32 ff.;
Luke xviii. 31 ff. — κατ᾿ ἰδίαν] διότι οὐκ ἔδει ταῦτα μαθεῖν
τοὺς πολλούς, ἵνα μὴ σκανδαλισθῶσιν, Euthymius Zigabenus.
There were others travelling along with them. — θανάτῳ]
dative of direction: *even to death*. See Winer, p. 197 f.
[E. T. 263]. This is in accordance with later Greek usage.
Comp. Wisd. ii. 20; 2 Pet. ii. 6; Lobeck, *ad Phryn.* p. 475;
Grimm's note on Wisd. as above. On the prediction of the
resurrection, see note on xvi. 21.

Ver. 20. Τότε] after the announcement in vv. 17–19.
Salome, His mother's sister (see note on John xix. 25), was
one of those women who were in the habit of accompanying
Jesus, xxvii. 56; Mark xv. 40, xvi. 1. She may have heard
from her sons what He, xix. 28, had promised the apostles. —
αἰτοῦσά τι] *making a request*. It is to anticipate to suppose τι
to imply *aliquid magni* (Maldonatus, Fritzsche). Comp. ver. 21,
τί θέλεις. On the *present* participle, see Kühner, II. 2, p. 622 f.;
Dissen, *ad Pind. Ol.* vii. 14; Bornem. *ad Xen. Anab.* vii. 7. 17.

Ver. 21. She thus designates the two most distinguished

positions in the Messiah's kingdom. For among Orientals the foremost place of honour was considered to be immediately on the right, and the next immediately on the left of the king, Joseph. *Antt.* vi. 11. 9 ; Wetstein and Paulus on this passage. She desired to see her sons not merely in the position of ordinary συγκληρονόμοι and συμβασιλεύοντες (Rev. iii. 21), but in that of the most distinguished *proceres regni.* — εἰπὲ ἵνα] as in iv. 3. The fact that the gentle and humble *John* should also have shared this wish (for both the disciples, in whose name also the mother is speaking, are likewise to be regarded as joining in the request, ver. 22, so that there cannot be said to be any essential difference between the present passage and Mark x. 35), shows how much his character must subsequently have been changed. Comp. Introduction to *John,* § 3.

Ver. 22. Οὐκ οἴδατε, κ.τ.λ.] *You do not understand what is involved in your request ;* you do not seem to be aware that the highest stages of συμβασιλεύειν (2 Tim. ii. 12 ; 1 Cor. iv. 8) in my kingdom cannot be reached without previously sharing in such sufferings as I have to endure. Jesus addresses the *two disciples themselves.* — δύνασθε] said with reference to *moral* ability. — τὸ ποτήριον] כּוֹס, figurative description of his fate generally, and of his sufferings in particular. See the exposition of Isa. li. 17 ; Jer. xlix. 12 ; Martyr. Polyc. 14.

Ver. 23. The disciples reply: δυνάμεθα, not because they did not quite understand what Jesus meant (ver. 18 f.), but because they were animated by a sincere though self-confident determination, such, too, as was afterwards sufficiently verified in the case of both, only in somewhat different ways. — οὐκ ἔστιν ἐμὸν δοῦναι, ἀλλ᾽ οἷς ἡτοίμ. ὑπὸ τοῦ πατρ. μ.] *sc.* δοθήσεται : is not *my* business (does not behove *me*) to give, but it will be given to those for whom it has been prepared (has been put in readiness, xxv. 34 ; 1 Cor. ii. 9) by my Father. For ἐμὸν ἐστί with infinitive, comp. Plat. *Legg.* ii. p. 664 B : ἐμὸν ἂν εἴη λέγειν. Jesus thus discourages the questionable request by frankly declaring that the granting of what has just been asked is one of those things which God has reserved to Himself; that it is a matter with which He, the Son, must not interfere. For another instance of such reservation on the part of the Father, see xxiv. 36 ; Mark xiii. 32. This evident meaning of the words is not to be explained away or modified. The former has been done by Chrysostom and his successors, also by Castalio, Grotius, Kuinoel, who took ἀλλά as equivalent to εἰ μή ; the latter by Augustine, Luther, according to whom the words *as man* ("secundum formam servi") are to be understood, and Bengel, who modifies οὐκ ἔστιν ἐμὸν δοῦναι by erroneously supplying the words: *till after my death.* Further, the words τὸ μὲν ποτήρ. μ. πίεσθε are to be regarded as expressing the Lord's *unfeigned trust and confidence* in the δυνάμεθα of the disciples ; He *feels confident that they will verify it by their actions.* His words, therefore, are only indirectly tantamount to a *prediction,* and that not exactly of *death by martyrdom,* which was certainly the fate of James, Acts xii., though not of John,[1] but of *suffering* generally in the interests of the Messiah's kingdom (Rom. viii. 17 ; 2 Cor. i. 5). It is probable, however, that the apocryphal story about John swallowing a *cup full of poison* (see Fabricius, *ad Cod. Apocr.* I. p. 576 ; Tischendorf, *Act. ap. apocr.* p. 269), and that without being anything the worse (Mark xvi. 18), as well as the legend about the attempt to scald him to death in boiling oil (Tertullian, *de praeser.* 36), owe their existence and propagation to the present passage. Origen views our Lord's words on this occasion in connection with the banishment of John to Patmos.

Ver. 24. Ἠγανάκτησαν] Jealousy of the two disciples who were thus aspiring to be first. Euthymius Zigabenus: οἱ δέκα τοῖς δυσὶ μαθηταῖς ἐφθόνησαν, τῶν πρωτείων ἐφιεμένοις.

Ver. 25 ff. Those ambitious desires which prompted the request of the sons of Zebedee have likewise a good deal to do

---

[1] The statement of Gregorius Hamartolos (quoted by Nolte in the *Tüb. theol. Quartalschr.* 1862, p. 466), to the effect that, in his λόγια, Papias declares that John was put to death by the Jews, cannot outweigh the testimony of the early church to the fact that he died a natural death. For the discussion of this point, see Hilgenfeld in his *Zeitschr.* 1865, p. 78 ff. ; Overbeck, *ibid.* 1867, p. 68 ff. ; Holtzmann in Schenkel's *Lex.* III. p. 333 ; Keim, III. p. 44 f. ; Steitz in the *Stud. u. Krit.* 1868, p. 487 ff.

with the displeasure of the other disciples. Accordingly, Jesus endeavours to check their ambition by insisting on the humble spirit of the servant as the way to true greatness in the ranks of His followers. — οἱ ἄρχοντες τῶν ἐθν.] the heathen rulers. — κατακυρ.] the intensive force of the compound verb serves to convey the idea of oppressive rule. Comp. Diod. Sic. xiv. 64, and the Sept. *passim;* see Schleusner; 1 Pet. v. 3 ; Acts xix. 16. Similarly with regard to the κατεξουσ., which occurs nowhere else, and which may be rendered : *they practise violence toward.* — αὐτῶν] refers in *both* instances to τ. ἐθνῶν. — οἱ μεγάλοι] *the magnates* (Hom. *Od.* xviii. 382, comp. μεγιστᾶνες, Mark vi. 21), "ipsis saepe dominis imperiosiores," Bengel. — οὐχ οὕτως ἐστιν ἐν ὑμῖν] it is not so among you. Observe the *present* (see critical notes); there is no such order of things among you. — μέγας] *great,* not equivalent to μέγιστος, but in the sense of: to occupy a high and distinguished place among you. In the sphere to which you belong, true greatness lies in doing service ; that is the principle on which you will act. Hence the future ἔσται; for, in the event of any one wishing to become great, he will aim at it by means of serving ; the latter is the *way to* the former. — πρῶτος] *one of the first* in point of rank, a sort of *climax* to μέγας, as διάκονος is to δοῦλος. The emphasis in the consequent clauses rests on those two predicates, and hence the emphatic word is placed in each case at the close.

Ver. 28. Ὥσπερ] " summum exemplum," Bengel. Comp. Phil. ii. 5 ; Rom. xv. 3 ; Polyc. *Phil.* 5 : ὃς ἐγένετο διάκονος πάντων. Observe here the consciousness, which Jesus had from the very first, that *to sacrifice himself* was His great divine mission. Comp. Dorner, *sündlose Vollk. Jesu,* p. 44 ff. — διακονηθῆναι] *to be waited upon,* as grandees are. — καὶ δοῦναι] *intensive;* adding on the *highest act,* the culminating point in the διακονῆσαι ; but δοῦναι is made choice of, because the ψυχή (*the soul,* as the principle of the life of the body) is conceived of as λύτρον (*a ransom*) ; for, through the shedding of the blood (xxvi. 28 ; Eph. i. 7), it becomes the τιμή of the redemption, 1 Cor. vi. 20, vii. 23. Comp. note on John x. 11. — ἀντὶ πολλῶν] ἀντί denotes substitution. That which is

given as a ransom takes the *place* (is given *instead*) of those who
are to be set free in consideration thereof. The λύτρον (Plat.
Legg. xi. p. 919 A, *Rep.* p. 393 D, Thuc. vi. 5. 4) is an ἀντί-
λυτρον (1 Tim. ii. 6), ἀντάλλαγμα (xvi. 26). Whether ἀντὶ
πολλῶν should be joined to λύτρον, which is the simpler
course, or connected with δοῦναι, is a matter of perfect indifference (in answer to Hofmann, *Schriftbew.* II. 1, p. 300) so
far as the meaning of ἀντί is concerned. In any case, that
meaning is strictly and specifically defined by λύτρον (כֹּפֶר),[1]
according to which ἀντί can only be understood in the sense
of *substitution* in the act of which the ransom is presented
as an equivalent to secure the deliverance of those on whose
behalf it is paid,—a view which is only confirmed by the fact
that in other parts of the New Testament this ransom is usually
spoken of as an *expiatory sacrifice*, xxvi. 28 ; John i. 29 ;
1 John iv. 10 ; Rom. iii. 25 ; Isa. liii. 10 ; 1 Pet. i. 18 f.,
iii. 18. *That* which they are redeemed *from* is the eternal
ἀπώλεια, in which, as having the wrath of God abiding upon
them (John iii. 36), they would remain imprisoned (John iii.
16 ; Gal. iii. 13 ; 2 Cor. v. 21 ; 1 Pet. ii. 24 ; Col. i. 14, ii.
13 f.) as in a state of hopeless bondage (Heb. ii. 15), unless the
guilt of their sins were expiated. — πολλῶν] The vicarious
death of Jesus may be described as having taken place for
all (Rom. v. 18 ; 1 Tim. ii. 6 ; 1 John ii. 2), or for *many*

---

[1] Ritschl, in the *Jahrb. f. D. Theol.* 1863, p. 222 ff., defines λύτρον as meaning something given by way of equivalent in order *to avert* death ; this, however, is not sufficient, for, throughout the Sept. also, in which כפר is rendered
by λύτρον (Ex. xxi. 30, xxx. 12 ; Num. xxxv. 31 f.; Prov. vi. 35, xiii. 8), *pretium
redemtionis* is found to be the specific meaning given to the word, although the
connection may sometimes admit *ex adjuncto* the additional idea of something
given for the purpose of *averting death.* The Sept. likewise adheres to the same
meaning in cases where other expressions are rendered by λύτρον, such as נְאֻלָּה
(Lev. xxv. 24, 51), הַפְּדֻיִם (Num. iii. 51), פִּדְיוֹן (Ex. xxi. 30), מְחִיר (Isa.
xlv. 13). Ritschl interprets our present passage as follows : "*I am come to
give away my life to God in sacrifice, that I may become the substitute of those
who could never hope to succeed in finding, either for themselves or others, any
adequate ransom as a means of securing their exemption from death ; but the
substitute only of those who, through faith and self-denying devotion to my person,
fulfil the condition on which alone the ransom furnished by me can procure the
hoped for exemption,*" p. 238.

(so also xxvi. 28; Heb. ix. 28), according as we regard it as an objective fact (that fact being: Jesus has given His life a ransom for *all* men), or look at it in relation to the subjective appropriation of its results on the part of individuals (which happens only in the case of believers). So in the present case, where, accordingly, πολλῶν is to be understood as meaning all who *believe* now and *will* believe hereafter (John xvii. 20).

Ver. 29. Comp. Mark x. 46 ff.; Luke xviii. 35 ff. — *Καὶ ἐκπορ. αὐτῶν ἀπὸ 'Ιεριχώ*] The Synoptists make no mention whatever of the visit to Ephraim and the journey to Bethany (mentioned in John xi. 54, xii. 1); indeed, their narrative (Matt. xxi. 1 f.) positively excludes at least the latter of these. This divergence, and not a mere want of precision, should be fairly acknowledged (comp. note on xxi. 1), and not explained away by means of ingenious conjectures (Paulus, Schleiermacher, Neander, comp. also Sieffert, who suppose that Jesus may have entered Bethany along with the rest of the pilgrims in the evening, and may have left it again next morning or the morning after; see, on the other hand, on John xii. 17 f., note). A further discrepancy is to be found in the fact that Luke represents the healing as having taken place ἐν τῷ ἐγγίζειν αὐτὸν εἰς 'Ιεριχ., and that Mark and Luke mention only one blind man, although the first mentioned divergence has been turned to account in the way of supporting the hypothesis that Matthew has blended together two distinct cases of healing, one of which is supposed to have taken place when Jesus was entering the town, the other when He was leaving it (Theophylact, Neander, Wieseler, Ebrard, Krafft). The difficulty connected with the mention of two men is not removed by a supposed reminiscence of ix. 27 ff. (Strauss), nor explained by supposing that the blind man of Bethsaida, Mark viii. 22, may have been included (Holtzmann, Volkmar); but it proves that, in point of authenticity, Matthew's account compares unfavourably with the characteristic narrative of Mark, which bears traces of being the original account of what took place. Comp. note on viii. 28 ff.

Ver. 31 f. *"Ινα σιωπήσ.*] Aim of ἐπετίμησεν αὐτοῖς. —

Euthymius Zigabenus says well: ἐπεστόμισεν αὐτοὺς εἰς τιμὴν τοῦ Ἰησοῦ, ὡς ἐνοχλοῦντας αὐτόν. Comp. xix. 13. They probably saw that He was just then in the act of conversing on some topic or other. — τί θέλετε ποιήσω ὑμῖν ;] The question is intended to increase their *confidence* by means of the *hope* which it excites. Comp. note on John v. 6. There is no need to supply ἵνα, but comp. note on xiii. 28.

Ver. 33 f. Ἵνα ἀνοιγῶσιν, κ.τ.λ.] answering the above question in terms of the object aimed at in the cry, ἐλέησον ἡμᾶς, of which ἵνα ἀνοιγ., κ.τ.λ. is the continuation. — ἥψατο] different from Mark and Luke, who represent Jesus as healing merely by the power of His *word.* — τῶν ὀμμάτων (see critical notes), used for variety, being, as far as the meaning is concerned, the same as ὀφθαλμοί. Comp. Xen. *Mem.* i. 4. 17 ; Plat. *Alc.* I. p. 133 B. — ἀνέβλ. αὐτ. οἱ ὀφθ.] *their eyes recovered the power of seeing ;* naïvely told. — ἠκολούθ. αὐτῷ] we cannot tell whether they followed him permanently, though this seems probable from Mark x. 46.

CHAPTER XXI.

VER. 1. πρὸς τὸ ὄρος] Instead of πρός, Lachm. and Tisch. have εἰς, following B C** 33, codd. of It. Or.(once). Correctly; πρός is taken from Mark xi. 1 ; Luke xix. 29. — Ver. 2. πορεύθητε] Lachm. Tisch. 8: πορεύεσθε, following important evidence. But the transcribers happened to be more familiar with πορεύεσθε (x. 6, xxii. 9, xxv. 9, 41). — For ἀπέναντι, Lachm. Tisch. 8 have κατέναντι, which, though sanctioned by important evidence, is borrowed from Mark and Luke. — ἀγάγετε, for which, with Lachm., ἄγετε should be read, is likewise taken from the parallel passages (see, however, on Mark xi. 2). — Ver. 3. With the Received text, Lachm. and Tisch. read ἀποστελεῖ, following B D H M ℵ, Vulg. It. Copt. Sahid. Arm. Or., while Matth. Griesb. Scholz, on the other hand, have adopted ἀποστέλλει. Important evidence on both sides. The connection seemed to require the future, which was acordingly introduced here and in Mark xi. 3. — Ver. 4. ὅλον] is to be deleted, with Lachm. and Tisch. 8, following C* D L Z ℵ, vss. Or. Chrys. Hil. Comp. i. 22, xxvi. 56.—Ver. 5. πῶλον] Lachm. Tisch.: ἐπὶ πῶλον, following B L N ℵ, 1, 124, vss. Correctly; in the Sept. there is only one ἐπί. — Ver. 6. The evidence of B C D 33 in favour of συνέταξεν (Lachm. Tisch. 7) is sufficient. Tisch. 8, with the Received text, reads προσέταξεν, the more usual form. — Ver. 7. For the first ἐπάνω αὐτῶν, Lachm. and Tisch. 8 read ἐπ᾽ αὐτῶν, following B L Z ℵ, 69, Or., with which we may class D and codd. of It., which have ἐπ᾽ αὐτόν. The transcriber would be apt mechanically to anticipate the subsequent ἐπάνω. — ἐπεκάθισεν (Elz.: ἐπεκάθισαν) is supported by decisive evidence (adopted by Matth. Griesb. Fritzsche, Scholz, Lachm. Tisch.), so that instead of supposing it to be taken from Mark xi. 7 (comp. John xii. 14), we should rather regard the reading of the Received text as derived from Luke xix. 35. — Ver. 8. ἐστρώννυον] Tisch. 8: ἔστρωσαν, following only D ℵ * Or. A repetition of ἔστρωσαν in the earlier part of the verse. — Ver. 9. προάγοντες] Lachm. Tisch.: προάγ. αὐτόν, following B C D L ℵ, min. vss. Or. Eus. This αὐτόν, which in itself is not indispensable, was still more apt to be omitted in con-

sequence of Mark xi. 9. — Ver. 11. Lachm. (B D ℵ, Or.) puts ὁ
προφ. before Ἰησοῦς; so also Tisch. 8.   But how current was the
use of the phrase, "Jesus of Nazareth!"— Ver. 12. τοῦ Θεοῦ]
deleted by Lachm., following B L ℵ, min. vss. and Fathers.   It
was omitted as superfluous, and from its not being found in
Mark and Luke, also in consequence of its not occurring elsewhere in the New Testament. — Ver. 13. ἐποιήσατε] Fritzsche,
Lachm. Tisch.: ποιεῖτε, following B L ℵ, 124, Copt. Aeth. Or.
Eus.   Correctly; ἐποιήσατε is from Luke.   Comp. on Mark xi. 17.
— Ver. 19. μηκέτι] Lachm. and Tisch.: οὐ μηκέτι, following, it
is true, only B L; but οὐ would readily be omitted, all the more
that Mark xi. 14 has simply μηκέτι. — Ver. 23. ἐλθόντι αὐτῷ]
Lachm. Tisch. 8: ἐλθόντος αὐτοῦ.   See on viii. 1. —Ver. 25. Ἰωάννου]
Lachm. and Tisch.: τὸ Ἰωάννου, which is sufficiently attested by
B C Z ℵ, Or.; τό was omitted as superfluous. — παρ᾽ ἑαυτ.]
Lachm.: ἐν ἑαυτ., following B L M** Z, min. Cyr.   Gloss in
accordance with xvi. 7, 8. — Ver. 28. μου] upon important evi-
dence, is with Fritzsche, Tisch. to be deleted as an interpolation.
— Ver. 30. ἑτέρῳ] So also Griesb. Scholz, Tisch.   The δευτέρῳ
(Lachm.) of the Received text is opposed by C* D E F G H K U
X Δ Π ℵ, min. vss. and Fathers, and, coming as it does after
πρώτῳ, looks like an exegetical gloss. — Ver. 31. πρῶτος] Lachm.:
ὕστερος.   Maintained by Rinck and Schweizer [1] in the *Stud. u.
Krit.* 1839, p. 944.   Comp. Ewald also, who, however, suggests
ὕστερον, sc. μεταμεληθείς.   Similarly Buttm. in the *Stud. u. Krit.*
1860, p. 343 ff.   ὕστερος is found in B, while D, vss. (also
codd. of It. and the Vulg.) and several Fathers read ἔσχατος.
Consequence of the transposition that had taken place in vv. 29,
30 (B, min. vss. and Fathers): ὁ δὲ ἀποκρ. εἶπεν Ἐγὼ, κύρ., καὶ
οὐκ ἀπῆλθεν.   Καὶ προσελθ. τῷ ἑτέρῳ εἶπ. ὡσ.   Ὁ δὲ ἀποκρ. εἶπεν Οὐ
θέλω, ὕστερον δὲ, κ.τ.λ.   But this transposition was the result of the
ancient interpretation of the two sons as referring to the Jews
and the Gentiles. — Ver. 32. οὐ] Lachm.: οὐδέ, following B, min.
Syr^cur and jer. Copt. Aeth. It. Vulg. Hilar.   The compound negative, the force of which had not been observed, would be omitted

---

[1] Schweizer explains thus : ὁ ὕστερος, sc. ἀπελθών (which Buttm. should not have
declared to be erroneous). The answer, he says, is hesitating and reluctant, perhaps
intentionally *ambiguous*. But coming after the question τίς ἐκ τῶν δύο, κ.τ.λ., the
simple ὁ ὕστερος can only be taken as equivalent to ὁ δεύτερος, as in Xen. *Hell.* i.
7. 6, *al.* Lachm. was of opinion that the answer was intended to be *inappropriate* (comp. already Jerome), though he ultimately decided in favour of the
view that the words λέγουσιν . . . Ἰησοῦς, which Or. omits, are spurious. See the
latter's *Praefat.* II. p. v. Tisch., Bleek, and others have correctly upheld the
reading of the Received text.

all the more readily that δέ occurs just before. — Ver. 33. τις after ἄνθρωπος (in Elz. Matth.) is deleted by Griesb. and more recent editors, in accordance with decisive evidence. — Ver. 38. κατά- σχωμεν] Lachm. and Tisch.: σχῶμεν, following B D L Z א, min. Or. Cyr. The compound form, for sake of greater precision. — Ver. 44. This whole verse is wanting in D, 33, Cant. Ver. Verc. Corb. 1, 2, Or. Eus. (?) Lucif. Cyr. (?); condemned by Griesb., bracketed by Lachm., deleted by Tisch. The external evidence is not sufficient to warrant deletion. Had the words been borrowed from Luke xx. 18, they would have been inserted after ver. 42, and the first half of the passage would have been in closer agreement with Luke (that is to say, the πᾶς would not have been left out). The omission, again, might well be due to a mistake on the part of the copyist, whose eye might pass at once from αὐτῆς καί to αὐτὸν καί. — Ver. 46. ὡς] Lachm. and Tisch.: εἰς, following B L א, 1, 22, Or. ὡς is from ver. 26, xiv. 5.

Ver. 1. Comp. Mark xi. 1 ff.; Luke xix. 29 ff. Καὶ ἦλθον εἰς Βηθφαγῆ] by way of giving greater precision to the foregoing ἤγγισαν εἰς Ἱεροσ. They had come *towards Beth- phage;* that is, as the connection shows (ver. 2), they had not actually *entered* the village, but were close upon it, so that it lay right before them; comp. on John iv. 5. Hard by them ("in latere montis Oliveti," Jerome) was the neighbouring village of Bethany (ver. 17), about which, however, and its position with reference to Bethphage (Robinson, *Pal.* II. p. 312), nothing more precise can now be said. Consequently there is no divergence from Mark and Luke, so that it is unnecessary to understand εἰς, *versus,* after ἦλθον (Fritzsche), which is distinct from, and more definite than, ἤγγισαν. — Of *Bethphage,* בֵּית פַּאגֵי, *house of figs,* no trace remains (Robinson, as above). It is not once mentioned in the Old Testament, though frequently in the Talmud. Buxtorf, p. 1691; Hug, *Einl.* I. p. 18. — τότε] an important juncture. "Non prius; vectura mysterii plena," Bengel. To any one travelling from Jericho, the holy city would be in full view at *Bethphage* (not at Bethany). And Jesus *makes due arrange- ments* for the entry; it is not something done simply to *gratify* the enthusiastic wishes of those about Him (Neander, de Wette, Weizsäcker); comp. Keim, III. p. 85 f.

REMARK.—The stay of Jesus at Bethany, recorded by John
(xii. 1 ff.), does not admit of being inserted into the account given
by the Synoptists (in answer to Ebrard, Wichelh. *Komment. über
d. Leidensgesch.* p. 149 ; Lichtenstein) ; we should rather say that
these latter expressly forbid the view that the night had been
passed at Bethany, all the more that they introduce the anointing (Matt. xxvi. 6 ff. ; Mark xiv. 3 ff.), and consequently the
stay of Jesus at this village *after* the triumphal entry, and
that not merely in the order of their narrative, but also in the
order of events (Matt. xxvi. 2 ; Mark xiv. 1).   This likewise in
answer to Wieseler, p. 391 f.—The tradition, to the effect that
the *triumphal entry took place on the Sunday (Palmarum)*, is in
no way inconsistent with the synoptic narrative *itself*, and
agrees at the same time with John xii. 1, 12, inasmuch as it
would appear from this evangelist that the day on which Jesus
arrived at Bethany was most probably the 8th of Nisan, which,
however, according to John's representation, must have been
Saturday (see note on John xii. 1).   Still, as regards the dates
of the passion week, there remains this fundamental divergence,
that, according to the Synoptists, the Friday on which Jesus
died was the 15th, while according to John (see note on John
xviii. 28) it was the 14th of Nisan ; and further, that John xii.
12 represents Jesus as having passed the night at Bethany
previous to His triumphal entry, while according to the synoptical account He appears to have gone at once from Jericho to
Jerusalem.   In any case, the most authentic view of this
matter is that of John, on *whose* authority, therefore, must rest
the tradition that *Sunday* was the day on which Christ rode
into the city.

Ver. 2 f. Εἰς τὴν κώμην, κ.τ.λ.] *Bethphage.* — εὐθέως]
essentially appropriate to the specific character of the instructions : *immediately*, after you have entered. — The mention of
two animals made by Matthew, though seemingly *at variance*
with Mark xi. 2, Luke xix. 30, John xii. 14, represents the
matter more *correctly* than the other evangelists, and is neither
to be explained symbolically (of Judaism and heathenism, Justin
Martyr), nor to be regarded as a reduplication on the part of
Matthew (Ewald, Holtzmann), nor to be traced to a misap-
prehension of the words of the prophet (de Wette, Neander,
Strauss, Hilgenfeld), who intends עַיִר וְעַל as an epexegetical
parallel to עַל־חֲמֹר ; for just in the same way are we to understand

καὶ ἐπὶ πῶλον, ver. 5, so that, according to Matthew as well, Jesus rides upon the *foal*, though *accompanied* by the mother, a detail which the other evangelists fail to notice. Moreover, it is simply arbitrary to assign a mythical character to the prediction of Jesus on the strength of Gen. xlix. 11 (Strauss; on the other hand, Bleek). — ὅτι] recitative. — ἀποστέλλει] so far from refusing, *He sends them away*. The *present* represents as already taking place what will immediately and certainly be realized. Comp. Mark iv. 29. In εὐθέως δέ, *but at once*, observe Jesus' marvellous *knowledge*, not merely of the fact that the animals would undoubtedly be found awaiting them exactly as He said they would be, but of the further fact that the people of the place are so loyal to Him as perfectly to understand the meaning of the ὁ κύριος, κ.τ.λ., and to find in those words sufficient reason for at once complying with His request. Comp. xxvi. 18. The idea of a magical virtue attaching to the use of the name Jesus (Strauss) is foreign to the text; while, on the other hand, we fail to satisfy the requirements of the three accounts of this incident by resolving it into a mere case of borrowing (Paulus) or requisition (Keim). — The simple account of John does not affect the credibility of the synoptic narrative (also in answer to Bleek). See note on John xii. 14 f.

Ver. 4 f. Ἵνα πληρωθῇ] not accidental, but in accordance with the divine purpose of fulfilling, etc. This quotation, which is a free rendering, partly of the original Hebrew and partly of the Septuagint, combines Isa. lxii. 11 (εἴπατε ... Σιών) and Zech. ix. 9, where the riding of the ideal Messianic king upon an ass is simply a representation, not indeed of absolute humility (Hengstenberg, *Christol.* III. p. 360 f.), for such riding is a sign of πραΰτης, but of a *peaceful* disposition; comp. Ewald, *Propheten*, I. p. 256, ed. 2. He does not come upon a war-horse, not ἅρματα ἐλαύνων ὡς οἱ λοιποὶ βασιλεῖς, Chrysostom. The incident in which Jesus then realized the recognised fulfilment of the prophecy (Hengstenberg, Ewald, Keim) would suggest the strained interpretation of the figure, and quite properly, inasmuch as Christ's riding into the city revealed the *typical* nature of the form in which the prophet embodied his prediction (Düsterdieck, *de rei propheticae natura ethica,* 1852, p. 78 f.). For the prophetic expression *daughter of Zion* (the locality of the town regarded as its mother), see Knobel's note on Isa. i. 8. Comp. Lam. i. 6. — σοί] Dative of ethical reference, common likewise in classical Greek along with ἔρχεσθαι. — καὶ ἐπὶ πῶλον] See note on ver. 2. καί is *epexegetical.* — υἱὸν ὑποζυγ.] בֶּן־אֲתֹנוֹת. For ὑποζύγιον, *beast of burden,* a term more frequently used in the Septuagint to designate the *ass,* comp. Herod. ix. 24, 39, 41; Xen. *Anab.* i. 3. 1; Lucian, *Cynic.* x.; Polyb. iii. 51. 4; 3 Esdr. v. 43; 2 Pet. ii. 16.

Ver. 7. They spread their outer garments upon *both* animals, being uncertain *which* of them Jesus intended to mount. — The (*second*) ἐπάνω αὐτῶν must necessarily be referred, with Theophylact, Euthymius Zigabenus, Castalio, Beza, Homberg, Fritzsche, Winer, p. 165 [E. T. 219], to the *garments,* in which case it is clear from ver. 5 that Jesus sat upon the *foal.* Were we to refer αὐτῶν to the *animals,* the result would be the absurd idea (which Strauss, B. Bauer, Volkmar make use of against Matthew) that Jesus mounted both of them *at once,* not *one after the other* (Fritzsche, Fleck), seeing that κ. ἐπεκάθισεν ἐπ. αὐτῶν denotes the instantaneous, finished act which followed the spreading of the garments. To suppose (Ebrard, Olshausen), by way of justifying the reference to the animals, that we have here a loose form of speech, corresponding to the German phrase: he leaps from the horses, and such like, is out of the question, for the simple reason that no such σύλληψις can be assumed in the case of ver. 5, all the less so that, from this verse, it would appear that it was the *dam* on which Jesus rode, with the foal walking by her side.

Ver. 8. Manifestations of respect, such as kings were usually greeted with on entering cities, 2 Kings ix. 13; Wetstein's note on this passage; Robinson, II. p. 383. — ὁ πλεῖστος ὄχλος] *the most of the people,* the greatest part of the multitude. Comp. Plat. *Rep.* p. 397 D; Thuc. vii. 78; Xen. *Anab.* iii. 2. 36. — ἑαυτῶν] states what the multitude did with *their own* garments, after the *disciples* had spread theirs upon the two beasts.

Ver. 9 ff. 'Ωσαννά] נָא הוֹשִׁיעָה, Ps. cxviii. 25, *bestow blessing !*—addressed to God. The dative is due to the meaning of the verb (*opitulare*) contained in ὠσαννά. — ὠσαννὰ ἐν τοῖς ὑψίστ.] *Grant blessing in the highest places* (Luke ii. 14), *i.e.* in the highest *heaven* (Eph. iv. 10), where Thy throne is fixed, and from which let it descend upon the Messiah. The interpretation of Fritzsche, Olshausen: let blessing be *proclaimed* (by the angels) in heaven! is far-fetched. No less so is that of de Wette, Bleek: let Hosanna be *confirmed* in heaven, let it be ratified by God! Nor is ἐν τ. ὑψ. equivalent to ὁ ὢν τ. ὑψ. (grant blessing, O Thou who art in heaven), as Beza, Vatablus, Calovius, Bengel, Kuinoel, are disposed to think. — ἐν ὀνόμ. κυρίου] *i.e.* as sent by God to be His representative, John v. 43. — Speaking generally, the exclamation may be described as an outburst of enthusiasm expressing itself, in a free and impromptu manner, in language borrowed from the hymn for the feast of Tabernacles, Ps. cxviii. (Succoth iv. 5). — ἐσείσθη] *was thrown into a state of commotion* (Pind. *Pyth.* iv. 484; Soph. *Ant.* 163), on account of the sensation created by this Messianic entry into the city. The excitement was contagious. — ὁ προφήτης] the *well-known* prophet. The crowds that *accompanied* Him had, in most explicit terms, designated Him the Messiah; but the less interested people of the city wished above all to ascertain His name and rank. Hence the full reply, 'Ἰησοῦς . . . Γαλιλ., in which the ὁ ἀπὸ Ναζαρ. τ. Γαλιλ. doubtless betrays some-what of the Galilean *consciousness* of the multitude, inasmuch as it was for most part composed of Galileans.

REMARK.—The triumphal entry of Jesus is not a final attempt to establish the Messianic kingdom in a political sense (*Wolfenb. Fragm.*), such a kingdom having been entirely foreign to His purpose and His function. It is rather to be regarded as His last public and solemn appearance as the Messiah,—an appearance which, coming as it did immediately before His passion, was on the one hand a matter of deep personal interest because of the necessary bearing it was felt to have upon the mission of His life; while, if taken in con-nection with what happened so soon after, it was calculated, on the other hand, to destroy all expectations of a merely political

kind. The time was now come when Jesus felt that, just
because He *was* the Messiah, it *behoved* Him to do something—
and for this He appropriates the prophet's symbol of the Prince
of Peace—by way of contrast to His practice hitherto of for-
bidding the publication of His Messiahship. This step, which,
from the fact of the crisis being so near, might now be taken
without risk, He had postponed till the eve of His death,—a
circumstance of the utmost significance as regarded the sense
in which His Messiahship was to be understood. *This*
incident, too, was one of the things for which His hour had
not previously come (John vi. 15). Comp. note on John vii.
5 f. Strauss asserts that there is here the possibility at least
of a mythical story, though his objections are far from being to
the point. See, on the other hand, Ebrard and Bleek. According to Wittichen, *Jahrb. f. D. Theol.* 1862, p. 365, Jesus did
not intend this incident to be regarded in any other light than
as an ordinary *festival procession*, but the multitude, *without
consulting Him*, turned it into an occasion for a Messianic
demonstration. This is not in keeping with the unusual preparations mentioned in ver. 2 ; comp. ver. 7.

Ver. 12. Different from Mark xi. 11, 15, where the narrative is more precise ; comp. Weiss' note on Mark. — In the
court of the Gentiles were the *tabernae*, הניות, where animals,
incense, oil, wine, and other requisites for sacrifice were exposed for sale. Lightfoot on this passage. — The *money-
changers* (κολλυβ., see Phrynichus, p. 440) exchanged on
commission (קובלין, Maimonides, *Shekal.* 3) ordinary money for
the two drachmae pieces which were used in paying the
temple tribute (see note on xvii. 24). — This cleansing of the
temple is, with Chrysostom, Paulus, Kuinoel, Tholuck, Olshausen, Kern, Ebrard, Baumgarten - Crusius, Schleiermacher,
Hengstenberg, Wieseler, to be regarded as the *second* that took
place, the first being that recorded in John ii. 13 ff., and
which occurred on the occasion of the first visit to Jerusalem.
The abuse having been repeated, there is no reason why Jesus
should not have repeated this purifying process, and that (in
answer to Hofmann, Luthardt, Hengstenberg) without any
essential difference. The absence, in the synoptical account,
of any allusion to a previous occasion, is sufficiently explicable
from the length of time that intervened, and from the fact

that the Synoptists take no notice generally of what took place during the earlier visit to Judea. The similarity of the *accompanying circumstances* may be accounted for from the similarity of the *incidents themselves ;* whereas the supposition that the cleansing took place only on one occasion would necessarily involve a chronological derangement extending to almost the whole period of Christ's ministry,—a derangement which can neither be fairly imputed to the synoptical narrative nor even conceived of as far as John is concerned, whose testimony is that of an eye-witness. This is not "wishy-washy criticism" (Keim), but it is based upon the authenticity of the fourth Gospel, as well as upon the weighty and unanimous testimony of the synoptical writers, to sacrifice whose authority for the sake of John would be both one-sided and violent. This, however, is what Wetstein, Lücke, Neander, de Wette, Bleek, Ewald, Weizsäcker have done. *Others*, again, have rejected the fourth evangelist's account, so far as its chronology is concerned, in favour of that of the Synoptists (Ziegler, Theile, Strauss, Baur, Weisse, Hilgenfeld, Schenkel, Keim). Comp., further, the remarks under John ii. 17.

Ver. 13. Free combination of Isa. lvi. 7 and Jer. vii. 11, and taken from the Sept. — κληθήσ.] how *sacred* the purpose for which it was intended, but *ye*, etc. — ποιεῖτε (see critical notes) censures this desecration of the temple as a thing in which they are *still persisting.* — σπήλαιον λῃστῶν] The *strong* language of the prophet (otherwise in John) was in keeping with the *emotion* that was awakened in Jesus. The use of such language is sufficiently *accounted* for by the fact that *avarice* had taken up its abode in those sacred precincts to carry on its huckstering and money-changing : τὸ γὰρ φιλοκερδὲς λῃστρικὸν πάθος ἐστι, Theophylact. Differently Fritzsche : "Vos undequaque pecuniam, animalia huc congerere sustinetis, ut latrones praedam comportant in speluncam," —where, however, due prominence is not given to the distinctive point of comparison, viz. the *robbery.* — In vv. 12, 13, Jesus acts with higher authority than that of a mere zealot (Num. xxv. 11) : He addresses Himself to the purifying of the temple and its worship with such a reforming energy as, according to Mal. iii. 1-3, befitted the *Messiah*. Comp. Bertholdt, *Christol.* p. 163 ; Ullmann, *Sündl.* p. 177. And the acquiescence of the astonished multitude is all the more intelligible on the occasion of *this* cleansing, that the indignant reformer had just celebrated His triumphal march into the city in the character of Messiah. But even on the *first* occasion, John ii., their acquiescence is sufficiently explicable from the sudden and decided nature of the proceeding, taken in connection with the spiritually - imposing character of the Lord's person and bearing ("*divinitatis majestas lucebat in facie*," Jerome), so that it is quite needless to resort to the hypothesis of a miracle (Origen, Jerome).

Ver. 14 ff. The insertion of vv. 14–16 from the apostolic tradition is peculiar to Matthew. — $\tau\grave{a}$ $\theta\alpha\upsilon\mu\acute{a}\sigma\iota\alpha$] the only instance of this usage in the New Testament, though very common in classical Greek and the Sept.: *the wonderful things,* viz. the cleansing of the temple and the miraculous cures. This combination has suggested the use of the more *comprehensive* term. — Ver. 16. $\dot{a}\kappa o\acute{\upsilon}\epsilon\iota\varsigma$ $\kappa.\tau.\lambda.$] in a tone of rebuke, implying that He was the occasion of such impropriety, and was tolerating it. — $\ddot{o}\tau\iota$] *recitative.* The reply of Jesus, so profoundly conversant with the true sense of Scripture, is as much as to say that this shouting of the children is altogether befitting, as being the *praise which, according to Ps.* viii. 3, *God has perfected.* — $\nu\eta\pi\acute{\iota}\omega\nu$ $\kappa.$ $\theta\eta\lambda\alpha\zeta\acute{o}\nu\tau\omega\nu$] In explaining the words of the psalm, there is no need to have recourse to the fact that children usually received suck for two and three years (Grimm's note on 2 Macc. vii. 27), nor even to the idea of the children being transformed into *adult* instruments in effecting the triumph of God's cause (Hofmann, *Weiss. u. Erf.* II. p. 118), but only to bear in mind that, as a genuine poet, the psalmist seemed to hear, in the noise and prattle of the *babes* and *sucklings,* a celebration of their Maker's praise. But, inasmuch as those children who shouted *in the temple* were not $\nu\acute{\eta}\pi\iota o\iota$ (*i.c.* in connection with $\theta\eta\lambda\acute{a}\zeta.$ *infantes,* Isa. xi. 8 ; 1 Cor. iii. 1), the scriptural warrant by which Jesus here justifies their hosannas may be said to be based upon an in-

ference *a minore ad majus.* That is to say, if, according to
Ps. viii. 3, God had already ordained praise from the mouths
of *sucklings,* how much more has He done so from the mouths
of those little ones who now *shouted hosanna!* The *former,*
though unable to speak, and still at the mother's breast, are
found praising God; how much more the *latter,* with their
hosanna cries! These last are shouted in honour of the
Messiah, who, however, is God's Son and Representative, so
that in *His* δόξα *God* is glorified (John xiii. 31, xiv. 13;
Phil. ii. 11), nay, God glorifies *Himself* (John xii. 28). — κ.
ηὐλίσθη ἐκεῖ] Consequently He did not *pass the night* in
the open air (in answer to Grotius), for neither in classical
Greek do we always find αὐλίζεσθαι used in the sense of
bivouacking (Apollonid. 14; Diod. Sic. xiii. 6). Comp. Tob.
iv. 14, vi. 10, ix. 5; Judg. xix. 9 f. — On Bethany, some
15 stadia from Jerusalem (John xi. 18), see Tobler, *Topogr.
v. Jerus.* II. p. 432 ff.; Robinson, *Pal.* II. p. 309 ff.; Sepp,
Jerus. u. d. heil. Land, I. p. 583 ff. At present it is only a
miserable village, known by the Arabic name of *el-Aziriyeh* (from
el-Azir, i.e. *Lazarus*). For the *name,* see note on John i. 28.

Ver. 19. Comp. Mark xi. 19 ff. Μίαν] "unam illo loco,"
Bengel. — ἐπὶ τῆς ὁδοῦ] The tree, which was by the side
of the public road (not on private property), stood *above
the road,* either projecting over it merely, or occupying an
eminence close to it, or the road itself may have been in a
ravine. It was a favourite practice to plant fig-trees by the
roadside, because it was thought that the dust, by absorbing
the exuding sap, was conducive to the better growth of the
fruit, Plin. *N. H.* xv. 19. — ἦλθεν ἐπ' αὐτήν] not: *con-
scendit arborem* (Fritzsche), but: *He went up to it. From
seeing the tree in foliage,* Jesus expected, of course (for it
was well known that the fig-tree put forth its fruit before
coming into leaf), to find fruit upon it as well, namely, the
early *boccôre,* which, as a rule, did not ripen till June,
and not the harvest-figs, *kermuse,* that had been on the
tree all winter, and the existence of which He could not
infer from seeing *leaves.* Comp. Tobler, *Denkbl. aus Jerus.*
p. 101 ff. On the *disappointed expectation* of Jesus, Bengel

observes : " maxima humanitatis et deitatis indicia uno tempore edere solitus est." It is a perversion of the text to say, with Chrysostom, Euthymius Zigabenus, that He did not expect to find fruit upon the tree, but went up to it merely for the purpose of working the miracle. Moreover, the hunger is alleged to have been only a σχηματίζεσθαι (Euthymius Zigabenus), or an *esuries sponte excitata* (Cornelius a Lapide). The account of the withering of the tree, contained in Mark xi. 12 ff., 19 f., is more precise and more original (in answer to Köstlin, Hilgenfeld, Keim). Matthew abridges.

Ver. 21 f. Instead of telling the disciples, in reply to their question, by what means *He* (in the exercise of His divine power) caused the tree to wither, He informs them how *they* too might perform similar and even greater wonders (John xiv. 12), namely, through an unwavering *faith* in Him (xvii. 20), a faith which would likewise secure a favourable answer to all their prayers. The participation in the life of Christ, implied in the πίστις, would make them partakers of the divine power of which He was the organ, would be a guarantee that their prayers would always be in harmony with the will of God, and so would prevent the promise from being in any way abused. — *The affair of the fig-tree* (τὸ τῆς συκῆς, comp. viii. 33) should neither be explained on *natural* grounds (Paulus says : Jesus saw that the tree was on the point of dying, and that He intimated this " in the popular phraseology " ! Comp. even Neander, Baumgarten - Crusius, Bleek), nor regarded as a *mythical* picture suggested by the parable in Luke xiii. 6 ff. (Strauss, de Wette, Weisse, Hase, Keim), but *as the miraculous result of an exercise of His will on the part of Jesus*,—such a result as is alone in keeping with the conception of Christ presented in the Gospel narrative. But the *purpose* of the miracle cannot have been to punish an inanimate object, nor, one should think, merely to make a display of miraculous power (Fritzsche, Ullmann), but *to represent in a prophetic, symbolical, visible form* the punishment which follows moral barrenness (Luke xiii. 6 ff.),—such a punishment as was about to overtake the Jews in particular, and the approach of which Jesus was presently to announce with solemn earnestness on the eve of His own death (vv. 28-44, xxii. 1-14, xxiii., xxiv., xxv.). It is true He does not make any express *declaration* of this nature, nor had He previously led the disciples to expect such (Sieffert); but this objection is met partly by the fact that the πῶς of the disciples' question, ver. 20, did not *require* Him to do so, and partly by the whole of the subsequent denunciations, which form an eloquent commentary on the silent withering of the fig-tree. — αἰτήσητε ἐν τῇ προσευχῇ] Comp. note on Col. i. 9: *what ye will have desired in your prayer.* — πιστεύοντες] Condition of the λήψεσθε. He who prays *in faith*, prays *in the name of Jesus*, John xiv. 13.

Ver. 23. Comp. Mark xi. 27 ff.; Luke xx. 1 ff. — Διδάσκοντι] while He was engaged in teaching. — ἐν ποίᾳ ἐξουσίᾳ] *in virtue of what kind of authority.* Comp. Acts iv. 7. The second question is intended to apply to *Him who has given* the authority; the first is general, and has reference to the *nature* of the authority (whether it be divine or human). — ταῦτα] *these things,* cannot point merely to the *cleansing of the temple* (Theophylact, Euthymius Zigabenus), which is too remote for such special reference. As little can the *teaching* by itself be intended (Grotius, Bengel), that being a matter in connection with the ministry of Jesus about which the Sanhedrim was comparatively unconcerned, and for which He did not need a higher authority. We should rather say that, in their ταῦτα, the questioners mean to include *all that up till that moment Jesus had done* and was still doing in Jerusalem, and therefore refer to the triumphal entry, the cleansing of the temple, the miraculous healing and the teaching in the temple, all which, taken together, seemed to betoken the Messianic pretender. Comp. de Wette, Bleek, Weizsäcker, p. 532; Keim, III. p. 112. The members of the Sanhedrim hoped either to hear Him acknowledge that the ἐξουσία was *divine,* or presumptuously assert that it was *self-derived,* so that in either case they might have something on which to found judicial proceedings against Him. They seem to have been a provisional deputation of the Sanhedrim appointed to discover a pretext for excommunicating Him. Comp. John i. 19.

Ver. 24 f. Jesus prudently frustrates their design by proposing in reply a puzzling question, which, in the circumstances, they did not know how to answer.— λόγον ἕνα] *a single word, a single question ;* not more.   The subject of the question itself is admirably chosen, seeing that the work of reform in which Jesus was engaged had a necessary connection with that of John ; both would stand and fall together. — πόθεν ἦν] *whence did it proceed ?*   The following alternative is explanatory : was it *from God,* who had commissioned John, or *from men,* so that he baptized simply on his own authority or that of his fellow-mortals ?   The latter was out of the question, if John was a prophet (ver. 26).   Comp., further, Acts v. 39. — διελογ. παρ' ἑαυτοῖς] *they deliberated by themselves,* privately κατ' ἰδίαν, *i.e. with each other,* during a brief pause for private consultation, before giving their decision, which was intimated in the subsequent ἀποκριθέντες τῷ Ἰησοῦ. διαλογίζεσθαι in this instance also denotes reflection combined with mutual *consultation.*   Comp. xvi. 7 ; Mark viii. 16 ; Luke xx. 14. — ἐπιστεύσατε αὐτῷ] λέγοντι πολλὰ καὶ μεγάλα περὶ ἐμοῦ, Euthymius Zigabenus.

Ver. 26 f. Φοβούμεθα τὸν ὄχλον] Those words are preceded by an *aposiopesis,* the import of which, however (Luke xx. 6), is indicated by the words themselves.—The language of embarrassment : " *But suppose we should say : From men ; we are afraid of the people,*" etc.   Comp. note on Acts xxiii. 9. — πάντες γὰρ, κ.τ.λ.] See on xiv. 5. — καὶ αὐτός] *He also* on His part ; for *as they* with their wretched οὐκ οἴδαμεν left the question of Jesus *unanswered,* so now *in like manner He* with His decided and humbling οὐδὲ ἐγώ (*neither do I*) *refuses to answer* theirs.

Vv. 28–32. Peculiar to Matthew, and doubtless taken from the collection of the sayings of the Lord.—Jesus now assumes the *offensive* in order to convince His adversaries of their own baseness. — τέκνα and τέκνον suggest the father's *love.* — Ver. 30. ἐγώ] is to be taken *elliptically,* and that with due regard at the same time to its *emphatic* character, in virtue of which it forms a contrast to the negative answer of the other son : *I,* sir, will go and work in the vineyard this very day.   The

κύριε expresses the hypocritical submission of the man. — *The
publicans and harlots* are represented by the *first* mentioned
son ; for previous to the days of John they refused to obey
the divine call (in answer to the command to serve Him,
which God addressed to them through the law and the prophets, they practically said : οὐ θέλω), but when John appeared
they accorded him the faith of their hearts, so that, in conformity with his preaching, they were now amending their
ways, and devoting themselves to the service of God.   The
members of the Sanhedrim are represented by the *second* son ;
for, while pretending to yield obedience to the law of God
revealed in the Scriptures (by the submissive airs which they
assumed, they practically uttered the insincere ἐγὼ, κύριε), they
in reality disregarded it, and, unlike the publicans and the
harlots, they would not allow themselves to be influenced by
the movement that followed the preaching of the Baptist, so
that neither the efforts of John nor the example of the publicans
and harlots had any effect upon them in the way of producing
conversion.   To understand by the two sons the *Gentiles* and
the *Jews*, is entirely against the context. — προάγουσιν
ὑμᾶς] as though the future entering into the Messianic kingdom were *now* taking place.   The *going before*, however, does
not necessarily imply that others are following.   Comp. xviii.
14. — ἐν ὁδῷ δικαιοσύνης] *in the way of righteousness, i.e.*
as one whose walk and conversation are characterized by
moral integrity.   ἐν ἀμέμπτῳ βίῳ (Theophylact), ἵνα καὶ ἀξιό-
πιστος φανῇ (Euthymius Zigabenus).   Comp. 2 Pet. ii. 21,
ii. 2 ; Prov. viii. 20, xii. 28, xvii. 23.   The *preaching* of
righteousness (de Wette, Bleek, Keim) would have been expressed by some such terms as ὁδὸν δικαιοσ. διδάσκων
(xxii. 16). — ἰδόντες] the fact, namely, that the publicans
and harlots believed Him. — οὐδὲ μετεμελ. ὕστ.] *did not even*
feel *penitent* afterwards (ver. 29), far less did you get the
length of actual conversion.   The example of those others
produced so little impression upon you.   The emphasis is not
on ὕστερ., but on μετεμ. — τοῦ πιστεῦσαι] Object of μετεμ.
ὕστ., *so as to believe Him.*

Ver. 33 ff. Comp. Mark xii. 1 ff.; Luke xx. 9 ff.   Jesus,

in ver. 28 ff., having shown His adversaries how base they are, now proceeds to do this yet more circumstantially in another parable (founded, no doubt, upon Isa. v. 1 ff.), in which, with a lofty and solemn earnestness, He lays bare to them the *full measure of their sin* against God (even to the killing of His Son), and announces to them the *punishment* that awaits them. — ὤρυξεν ἐν αὐτῷ ληνόν] *dug a wine-vat in it*. Comp. Xen. *Oec.* xix. 2 : ὁπόσον βάθος ὀρύττειν δεῖ τὸ φυτόν. This was a trough dug in the earth for the purpose of receiving the juice of the grape as it flowed down from the press through an aperture covered with a grating. See Winer, *Realw.* I. p. 653 f. — πύργον] *a tower*, for watching the vineyard. Such tower - shaped structures were then, and are still, in common use for this purpose (Tobler, *Denkbl.* p. 113. — ἐξέδοτο] *he let it out* (Pollux. i. 75 ; Herod. i. 68 ; Plat. *Parm.* p. 127 A ; Dem. 268, 9), namely, to be cultivated. Seeing that the proprietor himself collects the produce (vv. 34, 41), we must assume that the vineyard was let for a *money* rent, and not, as is generally supposed, for a share of the fruit. For nothing is said in this passage about payment in kind to the proprietor, including only *part* of the produce. Otherwise in Mark xii. 2 ; Luke xx. 10 ; comp. Weiss' note on Mark. — τοὺς καρποὺς αὐτοῦ] αὐτοῦ is often taken as referring to the *vineyard ;* but without reason, for there is nothing to prevent its being referred to the subject last mentioned. It was *his own fruit* that the master wished to have brought to him. The fruit of the vineyard, and the *whole* of it too, *belongs to him.* — ἐλιθοβόλησαν] *they stoned him* (xxiii. 37 ; John viii. 5 ; Acts vii. 58 f., xiv. 5 ; Heb. xii. 20), forms a *climax* to ἀπέκτ., as being a "species atrox" (Bengel) of this latter. — ἐντραπήσ.] a reasonable expectation. — εἶπον ἐν ἑαυτοῖς] *they said one to another.* — καὶ σχῶμεν τὴν κληρον. αὐτοῦ] *and let us obtain possession of his inheritance,* namely, the vineyard to which he is the heir. In these words they state not the *result* of the murder (as in Mark), but *what step they propose to take next.* After the death of the son, who is therefore to be regarded as an only one, they intend to lay claim to the property. — ἐξέβαλον κ.

ἀπέκτ.] differently in Mark xii. 8, hence also the transposition in D, codd. of It. This passage contains no allusion to the previous *excommunication* (Grotius), or to the crucifixion of Christ because it took place *outside of Jerusalem* (comp. Heb. xiii. 12 f.; so Chrysostom, Theophylact, Euthymius Zigabenus, Olshausen), but simply describes the *scene* in which the son on his arrival *is thrust out of the vineyard and murdered.*— The parable illustrates the hostile treatment experienced time after time by God's prophets (the δοῦλοι) at the hands of the leaders (the husbandmen) of the Jewish theocracy (the vineyard), — an institution expressly designed for the production of moral fruit,—and also shows how their self-seeking and love of power would lead them to put to death even Jesus, the Son, the last and greatest of the messengers from God. Comp. Acts vii. 51 f. Chrysostom, Theophylact, Euthymius Zigabenus, likewise find a meaning in the *hedge* (the law), the *wine-vat* (the altar), and the *tower* (the temple). So also Bengel, who sees in ἀπεδήμησεν an allusion to the "*tempus divinae taciturnitatis;*" while Origen takes it as re-ferring to the time when God ceased to manifest Himself in a visible shape.

Ver. 40 f. According to Mark and Luke, it is *Jesus* who replies. But how appropriate and how striking (comp. ver. 31) that the *adversaries themselves* are forced to pronounce their own condemnation (in answer to Schneckenburger, de Wette, Bleek) ! — κακοὺς κακῶς ἀπολέσει αὐτ.] as *despic-able creatures* (scoundrels), *He will miserably destroy them.* The collocation κακοὺς κακῶς serves to indicate in an emphatic manner the correspondence between the conduct in question and its punishment. See Wetstein's note ; Fritzsche, *Diss. in* 2 *Cor.* ii. p. 147 f. ; Lobeck, *Paralip.* p. 58. Comp. Eur. *Cycl.* 270 : κακῶς οὗτοι κακοὶ ἀπόλοινθ'; and, in general, Lobeck, *ad Soph. Aj.* 866 ; Elmsl. *ad Eur. Med.* 787. If we are to apply the parable in accordance with the order of thought, and, therefore, in conformity with the meaning intended by Jesus Himself, we cannot understand the coming of the κύριος and the execution of the punishment as denoting the *second advent and the last judgment.;* for, apart from the

fact that it is God and not Christ that is represented by
the κύριος, the words οἵτινες ἀποδώσουσιν, κ.τ.λ., would point
to the period *subsequent* to the advent and the judgment,—
a reference not in keeping with the sense of the passage.
The true reference is to the *destruction of Jerusalem,* the
shape in which the divine judgment is to overtake the then
guardians of the theocracy, whereupon this latter would be
entrusted to the care of other guides (*i.e.* the leaders of the
Christian church as representing the true Ἰσραὴλ τοῦ θεοῦ),
who as such will be called upon to undertake the duties
and responsibilities of their unfaithful predecessors.   Comp.
xxii. 7; John vii. 34; Eph. iv. 11 f.   Such are the things
which those hostile questioners " ἄκοντες προφητεύουσι "
(Euthymius Zigabenus). — ἐν τοῖς καιροῖς αὐτῶν] αὐτῶν
refers to the γεωργοί: *at the terms prescribed to them for
doing so.*

Ver. 42. The enemies of Jesus have answered correctly,
but they are not aware that they have thus pronounced their
own condemnation, since those who thrust out the Son that
was sent to them are no other than themselves.   To bring
this fully home to them (ver. 45), is the purpose of the
concluding words added by our Lord.   The quotation is
from the Septuagint version of Ps. cxviii. 22 f., which was
composed after the captivity, and in which the stone, according to the *historical* sense of the psalm, represents the
people of Israel, who, though rejected by the Gentiles, were
chosen by God to form the foundation-stone of His house
(the theocracy); while, according to the *typical* reference of
the passage (which the Rabbinical teachers also recognised,
see Schoettgen), it denotes the ideal head of the theocracy,
viz. the *Messiah.* — λίθον ὅν] *a stone which,* attraction of
very frequent occurrence. — ἀπεδοκίμ.] as not fit for being
used in the building. — οὗτος] *this,* and no other. —
κεφαλὴν γωνίας] רֹאשׁ פִּנָּה, *head of the corner,* i.e. *corner-
stone* (in Hesychius we find κεφαλίτης in the sense of
corner-stone; see Lobeck, *ad Phryn.* p. 700), is the metaphorical designation of Him on whom the stability and
development of the theocracy depend, without whom it would

fall to pieces, and in this respect He resembles that stone in a building which is indispensably necessary to the support and durability of the whole structure. The antitype here referred to is not the *Gentiles* (Fritzsche), but, as must be inferred from the connection of our passage with what is said about the Son being thrust out and put to death, from the further statement in ver. 44, and from the common usage throughout the New Testament (Acts iv. 11; Eph. ii. 20; 1 Pet. ii. 7), *the Messiah.* — ἐγένετο αὕτη] *did he become so* (viz. the corner-stone, κεφαλὴ γωνίας). Here the *feminine* is not a Hebraism for the *neuter* (as little is it so in 1 Sam. iv. 7; Ps. xxvii. 4), as Buttmann, *Neut. Gr.* p. 108 [E. T. 123], would have us suppose, but strictly grammatical, inasmuch as it refers to κεφ. γων.; and accordingly we find that in the Septuagint also זאת is rendered according to its contextual reference. To refer to γωνίας merely (Wetstein) is inadmissible, for this reason, that, in what precedes, κεφαλὴ γων. was the prominent idea. — καὶ ἔστι θαυμαστὴ, κ.τ.λ.] viz. this κεφαλὴ γων. " *Our* eyes," as referring to *believers*.

Ver. 43. Διὰ τοῦτο] *therefore,* because, according to the psalm just quoted, the rejected stone is destined to become the corner-stone. What is contained in the following announcement is the necessary consequence of the inversion of the order of things just referred to. The λέγω ὑμῖν, however, like the ἀφ᾽ ὑμῶν below, implies the obvious intermediate thought: " for it is you who reject this corner-stone." — ἀρθήσεται ἀφ᾽ ὑμῶν] for they, along with the whole Ἰσραὴλ κατὰ σάρκα represented by them, were by natural right the *owners* of the approaching Messianic kingdom, its theocratic heirs; comp. xiii. 38. — ἔθνει ποιοῦντι, κ.τ.λ.] Jesus is not here referring to the *Gentiles,* as, since Eusebius' time, many, and in particular Schenkel, Hilgenfeld, Keim, Volkmar, have supposed, but, as the use of the singular already plainly indicates, to the whole of the future subjects of the kingdom of the Messiah, *conceived of as one people,* which will therefore consist of Jews and Gentiles, that new Messianic people of God, which is to constitute the body politic in the kingdom that is about to be established,

1 Pet. ii. 9. *The fruits of the Messiah's kingdom* are those fruits which must be produced as the condition of admission (v 3 ff., xiii. 8). Hence, likewise, the use of the *present* ποιοῦντι; for Jesus regards the future subjects of the kingdom *as already anticipating its establishment by producing its fruits.* The *metaphor* is to be regarded as an echo of the parable of the vineyard. The *fruits themselves* are identical with those mentioned in Eph. v. 9; Gal. v. 22; Rom. vi. 22.

Ver. 44. After having indicated the future punishment in the merely negative form of ἀρθήσεται κ.τ.λ., Jesus now proceeds to announce it in *positive* terms, by means of parallelism in which, without dropping the metaphor of the stone, the person in question is first the subject and then the object. A solemn exhausting of the whole subject of the coming doom. *And whosoever will have fallen upon this stone* (whosoever by rejecting the Messiah shall have incurred the judgment consequent thereon) *shall be broken* (by his fall); *but on whomsoever it shall fall* (whomsoever the Messiah, as an avenger, shall have overtaken), *it shall winnow him,* i.e. throw him off like the chaff from the winnowing-fan. συνθλᾶσ-θαι *(to be crushed)* and λικμᾶσθαι, which form a climax, are intended to portray the execution of the Messianic judgments. λικμάω is not equivalent to *conterere, comminuere,* the meaning usually assigned to it in accordance with the Vulgate, but is rather to be rendered by *to winnow, ventilare* (*Il.* v. 500; Xen. *Oec.* xviii. 2. 6; Plut. *Mor.* p. 701 C; Lucian, *Gymnas.* xxv.; Ruth iii. 2; Ecclus. v. 10). See likewise Job xxvii. 21, where the Sept. employs this *figurative* term for the purpose of rendering the idea of *driving away as before a storm* (שער). Comp. Dan. ii. 44; Wisd. xi. 20. — Observe the *change* which the figure undergoes in the second division of the verse. The stone that previously appeared in the character of the corner-stone, lying at rest, and on which, as on a stone of stumbling (Isa. viii. 14 f.), some one falls, is now conceived of as rolling down with crushing force upon the man; the latter having reference to the whole of such *coming* (ver. 40) in judgment down to the second advent; the former expressing the same thought in a *passive* form, κεῖται εἰς πτῶσιν (Luke ii. 34).

Ver. 45 f. It was the hint contained in this concluding remark that led Jesus at once to follow up what had been already said with another parabolic address directed against His enemies. — οἱ ἀρχιερεῖς κ. οἱ Φαρισ.] identical with the οἱ ἀρχ. κ. οἱ πρεσβύτεροι of ver. 23, so that, in the present instance, the latter are designated by the *name of the party* to which they belonged. — ἔγνωσαν] what had now become clear to them from what was said, vv. 42-44. The confident manner in which they express themselves in ver. 41 bears up to that point no trace of such knowledge, otherwise we should have to suppose that they *consciously* pronounced their own condemnation. — εἰς (see critical remarks) προφή-την: *held Him as a prophet, i.e.* in Him they felt they possessed a prophet; on εἰς, which is met with in later writers in the sense of the predicate, see Bernhardy, p. 219.

CHAPTER XXII.

VER. 4. ἡτοίμασα] Following B C* D L א, 1, 22, 23, we should,
with Lachm. and Tisch., read ἡτοίμακα because of the preponderance of manuscript authority. — Ver. 5. ὁ μὲν . . . ὁ δέ] B L,
min. Or.: ὃς μὲν . . . ὃς δέ. So Fritzsche, Lachm. Tisch. To be
preferred on the strength of this external authority, particularly
as C* א, which have ὁ μὲν . . . ὃς δέ, cannot be regarded as counter-
evidence. — For εἰς τήν, Fritzsche, Lachm. Tisch. read ἐπὶ τήν,
following B C D א, min. Or. Correctly; εἰς is a mechanical
repetition of the one preceding. — Ver. 7. The Received text has
ἀκούσας δὲ ὁ βασ. Of the numerous readings, the simple ὁ δὲ βασιλεύς
is the one favoured by B L א, min. Copt. Sahid., while most of
the other witnesses have καὶ ἀκ. ὁ βασ. (so Fritzsche, Scholz,
Tisch. 7). Lachm. reads ὁ δὲ βασ. ἀκούσας, but only following min.
It. Vulg. Arm. Ir. Chrys. Eus. In presence of such a multiplicity of readings, we ought to regard the simple ὁ δὲ βασ. as
the original one (so also Tisch. 8), to which, in conformity with
Matthew's style (comp. on the reading of the Received text,
especially ii. 3), ἀκούσας was added, being inserted sometimes in
one place and sometimes in another. Many important witnesses
insert ἐκεῖνος after βασιλ. (D and codd. of It. Lucif. place . it
before), a reading which is also adopted by Scholz and Tisch. 7
(therefore: κ. ἀκούσας ὁ βασιλεὺς ἐκεῖνος). It is not found in B L
א, min. Copt. Sahid. codd. of It. Vulg. Ir. It, too, has been
inserted mechanically as being in accordance with Matthew's
usual manner; it would scarcely have been omitted as being
somewhat in the way because of the ἐκεῖνος which follows. —
Ver. 10. ὁ γάμος] Tisch. 8: ὁ νυμφών, following B* L א. A mistaken gloss, for νυμφών means the bride-chamber. — Ver. 13.
ἄρατε αὐτὸν καὶ ἐκβάλετε] Lachm. Tisch. 8: ἐκβάλετε αὐτόν,
following B L א, min. vss. and Fathers. The word ἄρατε, not
being needed to complete the picture, was struck out. The reading of the Received text ought to be maintained. The genuineness of the ἄρατε is likewise confirmed by the gloss ἄρατε αὐτὸν
ποδῶν κ. χειρῶν, which came to be substituted for δήσαντες αὐτοῦ
πόδ. κ. χεῖρας (so D, Cant. Verc. Ver. Colb. Corb. 2, Clar. Ir.

Lucif.). — Ver. 16. λέγοντες] Fritzsche, Lachm. Tisch. 8: λέγον-τας, following B L א, 27, vss. (?). An improper emendation. — Ver. 23. οἱ λέγοντες] Lachm. and Tisch. 8 have deleted the article, following B D M S Z א, min. Or., no doubt; but incorrectly, for it is indispensable, and would be readily enough overlooked in consequence of the OI which immediately precedes it. — Ver. 25. For γαμήσας, with Lachm. and Tisch., following B L א, min. Or. read γήμας, a form which the copyists would be very apt to exchange for one of more frequent occurrence in the New Testament. — For καὶ ἡ γυνή, ver. 27, read, with Tisch. 8, simply ἡ γυνή, in accordance with the preponderance of evidence. — Ver. 28. Instead of ἐν τῇ οὖν ἀναστ., we should, with Lachm. and Tisch., read ἐν τ. ἀναστ. οὖν, following B D L א, min. The reading of the Received text was intended to be an emendation as regards the position of the οὖν. — Ver. 30. ἐκγαμίζονται] Lachm. Tisch. 8: γαμίζονται, following B D L א, min. Clem. Or. (twice) Ath. Isid. The compound form, besides being obviously suggested by Luke, is intended to be more precise, so as to bring out the reference to women. Neither of the words belongs to the older Greek, hence the variations are not of a grammatical nature. — τοῦ θεοῦ] wanting in B D, 1, 209, vss. and Fathers. Deleted by Lachm. Left out, in accordance with Mark xii. 25. — Ver. 32. οὐκ ἔστιν ὁ θεὸς θεός] The second θεός is deleted by Lachm., following B L Δ, min. Copt. Sahid. Or. (?). It is likewise wanting in D א, min. Eus. Chrys., which authorities drop the article before the first θεός. Tisch. 8 follows them, simply reading οὐκ ἔστιν θεός. The sufficiently attested reading of the Received text is to be adhered to; it was simplified in accordance with Mark and Luke. — Ver. 35. καὶ λέγων] not found in B L א, 33, vss. Deleted by Lachm. and Tisch. 8. The omission, though opposed to Matthew's usual style (xii. 10, xvii. 10, xxii. 23, 41, xxvii. 11), is in accordance with Mark xii. 28. — Ver. 37. Ἰησοῦς] is to be deleted, with Lachm. and Tisch., following B L א, 33, Copt. Sahid. Inserted from Mark xii. 29. — ἔφη] having decisive evidence in its favour, is to be preferred to εἶπεν of the Received text. — Ver. 38. For πρώτη κ. μεγάλη, read, with Fritzsche, Lachm. Tisch.: ἡ μεγάλη κ. πρώτη, following B D (which latter, however, omits ἡ) L (which, however, inserts the article also before πρώτη) Z א, min: vss: Hilar.; πρώτη would be placed first as being the chief predicate. Comp. δευτέρα below. — Ver. 40. καὶ οἱ προφῆται κρέμανται] B D L Z א, 33, Syr. Vulg. It. Tert. Hil.: κρέμαται καὶ οἱ προφ. Recommended by Griesb., adopted by Fritzsche, Lachm. Tisch. The reading of the Received text is an exegetical correction. — Ver. 44. ὑποπόδιον] B D G L

Z Γ Δ ℵ, min. vss. Aug.: ὑποκάτω. Recommended by Griesb., adopted by Lachm. and Tisch. The reading of the Received text is taken from the Sept. and Luke.

Ver. 1. *Καὶ ἀποκρ. ὁ ᾽Ιησ. πάλιν εἶπεν, κ.τ.λ.*] In the full consciousness of His mission and His own superiority, Jesus replied (*ἀποκρ.*, see note on xi. 25) to their hostile *ζητεῖν*, which only fear of the people kept in check, by adding another parabolic address (*ἐν παραβ.* plural of the category). Olshausen and Keim are not justified in doubting this connection on the ground that xxi. 45 f. is, as they suppose, the formal *conclusion.* The parable as given in Luke xiv. 16 ff. is not a Pauline modification of the one before us (Baur, Hilgenfeld), but is rather to be regarded as representing an imperfect version of it which had found its way into the document consulted by Luke. *Others* are of opinion that the parable in Luke xiv. 16 ff. is the more original of the two, and that here it is interwoven with another (ver. 8 ff.), the introduction to which, however, has disappeared, and that, in the process, still a third feature (vv. 6, 7) has been added from the parable which precedes (Ewald, Schneckenburger, de Wette, Strauss, Weizsäcker, Keim, Scholten). But coming as it does after the remark of xxi. 45 f., a *somewhat copious* parable such as that before us, so far from being a mere heaping of passage upon passage, is intended to serve as a *forcible concluding address* directed against His obdurate enemies,—an address, too, which does not interrupt the connection, since it was delivered before those for whom it was intended had had time to withdraw (ver. 15). As, in presence of such obduracy, *thoughts* of the divine love and of the divine wrath could not but crowd into the mind of Jesus; so, on the other hand, there could not fail to be something corresponding to this in their parabolic *utterance.*

Ver. 2 f. On *γάμους ποιεῖν, to prepare a marriage feast,* comp. Wetstein and Xen. *de rep. Lac.* i. 6; Tob. viii. 19. Michaelis, Fischer, Kuinoel, Paulus are mistaken in supposing that what is meant is a *feast on the occasion of his son's accession to the throne.* — The Messiah is the *bridegroom* (xxv. 1 ; Rev. xxi. 2, 9), whose *marriage* represents the setting up of His kingdom. Comp. ix. 15, John iii. 29, and note on Eph.

v. 27. — καλέσαι] i.e. to tell those who had been previously invited that it was now time to come to the marriage. Comp. ver. 4; Luke xiv. 17. For instances of such repeated invitations, see Wetstein. — ἀνθρ. βασιλ.] as in xviii. 23 ; ὁμοιώθη, as in xiii. 24.

Ver. 4. Τὸ ἄριστον] not equivalent to δεῖπνον (see Luke xiv. 12 ; Bornemann, ad Xen. Cyr. ii. 3. 21), nor a *meal generally*, but in the sense of *breakfast, prandium* (towards *mid-day*, Joseph. *Antt.* v. 4. 2), with which the series of meals connected with marriage was to *begin*. — ἡτοίμακα (see critical remarks): *paratum habeo*. — καὶ πάντα] *and everything* generally.

Ver. 5 ff. Ἀμελήσαντες] *having paid no attention*, said with reference merely to those who went away ; for the others, ver. 6, conducted themselves in a manner *directly hostile*. This in answer to Fritzsche, who holds that Matthew would have expressed himself more precisely : οἱ δὲ ἀμελ., οἱ μὲν ἀπῆλθον . . . οἱ δὲ λοιποὶ, κ.τ.λ. Instead of so expressing himself, however, he leaves it to appear from the context that the first οἱ represents the *majority* of those invited, while the οἱ δὲ λοιποί constitute the remainder, so that the general form of expression (οἱ δὲ ἀμελ., κ.τ.λ.) finds its limitation in οἱ δὲ λοιποί. This limitation might also have been expressed by οἱ δέ alone, in the sense of *some, however* (see Kühner, II. 2, p. 808). — εἰς τὸν ἴδιον ἀγρόν] *to his own farm* (Mark v. 14, vi. 36), so that he preferred his own selfish interests to being present at the marriage of the royal prince, as was also the case with him who went to his merchandise. For ἴδιος, comp. note on Eph. v. 22.

Ver. 8. Οὐκ ἦσαν ἄξιοι] Comp. Acts xiii. 46. "*Praeteritum* indignos eo magis *praetermittit*," Bengel. To represent the expedition against the rebels, and the destruction of their city as actually taking place while the supper is being prepared, — a thing hardly conceivable in real life, — is to introduce an episode *quite in accordance with the illustrative character* of the parable, which after all is only a *fictitious* narrative. Comp., for example, the mustard seed which grows to a *tree ;* the olive on which the *wild branch* is engrafted, Rom. xi., etc.; see also note on xxv. 1 f.

Ver. 9. Ἐπὶ τὰς διεξόδους τῶν ὁδῶν] *to the crossings of*

the roads, where people were in the habit of congregating most.
It is evident from ver. 7, according to which the city is
destroyed, that what is meant is not, as Kypke and Kuinoel
suppose, the squares *in the city* from which streets branch
off, but the places where *the country roads* cross each other.
Comp. *Babyl. Berac.* xliii. 1.   Gloss.: "Divitibus in more
fuit, viatores pauperes ad convivia invitare."

Ver. 10. Ἐξελθόντες] from the palace of the king out
into the highways. — συνήγαγον] through their invitation,
which was accepted. — πονηρ. τε καὶ ἀγαθ.] not "locutio
quasi proverbialis," Bengel, but they proceeded on the principle of not inquiring whether the parties in question were at
the time morally bad or good, provided they only accepted
the invitation.   The separation between the bad and the good
was not to be made by them, but subsequently by the king
himself, and that according to a higher standard.   Accordingly,
the separation takes place in ver. 11 ff., where the man who
has no wedding garment represents the πονηροί. — ὁ γάμος]
not equivalent to νυμφών, but *the wedding* (i.e. *the marriage
feast*, as in ver. 8; comp. Hom. *Od.* iv. 3, *Il.* xviii. 491), was
full of guests.   The emphasis, however, is on ἐπλήσθη.

Ver. 11 f. Ἔνδυμα γάμου] *a dress suited for a marriage.*
Comp. χλανὶς γαμική, Aristoph. *Av.* 1693.   It is true that, in
interpreting this passage, expositors (Michaelis, Olshausen)
lay stress on the Oriental custom of presenting handsome
caftans to those who are admitted to the presence of royalty
(Harmer, *Beobacht.* II. p. 117; Rosenmüller, *Morgenl.* V.
p. 75 ff.); and they are all the more disposed to do so,
that such a custom is calculated to make it appear with
greater prominence that righteousness is a *free gift*, and
that, consequently, man's sin is so much the more heinous:
but neither can it be proved (not from Gen. xlv. 22; Judg.
xiv. 12; 2 Kings v. 22, x. 22; Esth. vi. 8, viii. 15) that
any such custom existed in ancient times, nor does the text
make any allusion to it whatever, although it would have
contributed not a little to bring out the idea of the parable.
That those invited, however, *should appear in festive attire* was
a matter of course, and demanded by the rules of ordinary

etiquette (see Dougt. *Anal.* II. p. 23). The only thing *intended to be represented* here is the *moral* δικαιοσύνη, which, by faith in Christ, men are required to assume after being called to the Messianic kingdom through μετάνοια. Comp. vi. 33, v. 20. So far, our Lord's adversaries themselves could understand the figure of the wedding garment. But, of course, the true inward basis of the *moral* δικαιοσύνη was to be sought in that righteousness which, as a free gift, and in virtue of the death of Jesus, would be bestowed on those who *believed* (comp. the Fathers in Calovius). The knowledge of this truth, however, had to be reserved for a later stage in the development ·of Christian doctrine. — ἑταῖρε] Comp. on xx. 13. — πῶς εἰσῆλθες, κ.τ.λ.] a question expressive of astonishment : how has it been possible for thee to come in hither (how couldst thou venture to do so), without, etc.? — μὴ ἔχων] *although thou hadst not.* Differently ver. 11 : οὐκ ἐνδεδυμ. Comp. Buttmann, *Neut. Gr.* p. 301 [E. T. 351].

Ver. 13. Δήσαντες, κ.τ.λ.] that is, to make it impossible for him to get loose in course of the ἐκβάλλεσθαι, as well as to secure against his escape subsequently from the σκότος ἐξώτερον. — αὐτοῦ πόδ.] *his* feet ; comp. on viii. 3. — For the διάκονοι of this passage (not δοῦλοι this time, for the servants waiting at the *table* are intended), see xiii. 41. — ἐκεῖ ἔσται, κ.τ.λ.] not the words of the king, but, as the future ἔσται indicates, a remark on the part of *Jesus,* having reference to the condition *hinted at* in the words τὸ σκότ. τ. ἐξώτ. See, further, on viii. 12.

Ver. 14. Γάρ] introduces the reason of the ἐκεῖ ἔσται, κ.τ.λ. *For,* so far from the mere calling availing to secure against eternal condemnation, *many,* on the contrary, are *called* to the Messiah's kingdom, but comparatively *few* are *chosen* by God actually to participate in it. This saying has a somewhat different purport in xx. 16 ; still in both passages the ἐκλογή is not, in the first instance, the judicial sentence, but the eternal decree of God ; a decree, however, which has not selected the future subjects of the kingdom in any arbitrary fashion, but has destined for this honour those who, by appropriating and faithfully maintaining the requisite δικαιοσύνη

(see on ver. 11 f.), will be found to possess the corresponding disposition and character.   Comp. xxv. 34.   Similarly,
too, in xxiv. 22 ; Luke xviii. 7.   It was, however, only a
legitimate consequence of the contemplation of history from
a religious point of view, if the Christian consciousness felt
warranted in attributing even this amount of human freedom
to the agency of God (Eph. i. 4 ; Phil. ii. 13), and had to be
satisfied, while maintaining the human element no less than
the divine, with leaving the problem of their unity unsolved
(see on Rom. ix. 33, Remark).

Teaching of the parable : When the Messianic kingdom is
about to be established, instead of those who have been ·
invited to enter it, *i.e.* instead of the people of Israel, who
will despise the (according to the plural) repeated invitations,
nay, who will show their contempt to some extent by a violent
behaviour (for which God will chastise them, and that before
the setting up of the kingdom, ver. 7), God will order the
Gentiles to be called to His kingdom.   When, however, it is
being established, He will single out from among the Gentiles
who have responded to the call such of them as turn out to
be morally disqualified for admission, and condemn them to
be punished in Gehenna. — The *first invitation,* and which is
referred to in the τοὺς κεκλημένους of ver. 3, is conveyed
through Christ ; the *successive invitations* which followed were
given through the *apostles,* who, ver. 9, likewise invite the
Gentiles.   Comp. xxviii. 19 ; Acts i. 8, xiii. 46. — Observe in
connection with τότε, ver. 8, that it is not intended thereby
to *exclude* the calling of the Gentiles *before* the destruction of
Jerusalem ; but *simultaneously* with this event the work of
conversion was to be directed in *quite a special manner* toward
the Gentiles.   The destruction of Jerusalem was to form the
signal for the gathering in of the *fulness* of the Gentiles
(Rom. xi. 25).   Thus the τότε marks a grand *epoch* in the
historical development of events, an epoch already visible to
the far-seeing glance of Jesus, though at the same time we are
bound to admit the discrepancy that exists between this passage and the very definite statement regarding the date of the
second advent contained in xxiv. 29.   As is clear from the

whole connection, we must not suppose (Weisse) that *the man without the wedding garment* is intended to represent *Judas ;* but see on ver. 12. What is meant is a Christian with the old man still clinging to him. Comp. on Rom. xiii. 14; Gal. iii. 27 ; Eph. iv. 24; Col. iii. 12.

REMARK.—The part of the parable extending from ver. 11 onwards was certainly not spoken, so far as its *immediate* reference is concerned, with a view to the Pharisees, but was essential to the completeness of the truths that were being set forth, inasmuch as, without that part, there would be no reference to the way in which the holiness of God would assert itself at the setting up of the Messianic kingdom. And the more this latter point is brought out, the more *applicable* did it become to the case of the *Pharisees* also, who would be able to infer from it what *their* fate was to be on that day when, even from among those who will be found to have accepted the invitation, God will single out such as appear without the garment of δικαιοσύνη, and consign them to the punishment of hell,

Ver. 15 ff. Comp. Mark xii. 13 ff.; Luke xx. 20 ff. — Οἱ Φαρισαῖοι] now no longer in their official capacity, as deputed by the Sanhedrim (xxi. 23, 45), but on their own responsibility, and as representing a *party* adopting a still bolder policy, and proceeding upon a new tack. — ὅπως] They *took counsel* (comp. λαβὼν αἵρεσιν, Dem. 947, 20), *expressly with a view to.* Not equivalent to πῶς, the reading in D, and originating in a mistaken gloss. Comp. xii. 14. For συμβούλιον, *consultation,* comp. xxvii. 1, 7, xxviii. 12 ; Mark iii. 6 ; Dio Cass. xxxviii. 43 ; classical writers commonly use συμβουλή, συμβουλία. *Others* (Keim included), without grammatical warrant, render according to the Latin idiom: *consilium ceperunt.* Euthymius Zigabenus correctly renders by: συσκέπτονται. — ἐν λόγῳ] *in an utterance, i.e.* in a statement which he might happen to make. This statement is conceived of as a *trap* or *snare* (παγίς, see Jacobs *ad Anthol.* VII. p. 409, XI. p. 93), into which if He once fell they would hold Him fast, with a view to further proceedings against Him. *Others* explain : δι' ἐρωτήσεως (Euthymius Zigabenus). But Jesus could not become *involved in the snare* unless He gave such an *answer* to their queries as they hoped to elicit. παγιδεύειν, *illaqueare*, is not met with in classical writers, though it frequently occurs in the Septuagint.

Ver. 16. The *Herodians* are not Herod's courtiers (Fritzsche, following Luther), but the political party among the Jews that sought to uphold the dynasty of the Herods, popular royalists, in opposition to the principle of a pure theocracy, though willing also to take part with the powerful Pharisees against the unpopular Roman sway, should circumstances render such a movement expedient. For other interpretations, some of them rather singular, see Wolf and Köcher *in loc.* The passage in Joseph. *Antt.* xiv. 15. 10, refers to different circumstances from the present. Comp. Ewald, *Gesch. Chr.* p. 97 ff. ; Keim, III. p. 130 ff. To regard (as is done by Origen, Maldonatus, de Wette, Winer, Neander, Volkmar) those here referred to as supporters of the *Roman sway* generally (and not merely of the *Herodian dynasty* in particular), is certainly not in accordance with the *name* they bear. We may further observe that no little cunning was shown by the orthodox hierarchy in selecting some of the younger members of their order (who as such would be less liable to be suspected) to co-operate with a party no less hostile than themselves to the Messianic pretender, with a view to betray Jesus into an answer savouring of *opposition* to the payment of the tribute. *This* was the drift of the flattering preface to their question, and upon His answer they hoped to found an accusation before the *Roman authorities.* Comp. Luke xx. 20. But though the plot miscarried, owing to the answer being in the *affirmative*, the Pharisees had at least succeeded in now getting the *Herodians* to assume a hostile attitude toward Jesus, while at the same time they would be able to turn the reply to good account in the way of rendering Him unpopular with the masses. — λέγοντες] that is, through their representatives. Comp. xi. 2, xxvii. 19. — διδάσκαλε, οἴδαμεν, κ.τ.λ.] Comp. with this *cunning*, though in itself so true an instance of *captatio benevolentiae*, the *sincere* one in John iii. 2. — ἀληθὴς εἶ] *true*, avoiding every sort of ψεῦδος in your dealings, either *simulando* or *dissimulando.* In what follows, and which is still connected with ὅτι, this is made more precise, being put both positively and negatively. — τὴν ὁδὸν τοῦ θεοῦ] *the way prescribed by God, i.e.* the behaviour of men to each other which God requires. Comp. τὴν δικαιοσύνην τ. θεοῦ, vi. 33 ; τὰ ἔργα τ. θεοῦ, John vi. 28 ; and so Ps. xxvii. 11 ; Wisd. v. 7 ; Bar. iii. 13. — ἐν ἀληθείᾳ] *truthfully*, as beseems the character of this way ; see on John xvii. 19. — οὐ μέλει σοι περὶ οὐδενός] *Thou carest for no man*, in Thy teaching Thou actest without regard to the persons of men. — οὐ γὰρ βλέπεις, κ.τ.λ.] giving the reason for the statement contained in οἴδαμεν, κ.τ.λ. : *for Thou lookest not to mere external appearances in men ;* to Thee it is always a matter of indifference in regard to a man's person whether he be powerful, rich, learned, etc., or the reverse ; therefore we are convinced, ὅτι ἀληθὴς εἶ καὶ τὴν ὁδὸν, κ.τ.λ. Πρόσωπον ἀνθρ. denotes the *outward manifestation* in which men present themselves (comp. on xvi. 3). Comp. θαυμάζειν πρόσωπον, Jude 16. The emphasis, however, is on οὐ βλέπεις. We have not here a " natural paraphrase " of the Hebrew idiom λαμβάνειν πρόσωπον (Luke xx. 21), which expresses another, though similar idea (in answer to de Wette; see on Gal. ii. 6). In classical Greek, β. εἰς πρ. τινος is used in the sense of being barefaced. See Bremi *ad Aeschin.* p. 370.

Ver. 17. Ἔξεστι] problem founded on theocratic one-sidedness, as though the Jews were still the independent people of God, according to their *divine* title to recognise no king but God Himself. Comp. Michaelis, *Mos. R.* III. p. 154. It was also on this ground that Judas the Gaulonite appears to have refused to pay the tribute. See Joseph. *Antt.* xviii. 1. 1. As to κῆνσος, not merely poll-tax, but land-tax as well, see on xvii. 25. — Καίσαρι] without the article, being used as a proper name. — ἢ οὔ] " flagitant responsum rotundum," Bengel.

Ver. 18. Τὴν πονηρίαν] for they concealed *malicious designs* (the reverse of ἁπλότης) behind their seemingly candid, nay, flatteringly put question, in which their object was to try (πειράζετε) whether He might not be betrayed

into returning such an answer as might be used in further
proceedings against Him.   Apropos of ὑποκριταί, Bengel
appropriately observes: "*verum* se eis ostendit, ut dixerant,
ver. 16;" but in the interrogative τί, *why*, is involved the
idea of: what is your design in putting such a question ?

Ver. 19. Τὸ νόμισμα τ. κ.] "nummum aliquem ejus
monetae, in qua tributum exigi solet," Grotius.   The tribute
was paid in Roman, not in Jewish money.   "Ubicunque
numisma regis alicujus obtinet, illic incolae regem istum pro
domino agnoscunt," Maimonides in *Gezelah* v. 18. — προ-
σήνεγκ. αὐτῷ δηνάρ.] they had such current coin upon them.

Ver. 21 f. "There He catches them in their own trap,"
Luther.   The pointing to the image and inscription furnishes
the questioners with ocular demonstration of the actual existence and practical recognition of Caesar's sway, and from
these Jesus infers not merely the lawfulness, but the *duty
of paying to Caesar what belongs to Caesar* (namely, the money,
which shows, by the stamp it bears, the legitimacy of the
existing rule) ; but He also recognises at the same time the
necessity of attending to their *theocratic* duties, which are not
to be regarded as in any way compromised by their political
circumstances : *and to God what is God's* (what you derive
from Him in virtue of *His* dominion over you).   By this is
not meant simply the *temple tribute*, nor the *repentance* which
God may have desired to awaken through punishing them
with a foreign rule (Ebrard), nor merely the life of the soul
(Tertullian, Erasmus, Neander) ; but everything, in short, of a
material, religious, and ethical nature, which God, as sovereign
of the theocratic people, is entitled to exact from them as
His due.   By the τὰ Καίσαρος, on the other hand, we are not
to understand merely the *civil tax*, but everything to which
Caesar was entitled in virtue of his legitimate rule over the
theocratic nation.   So with this reply Jesus disposes of the
ensnaring question, answering it immediately with decision and
clearness, and with that admirable tact which is only met with
where there is a moral insight into the whole domain of duty ;
in a quick and overpowering manner He disarmed His adversaries, and laid the foundation for the Christian doctrine which

was more fully developed afterwards (Rom. xiii. 1 ff.; 1 Tim. ii. 1 f.; 1 Pet. ii. 13 f., 17), that it is the duty of the Christian not to rebel against the existing rulers, but to *conjoin* obedience to their authority with obedience to God. At the same time, there cannot be a doubt that, although, in accordance with the question, Jesus chooses to direct His reply to the first and not to the second of those two departments of duty (in answer to Klostermann's note on Mark), the second is to be regarded as the unconditional and absolute standard, not only for the first of the duties here mentioned (comp. Acts v. 29), but for every other. Chrysostom observes that : what is rendered to Caesar must not be τὴν εὐσέβειαν παραβλάπτοντα, otherwise it is οὐκέτι Καίσαρος, ἀλλὰ τοῦ διαβόλου φόρος καὶ τέλος. Thus the second part of the precept serves to dispose of any collision among our duties which accidental circumstances might bring about (Rom. xiii. 5). According to de Wette, Jesus, in the first part of His reply, does not refer the matter inquired about to the domain of conscience at all, but treats it as belonging only to the sphere of politics (Luke xii. 14), and then adds in the second part: "You can and ought to serve God, in the first place, with your moral and religious dispositions, and should not mix up with His service what belongs to the domain of civil authority." But such a severance of the two is not in accordance with the context; for the *answer* would in that case be an answer to an *alternative question* based on the general thought : is it lawful to be subject to Caesar, or to God only ? Whereas the reply of Jesus is : you ought to do *both things*, you ought to be subject to God *and* to Caesar as well; the one duty is *inseparable* from the other ! Thus our Lord *rises* above the *alternative*, which was based on theocratic notions of a one-sided and degenerate character, to the higher *unity of the true theocracy*, which demands no revolutions of any kind, and also looks upon the right moral conception of the existing civil rule as necessarily part and parcel of itself (John xix. 11), and consequently a simple yes or no in reply to the question under consideration is quite impossible. — ἀπόδοτε] the ordinary expression for *paying what it is one's duty to pay*,

as in xx. 8, xxi. 41 ; Rom. xiii. 7. — Ver. 22. ἐθαύμασαν]
" conspicuo modo ob responsum tutum et verum," Bengel. Οὐκ
ἐπίστευσαν δέ, Euthymius Zigabenus.

Ver. 23. Comp. Mark xii. 18 ff. ; Luke xx. 27 ff. ; Matthew
condenses. — Οἱ λέγοντες μὴ εἶναι ἀνάστ.] who assert, etc.,
serving to account for the question which follows. On the
necessity of the article, inasmuch as the Sadducees do not
say to Jesus that there is no resurrection, but because their
regular confiteor is here quoted, comp. Kühner ad Xen. ii.
7. 13 ; Mark xii. 18 : οἵτινες λέγουσι.

Ver. 24 ff. A free citation of the law respecting levirate
marriage, Deut. xxv. 5, and that without following the Septuagint, which in this instance does not render בם by the
characteristic ἐπιγαμβρ. If a married man died without male
issue, his brother was required to marry the widow, and to
register the first-born son of the marriage as the son of the
deceased husband. See Saalschütz, M. R. p. 754 ff. ; Ewald,
Alterth. p. 276 ff. ; Benary, de Hebraeor. leviratu, Berl. 1835.
As to other Oriental nations, see Rosenmüller, Morgenl. V. p. 81;
Bodenstedt, d. Völker des Kaukasus, p. 82 ; Benary, p. 31 ff.
— ἐπιγαμβρεύειν, to marry as brother-in-law (levir. יבם).
Comp. Gen. xxxviii. 8 ; Test. XII. patr. p. 599. Differently
ἐπιγαμβρ. τινι in 1 Macc. x. 54; 1 Sam. xviii. 22. — ἕως
τῶν ἑπτά] until the seven, i.e. and in the same manner they
continued to die until the whole seven were dead. Comp.
xviii. 22 ; 1 Macc. ii. 38. — ὕστερον πάντων] later than all
the husbands.

Ver. 28. Founding upon this alleged incident (which was
undoubtedly a silly invention got up for the occasion, Chrysostom), as being one strictly in accordance with the law, the
Sadducees now endeavour to make it appear that the doctrine
of the resurrection—a doctrine which, for the purpose of being
able to deny it, they choose to apprehend in a gross material
sense — is irreconcilable with the law ; while, by their fancied
acuteness, they try to involve Jesus Himself in the dilemma
of having to give an answer either disadvantageous to the law
or favourable to their doctrine. — γυνή] Predicate.

Ver. 29. Jesus answers that, in founding upon Deut. xxv. 5

the denial of the resurrection, which their question implies, they are *mistaken*, and that in a twofold respect : (1) they do not understand the *Scriptures, i.e.* they fail to see how that doctrine actually underlies many a scriptural utterance ; and (2) they do not sufficiently realize the extent of *the power of God*, inasmuch as their conceptions of the resurrection are purely material, and because they cannot grasp the thought of a higher corporeality to be evolved from the material body by the divine power. And then comes an illustration of the latter point in ver. 30, and of the former in ver. 31.

Ver. 30. Ἐν γὰρ τῇ ἀναστάσει] not: *in the resurrection life*, but, as in ver. 28 : *at the resurrection* (in answer to Fritzsche), which will be signalized not by marrying or giving in marriage, but by ushering in a state of things in which men will be like the angels, therefore a higher form of existence, from which the earthly conditions of life are eliminated, in which human beings will be not indeed disembodied, but endowed with a glorified corporeality, 1 Cor. xv. 44. The cessation of human propagation, not the abolition of the distinction of sex (Tertullian, Origen, Hilary, Athanasius, Basil, Grotius, Volkmar), is essentially implied in the ἀφθαρσία of the spiritual body. Comp. Luke xx. 36.— γαμοῦσιν] applies to the *bridegroom ;* γαμίζονται (Apoll. *de Synt.* p. 277, 13), on the other hand, to *daughters* who *are given in marriage* by their parents.— ἀλλ' ὡς ἄγγελοι, κ.τ.λ.] *but they are as the angels of God in heaven.* ἐν οὐρανῷ belongs not to εἰσί, but to ἄγγελοι τ. θεοῦ, because the partakers in the resurrection (and the Messianic kingdom) are not understood to be in heaven (xxv. 31 ff.; 1 Cor. xv. 52 ; 2 Pet. iii. 13 ; not inconsistent with 1 Thess. iv. 17). It is obvious from our passage—in which the likeness to the angels has reference to the nature of the future *body*—that the angels are to be conceived of not as mere spirits, but as possessing a supramundane corporeality. This is necessarily presupposed in the language before us. Comp. 1 Cor. xv. 40 ; Phil. ii. 10 ; Hahn, *Theol. d. N. T.* I. p. 267 ; Weiss, *Bibl. Theol.* p. 68 ; Kahnis, *Dogm.* I. p. 556. The δόξα of the angels is essentially connected with their corporeality (in opposition to Delitzsch, *Psychol.* p. 66). — While a similar idea of the future body and the future mode of existence is met with in Rabbinical writers (see Wetstein), it is also conjoined, however, with the gross materialistic view : " Mulier illa, quae duobus nupsit in hoc mundo, priori restituitur in mundo futuro," *Sohar Gen.* f. xxiv. 96.

Ver. 31 f. *But with reference to the resurrection,* set over against the foregoing ἐν γὰρ τῇ ἀναστ. ; the sequence of the address is indicated by the prepositions. περὶ τῆς ἀναστ. should be taken along with οὐκ ἀνέγνωτε. — ὑμῖν] imparts the vivacity of individuality to the words of Jesus. The quotation is from Ex. iii. 6. His opponents had cited a passage from the law ; with a passage from the law Jesus confutes them, and thus combats them with their own weapons. It is wrong to refer to this in support of the view that the Sadducees accepted *only the Pentateuch* as authoritative scripture (Tertullian, Origen, Jerome, Luther, Paulus, Olshausen, Süskind in the *Stud. u. Krit.* 1830, p. 665). Yet these aristocrats regarded the law, and the mere letter of the law too, as possessing supreme authority. — οὐκ ἔστιν ὁ θεὸς, κ.τ.λ.] This is the *major proposition* of a syllogism, in terms of which we are warranted in recognising in the passage here quoted a scriptural testimony in favour of the resurrection. The Sadducees had failed to draw the inference thus shown to be deducible from the words ; hence ver. 29 : μὴ εἰδότες τὰς γραφάς, a fact which Jesus has now confirmed by the illustration before us. *The point of the argument* does not turn upon the present εἰμί (Chrysostom, and those who follow him), but is to this effect : seeing that God calls Himself the God of the patriarchs, and as He cannot sustain *such* a relation toward the dead, *i.e.* those who are absolutely dead, who have ceased to exist (οὐκ ὄντων καὶ καθάπαξ ἀφανισθέντων, Chrysostom), but only toward the living, it follows that the deceased patriarchs must be living,—living, that is, in Sheol, and living as ἀναστῆναι μέλλοντες (Euthymius Zigabenus). Comp. Heb. xi. 16. The similar inference in Menasse f. Isr. *de Resurr.* i. 10. 6, appears to have been deduced from the passage before us. Comp. Schoettgen, p. 180.

Ver. 33. Οἱ ὄχλοι] ἀπόνηροι καὶ ἀδέκαστοι, Euthymius Zigabenus. Comp. vii. 28.

Ver. 34. The following conversation respecting the great commandment is given in Mark xii. 28 ff. with such characteristic detail, that Matthew's account cannot fail to have the appearance of being *incomplete*, and, considering the bias of the incident (see note on ver. 35), to look as if it represented a *corrupt* tradition. In Luke x. 25 ff. there is a similar conversation, which, however, is not given as another version of that now before us, but as connected with a different incident that took place some time before. — οἱ δὲ Φαρισ.] Comp. ver. 15. They had already been baffled, and had withdrawn into the background (ver. 22); but the victory of Jesus over the Sadducees provoked them to make one more attempt, not to avenge the defeat of those Sadducees (Strauss), nor to display their own superiority over them (Ebrard, Lange), —neither view being hinted at in the text, or favoured by anything analogous elsewhere,—but, as was the object in every such challenge, to tempt Jesus, if that were at all possible, to give such an answer as might be used against Him, see ver. 35. — ἀκούσαντες] whether while present (among the multitude), or when absent, through the medium, perhaps, of their spies, cannot be determined. — συνήχθησαν ἐπὶ τὸ αὐτό] for the purpose of concerting measures for a new attack. Consequently the νομικός of ver. 35 had to be put forward, and, while the conversation between Jesus and him is going on, the parties who had deputed him gather round the speakers, ver. 41. There is, accordingly, no reason to apprehend any discrepancy (Köstlin) between the present verse and ver. 41. — ἐπὶ τὸ αὐτό] *locally*, not said with reference to their *sentiments*. See on Acts i. 15; Ps. ii. 2.

Ver. 35. Νομικός] the only instance in Matt.; it is met with in none of the other Gospels except that of Luke. It occurs, besides, in Tit. iii. 13. The word is used to signify one who is *conversant with the law*, ἐπιστήμων τῶν νόμων (Photius), Plut. *Sull.* 36; Strabo, xii. p. 539; Diog. L. vi. 54; Epictet. i. 13; *Anthol.* xi. 382. 19. It is impossible to show that there is any essential difference of meaning between this word and γραμματεύς (see note on ii. 4); comp. on the contrary, Luke xi. 52, 53. — The term νομικός is more specific (*jurisconsultus*), and more strictly Greek; γραμματεύς, on the other hand, is more general (*literatus*), and more Hebrew in its character (סֹפֵר). The latter is also of more frequent occurrence in the Apocr.; while the former is met with only in 4 Macc. v. 3. In their character of *teachers* they are designated νομοδιδάσκαλοι, Luke v. 17; Acts v. 37; 1 Tim. i. 7. — πειράζων αὐτόν] different from Mark xii. 28 ff., and indicating that the question was dictated by a malicious intention (Augustine, Grotius). The *ensnaring character of the* question was to be found in the circumstance that, if Jesus had specified any particular ποιότης of a great commandment (see on ver. 36), His reply would have been made use of, in accordance with the casuistical hair-splitting of the schools, for the purpose of assailing or defaming Him on theological grounds. He specifies, however, *those two commandments themselves*, in which *all* the others are essentially included, thereby giving His answer indirectly, as though He had said: supreme love to God, and sincerest love of our neighbour, constitute the ποιότης about which thou inquirest. This love must form the principle, spirit, life of all that we do.

Ver. 36 f. *What kind of a commandment* (qualitative, comp. xix. 18) *is great in the law*; what must be the nature of a commandment in order to constitute it *great?* The commandment, then, which Jesus singles out as the great one κατ᾽ ἐξοχήν, and which, as corresponding to the subsequent δευτέρα, He places at the head of the whole series (ἡ μεγάλη κ. πρώτη, see the critical notes) in that of Deut. vi. 5, quoted somewhat freely after the Sept. — κύριον τὸν θεόν σου] אֶת יְהוָֹה אֱלֹהֶיךָ, in which regular designation τὸν θεόν σου is *in apposition*, consequently not to be rendered: "*utpote* Dominum tuum," Fritzsche.—Love to God must fill the whole *heart*, the entire inner sphere in which all the workings of the personal consciousness originate (Delitzsch, *Psychol.* p. 248 ff.; Krumm, *de notionib. psych. Paul.* § 12), the whole *soul*, the whole faculty of feeling and desire, and the whole *understanding*, all the powers of thought and will, and must determine their operation. We have thus an enumeration of the different elements that go to make up τὸ δεῖν ἀγαπᾶν τὸν θεὸν ὁλοψύχως, τοῦτό ἐστι τὸ διὰ πάντων τῶν τῆς ψυχῆς μερῶν καὶ δυνάμεων αὐτῷ προσέχειν (Theophylact), the complete harmonious self-dedication of the *entire* inner man to God, as to its highest good. Comp. Weiss, *Bibl. Theol.* p. 81, ed. 2.

Ver. 39. *But a second is like unto it,* of the same nature and character, possessing to an equal extent the ποιότης (ὅτι αὕτη ἐκείνην προοδοποιεῖ, καὶ παρ' αὐτῆς συγκροτεῖται πάλιν, Chrysostom), which is the necessary condition of greatness, and therefore no less radical and fundamental. Comp. 1 John iv. 16, 20, 21; Matt. xxv. 40, 45. Euthymius Zigabenus: ἀλληλοχοῦνται κ. φεράλληλοί εἰσιν αἱ δύο. We should not adopt the reading ὁμοία αὕτη, recommended by Griesbach, following many Uncials and min. (but in opposition to the vss.); nor again that of Fritzsche, ὁμοία αὐτῇ, αὕτη (conjecture). The former was presumed (comp. Mark xii. 31) to be a necessary emendation, because from the commandment being immediately added, the demonstrative seemed requisite by way of introducing it. Moreover, according to the context, there would be no need for the dative in the case of ὅμοιος. The commandment is quoted from Lev. xix. 18, after the Sept. — ἀγαπήσεις] This, the inward, moral esteem, and the corresponding behaviour, may form the subject of a command, though the same cannot be said of φιλεῖν, which is love as a matter of *feeling.* Comp. on v. 44, and see in general Tittmann, *Syn.* p. 50 ff. The φιλία τοῦ κόσμου (Jas. iv. 4), on the other hand, may be *forbidden ;* comp. Rom. viii. 7 ; the φιλεῖν of one's own ψυχή (John xii. 25), and the μὴ φιλεῖν τὸν κύριον (1 Cor. xvi. 22), may be *condemned,* comp. also Matt. x. 37. — ὡς σεαυτ.] as thou shouldst love *thyself,* so as to cherish toward him *no less than toward thyself* that love which God would have thee to feel, and to act toward him (by promoting his welfare, etc., comp. vii. 12) in such a manner that your conduct may be in accordance with this loving spirit. Love must do away with the distinction between I and Thou.

Bengel: "Qui Deum amat, se ipsum amabit *ordinate, citra philautiam*," Eph. v. 28.

Ver. 40. *Those* two commandments contain the fundamental principle of the whole of the commandments in the Old Testament. — ταύταις] with emphasis: *these* are the two commandments on which, etc. — κρέμαται] *depends* thereon, so that those commandments constitute the basis and essential condition of the moral character of all the others, Rom. xiii. 8 f.; Gal. v. 14. Comp. Plat. *Legg.* viii. p. 831 C: ἐξ ὧν κρεμαμένη πᾶσα ψυχὴ πολίτου. Pind. *Ol.* vi. 125; Xen. *Symp.* viii. 19; Gen. xliv. 30; Judith viii. 24. — καὶ οἱ προφῆται] so far as the *preceptive* element in them is concerned. Comp. on v. 17. Thus Jesus includes more in His reply than was contemplated by the question (ver. 36) of the νομικός.

Ver. 41. Comp. Mark xii. 35 ff.; Luke xx. 41 ff. Jesus, in His turn, now proceeds to put a question to the Pharisees (who in the meantime have gathered round Him, see on ver. 34), for the purpose, according to Matthew's view of the matter (ver. 46), of convincing them of their own theological helplessness, and that in regard to the problem respecting the title "Son of David," to which David himself bears testimony, and with the view of thereby escaping any further molestation on their part. According to de Wette, the object was: to awaken a higher idea of His (non-political) mission (Neander, Baumgarten-Crusius, Bleek, Schenkel, Keim). This view, however, is not favoured by the context, which represents Jesus as victor over His impudent and crafty foes, who are silenced and then subjected to the castigation described in ch. xxiii.

Ver. 43 f. Πῶς] *how is it possible, that*, etc.—In His question Jesus starts with what was a universal *assumption* in His day, viz. that David was the author of Ps. cx., which, however, is *impossible*, the fact being that it was only composed in the time of this monarch, and *addressed to him* (see Ewald on this psalm). The fact that Jesus shared the opinion referred to, and entertained no doubt as to the accuracy of the title of the psalm, is not to be questioned, though it should

not be made use of, with Delitzsch and many others, for the
purpose of proving the Davidic authorship of the composition;
for a historico-critical question of this sort could only belong
to the sphere of Christ's *ordinary national* development, which,
as a rule, would necessarily bear the impress of His time.
With ἐν πνεύμ. before us, the idea of *accommodation* or of a
play upon logic is not to be thought of, although Delitzsch
himself maintains that something of the kind is possible.
Among the unwarrantable and evasive interpretations of
certain expositors is that of Paulus, who thinks that the object
of the question of Jesus from beginning to end was the *historico-
critical* one of persuading His opponents that the psalm was
not composed by David, and that it contains no reference to
the Messiah.[1]— ἐν πνεύματι] meaning, perhaps, that He did
not do so on His own authority, but *impulsu* Spiritus Sancti
(2 Pet. i. 21); Luke ii. 27; 1 Cor. xii. 3; Rom. viii. 15,
ix. 2. David was regarded as a prophet, Acts ii. 30, i. 16.
— αὐτόν] *the Messiah;* for the personage in the psalm is a
prophetic *type* of the *Messiah;* as also the Rabbinical teachers
recognised in him one of the foremost of the Messianic predictions (Wetstein, Schoettgen), and only at a later period
would they hear of any other reference (Delitzsch on Heb.
i. 13, and on Ps. cx.). — ἕως ἂν θῶ, κ.τ.λ.] see on 1 Cor.
xv. 25.

Ver. 45 f. Εἰ οὖν Δαυείδ, κ.τ.λ.] The emphasis rests on
the correlative terms κύριον and υἱός : If, then, as appears from
this language of the psalm, David, whose *son* He is, according to your express confession, still calls Him *Lord,* how is this
to be reconciled with the fact that He is at the same time the

---

[1] For the correct view of this matter, see Diestel in the *Jahrb. f. D. Theol.*
1863, p. 541 f.; see also the pointed elucidation, as well as refutation of the
other interpretations, in Keim, III. p. 154 ff.; comp. Gess, I. p. 128 f. Then
there is the explanation, frequently offered since Strauss suggested it, and which
is to the effect that Jesus wished to cast discredit upon the currently received
view regarding Messiah's descent from David, and that He Himself was not
descended from David,—a circumstance which is supposed to have undoubtedly
stood in the way of His being recognised as the Messiah (Schenkel, Weisse,
Colani, Holtzmann); all which is decidedly at variance with the whole of the
New Testament, where the idea of a non-Davidic Messiah would be a *contradictio
in adjecto.*

psalmist's *son*? Surely that styling of Him as *Lord* must seem incompatible with the fact of such *son*ship! The difficulty might have been solved in this way: according to His human descent He is David's *son*; but, according to His divine origin as the Son of God, from whom He is sprung, and by whom He is sent (xi. 27, xvii. 26; John i. 14, 18, vi. 46, vii. 28 f.; Rom. i. 3 f.),—in virtue of which relation He is superior to David and all that is merely human, and, by His elevation to the heavenly δόξα (Acts ii. 34), destined to share in the divine administration of things in a manner in keeping with this superiority,—He is by David, speaking under the influence of the Holy Spirit, called his *Lord*. The Pharisees understood nothing of this twofold relation, and consequently could not discern the true majesty and destiny of the Messiah, so as to see in Him both David's *Son* and *Lord*. Hence not one of them was found capable of answering the question as to the πῶς . . . ἐστι. Observe that the question does not *imply a negative*, as though Jesus had asked, μὴ υἱὸς αὐτοῦ ἐστι; — οὐκέτι] "Nova dehinc quasi scena se pandit," Bengel.

CHAPTER XXIII.

VER. 3. τηρεῖν] after ὑμῖν is deleted by Fritzsche, Lachm. and
Tisch., following Mill. It is wanting in very important authorities. A gloss, for which certain authorities have ποιεῖν. —
τηρεῖτε κ. ποιεῖτε] Lachm.: ποιήσατε κ. τηρεῖτε. So also Tisch.
This is the original reading (B L Z ℵ** 124, Hilar.) ; for the
sake of uniformity, ποιήσατε was changed into ποιεῖτε (D, 1, 209,
Eus. Dam.) ; but the transposed order τηρ. κ. π. is an ancient
logical correction (as old as Syr. Vulg. It.). — Ver. 4. For γάρ
Lachm. and Tisch. read δέ, following weighty attestation. Correctly ; γάρ was meant to be more precise. — καὶ δυσβαστ.]
deleted by Tisch. 8, following L ℵ, vss. Ir. But the evidence
in favour of the words is too strong, and their omission on
account of the two καί's might so readily occur that they must
not be regarded as an interpolation from Luke xi. 46. — τῷ δέ]
Lachm. Tisch. 8 : αὐτοὶ δὲ τῷ, following B D L ℵ, and two min.
vss. and Fathers. Exegetical amplification after Luke xi. 46. —
Ver. 5. For δέ after πλατύν. Lachm. Tisch. 8 have γάρ, in accordance with B D L ℵ, min. vss. Chrys. Damasc. See on ver. 4.
— τῶν ἱματ. αὐτ.] deleted by Lachm. and Tisch., following B
D ℵ, 1, 22, vss. Correctly ; an explanatory addition. — Ver. 6.
For φιλ. τε we should, with Lachm. and Tisch., read φιλ. δέ, in
accordance with decisive evidence. — Ver. 7. Lachm. and Tisch. 8
have ῥαββί only once, following B L Δ ℵ, min. vss. and Fathers.
But how easily may the reduplication have been overlooked,
both on its own account and in consequence of its not occurring
in the instance immediately following ! Comp. on Mark xiv. 45.
— Ver. 8. καθηγητής] Fritzsche, Lachm., and Tisch., following
Grotius, Mill, and Bengel, read διδάσκαλος, which Rinck also approves. No doubt καθηγητ. has a very decided preponderance of
evidence in its favour (of the uncials only B U ℵ**? read διδάσκ.);
but, owing to ver. 10, it is so utterly inappropriate in the
present instance, that it must be regarded as an old and clumsy
gloss inserted from ver. 10 (namely, καθηγητὴς ὁ Χριστός, according
to the reading of Elz. Scholz). By this it was merely intended
to intimate that it is Christ that is referred to here as well as

in ver. 10 below. — Ver. 10. εἶς γάρ ὑμῶν ἐστιν ὁ καθηγ.]
Lachm. and Tisch.: ὅτι καθηγητὴς ὑμῶν ἐστιν εἶς. The latter is
the best attested reading ; that of the Received text is to conform with ver. 8 f. — In the *Textus receptus* the two verses, 13
and 14, stand in the following order: (1) οὐαί . . . εἰσελθεῖν; (2)
οὐαί . . . χρῆμα, in opposition to E F G H K M S U V Γ Δ Π, vss.
and Fathers. On this evidence Griesbach, Scholz, Fritzsche
have adopted the transposed order. But οὐαί . . . χρῆμα (in Elz.
ver. 14) is wanting in B D L Z ℵ, min. vss. and Fathers (Origen
as well), and is correctly deleted by Lachm. and Tisch., although
defended by Rinck and Keim. An interpolation from Mark
xii. 40 ; Luke xx. 47. — Ver. 17. τίς γάρ μείζων] Lachm.: τί γάρ
μεῖζον, but, undoubtedly, on the evidence of Z only. The vss.
(Vulg. It.) can have no weight here. — ἁγιάζων] Lachm. and
Tisch.: ἁγιάσας, following B D Z ℵ, Cant.; Vulg. has *sancti-
ficat.* The *present* participle is from ver. 19, where there is no
difference in the reading. — Ver. 19. μωροί καί] is wanting in
D L Z ℵ, 1, 209, and several vss., also Vulg. It. Bracketed by
Lachm., condemned by Rinck, deleted by Tisch. ; and justly so,
because there was no motive for omitting the words, while their
insertion would be readily suggested by ver. 17. — Ver. 21.
For κατοικήσαντι Elz. Lachm. Tisch. 8 have κατοικοῦντι, following
B H S ℵ, min., the force of the aorist not being apprehended.
— Ver. 23. Elz.: ταῦτα ἔδει ; but Griesb., Fritzsche, Lachm.,
Tisch. 7 have adopted ταῦτα δὲ ἔδει. In both cases the evi-
dence is considerable ; but how readily might δὲ be omitted
before ἔδει through oversight on the part of the transcriber ! —
Ver. 25. ἐξ] is wanting in C D, min. Chrys. Deleted by Lachm.
It had been omitted as unnecessary. — Elz. Lachm. Tisch.
read ἀκρασίας, instead of which Griesb. and Scholz have ἀδικίας.
The evidence is very much divided, being strong on both sides ;
ἀκρασίας is to be preferred. This word, the only other instance
of which in the N. T. is at 1 Cor. vii. 5, appeared to be inappropriate, and came to be represented by a variety of glosses
(ἀκαθαρσίας, πλεονεξίας, ἀδικίας, πονηρίας). — Ver. 26. αὐτῶν]
Fritzsche, Lachm., Tisch.: αὐτοῦ, following B* D E* min. Aeth.
Verc. This αὐτοῦ is bound up with the omission of καὶ τῆς
παροψ. in D, min. Cant. Verc. Clem. Chrys. Ir. (deleted by
Tisch.). Those words, however, are evidently an insertion from
ver. 25, an insertion, moreover, which is inconsistent with αὐτοῦ,
so that the words ought to be deleted and αὐτοῦ preferred to
αὐτῶν. — Ver. 27. παρομοιάζετε] Lachm.: ὁμοιάζετε, only on the
evidence of B, 1. The preposition has been left out, probably
because the compound form is not found elsewhere in the N. T.

— Ver. 30. ἤμεθα, instead of ἦμεν of the Received text, is supported by decisive evidence.— Ver. 34. καὶ ἐξ αὐτ.] in the first case καὶ is wanting in B M Δ Π א, min. codd. of It. Syr. Arm. Or.(once). Deleted by Lachm. and Tisch.; but how readily may *this* καὶ have been omitted since the next clause opens with καὶ! — Ver. 36. Before ἥξει, Griesb., followed by Matth., Fritzsche, Scholz, inserted ὅτι, which, however, Lachm. and Tisch. have deleted again. ὅτι has important evidence both for and against. A common interpolation.—ταῦτα πάντα] The order πάντα ταῦτα (Lachm. Tisch. 7) is well attested, though there is a preponderance of evidence (C D א, etc., Vulg. It.) for the reading of the Received text. — Ver. 37. νοσσία ἑαυτῆς] Lachm. has deleted ἑαυτ., but only on the evidence of B, vss. Clem.(once) Or.(once) Cypr. Hil., and notwithstanding the probable omission of the pronoun as apparently superfluous. Had it been inserted from Luke xiii. 34, it would have been placed between τά and νοσσία. For ἑαυτῆς Tisch. reads αὐτῆς, following B** D, marg. M Δ א* 33, Clem.(once) Eus. Cyr. Theodoret. The reflective might be easily overlooked, as was often the case. — Ver. 38. ἔρημος is wanting in B L Copt.* Corb. 2, Or. Deleted by Lachm.; to be maintained on account of the preponderating evidence in its favour, though in the case of Luke xiii. 35 it is inserted as a gloss from Matthew.

Ver. 1. After the Pharisees have been thus *silenced*, there now follows the decisive and direct *attack* upon the hierarchs, in a series of overwhelming denunciations extending to ver. 39, and which, uttered as they are on the eve of His death, form a kind of Messianic σημεῖον through which Jesus seeks to testify against them. Luke has inserted at ch. xi. portions of this discourse in an order different from the original; but he. has given in the present connection, like Mark xii., only a few fragments, so that, keeping in view that a collection of our Lord's sayings was made by Matthew, and considering the originality in respect of matter and arrangement which characterizes the grand utterances now before us, the preference must be accorded to the report furnished by this apostle (in answer to Schleiermacher, Schulz, Schneckenburger, Olshausen, Volkmar). The entire discourse has so much the character of a living whole, that, although much that was spoken on other occasions may perhaps be mixed up with it, it is scarcely possible to disjoin such passages from those that are essentially

original. Ewald thinks that the discourse is made up of
passages that were probably original, though uttered on
very different occasions; Holtzmann has recourse to the
hypothesis that the evangelist has derived his account from
a supposed special source, the same as that on which ch. v.
is based; in answer to the latter, see Weiss, 1864, p. 114.
Observe that the ὄχλοι are mentioned first, because the first
part of the discourse on to ver. 7 is directed to them, then the
μαθηταί are addressed in vv. 8–12, whereupon in ver. 13 ff.
we have the withering apostrophe to the Pharisees who were
present, and that for the purpose of warning the ὄχλοι and
the μαθηταί to beware of them; and finally, the concluding
passage, ver. 37 ff., containing the pathetic exclamation over
Jerusalem.   The glance, the gesture, the attitude, the matter
and the language, were such that there could be no doubt who
were immediately aimed at in the various sections of the discourse.   We may imagine the scene in the temple to have been
as follows: in the *foreground,* Jesus with His *disciples ;* a little
farther off, the ὄχλοι ; more *in the background,* the Pharisees,
who in xxii. 46 are spoken of as having withdrawn.

Ver. 2. The phrase: " *to sit in Moses' seat* " (in the seat
which Moses had occupied as lawgiver), is borrowed not from
Ex. xviii. 13, but refers to the later practice of having chairs
for teachers (comp. Acts xxii. 3), and is intended as a figurative mode of describing the functions of one who " *acts as a
public teacher of the Mosaic law,*" in discharging which functions
the teacher may be regarded as the representative and *successor
of Moses.*   Accordingly, in Rabbinical writers, one who suc-
ceeds a Rabbi as the representative of his school is described
as יֹשֵׁב עַל־כִּסְאוֹ.   See Vitringa, *Synag.* p. 165 f. — ἐκάθισαν]
have seated themselves, have assumed to themselves the duties
of this office.   In the whole of this phraseology one cannot
fail to detect an allusion to the pretensions and self-seeking
character of the Pharisees.   Comp. 2 Thess. ii. 4.

Ver. 3. Οὖν] inasmuch as they speak as teachers and
interpreters of *the Mosaic law.* — πάντα . . . ὅσα] Limitations
of the sense, which lie outside the point of view marked out
by the expression " Moses' seat," — as though Jesus had in

view only the *moral part of the law* (Chrysostom), or contemplated merely what had reference to the *theocratic polity* (Lange), or meant simply to speak *comparatively* (Bleek),— are in opposition to the text, and are of an arbitrary character, all the more so that the multitude was assumed to possess sufficient *capacity for judging* as to how much of the teaching was binding upon them, and how much was not. The words are addressed to the ὄχλοι, whom Jesus had neither the power nor the wish to release from their obligations in respect to the manifest teachings of the law. But having a regard to the glaring inconsistency between the *teaching* and the *conduct* of their pharisaic instructors, and considering His own fundamental principle with regard to the obligatory character of the law, ver. 18 f., He could not have spoken otherwise than He did when He inculcated upon the people the duty of complying with the *words* while refusing to imitate the *conduct* of those instructors. This utterance was conservative, as befitted the needs of the people, and unsparingly outspoken, as the conduct of the Pharisees deserved; but, in opposition to both Pharisees and people, it guarded the holiness of the law. Observe that He is here speaking of the Pharisees in their special capacity as *teachers of the Mosaic law* (Augustine, Calvin, Grotius, Bengel), so that His language is at variance neither with xvi. 6 nor with the axiom given in xv. 13; Acts v. 29. — ποιήσατε κ. τηρεῖτε (see critical notes): *aorist* and *present:* do it, and observe it constantly. See Kühner, II. 1, p. 158 f.

Ver. 4. Comp. Luke xi. 46. — In δεσμεύουσι δέ (see critical notes), the δέ introduces an instance of their λέγουσι καὶ οὐ ποιοῦσι of a peculiarly oppressive character. — The *binding* (tying up into a bundle portions from the various elements, comp. Judith viii. 3) of *heavy burdens* is an expression intended to represent the connecting together of a number of requirements and precepts, so that, from their accumulation, they become difficult to fulfil. — τῷ δὲ δακτύλῳ αὐτῶν, κ.τ.λ.] *but are themselves indisposed to move them even with their finger,* in the direction, that is, of their fulfilment. The emphasis rests on τῷ δακτύλῳ; they will not move the burdens with their *finger,* far less would they bear them upon their *shoulders.*

Vv. 5-7. Comp. Luke xi. 43 f. — φυλακτήρια, amulets, were the תְּפִלִּין, the strips of parchment with passages of Scripture, viz. Deut. xi. 13–22, vi. 4-10, Ex. xiii. 11–17, 1–11, written upon them. They were enclosed in small boxes, and, in accordance with Ex. xiii. 9, 16, Deut. vi. 8, xi. 18, worn during prayer, some on the forehead, some on the left arm next the heart. They were intended to remind the wearer that it was his duty to fulfil the law with head and heart, and, at the same time, to serve the purpose of protecting him from the influence of evil spirits. Joseph. *Antt.* iv. 8. 13 ; Lund, *Jüd. Heiligth.*, ed. Wolf, p. 898 ff.; Keil, *Arch.* I. p. 342 f. — πλατύνουσι] *they broaden* their φυλακτήρια, *i.e.* they make them broader than those of others, in order that they may thereby become duly conspicuous. Corresponding to this is: μεγαλύνουσι, *they enlarge.* On the κράσπεδα, see on ix. 20. — τὴν πρωτοκλισίαν] *the foremost couch at table, i.e.* according to Luke xiv. 8 ff. (Joseph. *Antt.* xv. 2. 4), the *uppermost* place on the divan, which the Greeks also regarded as the place of honour (Plut. *Symp.* p. 619 B). The Persians and Romans, on the other hand, looked upon the place *in the middle* as the most distinguished. The term is met with only in the synoptical Gospels and the Fathers. Suidas: πρωτοκλισία· ἡ πρώτη καθέδρα. — ῥαββί, ῥαββί] רַבִּי, רִבִּי (διδάσκαλε, John i. 39 ; with *yod* paragogic). The reduplication serves to show how *profound* the reverence is. Comp. Mark xiv. 15 ; Matt. vii. 21 f. For the view that *Rabbi* (like our " Dr.") was the title used in addressing learned teachers as early as the time of Jesus (especially since Hillel's time), see Lightfoot, also Pressel in Herzog's *Encykl.* XII. p. 471 ; Ewald, *Gesch. Chr.* p. 305.

Vv. 8–12. Ὑμεῖς] with which the discourse is suddenly turned to the disciples, is placed first[1] for sake of emphasis, and forms a contrast to the Pharisees and scribes. — μὴ

---

[1] In consequence of this address to the disciples, Holtzmann, p. 200, regards the whole discourse, in the form in which it has come down to us, as an historical impossibility. Observe, however, the impassioned and lively way in which the topics are varied so as to suit exactly the different groups of which the audience was composed (see on ver. 1).

κληθῆτε] neither wish nor allow it. — πάντες δέ] so that no one may violate the fraternal tie on the ground of his supposed superiority as a teacher. — καὶ πατέρα, κ.τ.λ.] The word πατέρα, by being placed at the beginning, becomes emphatic, and so also ὑμῶν, by being separated from πατέρα to which it belongs: And you must not call any one *father* of you upon earth, *i.e.* you must not apply the teacher's title "*our father*" (אב, see Buxtorf, p. 10, 2175; Ewald as above) to any mere man. Comp. Winer, p. 549 [E. T. 738]. — Ver. 10. *Neither are you to allow yourselves to be called leaders* (in the scholastic sense), *for the leader of you is One* (see critical notes), *the Messiah.* For examples of the way in which Greek philosophers were addressed by their disciples, see Wetstein. — ὁ δὲ μείζων ὑμῶν, κ.τ.λ.] But among you greatness is to be indicated quite otherwise than by high-sounding titles: *the greater among you, i.e.* he among you who would surpass the others in true dignity, *will be your servant.* Comp. ver. 12. This is a saying of which Jesus makes very frequent use (Luke xiv. 11, xviii. 14). Comp. xx. 26 f.; also the *example* of Jesus in the washing of the disciples' feet, and Phil. ii. 6 f. — ταπεινωθ. . . . ὑψωθ.] that is, on the occasion of the setting up of my kingdom.

REMARK.—The prohibitions, ver. 8 ff., have reference to the *hierarchical* meaning and usage which were at that time associated with the titles in question. The teacher's titles *in themselves* are as legitimate and necessary as his *functions;* but the hierarchy, in the form which it assumed in the Catholic church with the "holy *father*" at its head, was contrary to the spirit and mind of Jesus. Apropos of ver. 11, Calvin appropriately observes: "Hac clausula ostendit, se non sophistice litigasse de *vocibus,* sed *rem* potius spectasse."

Ver. 13. Here begins the direct and withering apostrophe of Jesus to His *adversaries* themselves who are still present, this part of the address consisting of *seven woes,* and extending to ver. 36. For the spurious ver. 14, *Elz.,* concerning the devouring of widows' houses, see the critical remarks. The *characteristic feature* in this torrent of woes is its intense righteous indignation, such as we meet with in the prophets

of old (comp. Isa. v. 8, x. 1 ; Hab. ii. 6 ff.),—an indignation
which abandons the objects of it as past all hope of amendment,
and cuts down every bridge behind them.   To Celsus (in Origen,
ii. 76) all this sounded as mere empty threat and scolding.
— ὅτι] assigns the reason of this οὐαί. — κλείετε, κ.τ.λ.] The
approaching kingdom of the Messiah is conceived of under the
figure of a palace, the doors of which have been thrown open
in order that men may enter.   But such is the effect of the
opposition offered to Christ by the scribes and Pharisees, that
men withhold their belief from the Messiah who has appeared
among them, and show themselves indifferent to the δικαιοσύνη,
necessary in order to admission into the kingdom from which
they are consequently excluded.   Comp. Luke xi. 52.   *They
thus shut the door of the kingdom in men's faces.* — ὑμεῖς γὰρ,
κ.τ.λ.] explanatory reason. — τοὺς εἰσερχομ.] who are trying,
who are endeavouring to obtain admission.   See Bernhardy,
p. 370 f.

Ver. 15. Instead of helping men into the Messiah's kingdom,
what *contemptible efforts to secure proselytes* to their own way
of thinking !   This representation of pharisaic zeal is doubtless hyperbolical, though it is, at the same time, based upon
actual journeyings for the purpose of making converts (Joseph.
Antt. xx. 2. 4).   On Jewish proselytism generally, see Danz
in Meuschen, *N. T. ex Talm. ill.* p. 649. Wetstein's note on this
passage. — ἕνα] a single. — καὶ ὅταν γένηται] sc. προσή-
λυτος. — υἱὸν γεέννης] *one fit for Gehenna,* condemned to
be punished in it.   Comp. on viii. 12 ; John xvii. 12. —
διπλότερον ὑμῶν] is commonly taken in an *adverbial* sense
(Vulg.: *duplo quam*), a sense in which it is consequently to
be understood in the corresponding passage of Justin (*c. Tr.*
122): νῦν δὲ διπλότερον υἱοὶ γεέννης, ὡς αὐτὸς εἶπε, γίνεσθε.
Coming as it does after υἱόν, it is more natural to regard
it, with Valla, as an *adjective : who is doubly more so than
you are.* For the *comparative* itself, comp. App. *Hist. praef.*
10 : σκεύη διπλότερα τούτων.   But it is still rendered doubtful whether διπλότερον is to be taken in an adverbial or
adjective sense by a passage from Justin as above : οἱ δὲ
προσήλυτοι οὐ μόνον οὐ πιστεύουσιν, ἀλλὰ διπλότερον ὑμῶν

βλασφημοῦσι. This passage is likewise unfavourable to Kypke's interpretation : *fallaciorem,* which adjective would be of a more specific character than the context would admit of. *But in how far was Jesus justifiable in using the words* διπλότερον ὑμῶν? According to Chrysostom, Theodore of Mopsuestia, Euthymius Zigabenus : in consequence of the evil example of him who made the convert, which was such that " ex malo ethnico fit pejor Judaeus " (Erasmus) ; according to de Wette : in consequence of the high estimate in which the teachers are held by their disciples, and because superstition and error usually appear with a twofold greater intensity in the taught than in the teachers ; according to Olshausen : because the converted heathen had not the advantage of enjoying the spiritual aid to be found in Mosaism ; according to Bleek : because it was common also to admit as converts those who were influenced by mere external considerations. According to the context (ποιεῖτε) : on account of the manner in which the proselytes *continued* to be influenced and wrought upon by those who converted them, in consequence of which they were generally found to become more bigoted, more unloving, and more extreme than their instructors, and, of course, necessarily more corrupt.

Ver. 16. A new point, and one so peculiarly heinous that a somewhat larger portion of the denunciatory address is devoted to it. — ἐν τῷ ναῷ] as in the Mischna we frequently meet with such expressions as : *per habitaculum hoc,* רמעז הזה. See Wetstein and Lightfoot. — ἐν τῷ χρυσῷ τοῦ ναοῦ] *by the gold which belongs to the temple,* the ornaments, the vessels, perhaps also the gold in the sacred treasury (to which latter Jerome, Maldonatus, refer). We nowhere meet with any example of such swearing, and the subject of *Corban* (xv. 5) is foreign to our passage (Lightfoot), inasmuch as there is no question of τοῦς in the present instance. For ἐν with ὀμνύειν, comp. on v. 34. — οὐδέν ἐστιν] *it* (the oath) *is nothing,* is of no consequence. It is not the person swearing who is the subject, but ὃς ἂν ὀμόσῃ, κ.τ.λ., form an absolute nominative, as in vii. 24, x. 14, xiii. 12. — ὀφείλει] *is indebted,* bound to keep the oath.

Ver. 17 ff. *Γάρ*] Justifies the preceding epithets. — *μείζων*] *of greater consequence*, and consequently more binding, as being a more sacred object by which to swear. The reason of the *μείζων* lies in *ὁ ἁγιάσας τὸν χρυσόν*, according to which the consecrated relation is conceived of as one between the temple and the gold, that has been *brought about* (otherwise if *ἁγιάζων* be read) by the connecting of the latter with the former. — *τὸ δῶρον*] the *offering* (v. 23), as laid upon the altar, it belongs to God.

Vv. 20–22. *Οὖν*] inference from ver. 19; because the greater, from which the less (the *accessorium*), as being bound up with it, derives its sanctity, necessarily includes that less. — *ὁ ὀμόσας ... ὀμνύει*] The *aorist* participle represents the *thing as already in the course of being done* (Kühner, II. 1, p. 134, *ad Xen. Mem.* i. 1. 18): he who has proceeded to swear by the altar, swears (*present*), according to the point of view indicated by *οὖν*, not merely by the altar, but at the same time by all that is upon it as well. — Ver. 21. No longer dependent on *οὖν*; but two other examples of swearing are adduced independently of the former, in each of which even the highest of all, God Himself, is understood to be included. Accordingly we find the objects presented in a different relation to one another. Formerly the greater included the less, now the converse is the case. But though differing in this respect, there is in both instances a perfect agreement as to the sacred and binding character of the oaths.—*κατοικήσαντι*] *who made it his dwelling-place*, took up his abode in it (after it was built). Comp. Jas. iv. 5; Luke ii. 49. — Ver. 22 [1]. Comp. on v. 34.

Ver. 23. Comp. Luke xi. 39 ff. — In accordance with certain traditional enactments (*Babyl. Joma*, f. lxxxiii. 2), the Pharisees extended the legal prescriptions as to tithes (Lev. xxvii. 30; Num. xviii. 21; Deut. xii. 6 f., xiv. 22–27) so as to include even the most insignificant vegetable products, such

---

[1] The opposite of ver. 22 occurs in *Schevuoth*, f. xxxv. 2: "Quia praeter Deum, coeli et terrae creatorem, datur etiam ipsum coelum et terra, indubium esse debet, quod is, qui per coelum et terram jurat non per eum juret, qui illa creavit, sed per illas ipsas creaturas."

as mint, anise, and cummin. See Lightfoot and Wetstein on this passage. Ewald, *Alterth.* p. 399. — τὰ βαρύτερα τοῦ νόμου] *the weightier things, i.e.* the more important (*graviora*) elements of the law (comp. Acts xxv. 7), not: the things *more difficult of fulfilment* (*difficiliora*, as Fritzsche), which interpretation is indeed grammatically admissible (1 John v. 3), but must be rejected, because, according to the context (see ver. 24), Jesus was comparing the important with the less important, and most probably had in view the analogy of the praecepta *gravia* (חמורים) et *levia* (קלים) of the Jewish doctors (see Schoettgen, p. 183). — τὴν κρίσιν] comp. Ps. xxxiii. 5 ; not: *righteousness* (the usual interpretation), a sense in which the term is never used (comp. on xii. 18), but *judgment,* i.e. *deciding for the right as against the wrong.* Comp. Bengel and Paulus. The κρίσις is the *practical manifestation* of righteousness. — τὴν πίστιν] *faithfulness,* Jer. v. 1 ; Rom. iii. 3 ; Gal. v. 22 ; and see on Philem. 5. The opposite of this is ἀπιστία, *perfidia* (Wisd. xiv. 25, frequent in classical writers). — ταῦτα] the βαρύτερα just mentioned, not the tithing of mint, etc. (Bengel). — ἔδει] *oportebat.* See Kühner, II. 1, p. 176 f. Those were the duties which had *been neglected.* — μὴ ἀφιέναι] scarcely so strong as the positive ποιῆσαι. Observe the contrasts : What you *have neglected* you ought to have *done,* and at the same time not *have neglected* what you are *in the habit of doing,*—the former being of paramount importance ; the subordinate matter, viz. your painful attention to tithes, is not superseded by the higher duties, but only kept in its proper place.

Ver. 24. The Jews were in the habit of straining their wine (διϋλίζ., Plut. *Mor.* p. 692 D), in order that there might be no possibility of their swallowing with it any unclean animal, however minute (Lev. xi. 42). Buxtorf, *Lex. Talm.* p. 516. Comp. the *liquare vinum* of the Greeks and Romans ; Mitscherlich, *ad Hor. Od.* i. 11. 7 ; Hermann, *Privatalterth.* § xxvi. 17. Figurative representation of the painful scrupulosity with which the law was observed. — τὸν κώνωπα] a kind of attraction for *percolando removentes muscam* (*that found in the wine,* τὸν κ.*), just as in classical writers the phrase καθαίρειν τι is often used to express *the removing of anything by cleansing*

(Hom. *Il.* xiv. 171, xvi. 667; Dio Cass. xxxvii. 52). κώνωψ
is not a *worm* found in *sour* wine (Bochart, Bleek), but, as
always, a *gnat.* In its attempt to suck the wine, it falls in
amongst it. — τὴν δὲ κάμηλ. καταπίν.] proverbial expression,
τὰ μέγιστα δὲ ἀπαρατηρήτως ἁμαρτάνοντες, Euthymius Zigabenus. Observe at the same time that the camel is an *unclean*
animal, Lev. xi. 4.

Ver. 25. *But inwardly they* (the cup and the plate) *are
filled from extortion and excess* (ἀκρασίας, see critical notes).
That with which they are filled, viz. the wine and the meat, *has
been obtained* through extortion and excess. Plunder (Heb. x.
34, common in classical writers) and exorbitance have contributed to fill them. On γέμειν ἐκ, see on John xii. 3. The
simple genitive (ver. 27) would only be equivalent to: *they
are full of plunder*, etc. — ἀκρασίας] a later form of ἀκρα-
τείας. See on 1 Cor. vii. 5.

Ver. 26. Καθάρισον πρῶτον, κ.τ.λ.] *i.e.* let it be your
first care (πρῶτον, as in vi. 33, vii. 5, and elsewhere), to see
that the wine in the cup is no longer procured by extortion
and exorbitance. — ἵνα γένηται, κ.τ.λ.] not: " ut tum recte
etiam externae partes possint purgari," Fritzsche, but with
the emphasis on γένηται: in order that what you aim at
may then *be effected*, viz. the purity of the outside as well,
—in order that, then, the outside of the cup also may
not merely *appear* to be clean through your washing of it,
but may actually *become* so, by losing *that* impurity which,
in spite of all your cleansing, still adheres to it (which
it contracts, as it were, from its contents), simply because
it is filled with that which is procured through immoral
conduct. The external cleansing is not declared to be unnecessary (de Wette), nor, again, is it intended to be regarded
as the true one, which latter can only be brought about
after the purifying of the contents has been effected. Bengel
fitly observes : " alias enim illa mundities externa non est
mundities." That which is insisted on with πρῶτον is to be
attended to in the first place.

Ver. 27 f. The graves were whitewashed with lime (κονία)
every year on the 15th of Adar (a custom which Rabbinical

writers trace to Ezek. xxxix. 15), not for the purpose of
ornamenting them, but in order to render them so conspicuous
as to prevent any one defiling himself (Num. xix. 16) by
coming into contact with them. For the passages from
Rabbinical writers, see Lightfoot, Schoettgen, and Wetstein.
A kind of ornamental appearance was thus imparted to the
graves. In Luke xi. 44, the illustration is of a totally different character. — ὑποκρίσ. κ. ἀνομ.] (immorality): both as
representing their disposition. Thus, morally speaking, they
were τάφοι ἔμψυχοι, Lucian, D. M. vi. 2.

Ver. 29 ff. Comp. Luke xi. 47 ff. — The οἰκοδομεῖν of the
tombs of the prophets and the κοσμεῖν of the sepulchres of the
righteous (the Old Testament saints, comp. ver. 35, xiii. 17;
Heb. xi. 23); this preserving and ornamenting of the sacred
tombs by those who pretended to be holy was accompanied
with the self-righteous declaration of ver. 30. On the ancient
tombs of a more notable character, see, in general, Robinson,
Pal. II. p. 175 ff., and on the so-called " tombs of the prophets "
still existing, p. 194. Tobler, Topogr. v. Jerus. II. p. 227 ff. —
εἰ ἤμεθα, κ.τ.λ.] not: if we had been, but: if we were (comp.
on John xi. 21), if we were living in the time of our fathers,
certainly we would not be, etc. — ὥστε μαρτυρεῖτε ἑαυτοῖς,
κ.τ.λ.] Thus (inasmuch as you say τῶν πατέρων ἡμῶν) you
witness against yourselves (dative of reference, Jas. v. 3), that you
are the sons, etc. υἱοί contains a twofold meaning. From τῶν
πατέρ. ἡμ., in which the Pharisees point to their bodily descent,
Jesus likewise infers their kinship with their fathers in respect
of character and disposition. There is a touch of sharpness in
this pregnant force of υἱοί, the discourse becoming more and
more impassioned. " When you thus speak of your fathers, you
yourselves thereby testify to your own kinship with the mur-
derers of the prophets." De Wette's objection, that this interpretation of υἱοί would be incompatible with what is said by
way of vindicating themselves at ver. 30, does not apply, because
Jesus feels convinced that their character entirely belies this
self-righteous utterance, and because He wishes to make them
sensible of this conviction through the sting of a penetration
that fearlessly searches their hearts and reads their thoughts.

—— ἐν τῷ αἵματι] *i.e.* the crime of shedding their blood. On αἷμα in the sense of *caedes*, see Dorvill. *ad Charit.* p. 427. For ἐν, see on Gal. vi. 6.

Ver. 32. Quite in keeping with the deepening intensity of this outburst of indignation is the bitter *irony* of the imperative πληρώσατε (comp. xxv. 45), the mere *permissive* sense of which (Grotius, Wetstein, Kuinoel) is too feeble.[1] This *filling up* of the measure (of the sins) of the fathers *was brought about* by their sons ("haereditario jure," Calvin), when they put Jesus Himself as well as His messengers to death. —— καὶ ὑμεῖς] *ye also.* The force of καί is to be sought in the fact that πληρώσατε, κ.τ.λ., is intended to indicate a line of conduct corresponding to and supplementing that of the fathers, and in regard to which the *sons also* must take care not to come short.

Ver. 33. Πῶς φύγητε] Conjunctive, *with a deliberative force: how are you*, judging from your present character, *to escape from* (see on iii. 7), etc. Comp. xxvi. 54; Mark iv. 30; Hom. *Il.* i. 150: πῶς τίς τοι πρόφρων ἔπεσιν πείθηται Ἀχαιῶν;—The κρίσις τῆς γεένν. means the pronouncing of the sentence which condemns to Gehenna. The phrase *judicium Gehennae* is also of very frequent occurrence in Rabbinical writers. See Wetstein. The judgment comes when the measure is full. Comp. 1 Thess. ii. 16.

Ver. 34. Διὰ τοῦτο] must be of substantially the same import as ὅπως ἔλθῃ ἐφ' ὑμᾶς in ver. 35. *Therefore*, in order that ye may not escape the condemnation of hell (ver. 33), *behold, I send to you . . . and ye will,* etc.; καὶ ἐξ αὐτῶν is likewise dependent on διὰ τοῦτο. Awful unveiling of the divine decree. *Others* have interpreted as follows: διότι μέλλετε πληρῶσαι τὸ μέτρον τῆς κακίας τῶν πατέρων ὑμῶν (Euthymius Zigabenus, Fritzsche), thus arbitrarily disregarding what immediately precedes (ver. 33). Moreover, without any hint what-

---

[1] The readings ἐπληρώσατε (D II, min.) and πληρώσητε (B* min. vss.) are nothing but traces of the difficulty felt in regard to the imperative. The former is preferred, though at the same time erroneously interpreted by Wilke, *Rhetor.* p. 367 ; the latter, again, is adopted by Ewald, who regards κ. ὑμεῖς πληρώσητε as also dependent on ἵνα.

ever in the text of Matthew, ἰδού, ἐγὼ ἀποστέλλω, κ.τ.λ., has
sometimes been taken for a quotation from some lost apocryphal
prophecy, ἔφη ὁ θεός, or some such expression, being understood (van Hengel, *Annotatio*, p. 1 ff., and Paulus, Strauss,
Ewald, Weizsäcker),—a view borne out, least of all, by Luke
xi. 49, which passage accounts for the unwarrantable interpretation into which Olshausen has been betrayed.[1] The corresponding passage in Luke has the appearance of belonging to
a later date (in answer to Holtzmann and others). Comp. on
Luke xi. 49. — ἐγώ] is uttered not by God (Ewald, Scholten),
but by *Jesus*, and that under a powerful sense of His Messianic
dignity, and with a boldness still more emphatically manifested
by the use of ἰδού. Through this ἐγὼ ἀποστέλλω, κ.τ.λ., Jesus
gives it to be understood that it is *Himself* who, in the future
also, is still to be the *object* of hatred and persecution on the
part of the Pharisees (comp. Acts ix. 5). — προφήτας κ.
σοφοὺς κ. γραμμ.] by whom He means His apostles and other
teachers (Eph. iv. 11), who, in respect of the Messianic
theocracy, would be what the Old Testament prophets were,
and the Rabbins (חֲכָמִים) and scribes of a later time ought to
have been, in the Jewish theocracy. For the last-mentioned
order, comp. xiii. 52. Olshausen is of opinion that the *Old
Testament prophets themselves must also* have been intended
to be included, and that ἀποστέλλω (which represents the
near and certain future as already present) must indicate
" God's pure and eternal present." The subsequent *futures*

---

[1] " Jesus," he says, " is here speaking as the very impersonation of wisdom ;
Matthew has omitted the quotation formula, because his object was to represent
Jesus as the one from whom the words originally and directly emanate ; but the
original form of the passage is that in which it is found in Luke." Strauss,
in Hilgenfeld's *Zeitschr.* 1863, p. 84 ff., also has recourse to the hypothesis of a
lost book, belonging, as he thinks, to a date subsequent to the destruction of
Jerusalem, and written by a Christian, and in which the messengers in question
are understood to be those whom God has been sending from the very earliest
times. In this Strauss, following in the wake of Baur, is influenced by anti-
Johannine leanings. According to Ewald, a volume, written shortly after the
death of the prophet Zechariah in the fifth century before Christ, but which
is now lost, was entitled ἡ σοφία τοῦ θεοῦ. The σταυρώσετε, he thinks, was inserted by Matthew himself. Bleek, in the *Stud. u. Krit.* 1853, p. 334, and in
his commentary, agrees in the main with Ewald.

ought to have prevented any such construction being put
upon the passage. For γραμμ., comp. xiii. 52. — καὶ ἐξ
αὐτῶν] οὐ πάντες (Euthymius Zigabenus), but more emphatic than if we had had τινάς besides : *and from their
ranks ye will murder*, etc., so that the actions are conceived
of *absolutely* (Winer, p. 552 [E. T. 743]). The same words
are solemnly repeated immediately after. — καὶ σταυρώ-
σετε] *and among other ways of putting them to death, will
crucify them, i.e.* through the Romans, for crucifixion was
a *Roman* punishment. As a historical case in point, one
might quote (besides that of Peter) the crucifixion of *Simeon*,
a brother of Jesus, recorded by Eusebius, *H. E.* iii. 32.
The meagreness, however, of the history of the apostolic
age must be taken into account, though it must not be
asserted that in σταυρώσετε Jesus was referring to *His own
case* (Grotius, Fritzsche, Olshausen, Lange). He certainly
speaks with reference to the *third* class of divine messengers,
the class whom He is *now sending* (Calov.), but not from the
standpoint of His eternal, ideal existence (Olshausen), nor in
the name of God (Grotius), and then, again, from the standpoint of His personal manifestation in time (Olshausen),
fancies for which there is no foundation either in Luke xi. 49
or in the text itself. Jesus does not contemplate *His own*
execution in what is said at ver. 32. — ἐν ταῖς συναγωγ.]
x. 17. — ἀπὸ πόλεως εἰς πόλιν] x. 23. Comp. Xen. *Anab.*
v. 4. 31 : εἰς τὴν ἑτέραν ἐκ τῆς ἑτέρας πόλεως.

Ver. 35. Ὅπως ἔλθῃ, κ.τ.λ.] Teleology of the divine decree:
in order that all the righteous (innocent) *blood* (Jonah i. 14 ;
Joel iii. 19 ; Ps. xciv. 21 ; 1 Macc. i. 37) *may come upon you,
i.e.* the punishment for shedding it. Comp. xxvii. 25. The
scribes and Pharisees are regarded as the *representatives* of the
people, and for whom, as their leaders, they are held *responsible.* — αἷμα] "ter hoc dicitur uno hoc versu, magna vi,"
Bengel. And it is δίκαιον, because it contains the *life* (see on
Acts xv. 20). Comp. Delitzsch, *Psych.* p. 242. — ἐκχυνόμε-
νον] *present*, conceived of as a thing going on in the present,
Kühner, II. 1, p. 116. A vivid picture, in which we seem
to see the blood still actually flowing. On the later form

ἐκχύνω for ἐκχέω, see Lobeck, *ad Phryn.* p. 726. — ἐπὶ τῆς γῆς] according to the canonical narrative (see below). — *Ζαχαρίου υἱοῦ Βαραχίου*] refers to 2 Chron. xxiv. 20, where Zechariah, son of Jehoiada, is said to have been stoned to death by order of King Joash, ἐν αὐλῇ οἴκου κυρίου. Comp. Joseph. *Antt.* ix. 8. 3. The detail contained in μεταξὺ, κ.τ.λ., renders the narrative more precise, and serves to emphasize the *atrocious character* of a deed perpetrated, as this was, on so sacred a spot. Since, according to the arrangement of the books in the Hebrew Canon, Genesis stood at the beginning and 2 Chronicles at the end, and since the series here indicated opens with the case of Abel (Gen. iv. 10 ; Heb. xi. 4), so this (2 Chron. xxiv. 20) is regarded as the *last* instance of the murder of a prophet, although, chronologically, that of Urijah (Jer. xxvi. 23) belongs to a more recent date. The Rabbinical writers likewise point to the murder of this Zacharias as one of a peculiarly deplorable nature ; see *Targum Lam.* ii. 20 ; Lightfoot on our passage. And how admirably appropriate to the scope of this passage are the words of the dying Zechariah : יֵרֶא יְהֹוָה וְיִדְרֹשׁ, 2 Chron. xxiv. 22 ; comp. with Gen. iv. 10 ! If *this latter* is the Zacharias referred to in the text, then, inasmuch as the assumption that his father had two names (*scholion* in Matthaei, Chrysostom, Luther, Beza, Grotius, Elsner, Kanne, *bibl. Unters.* II. p. 198 ff.) is no less arbitrary than the supposition that υἱοῦ Βαραχ. is a gloss (Wassenbergh, Kuinoel), there must, in any case, be some *mistake in the quoting of the father's name* (de Wette, Bleek, Baumgarten-Crusius). It is probable that Jesus Himself did not mention the father's name at all (Luke xi. 51), and that it was introduced into the text from oral tradition, into which an error had crept from confounding the person here in question with the better known *prophet* of the same name, and whose father was called Barachias (Zech. i. 1). Comp. Holtzmann, p. 404. This tradition was followed by Matthew ; but in the Gospel of the Hebrews the wrong name was carefully avoided, and the correct one, viz. *Jehoiada*, inserted instead (Hilgenfeld, *N. T. extra can.* IV. p. 17, 11). According to *others*, the person referred to is *that* Zacharias

who was murdered at the commencement of the Jewish war,
and whose death is thus recorded by Joseph. *Bell.* iv. 6. 4:
δύο δὲ τῶν τολμηροτάτων (ζηλωτῶν) προσπεσόντες ἐν μεσῷ
τῷ ἱερῷ διαφθείρουσι τὸν Ζαχαρίαν υἱὸν τοῦ Βαρούχου.
So Hammond, Krebs, Hug, Credner, *Einl.* I. p. 207, Gfrörer,
Baur, Keim. It is the opinion of Hug that Jesus, as speaking prophetically, made use of the future tense, but that
Matthew substituted a past tense instead, because when this
Gospel was written the murder had already been committed
(after the conquest of Gamala). Keim likewise finds in this
a hint as to the date of the composition of Matthew. But
apart from the fact that the names Barachias and Baruch are
not one and the same, and that the reading in the passage
just quoted from Josephus is doubtful (Var. Βαρισκαίου), the
alleged substitution of the aorist for the future would be so
flagrantly preposterous, that a careful writer could scarcely
be expected to do anything of the sort. As against this whole
hypothesis, see besides Theile in Winer's *neu. krit. Journ.* II.
p. 405 ff., Kuhn in the *Jahrb. d. Theol.* I. p. 350 ff.
Finally, we may mention, only for the sake of recording them,
the ancient opinions (in Chrysostom and Theophylact) that
the Zacharias referred to in our passage was either the minor
prophet of that name, or the father of the Baptist (see *Prot-
evang. Jac.* 23). The latter view is that of Origen, Basil,
Gregory of Nyssa, Theophylact, and several others among the
Fathers (see Thilo, *Praef.* p. lxiv. f.); and recently of Müller
in the *Stud. u. Krit.* 1841, p. 673 ff. — μεταξὺ τοῦ ναοῦ,
κ.τ.λ.] between the temple proper and the altar of burnt-
offerings in the priests' court.

Ver. 36. Ἥξει] Put first for sake of emphasis: *shall come,*
shall inevitably come upon, etc. Comp. ix. 15, xxvii. 49.
— πάντα ταῦτα] according to the context: *all this shedding
of blood, i.e.* the punishment for it. — ἐπὶ τ. γενεὰν ταύτ.]
See on xi. 16; *upon this generation,* which was destined to
be overtaken by the destruction of Jerusalem and the judgments connected with the second coming (ver. 38 f.), comp.
on xxiv. 34.

Ver. 37 ff. After denouncing all those woes against the

scribes and Pharisees, the departing Redeemer, looking with sad eye into the future, sets the *holy city* also—which He sees hastening to its destruction under the false guidance of those leaders — in a living connection with the tragic contents of ver. 34 ff., but in such a way that his parting words are no longer *denunciations of woe*, but the deep wail of a heart wounded, because *its love has been despised.* Thus ver. 37 ff. forms an appropriate conclusion to the whole drama of the discourse. Luke xiii. 34 introduces the words in a historical connection entirely different. — The *repetition* of the name of Jerusalem is here ἐμφαντικὸς ἐλέος, Euthymius Zigabenus. — ἀποκτείνουσα, κ.τ.λ.] The *present* participles denote the *usual* conduct : *the murderess, the killer with stones.* — πρὸς αὐτήν] *to her ;* because the attributive participial clause from being in the *nominative* places the subject addressed under the point of view of the *third* person, and only then proceeds (ποσάκις . . . τέκνα σου) with the vocative of *address* in Ἰερουσαλήμ. Comp. Luke i. 45 ; Job xviii. 4 ; Isa. xxii. 16. With Beza and Fritzsche, αὐτήν might be read and taken as equivalent to σεαυτήν ; but αὐτήν is to be preferred, for this reason, that there is here no such special emphasis as to call for the use of the reflective pronoun (we should expect simply πρός σε in that case). — ποσάκις, κ.τ.λ.] The literal meaning of which is : " How often I have wished to take thy citizens under my loving protection as Messiah ! " For the metaphor, comp. Eurip. *Herc. Fur.* 70 f., and the passages in Wetstein, Schoettgen, p. 208 (Rabbinical writers speak of the Shechinah as gathering the proselytes under its wings). Observe ἑαυτῆς : her *own* chickens. Such was the *love* that I felt toward you. On the form νοσσ. for νεοσσ., see Lobeck, *ad Phryn.* p. 206. οὐκ ἐθελήσατε] sc. ἐπισυναχθῆναι ; they *refused* (Nägelsbach on *Il.* iii. 289 ; Baeumlein, *Partik.* p. 278), namely, to have faith in him as the Messiah, and consequently the *blame* rested with *themselves.* This refusal was their actual κρῖμα, John ix. 39.

Ver. 38 f. Ἀφίεται ὑμῖν ὁ οἶκος ὑμ.] *your house is abandoned to your own disposal ;* the time for divine help and protection for your city is now gone by ! For the meaning, comp. Joseph. *Antt.* xx. 8. 5. The *present* implies the tragic and decisive *ultimatum*. The ἔρημος, which is to be retained on critical grounds (see critical notes), intimates what is to be the *final result* of this abandonment, viz. the destruction of Jerusalem (ἐρήμωσις, xxiv. 45 ; Luke xxi. 20); on the proleptic use of the adjective, comp. on xii. 13, and Kühner, II. 1, p. 236. According to the context, ὁ οἶκος ὑμῶν can only mean Ἰερουσαλήμ, ver. 37 (Bleek), in which their children *dwell ;* not the city *and the country at large* (de Wette and earlier expositors, in accordance with Ps. lxix. 25), nor the whole *body of the Jewish people* (Keim), nor the *temple* (Jerome, Theophylact, Euthymius Zigabenus, Calvin, Olearius, Wolf, Michaelis, Kuinoel, Neander, Baumeister in Klaiber's *Stud.* II. p. 67 f. ; Hofmann, *Schriftbew.* II. 2, p. 92 ; Ewald). — Ver. 39 proceeds to account for this ἀφίεται ὑμῖν, κ.τ.λ. Were your city any longer to be shielded by the divine protection, I would still linger among you ; but I now leave you, and it is certain that henceforth (His presence among them, as He knows, being about to cease with His death, comp. xxvi. 64) you will not see me again until my second coming (not : in the destruction of Jerusalem, Wetstein), when I shall appear in the glory of the Messiah, and when, at my approach, you will have saluted (εἴπητε, *dixeritis*) me, whom you have been rejecting, with the Messianic confession εὐλογη- μένος, κ.τ.λ. (xxi. 9). This is not to be understood of the *conversion of Israel* (Rom. xi. ; Rev. xi.) in its development down to the second coming (Bengel, Köstlin, Hofmann, Lange, Schegg, Auberlen, Ewald) ; for Jesus is addressing *Jerusalem,* and threatening it with the *withdrawal* of God's superintend- ing care, and that *until the second appearing* of Messiah (ὁ ἐρχόμενος), and hence He cannot have had in view an inter- vening μετάνοια and regeneration of the city. No ; the abandonment of the city on the part of God, which Jesus here announces, is ultimately to lead to her destruction ; and then, at His second appearing, which will follow immediately upon the ruin of the city (xxiv. 29), His obstinate enemies will be constrained to join in the loyal greeting with which the Messiah will be welcomed (xxi. 9), for the manifestation of

His glory will sweep away all doubt and opposition, and *force them at last to acknowledge and confess Him* to be their Deliverer. A truly tragic feature at the close of this moving address in which Jesus bids farewell to Jerusalem, not with a *hope*, but with the certainty of ultimate, though sorrowful, *victory*. Euthymius Zigabenus very justly observes in connection with ἕως ἂν εἴπητε, κ.τ.λ.: καὶ πότε τοῦτο εἴπω-σιν; ἑκόντες μὲν οὐδέποτε· ἄκοντες δὲ κατὰ τὸν καιρὸν τῆς δευτέρας αὐτοῦ παρουσίας, ὅταν ἥξει μετὰ δυνάμεως καὶ δόξης πολλῆς, ὅταν οὐδὲν αὐτοῖς ὄφελος τῆς ἐπιγνώσεως. Comp. Theophylact, Calvin, Gerhard, Calovius. Wieseler, p. 322, despairing of making sense of the passage, has gone the length of maintaining that some ancient reader of Matthew has inserted it from Luke. This view might seem, no doubt, to be favoured by the use, in the present instance, of Ἰερουσαλήμ, ver. 37, the form in which the word regularly appears in Luke, and for which, on every other occasion, Matthew has Ἱεροσό-λυμα; but it might very easily happen that, in connection with an utterance by Jesus of so remarkable and special a nature, the form given to the name of the city in the fatal words addressed to her would become so stereotyped in the Greek version of the evangelic tradition, that here, in particular, the Greek translator of Matthew would make a point of not altering the form " Ἰερουσαλήμ," which had come to acquire so fixed a character as part of the utterance before us.

REMARK.—It is fair to assume that Christ's exclamation over Jerusalem presupposes that the capital had repeatedly been the scene of His ministrations, which coincides with the visits on festival occasions recorded by John. Comp. Acts x. 39, and see Holtzmann, p. 440 f.; Weizsäcker, p. 310. Those who deny this (among them being Hilgenfeld, Keim) must assume, with Eusebius in the *Theophan.* (*Nova bibl. patr.* iv. 127), that by the children of Jerusalem are meant the *Jews in general*, inasmuch as the capital formed the centre of the *nation ;* comp. Gal. iv. 25. Baur himself (p. 127) cannot help seeing the far-fetched character of this latter supposition, and consequently has recourse to the unwarrantable view that we have before us the words of a prophet speaking in the name of God,—words which were first put into the mouth of Jesus in their present form, so that, when they were uttered, ποσάκις would be intended to refer to the whole series of prophets and messengers, who had come in God's name ; just as Origen had already referred them to Moses and the prophets as well, in whom Christ was supposed to have been substantially present ; comp. Strauss in Hilgenfeld's *Zeitschr.* 1863, p. 90.

CHAPTER XXIV.

VER. 2. For ὁ δὲ Ἰησοῦς we should read, with Lachm. and Tisch., ὁ δὲ ἀποκριθείς, following important evidence. The insertion of the subject along with the participle led to the omission of the latter. — οὐ βλέπετε] Fritzsche: βλέπετε, following D L X, min. vss. and Fathers. Ancient (It. Vulg.) correction for sake of the sense, after Mark xiii. 2. — For πάντα ταῦτα we should read, with Lachm. Fritzsche, Tisch. 8, ταῦτα πάντα, in accordance with a preponderance of evidence. — ὃς οὐ] Elz.: ὃς οὐ μή, against decisive evidence. Mechanical repetition of the preceding οὐ μή. — Ver. 3. τῆς συντελ.] The article is wanting in B C L ℵ, min. Cyr. (in the present instance), and has been correctly deleted by Lachm. and Tisch. Superfluous addition. — Ver. 6. πάντα] is wanting, no doubt, in B D L ℵ, min. vss., and has been deleted by Lachm. and Tisch. 8, but it had been omitted in conformity with Mark xiii. 7; while in some of the witnesses we find ταῦτα, in accordance with Luke xxi. 9, and in some others, again, πάντα ταῦτα (Fritzsche: ταῦτα πάντα). The various corrections were occasioned by the unlimited character of πάντα. — Ver. 7. καὶ λοιμοί] is wanting in B D E* ℵ, min. Cant. Ver. Verc. Corb. 2, Hilar. Arnob. Deleted by Lachm. and Tisch. 8. Other witnesses reverse the order of the words, which is strongly favoured by Luke. All the more are they to be regarded as inserted from Luke xxi. 11. — Ver. 9. Elz. has ἐθνῶν. But the reading τῶν ἐθνῶν has a decided preponderance of evidence in its favour; and then how easily might τῶν be overlooked after πάντων! The omission of τῶν ἐθνῶν in C, min. Chrys. was with a view to conformity with Mark and Luke. — Ver. 15. ἑστώς] Fritzsche, Lachm. and Tisch.: ἑστός, following a preponderance of MS. authority (including B* ℵ), and correctly. The transcribers have contracted into ἑστώς what, strictly speaking, should be spelt ἑσταός, though the spelling ἑστός is also met with in classical writers. — Ver. 16. ἐπί] Lachm.: εἰς, following B D Δ, min. Fathers. Adopted from Mark xiii. 14; Luke xxi. 21. Mark is likewise the source of the reading καταβάτω, ver. 17, in B D L Z ℵ, min. Or. Caes. Isid.

Chrys., and which Fritzsche, Lachm. Tisch. 8 have adopted. —
For τι ἐκ, as in Elz., read, with Lachm. and Tisch., τὰ ἐκ, following decisive evidence. — Ver. 18. τὰ ἱμάτια] τὸ ἱμάτιον, no
doubt, has weighty evidence in its favour, and is approved by
Griesb. and adopted by Lachm. and Tisch. 8, but it is taken
from Mark xiii. 16. — Ver. 20. The simple σαββάτῳ (Elz.: ἐν
σαββ.) is supported by decisive evidence. — Ver. 23. πιστεύσητε]
Lachm.: πιστεύετε, following only B* Or. Taken from Mark
xiii. 21. — Ver. 24. For πλανῆσαι Tisch. 8 has πλανηθῆναι, following D ℵ, codd. of It. Or.ᶦⁿᵗ and several other Fathers. The
reading of the Received text is, no doubt, supported by preponderating evidence; but how readily might the active have
been substituted for the passive in conformity with vv. 5, 11!
— Ver. 27. καί is, with Scholz, Lachm. Tisch., to be deleted
after ἔσται, in accordance with decisive evidence. Inserted in
conformity with the usual mode of expression; in vv. 37, 39
we should likewise delete the καί, which Tisch. 8 retains in
ver. 39. — Ver. 28. γάρ] deleted by Lachm. and Tisch. 8, following B D L ℵ, min. vss. and Fathers. Correctly. A common
insertion of the connecting particle. This is more probable than
the supposition that a fastidious logic took exception to the
kind of connection. — Ver. 30. τότε κόψ.] The omission of τότε
by Tisch. 8 is without adequate evidence, having among the
uncials only that of ℵ*. Had the words been inserted in
accordance with Mark xiii. 26, Luke xxi. 27, they would have
been placed before ὄψονται. — Ver. 31. φωνῆς] is not found in
L Δ ℵ, min. Copt. Syr. and several Fathers. Being awkward
and superfluous, it was in some cases omitted altogether, in
others (Syr.ʲᵉʳ· Aeth., also Syr.ᴾ·, though with an asterisk at φων.)
placed before σαλπ., and sometimes it was conjoined with σαλπ.
by inserting καί after this latter (D, min. Vulg. It. Hilar. Aug.
Jer.). — For the second ἄκρων Lachm. has τῶν ἄκρ., following only
B, 1, 13, 69. — Ver. 34. After λέγω ὑμῖν, Lachm., in accordance
with B D F L, min. It. Vulg. Or., inserts ὅτι, which, however,
may readily have crept in from Mark xiii. 30; Luke xxi. 32.
— Ver. 35.[1] Griesb. and the more recent editors (with the exception, however, of Matth. and Scholz) have adopted παρελεύσεται in preference to the παρελεύσονται of Elz., following B D L,
min. Fathers. The plural is taken from Mark xiii. 31; Luke
xxi. 33. — Ver. 36. Before ὥρας Elz. has τῆς, which, though
defended by Schulz, is condemned by decisive evidence. Super-

---

[1] The omission of this whole verse by ℵ*, an omission sanctioned neither by
earlier nor by later evidence, is simply an error of the transcriber.

fluous addition. Comp. ver. 3. — After οὐρανῶν Lachm. and Tisch. 8 have οὐδὲ ὁ υἱός, in accordance with B D א, min. codd. of It. Syr.ʲᵉʳ· Aeth. Arm. Chrys. Or.ⁱⁿᵗ Hil. Ambr., etc. For a detailed examination of the evidence, see Tisch. The words are an ancient interpolation from Mark xiii. 32. Had it been the case that they originally formed part of our passage, but were deleted for dogmatic reasons, it is certain that, having regard to the christological importance sometimes ascribed to them (" gaudet Arius et Eunomius, quasi ignorantia magistri," Jerome), they would have been expunged from Mark as well. The interpolation was all the more likely to take place in the case of Matthew, from its serving to explain μόνος (which latter does not occur in Mark). — Elz. Scholz, and Tisch. 7 have μου after πατήρ. Defended by Schulz, though deleted by Griesb. Lachm. Tisch. 8. It is likewise adopted by Fritzsche, who, however, deletes the following μόνος, which is wanting only in Sahid. In deference to the ordinary usage in Matthew (vii. 21, x. 32 f., etc.), μου should be restored. It is wanting, no doubt, in B D L Δ Π א, min. vss. and Fathers, but it may readily enough have been omitted in consequence of the MO immediately following it, all the more that it is not found in Mark. — Ver. 37. δέ] Lachm.: γάρ, following B D I, vss. Fathers. An exegetical gloss. — Ver. 38. ταῖς πρό] is deleted by Fritzsche and Tisch. 7, in accordance with some few, and these, too, inadequate witnesses (Origen, however). Coming as it does after ver. 37, it had been mechanically omitted; it can scarcely have been inserted as the result of reflection. Before ταῖς Lachm. has ἐκείναις, following B D (which latter omits ταῖς), codd. of It.,—a reading which ought to be adopted, all the more because in itself it is not indispensable, and because it was very apt to be omitted, in consequence of the similarity in the termination of the words. — For ἐκγαμίζοντες read γαμίζοντες, with Tisch. 8, following D א, 33, Chrys.; comp. on xxii. 30.—Ver. 40. For ὁ εἷς Fritzsche, Lachm. and Tisch. have simply εἷς in both instances, following B D 1 L א, min. (Δ and Chrys. leave out the article only in the first case). For sake of uniformity with ver. 41. — Ver. 41. μυλῶνι] Lachm. and Tisch.: μύλῳ, following preponderating evidence; the reading of the Received text is intended to be more precise. — Ver. 42. ὥρᾳ] Lachm. and Tisch.: ἡμέρᾳ. So B D I Δ א, min. Ir. Cyr. Ath. Hilar. and vss. The reading of the Received text is by way of being more definite. Comp. ver. 44. — Ver. 45. αὐτοῦ after κύριος is wanting in important witnesses (deleted by Lachm. and Tisch. 8), but it must have been left out to conform with Luke xii. 42. — θεραπείας] Lachm. and Tisch.:

οἰκετείας, following B I L Δ, min. Correctly; from the word
not occurring elsewhere in the New Testament, it would be
explained by the gloss οἰκίας (א, min. Ephr. Bas. Chrys.), or at
other times by θεραπ. — For the following διδόναι read δοῦναι, with
Griesb. Fritzsche, Lachm. Tisch., in accordance with preponderating evidence. — Ver. 46. ποιοῦντα οὕτως] Lachm. and
Tisch.: οὕτως ποιοῦντα, following B C D I L א, min. Vulg. It. Aeth.
Ir. Hil.   The reading of the Received text is from Luke xii. 43.
— Ver. 48. The order μου ὁ κύριος is favoured by a preponderance
of evidence, and, with Lachm. and Tisch., ought to be preferred.
Lachm. and Tisch. 8 omit ἐλθεῖν, though on somewhat weaker
evidence; ἐλθεῖν is further *confirmed* by the reading ἔρχεσθαι in
min. Or. Bas., which is taken from Luke xii. 45. The infinitive not being *indispensable* (comp. xxv. 5), was passed over. —
Ver. 49. αὐτοῦ, which is wanting in Elz. (and Tisch. 7), has
been restored by Griesb. Lachm. and Tisch. 8, in accordance
with preponderating evidence.   Similarly with regard to ἐσθίῃ
δὲ καὶ πίνῃ (for ἐσθίειν δὲ καὶ πίνειν in Elz.), which has decisive
evidence in its favour, and is an altered form of Luke xii. 45.

Ver. 1. On the following discourse generally, see: Dorner,
de orat. Chr. eschatologica, 1844; R. Hofmann, *Wiederkunft
Chr. u. Zeichen d. Menschensohnes*, 1850; Hebart, *d. zweite
sichtb. Zuk. Chr.* 1850; Scherer in the *Strassb. Beitr.* 1851,
II. p. 83 ff.; E. J. Meyer, *krit. Comment. zu d. eschatolog.
Rede Matth.* xxiv., xxv., I., 1857; Cremer, *d. eschatolog.
Rede Matth.* xxiv., xxv., 1860; Luthardt, *Lehre v. d. letzten
Dingen*, 1861; Hoelemann, *Bibelstudien*, 1861, II. p. 129 ff.;
Auberlen in the *Stud. u. Krit.* 1862, p. 213 ff.; Pfleiderer in
the *Jahrb. f. D. Theol.* 1868, p. 134 ff.; Kienlen, *ibid.* 1869,
p. 706 ff., and *Commentaire sur l'apocalypse*, 1870, p. 1 ff.;
Wittichen, *Idee d. Reiches Gottes*, 1872, p. 219 ff.; Weissenbach, *d. Wiederkunfts-gedanke Jesu*, 1873, p. 69 ff., comp.
his *Jesu in regno coel. dignitas*, 1868, p. 79 ff.; Colani, *Jésus
Christ et les croyances messian. de son temps*, ed. 2, 1864,
p. 204 ff.—The parallel passages are Mark xiii., Luke xxi.
Luke, however, in accordance with his own independent way
of treating his narrative, does not merely omit many particulars
and put somewhat differently many of those which he records
(as is likewise the case with Mark), but he introduces not a
few in a different, and that an earlier historical connection

(ch. xii. 17). But this would not justify us, as Luther, Schleiermacher, Neander, Hase suppose, in using Luke's narrative for correcting Matthew (Strauss, II. p. 337 f.; Holtzmann, p. 200 ff.), to whom, as the author of the collection of our Lord's sayings, precedence in point of authority is due. It must be admitted, however, that it is precisely the eschatological discourses, more than any others, in regard to which it is impossible to determine how many modifications of their original form may have taken place[1] under the influence of the ideas and expectations of the apostolic age, although the shape in which they appeared first of all was given to them, not by Mark (Holtzmann, p. 95; see, on the other hand, Weiss), but by Matthew in his collection of the sayings of our Lord. This is to be conceded without any hesitation. At the same time, however, we must as readily allow that the discourse is characterized by all the unity and consecutiveness of a skilful piece of composition, and allow it all the more that any attempt to distinguish accurately between the original elements and those that are not original (Keim) only leads to great uncertainty and diversity of opinion in detail. But the idea that portions of a Jewish (Weizsäcker) or Judaeo-Christian (Pfleiderer, Colani, Keim, Weissenbach) apocalyptic writing have been mixed up with the utterances of Jesus, appears not only unwarrantable in itself, but irreconcilable with the early date of the first two Gospels, especially in their relation to the collection of our Lord's sayings ($\lambda o \gamma i a$). — $\dot{\epsilon} \xi \epsilon \lambda \theta \dot{\omega} \nu$] from the temple, xxi. 23. — $\dot{\epsilon} \pi o \rho \epsilon \dot{\upsilon} \epsilon \tau o \ \dot{a} \pi \dot{o} \ \tau o \hat{\upsilon} \ \dot{\iota} \epsilon \rho o \hat{\upsilon}$] *He went away from the temple*, withdrew to some distance from it. Comp. xxv. 41. For this interpretation we require neither a *hyperbaton* (Fritzsche, de Wette), according to which $\dot{a} \pi \dot{o} \ \tau. \ \dot{\iota} \epsilon \rho o \hat{\upsilon}$

---

[1] Although the contents of the discourse itself, as well as the earlier date of the first two Gospels generally, decidedly forbid *the* supposition that it was not composed till after the destruction of Jerusalem, and that, consequently, it assumes this latter to have already taken place (Credner, Baur, Köstlin, Hilgenfeld, Volkmar). If this supposition were correct, the discourse would have to be regarded as a late product of the apostolic age, and therefore as a *vaticinium post eventum*. Further, the eschatological views of the apostolical Epistles, though they presuppose corresponding teaching on the part of Jesus, by no means imply any knowledge of the specific discourses in ch. xxiv., xxv. (in answer to E. J. Meyer, p. 50 ff.).

would belong to ἐξελθών,[1] nor the accentuation ἄπο (Bornemann
in the *Stud. u. Krit.* 1843, p. 108 f.). — τὰς οἰκοδομὰς τοῦ
ἱεροῦ] not merely τοῦ ναοῦ, but the whole of the buildings
connected with the temple, all of which, with the ναός and
the porches and the courts, constituted the ἱερόν.   Comp. on
iv 5.   The magnificent structures (Joseph. *Bell.* v. 5. 6, vi.
4. 6, 8 ; Tac. *Hist.* v. 8. 12) were not then finished as yet, see
on John ii. 21.—Even Chrysostom, Erasmus, and Bengel
did not fail to perceive that what *led* the disciples to direct the
attention of Jesus to the temple-buildings was the announcement contained in xxiii. 38, which, though it did not refer
exclusively to the temple, necessarily *included* the fate of
this latter as well.   This the disciples could not but notice ;
and so, as they looked back and beheld the splendours of the
entire sacred edifice, they could not help asking Jesus further
to explain Himself, which He does at 'once in ver. 2, and
in terms corresponding with what He had announced in
xxiii. 38.

Ver. 2. Οὐ[2] βλέπετε ταῦτα πάντα (see critical notes)
does not mean : " *do not gaze so much at all this* " (Paulus),
in which case μή, at least, would be required ; nor : " *are you
not astonished at all this magnificence* " (de Wette, following
Chrysostom) ? which would be to import a different meaning
into the simple βλέπετε ; but : *ye see not all this*, by which, of
course, Jesus does not intend the mere temple-buildings *in
themselves considered*, but *the doom which awaits all those
splendid edifices*,—a doom which He at once proceeds to reveal.
Instead of having an eye to perceive all this, to them everything looked so magnificent ; they were βλέποντες οὐ βλέποντες (xiii. 13), so that they were incapable of seeing the
true state of matters as regarded the temple ; it was hid from
their eyes.   The more vividly Jesus Himself foresaw the

---

[1] This supposition, indeed, has likewise led to the transposition : ἀπὸ (Lachm.:
ἐκ, following B) τοῦ ἱεροῦ ἐπορεύετο (B D L Δ ℵ, min. vss. Fathers), which order is
adopted by Tisch. 8.

[2] Among modern critics, Kuinoel, Fritzsche, Baumgarten-Crusius, Ewald,
Bleek, have decided in favour of omitting οὐ, as approved by Griesbach and
Schulz.   Among those belonging to an earlier date, Casaubon says distinctly,
with regard to the negative : " hic locum *non potest* habere."

coming ruin; the more distinct the terms in which He had just been pointing to it, xxiii. 38; the deeper the emotion with which He had taken that touching farewell of the temple; the fuller, moreover, the acquaintance which the disciples must have had with the prophecy in Dan. ix.; and the greater the perplexity with which, as the Lord was aware, they continued to regard His utterance about the temple, xxiii. 38; so much the more intelligible is this introductory passage, in which Jesus seeks to withdraw their attention from what presents itself to the mere outward vision, and open their eyes in order that as $μὴ$ $βλέποντες$ $βλέπωσι$ (John ix. 39). Further, it is better to take this pregnant utterance in an *affirmative* rather than in an *interrogative* sense, as is usually done, because there is no preceding *assertion* on the part of the disciples to which the question of *surprise* might be said to correspond. Grulich (*de loci Matth.* xxiv. 1, 2, *interpret.*, 1839) places the emphasis on $πάντα$: " videtis quidem $ταῦτα$, sed non videtis $ταῦτα$ $πάντα$ (nimirum templi desolationem, etc.)." So also Hoelemann. This is improbable, if for no other reason than the ordinary usage as regards $ταῦτα$ $πάντα$, which has no such refinement of meaning anywhere else. Jesus would simply have said: $οὐ$ $πάντα$ $βλέπετε$. Bornemann, as above, after other attempts at explanation, finds it simplest to interpret as follows: *ye see not; of all this, believe me, not one stone will remain upon another*, etc. He thinks that what Jesus meant to say was: $ταῦτα$ $πάντα$ $καταλυθή$-$σεται$, but that He interrupts Himself in order to introduce the asseveration $ἀμὴν$ $λέγω$ $ὑμῖν$, and so breaks the construction. That Jesus, however, would not merely have broken the construction, but still more would have used the words $οὐ$ $μὴ$ $ἀφεθῇ$ without any logical reference to $ταῦτα$ $πάντα$, is clearly indicated by $ὧδε$, which therefore contradicts the explanation just given. — $ὃς$ $οὐ$ $καταλυθ.$] For $οὐ$, see Winer, p. 448 [E. T. 604]; Buttmann, p. 305 [E. T. 355]. Not a stone will be left upon another without being thrown down. Occurring as it does in a prophetical utterance, this *hyperbolical* language should not be strained in the least, and certainly it ought not to be made use of for the purpose of disproving the genuineness of the passage; see, as against this abuse, Keim, III. p. 190 ff. ; Weissenbach, p. 162 ff. And on account of Rev. xi. 1 ff., comp. also Weizsäcker, p. 548 f.

Ver. 3. Κατ' ἰδίαν] unaccompanied by any but such as belonged to the number of the Twelve, because they were going to ask Him to favour them with a secret revelation. Differently Mark xiii. 3. — ταῦτα] those disastrous events of ver. 2. — καὶ τί τὸ σημεῖον, κ.τ.λ.] The disciples assume, as matter of course, that immediately after the destruction in question the Lord will appear, in accordance with what is said xxiii. 39, for the purpose of setting up His kingdom, and that with this the current (the pre-Messianic) era of the world's history will come to an end. Consequently they wish to know, *in the second place* (for there are only *two* questions, not *three*, as Grotius, Ebrard suppose), what is to be the sign which, after the destruction of the temple, is to precede this second coming and the end of the world, that by it they may be able to recognise the approach of those events. The above assumption, on the part of the disciples, is founded on the doctrine respecting the הבלי המשיח, *dolores Messiae*, derived from Hos. xiii. 13. See Schoettgen, II. p. 550; Bertholdt, *Christol.* p. 43 ff. — τῆς σῆς παρουσίας] After his repeated intimations of future suffering and death, the disciples could not conceive of the *advent* of Jesus (1 Cor. xv. 23 ; 1 Thess. ii. 19 ; in the Gospels peculiar to Matthew) to set up His kingdom and make a permanent stay in any other way than as a solemn *second coming.* After His resurrection they expected the *Risen One* straightway to set up His kingdom (Acts i. 6),—a very natural expectation when we bear in mind that the resurrection was an unlooked-for event; but, after the ascension, their hopes were directed, in accordance with the express promises of Jesus, to the coming *from heaven,* which they believed was going to take place ere long, Acts i. 11, iii. 20 f., *al.,* and the numerous passages in the New Testament Epistles. Comp. Wittichen in the *Jahrb. f. Deutsche Theol.* 1862, p. 354 ff. Observe, too, the emphatic σῆς coming after the general expression ταῦτα. — καὶ συντελ. τοῦ αἰῶνος] In the Gospels we find no trace of the millenarian ideas of the Apocalypse. The τοῦ αἰῶνος, with the article, but not further defined, is to be understood as referring to the *existing*, the then *current* age of the world, *i.e.* to the αἰὼν οὗτος, which is brought to a close (συντέλεια) with the second coming, inasmuch as, with this latter event, the αἰὼν μέλλων begins. See on xiii. 39. The second coming, the resurrection and the last judgment, fall upon the ἐσχάτη ἡμέρα (John vi. 39, xi. 24), which, as it will be the last day of the αἰὼν οὗτος in general, so of the ἐσχά-των ἡμερῶν (Acts ii. 17 ; 2 Tim. iii. 1 ; Jas. v. 3 ; Heb. i. 2 ; 2 Pet. iii. 3) in particular, or of the καιρὸς ἔσχατος (1 Pet. i. 5), or of the χρόνος ἔσχατος (Jude 18 ; 1 Pet. i. 20), which John likewise calls the ἐσχάτη ὥρα (1 John ii. 18). This concluding period, which terminates with the last day, is to be characterized by abounding distress and wickedness (see on Gal. i. 4). The *article* was unnecessary before συντελείας, seeing that it is followed by the genitive of specification ; Winer, p. 118 f. [E. T. 155].

Ver. 4. The *reply* of Jesus is directed, in the first instance, to the *second* question (τί τὸ σημεῖον, κ.τ.λ.), inasmuch as He indicates, as the discourse advances, the things that are to pre-cede His second coming, till, in ver. 28, He reaches the point which borders immediately upon the latter event (see ver. 29). But this answer to the second question involves, at the same time, an indirect answer to the first, in so far as it was possible to give this latter at all (for see ver. 36), and in so far as it was advisable to do so, if the watchfulness of the disciples was to be maintained. The discourse proceeds in the following order down to ver. 28 : first there is a warning with regard to the appearing of false Messiahs (extending to ver. 5), then the announcement of the *beginning* and *development* of the *dolores Messiae* on to their termination (vv. 6–14), and finally the hint that these latter are to *end* with the destruction of the temple and the accompanying disasters (vv. 15–22), with a repetition of the warning against false Messiahs (vv. 23–28). Ebrard (*adv. erroneam nonnull. opinion., qua Christus Christique apost. existumasse perhibentur, fore ut univ. iudicium ipsor. actate superveniret*, 1842) finds in vv. 4–14

the reply of Jesus to the disciples' *second* question.   He thinks
that in ver. 15 Jesus passes to the first, and that in ver. 29
He comes back "ad σημεῖον τῆς ἑαυτοῦ παρουσίας κατ᾽
ἐξοχήν, *i.c.* ad secundae quaestionis partem priorem."   This
supposition is simply the result of an imperious dogmatic pre-
conception, and cannot be justified on any fair exegetical
principle.   See below.   Dorner, who spiritualizes the discourse, understands vv. 4–14 as setting forth the nature of
the gospel and its necessary development, while he regards
what follows, from ver. 15 onward, as describing the historical
"decursum Christianae religionis;" he thinks that Jesus
desired by this means to dispel the premature Messianic
hopes of the disciples, and make them reflect on what they
must bear and suffer "ut evangelium munere suo *historico*
perfungi possit."

Vv. 4, 5. In the first place—and how appropriate and
necessary, considering the eagerness of the disciples for the
second coming!—a *warning against false Messiahs*, and then
ver. 6 f. the first, far off, indirect prognostics of the second
advent, like the roll of the distant thunder. — ἐπὶ τ. ὀνόμ.
μου] *on the strength of my name*, so that they *rest* their claims
upon the name of *Messiah*, which they arrogate to themselves.
Comp. xviii. 5.   The following λέγοντες, κ.τ.λ. is epexegetical.
We possess no *historical* record of any false Messiahs having
appeared *previous to the destruction of Jerusalem* (Barcochba
did not make his appearance till the time of Hadrian); for
Simon Magus (Acts viii. 9), Theudas (Acts v. 36), the
Egyptian (Acts xxi. 38), Menander, Dositheus, who have been
referred to as cases in point (Theophylact, Euthymius Zigabenus,
Grotius, Calovius, Bengel), did not pretend to be the *Messiah*.
Comp. Joseph. *Antt.* xx. 5. 1 ; 8. 6 ; *Bell.* ii. 13. 5.   Then as
for the period *subsequent to the destruction of the capital*, it is
not here in question (in answer to Luthardt, Cremer, Lange) ;
for see on ver. 29.   And consequently it cannot have been
intended, as yet, to point to such personages as Manes, Mon-
tanus, and least of all Mohammed.

Ver. 6. Δέ] continuative: but to turn now from this preliminary warning to your question itself—ye will hear, etc.

This reply to the disciples' question as to the events that were to be the *precursors* of the destruction of the temple (comp. πότε, ver. 3), is so framed that the prophetic outlook is directed first to the more general aspect of things (to what is to take place on the theatre of the *world at large*, vv. 6–8), and then to what is of a more special nature (to what concerns the *disciples* and the community of *Christians*, vv. 9–14). For the *future* μελλήσ. (*you will have to*), comp. 2 Pet. i. 12 ; Plat. *Ep.* vii. p. 326 C. — πολέμους κ. ἀκοὰς πολέμων] said with reference to wars *near at hand*, the din and tumult of which are actually heard, and to wars *at a distance*, of which nothing is known except from the *reports* that are brought home. — ὁρᾶτε, μὴ θροεῖσθε] *take care, be not terrified.* For θροεῖσθε, comp. 2 Thess. ii. 2 ; Song of Sol. v. 4 ; on the two imperatives, as in viii. 4, 15, ix. 30, see Buttmann, *Neut. Gr.* p. 209 [E. T. 243]. — δεῖ γὰρ πάντα γενέσθαι] they are not to be terrified, *because it is necessary that all that should take place.* The reflection that it is a matter of *necessity* in pursuance of the divine purpose (xxvi. 54), is referred to as calculated to inspire a calm and reassured frame of mind. πάντα is to be understood as meaning : *everything that is then to happen*, not specially (τὰ πάντα, ταῦτα πάντα, comp. critical notes) the matters indicated by μελλήσετε . . . πολέμων, but rather that : nothing, which begins to take place, can stop short of its full accomplishment. The emphasis, however, is on δεῖ. — ἀλλ' οὔπω ἐστὶ τὸ τέλος] *however, this will not be as yet the final consummation*, so that you will require to preserve your equanimity still further. Comp. Hom. *Il.* ii. 122 : τέλος δ' οὔ πώ τι πέφανται. τὸ τέλος cannot mean the συντέλεια, ver. 3 (Chrysostom, Ebrard, Bleek, Lange, Cremer, Auberlen, Hoelemann, Gess), but, as the context proves by the correlative expression ἀρχὴ ὠδίνων, ver. 8, and by τὸ τέλος, ver. 14, comp. with οὖν, ver. 15, *the end of the troubles at present under consideration.* Inasmuch, then, as these troubles are to be straightway followed by the world's last crisis and the signs of the Messiah's advent (vv. 29, 30), τὸ τέλος must be taken as referring to *the end of the dolores Messiae.* This end *is* the laying waste of the temple and the unparalleled desolation of the land that is to accompany it. Ver. 15 ff. This is also substantially equivalent to de Wette's interpretation : " the decisive winding up of the present state of things (and along with it the climax of trouble and affliction)."

Ver. 7. Γάρ] it is not quite the end as yet ; *for* the situation will become still more turbulent and distressing : *nation will rise against nation, and kingdom against kingdom*, etc. We have here depicted in colours borrowed from ancient prophecy (Isa. xix. 2), not only those risings, becoming more and more frequent, which, after a long ferment, culminated in the closing scene of the Jewish war and led to the destruction of Jerusalem, but also those convulsions in nature by which they were accompanied. That this prediction was fulfilled *in its general aspects* is amply confirmed, above all, by the well-known accounts of Josephus ; but we are forbidden by the very nature of genuine prophecy, which cannot and is not meant to be restricted to isolated points, either to assume or try to prove that such and such historical events are special literal fulfilments in concrete of the individual features in the prophetic outlook before us, — although this has been attempted very recently, by Köstlin in particular. As for the Parthian wars and the risings that took place some ten years after in Gaul and Spain, they had no connection whatever with Jerusalem or Judaea. There is as little reason to refer (Wetstein) the πολέμους of ver. 6 to the war waged by Asinaeus and Alinaeus against the Parthians (Joseph. *Antt.* xviii. 9. 1), and the ἀκοὰς πολέμων to the Parthian declaration of war against King Izates of Adiabene (Joseph. *Antt.* xx. 3. 3), or to explain the latter (ἀκοὰς πολέμων) of the struggles for the imperial throne that had broken out after the death of Nero (Hilgenfeld). Jesus, who sees rising before Him the horrors of war and other calamities connected, ver. 15, with the coming destruction of Jerusalem, presents *a picture* of them to the view of His hearers. Comp. 4 Esdr. xiii. 21; *Sohar Chadasch,* f. viii. 4 : " Illo tempore bella in mundo excitabuntur ; gens erit contra gentem, et urbs contra urbem : angustiae multae contra hostes Israelitarum innovabuntur." *Beresch. Rabba,* 42 f., 41. 1 : " Si videris regna contra se invicem insurgentia,

tunc attende, et adspice pedem Messiae." — λιμοὶ κ. σεισμοί]
see critical notes. Nor, again, is this feature in the prediction
to be restricted to some such special famine as that which
occurred during the reign of Claudius (Acts xi. 28), too early
a date for our passage, and to one or two particular cases of
earthquake which happened in remote countries, and with which
history has made us familiar (such as that in the neighbourhood of Colossae, Oros. *Hist.* vii. 7, Tacit. *Ann.* xiv. 27, and
that at Pompeii). — κατὰ τόπους] which is applicable only
to σεισμοί, as in Mark xiii. 8, is to be taken distributively
(Bernhardy, p. 240 ; Kühner, II. 1, p. 414) : *locatim,* travelling from one district to another. The equally grammatical
interpretation : *in various localities here and there* (Grotius,
Wetstein, Raphel, Kypke, Baumgarten-Crusius, Köstlin, Bleek),
is rather too feeble to suit the *extraordinary* character of the
events referred to. In vv. 6, 7, Dorner finds merely an embodiment of the thought : " evangelium gladii instar dissecabit
male conjuncta, ut vere jungat ; naturae autem phaenomena
concomitantia quasi depingent motus et turbines in spiritu-
alibus orbibus orturos."

Ver. 8. *But all this will be the beginning of woes* (Euthymius
Zigabenus : προοίμια τῶν συμφορῶν), will stand in the same
relation to what is about to follow, as the *beginning* of the
birth - pangs does to the much *severer* pains which come
after. It is apparent from ver. 7 that ἔσται is understood.
The figure contained in ὠδίνων is to be traced to the popular
way of conceiving of the troubles that were to precede the
advent of the Messiah as חבלי המשׁיח. Comp. on ver. 3.

Ver. 9. Jesus now exhibits the *sequel* of this universal
beginning of woes in its special bearing upon the *disciples
and the whole Christian community.* Comp. on x. 17 ff. —
τότε] *then,* when what is said at ver. 7 will have begun.
Differently in Luke xxi. 12 (πρὸ δὲ τούτων), where, though
τότε is not in any way further defined (Cremer), we have
clearly a correction in order to adapt the expression to the
persecutions that in the evangelist's time had already *begun.*
Seeing that the expressions are distinctly *different* from each
other, it is not enough to appeal to the " *elasticity* " of the τότε

(Hoelemann). — ἀποκτενοῦσιν ὑμᾶς] spoken *generally*, not
as intimating, nor even presupposing (Scholten), the death of
all of them. After παραδώσ. ὑμᾶς the current of prophetic
utterance flows regularly on, leaving to the hearers themselves
to make the necessary distinctions. — καὶ ἔσεσθε μισού-
μενοι] It is a mistake to suppose that we have here a reference
to Nero's persecution (proceeding upon an erroneous interpretation of the well-known " odio humani generis " in Tacit.
Ann. xv. 44, see Orelli on the passage), because it is the
disciples that are addressed ; and to regard them as the representatives of Christians *in general*, or as the *sum total of the
church* (Cremer), would be arbitrary in the highest degree ; the
discourse does not become general in its character till ver. 10.
Comp. 1 Cor. iv. 13. — ὑπὸ πάντων τ. ἐθνῶν] *by all nations*.
What a confirmation of this, in all *general* respects, is furnished by the history of the apostles, so far as it is known to
us ! But we are not justified in saying more, and especially
when we take into account the prophetic colouring given to
our discourse, must we beware of straining the πάντων in
order to favour the notion that the expression contains an
allusion to the vast and long-continued efforts that would
be made to disseminate the gospel throughout the world
(Dorner) ; let us repeat that it is the *apostles* who are in
question here. Comp. x. 17 f., 22.

Ver. 10. Καὶ τότε] *and then*, when those persecutions
will have broken out against you. — σκανδαλισθήσονται
πολλοί] *many will receive a shock*, *i.e.* many Christians will
be tempted to relapse into unbelief, see on xiii. 21. For the
converse of *offenduntur* in this sense, see ver. 13. Consequence of this falling away: καὶ ἀλλήλους παραδώσ.] *one
another*, *i.e.* the Christian who has turned apostate, him who
has continued faithful. What a climax the troubles have
reached, seeing that they are now springing up in the very
heart of the Christian community itself !

Ver. 11. Besides this ruinous apostasy in consequence of
persecution from without, there is the propagation of error by
false Christian teachers living in *the very bosom* of the church
itself (comp. vii. 15). These latter should not be more

precisely defined (Köstlin : " extreme antinomian tendencies ; "
Hilgenfeld : " those who adhere to Pauline views ; " comp.
also Weiss, *Bibl. Theol.* p. 586, ed. 2). The history of the
apostolic age has sufficiently confirmed this prediction, Acts
xx. 30 ; 1 John iv. 1.

Ver. 12. *And in consequence of the growing prevalence of
wickedness* (as the result of what is mentioned in vv. 10, 11),
the love of the greater number will become cold ; that pre-
dominance of evil within the Christian community will
have the effect of cooling the brotherly love of the majority
of its members. The moral degeneracy within the pale of
that community will bring about as its special result a pre-
vailing want of charity, that specific contrast to the true
characteristic of the Christian life (Gal. v. 6 ; 1 Cor. xiii. 1 ff. ;
1 John iv. 20). For ἀνομία, the opposite of moral compliance
with the law of God (= ἁμαρτία, 1 John iii. 4), comp. vii. 23,
xiii. 41, xxiii. 28 ; 2 Cor. vi. 14 ; 2 Thess. ii. 7. For ψύγειν
with γ, comp. Lobeck, *ad Phryn.* p. 318. — τῶν πολλῶν] are
not the πολλοί mentioned in ver. 10 (Fritzsche), whose love,
as that verse informs us, is already changed into hatred, but
the *multitude*, the *mass*, the great body (Kühner, II. 1, p. 548 ;
Ast, *Lex. Plat.* III. p. 148) of Christians. In the case of those
who were distinguished above the ordinary run of Christians,
no such cooling was to take place ; but yet, as compared with
the latter, they were only to be regarded as ὀλίγοι. According
to Dorner, vv. 11, 12 apply not to the apostolic age, but
to a subsequent stage in the history of the church. But
such a view is inconsistent with the numerous testimonies to
be met with in the Epistles, with the apprehensions and
expectations regarding impending events to which they give
expression. Comp. on Gal. i. 4.

Ver. 13. Ὁ δὲ ὑπομείνας] contrast to what in the σκαν-
δαλισθήσ. πολλοί of ver. 10 and the πλανήσ. πολλούς of ver.
12 is described as apostasy, partly from the faith generally,
and partly (ver. 12) from the *true* Christian faith and life.
Comp. x. 22. According to Fritzsche, it is only the persevering *in love* that is meant, so that the contrast has
reference merely to ψυχήσεται, κ.τ.λ. But according to our

interpretation, the contrast is more thorough and better suited to the terms of the passage. — εἰς τέλος] not *perpetuo* (Fritzsche), which, as the connection shows (ver. 6), is too indefinite; but: *unto the end, till the last*, until the troubles will have come to an end, which, as appears from the context (σωθήσεται), will, in point of fact, be coincident with the second advent. Comp. vv. 30, 31, x. 22. The context forbids such interpretations as: *unto death* (Elsner, Kuinoel, Ebrard), *until the destruction of Jerusalem* (Krebs, Rosenmüller, R. Hofmann), σωθήσεται being referred in the latter case to the flight of the Christians to Pella (Eusebius, *H. E.* iii. 5). Of course ver. 13 describes the " sanam hominis Christiani dispositionem spiritualem ad eschatologiam pertinentem "(Dorner), always on the understanding, however, that the second advent is *at hand*, and that the " homo Christianus " *will live to see it.*

Ver. 14. Having just uttered the words εἰς τέλος, Christ now reveals the prospect of a *most encouraging state of matters* which is immediately to *precede* and usher in the consummation indicated by this εἰς τέλος, namely, the preaching of the gospel throughout the whole world in spite of the hatred and apostasy previously mentioned (vv. 9, 10 ff.); ὅτι οὐδὲν τῶν δεινῶν περιγενήσεται τοῦ κηρύγματος, Euthymius Zigabenus. The substantial fulfilment of this prediction is found in the missionary labours of the apostles, above all in those of Paul; comp. Acts i. 9; Rom. i. 14, x. 18, xv. 19; Matt. xxviii. 19; Col. i. 23; Clem. 1 *Cor.* v. — τοῦτο τὸ εὐαγγ.] According to de Wette, the author here (and xxvi. 13) so far forgets himself as to allude to the gospel *which he was then in the act of writing.* The τοῦτο here may be accounted for by the fact that Christ was there and then engaged in preaching the gospel of the Messiah's kingdom, inasmuch as eschatological prediction undoubtedly constitutes an essential *part* of the gospel. Consequently: " hoc evangelium, quod nuntio."— ἐν ὅλῃ τῇ οἰκουμ.] must not be limited to the *Roman empire* (Luke ii. 1), but should be taken quite *generally: over the whole habitable globe*, a sense which is alone in keeping with Jesus' consciousness of His Messianic mission, and with the πᾶσι τοῖς ἔθνεσι which follows. — εἰς μαρτύριον, κ.τ.λ.] *in order that testimony may be borne before all nations,* namely, *concerning me and my work,* however much they may have hated you for my name's sake. The interpretation of the Fathers: εἰς ἔλεγχον, is therefore substantially in accordance with the context (ver. 9), though there was no need to import into the passage the idea of the *condemnation* of the heathen, which condemnation would follow as a *consequence* only in the case of those who might be found to reject the testimony. There are *other* though arbitrary explanations, such as . " ut nota illis esset pertinacia Judaeorum " (Grotius), or : "ut gentes testimonium dicere possint harum calamitatum et insignis pompae, qua Jesus Messias in has terras reverti debeat" (Fritzsche), or : " ita ut *crisin* aut vitae aut mortis adducat " (Dorner). — καὶ τότε] *and then,* when the announcement shall have been made throughout the whole world. — τὸ τέλος] the end of the troubles that are to precede the Messiah's advent, correlative to ἀρχή, ver. 8. Comp. ver. 6 ; consequently not to be understood in this instance either as referring to the *end of the world* (Ebrard, Bleek, Dorner, Hofmann, Lange, Cremer), which latter event, however, will of course announce its approach by catastrophes in nature (ver. 29) *immediately after* the termination of the *dolores Messiae.*

Ver. 15. See Wieseler in the *Götting. Vierteljahrschr.* 1846, p. 183 ff. ; Hengstenberg, *Christol.* III. p. 116 ff. More precise information regarding this τέλος. — οὖν] *therefore,* in consequence of what has just been stated in the καὶ τότε ἥξει τὸ τέλος. According to Ebrard and Hoelemann, οὖν indicates a *resuming of the previous subject* (Baeumlein, *Partik.* p. 177 ; Winer, p. 414 [E. T. 555]): "Jesus ad *primam questionem revertitur,* praemisso secundae quaestionis responso." But even Ebrard himself admits that Jesus has *not as yet* made any direct reference to the disciples' first question, ver. 3, accordingly he cannot be supposed to *recur* to it with a mere οὖν. Wieseler also takes a similar view of οὖν. He thinks that it is used by way of resuming the thread of the conversation, which had been interrupted by the preliminary warning inserted at vv. 4–14. But this conversation, which the disciples had introduced, and in which, moreover, vv. 4–14 are by no means of the nature

of a mere warning, has not been interrupted at all. According
to Dorner, οὖν marks the transition from the eschatological
principles contained in vv. 4–14 to the *applicatio eorum his-
torica s. prophetica,* which view is based, however, on the
erroneous assumption that vv. 4–14 do not possess the
character of concrete eschatological prophecy.   The predictions before us respecting the Messianic woes become more
threatening till just at this point they reach a climax. — τὸ
βδέλυγμα τῆς ἐρημώσεως] *the abomination of desolation ;*
the genitive denotes that in which the βδέλυγμα specifically
consists and manifests itself as such, so that the idea, "the
abominable desolation," is expressed by the use of another
substantive instead of the adjective, in order to bring out the
characteristic attribute in question ; comp. Ecclus. xlix. 2 ;
Hengstenberg: the abomination, which *produces* the desolation.   But in Daniel also the ἐρήμωσις is the leading
idea.   The Greek expression in our passage is not exactly
identical with the Septuagint[1] rendering of שִׁקּוּצִים מְשֹׁמֵם, Dan.
ix. 27 (xi. 31, xii. 11). Comp. 1 Macc. i. 54, vi. 7.   In this
prediction it is not to *Antichrist,* 2 Thess. ii. 4 (Origen,
Luthardt, Klostermann, Ewald), that Jesus refers ; nor, again,
is it to the *statue of Titus,* which is supposed to have been
erected on the site of the temple after its destruction (Chrysostom, Theophylact, Euthymius Zigabenus) ; nor to that of
Caligula, which is *said* (but see Krebs, p. 53) to have been

[1] In the Hebrew of the passage referred to in Daniel the words are not intended
to be taken together (Hävernick, von Lengerke on Dan. ix. 27, Hengstenberg,
Christol. III. p. 103 f.).   They are, moreover, very variously interpreted ; von
Lengerke (Hengstenberg), for example : "the destroyer comes over the pinnacles
of abomination ;" Ewald (Auberlen): "and that on account of the fearful height of
abominations;" Wieseler: "and that because of the destructive bird of abomination" (referring to the eagle of Jupiter Olympius, to whom Epiphanes dedicated
the temple at Jerusalem, 2 Macc. vi. 2); Hofmann, *Weissag. u. Erf.* I. p. 309 :
"and that upon an offensive idol cover" (meaning the veil with which the
altar of the idol was covered).   My interpretation of the words in the original
(וְעַל כְּנַף שִׁקּוּצִים מְשֹׁמֵם) is this : *the destroyer (comes) on the wing of abominations,* and that until, etc.   Comp. Keil.   Ewald on *Matthew,* p. 412,
takes כְּנַף as a paraphrase for τὸ ἱερόν.   The Sept. rendering is probably from
such passages as Ps. lvii. 2.   For other explanations still, see Hengstenberg,
Christol. III. p. 123 ff. ; Bleck in the *Jahrb. f. D. Theol.* 1860, p. 93 ff.

set up within the temple; nor even to the equestrian statue of *Hadrian* (all which Jerome considers possible), which references would imply a period too early in some instances, and too late in others. It is better, on the whole, not to seek for any more special reference (as also Elsner, Hug, Bleek, Pfleiderer have done, who see an allusion to the sacrilegious acts committed by the *zealots in the temple*, Joseph. *Bell.* iv. 6. 3), but to be satisfied with what the words themselves plainly intimate : *the abominable desolation on the temple square*, which was historically realized in the doings of the heathen conquerors during and after the capture of the temple, though, at the same time, no special stress is to be laid upon the heathen *standards* detested by the Jews (Grotius, Bengel, Wetstein, de Wette, Ebrard, Wieseler, Lange), to which the words cannot refer. Fritzsche prefers to leave the $\beta\delta\epsilon\lambda$. τ. $\dot{\epsilon}\rho$. without any explanation whatever, in consequence of the $\dot{o}$ $\dot{a}\nu\alpha\gamma\iota\nu\dot{\omega}\sigma\kappa$. $\nu o\epsilon\dot{\iota}\tau\omega$, by which, as he thinks, Jesus meant to indicate that the reader was to find out the prophet's meaning for himself. The above general interpretation, however, is founded upon the text itself; nor are we warranted by Dan. ix. 27 in supposing any reference of a very special kind to underlie what is said. The idea of a desecration of the temple by *the Jews themselves* (Hengstenberg), or of the *corrupt state of the Jewish hierarchy* (Weisse, *Evangelienfr.* p. 170 f.), is foreign to the whole connection. — $\tau\dot{o}$ $\dot{\rho}\eta\theta\dot{\epsilon}\nu$ $\delta\iota\dot{a}$ $\Delta a\nu$. τ. $\pi\rho o\phi$.] *what has been said* (expressly mentioned) by Daniel, not: " which is an expression of the prophet Daniel " (Wieseler); for the important point was not the prophetic *expression*, but the *thing* itself indicated by the prophet. Comp. xxii. 31. — On $\dot{\epsilon}\sigma\tau\dot{o}s$, see critical notes, and Kühner, I. p. 677. — $\dot{\epsilon}\nu$ $\tau\dot{o}\pi\dot{\omega}$ $\dot{a}\gamma\dot{\iota}\dot{\omega}$] *in the holy place; i.e.* not the *town* as invested by the Romans (so Hoelemann and many older expositors, after Luke xxi. 20), but the *place of the temple* which has been in question from the very first (ver. 2), and which Daniel has in view in the passage referred to. The designation selected forms a tragic contrast to the $\beta\delta\dot{\epsilon}\lambda\upsilon\gamma\mu a$; comp. Mark xiii. 14 : $\dot{o}\pi o\upsilon$ $o\dot{\upsilon}$ $\delta\epsilon\hat{\iota}$. *Others,* and among them de Wette and Baumgarten-Crusius

(comp. Weiss on Mark), understand the words as referring
to *Palestine*, especially to the *neighbourhood of Jerusalem*
(Schott, Wieseler), or to *the Mount of Olives* (Bengel), because
it is supposed that it would have been too late to seek to
escape after the temple had been captured, and so the flight
of the Christians to Pella took place as soon as the war
began.   The ground here urged, besides being an attempt to
make use of the special form of its historical fulfilment in
order to correct the prophetic picture itself, as though this
latter had been of the nature of a special prediction, is irrelevant, for this reason, that in ver. 16 the words used are not
"*in Jerusalem*," but ἐν τῇ Ἰουδαίᾳ; see on ver. 16.   Jesus
means to say : When the abomination of desolation will have
marred and defaced the symbol of the *divine guardianship of
the people*, then everything is to be given up as lost, and
safety sought only by fleeing from Judaea to places of greater
security among the mountains. — ὁ ἀναγινώσκων νοείτω]
let the reader understand ! (Eph. iii. 4).   Parenthetical observation by the *evangelist*, to impress upon his readers the precise
point of time indicated by Jesus at which the flight is to
take place upon the then impending (not already present,
Hug, Bleek) catastrophe.   Chrysostom, Euthymius Zigabenus,
Paulus, Fritzsche, Kaeuffer, Hengstenberg (*Authent. d. Dan.* p.
258 ff.), Baumgarten-Crusius, Ewald, ascribe the observation
to *Jesus*, from *whose* lips, however, one would have expected,
in the flow of living utterance, and according to His manner
elsewhere, an expression similar to that in xi. 15, xiii. 9, or
at least ὁ ἀκούων νοείτω.   We may add that our explanation
is favoured by Mark xiii. 14, where τὸ ῥηθὲν ὑπὸ Δαν. τοῦ
προφ. being spurious, it is consequently the reader, not of
Daniel, but of the *gospel*, that is meant.   Hoelemann incorrectly
interprets : "*he who has discernment*, let him understand it "
(alluding to Dan. xii. 11); ἀναγινώσκ. is never used in the
New Testament in any other sense than that of *to read*.

Ver. 16 ff. Apodosis down to ver. 18. — οἱ ἐν τ. Ἰουδ.]
means those who may happen to be living in the *country*
of Judaea (John iii. 22), in contradistinction to Jerusalem
with its holy place, the abominations in which are to be

the signal for flight. — μὴ καταβαινέτω, κ.τ.λ.] Some have
conceived the idea to be this : " ne per scalas interiores, sed
exteriores descendat," Bengel (Grotius, Wetstein) ; or : *let him*
flee over the roofs (over the lower walls, separating house from
house, till he comes to the city wall, Michaelis, Kuinoel,
Fritzsche, Paulus, Winer, Kaeuffer). *Both* views may be
taken each according to circumstances. — τὰ ἐκ τῆς οἰκίας
αὐτοῦ] common attraction for τὰ ἐν τῇ οἰκίᾳ ἐκ τῆς οἰκίας.
See Kühner, I. 474, and *ad Xen. Mem.* iii. 6. 11 ; Winer,
p. 584 [E. T. 784]. — ἐν τῷ ἀγρῷ] where, being at work,
he has no upper garment with him. — People will have to
flee *to save their lives* (ver. 22) ; not according to the idea
imported by Hofmann : to escape the otherwise too powerful
temptation to deny the Lord.   This again is decisively refuted
by the fact that, in vv. 16–19, it is not merely the *disciples*
or *believers* who are ordered to flee, but the summons to do
so is *a general one.*   What is said with reference to the flight
does not assume an *individualizing* character till ver. 20.

Ver. 19. Αἱ μὲν γὰρ ἔγκυοι οὐ δυνήσονται φεύγειν, τῷ
φορτίῳ τῆς γαστρὸς βαρυνόμεναι· αἱ δὲ θηλάζουσαι διὰ τὴν
πρὸς τὰ τέκνα συμπάθειαν, Theophylact.

Ver. 20. "Ἵνα] *Object* of the command, and therefore its
purport ; Mark xiv. 35 ; Col. i. 9. — μηδὲ σαββάτῳ] without ἐν, as in xii. 1 ; Winer, p. 205 [E. T. 274]. On the
Sabbath the rest and the solemnities enjoined by the law, as
well as the short distance allowed for a Sabbath-day's journey
(2000 yards, according to Ex. xvi. 29 ; see Lightfoot on Luke
xxiv. 50 ; Acts i. 12 ; Schoettgen, p. 406), could not but
interfere with the necessary haste, unless one were prepared
in the circumstances to ignore all such enactments.   Taken
by themselves, the words μηδὲ σαββάτῳ seem, no doubt, to
be inconsistent with Jesus' own liberal views regarding the
Sabbath (xii. 1 ff.; John v. 17, vii. 22); but he is speaking
from the standpoint of *His disciples,* such a standpoint as they
occupied *at the time He addressed them,* and which was destined
to be outgrown only in the course of a later development of
ideas (Rom. xiv. 5 ; Col. ii. 6).   As in the case of χειμῶνος,
what is here said is simply with a view to everything being

avoided calculated to interfere with their hasty flight.   Comp.
x. 23.

Ver. 21. Those hindrances to flight are all the more to
be deprecated that the troubles are to be unparalleled, and
therefore a rapid flight will be a matter of the most urgent
necessity. — ἕως τοῦ νῦν] *usque ad hoc tempus*, Rom. viii. 22.
Κόσμου is not to be supplied here (Fritzsche).   See, on the
other hand, Mark xiii. 19; 1 Macc. ii. 33; Plat. *Parm.*
p. 152 C, *Ep.* xiii. p. 361 E.   On the threefold negative οὐδὲ
οὐ μή, see Bornemann in the *Stud. u. Krit.* 1843, p. 109 f.
For the expression generally, Plat. *Tim.* p. 38 A : οὐδὲ γενέσθαι ποτὲ οὐδὲ γεγονέναι νῦν οὐδ᾽ εἰσαῦθις ἔσεσθαι ; Stallbaum,
ad Rep. p. 492 E.

Ver. 22. *And unless those days had been shortened*, those,
namely, of the θλίψις μεγάλη (ver. 29), etc.   This is to
be understood of the *reduction of the number* of the days
over which, but for this shortening, the θλίψις would have extended, not of the *curtailing of the length of the day* (Fritzsche),
—a thought of which Lightfoot quotes an example from Rabbinical literature (comp. the converse of this, Josh. x. 13),
which, seeing that there is a *considerable number* of days,
would be to introduce an element of a very extraordinary
character into the usual ideas connected with the acceleration
of the advent (1 Cor. vii. 29).   Rather comp. the similar idea,
which in Barnab. iv. is ascribed to Enoch. — ἐσώθη] used here
with reference to the *saving of the life* (viii. 25, xxvii. 40, 42,
49, and frequently); Euthymius Zigabenus: οὐκ ἂν ὑπεξέ-
φυγε τὸν θάνατον.   Hofmann incorrectly explains: saved from
denying the Lord. — πᾶσα σάρξ] *every flesh*, i.e. *every mortal
man* (see on Acts ii. 16), would not be rescued, *i.e. would
have perished*.   Comp. for the position of the negative, Fritzsche,
Diss. II. on 2 *Cor.* p. 24 f.   The limitation of πᾶσα σάρξ to
the Jews and Christians belonging to town or country who are
found *in immediate contact with the theatre of war*, is justified
by the context.   The ἐκλεκτοί are *included*, but it is not these
alone who are meant (Hofmann). — The aorist ἐκολοβ. conveys
the idea that the shortening was resolved upon *in the counsels
of the divine compassion* (Mark xiii. 20), and its relation to

the aorist ἐσώθη in the apodosis is this . had the shortening of the period over which the calamities were to extend not taken place, this would have involved the utter destruction of all flesh. The *future* κολοβωθήσ. again conveys the idea that the *actual* shortening *is being* effected, and therefore that the case supposed, with the melancholy consequences involved in it, *has been averted.* — διὰ δὲ τοὺς ἐκλεκτούς] *for sake of the chosen* (for the Messianic kingdom), in order that they might be preserved for the approaching advent. That in seeking to save the righteous, God purposely adopts a course by which He may save others at the same time, is evident from Gen. xviii. 13 ff. But the ἐκλεκτοί (see on xxii. 14) are those who, at the time of the destruction of the capital, are *believers* in Christ, and are found *persevering in their faith in Him* (ver. 13); not the future *credituri* as well (Jahn in Bengel's *Archiv.* II. 1; Schott, *Opusc.* II. p. 205 ff.; Lange, following Augustine, Calovius), which latter view is precluded by the εὐθέως of ver. 29. — There is a certain *solemnity* in the repetition of the same words κολοβ. αἱ ἡμέραι ἐκεῖναι. Ebrard lays stress upon the fact, as he supposes, that our passage describes a calamity " cui finis sit imponendus, et quae ab aetate paulo saltem feliciore sit excipienda," and accordingly infers that the idea of the immediate end of the world is thereby excluded. But the *aetas paulo saltem felicior*, or the supposition that there is any interval at all between the θλίψις μεγάλη and ver. 29, is foreign to the text; but the *end* of the above-mentioned disaster is to take place in order that what is stated at ver. 29 may follow it *at once.*

Ver. 23 ff. Τότε] *then*, when the desolation of the temple and the great θλίψις shall have arrived, false Messiahs, and such as falsely represent themselves to be prophets, will again come forward and urge their claims with greater energy than ever, nay, in the most seductive ways possible. Those here referred to are different from the pretenders of ver. 4 f. The excitement and longing that will be awakened in the midst of such terrible distress will be taken advantage of by impostors with pretensions to miracle-working, and then how dangerous they will prove! By such early expositors as Chrysostom and those who come after him, ver. 23 was supposed to mark the transition to the subject of the advent, so that τότε would pass over the whole period between the destruction of Jerusalem and the second advent; while, according to Ebrard (comp. Schott), the meaning intended by Jesus in vv. 23, 24 is, that after the destruction of the capital, the condition of the church and of the world, described in vv. 4-14, " *in posterum quoque mansurum esse.*" Such views would have been discarded if due regard had been paid to the τότε by which the point of time is precisely defined, as well as to the circumstance that the allusion here is *merely* to the coming forward of false Christs and false prophets. Consequently we should also beware of saying, with Calovius, that at this point Christ passes to the subject of His *adventus spiritualis per evangelium.* He is still speaking of that period of distress, ver. 21 f., which *is to be immediately followed*, ver. 29, by the second advent. — ψευδόχριστοι] those who falsely claim to be Messiah; nothing is known regarding the historical fulfilment of this. Jonathan (Joseph. *Bell.* vii. 11. 3) and Barcochba (see on ver. 5) appeared at a later period. — ψευδοπροφῆται] according to the context, not Christian teachers (ver. 11), in the present instance, but *such as pretended to be sent by God, and inspired to speak to the people in the season of their calamity*,— deceivers similar to those who had tried to impose upon their fellow-countrymen during the national misfortunes of earlier times (Jer. xiv. 14, v. 13, vi. 13, viii. 10). Comp. Joseph. *Bell.* ii. 13. 4 : πλάνοι γὰρ ἄνθρωποι καὶ ἀπατῶντες προσχήματι θειασμοῦ νεωτερισμοὺς καὶ μεταβολὰς πραγματευόμενοι, δαιμονᾶν τὸ πλῆθος ἀνέπειθον, κ.τ.λ. *Others* suppose that the reference is to such as sought to pass for *Elijah* or some other prophet *risen from the dead* (Kuinoel), which would scarcely agree with the use of a term so general as the present ; there are those also who think it is the *emissaries of the false Messiahs* who are intended (Grotius).— δώσουσι] not : *promise* (Kypke, Krebs), but : *give*, so as to suit the idea involved in σημεῖα. Comp. xii. 39 ; Deut. xiii. 1. — On σημεῖα καὶ τέρατα, between which there is no *material* difference, see on Rom. xv. 19. Miracles may also be performed by Satanic agency,

2 Thess. ii. 9. — ὥστε πλανηθῆναι (see critical notes): *so that the very elect may be led astray* (Kühner, II. 2, p. 1005) if possible (εἰ δυνατόν: *si fieri possit;* "conatus summus, sed tamen irritus," Bengel). — Ver. 25. Διαμαρτύρεται ἐξασφαλιζόμενος, Euthymius Zigabenus. Comp. John xiv. 29.

Ver. 26. Οὖν] according to the tenor of this my prediction. Ver. 26 does not stand to ver. 23 in the relation of a strange *reduplication* (Weiss), but as a rhetorical amplification which is brought to an emphatic close by a repetition of the μὴ πιστεύσητε of ver. 23. — ἐστί] the Messiah, ver. 23. — ἐν τοῖς ταμείοις] the article is to be taken *demonstratively,* while the plural denotes the inner rooms of a house. According to Fritzsche, we have here the *categorical* plural (see on ii. 20): "en, ibi est locorum, quae conclavia appellantur." That would be too vague a pretence. The phraseology here made use of: *in the wilderness—in the inner rooms of the house* —is simply apocalyptic *imagery.* "*Ultra* de deserto et penetralibus quaerere non est sobrii interpretis," Maldonatus.

Ver. 27. *Reason why* they were not to listen to such assertions. The advent of the Messiah will not be of such a nature that you will require to be directed to look here or look there in order to see him ; but it will be as the lightning, which, as soon as it appears, suddenly announces its presence *everywhere;* οὕτως ἔσται ἡ παρουσία ἐκείνη, ὁμοῦ πανταχοῦ φαινομένη διὰ τὴν ἔκλαμψιν τῆς δόξης, Chrysostom. Not as though the advent were not to be connected with some locality or other upon earth, or were to be invisible altogether (R. Hofmann); but what is meant is, that when it takes place, it will all of a sudden openly display itself in a glorious fashion *over the whole world.* Ebrard (comp. Schott) is wrong in supposing that the point of comparison lies only in the circumstance that the event comes *suddenly and without any premonition.* For certainly this would not tend to show, as Jesus means to do, that the assertion: he is in the wilderness, etc., is an *unwarrantable* pretence.

Ver. 28. Confirmation of the truth that the advent will announce its presence everywhere, and that from the point of view of the retributive punishment which the coming One

will be called upon everywhere to execute. The emphasis of
this figurative adage is on ὅπου ἐὰν ᾖ and ἐκεῖ: " *Wherever*
the carcase *may happen to be, there* will the eagles be gathered
together,"—on no spot where there is a carcase will this
gathering fail, so that, when the Messiah shall have come,
He will reveal Himself everywhere in this aspect also (namely,
as an avenger). Such is the sense in which this saying was
evidently understood as early as the time of Luke xvii. 37.
The *carcase* is a metaphorical expression denoting the *spiritually
dead* (viii. 22 ; Luke xvi. 24) who are doomed to the Messianic
ἀπώλεια, while the words συναχθήσονται (namely, at the
advent) οἱ ἀετοί convey the same idea as that expressed in
xiii. 41, and which is as follows : the *angels*, who are sent forth
by the Messiah for the purpose, συλλέξουσιν ἐκ τῆς βασιλείας
αὐτοῦ πάντα τὰ σκάνδαλα, καὶ βαλοῦσιν αὐτοὺς εἰς τὴν κάμινον
τοῦ πυρός, the only difference being, that in our passage
the prophetic imagery depicting the mode of punishment is
not that of consuming by fire, and that for the simple reason
that the latter would not harmonize with the idea of the carcase
and the eagles (Bleek, Luthardt, Auberlen). *Others* (Lightfoot, Hammond, Clericus, Wolf, Wetstein) have erroneously
supposed that the *carcase* alludes to *Jerusalem* or the *Jews*,
and that the *eagles* are intended to denote the Roman legions
with their standards (Xen. *Anab.* i. 10. 12 ; Plut. *Mar.* 23).
But it is the *advent* that is in question ; while, according to
vv. 23–27, ὅπου ἐὰν ᾖ cannot be taken as referring to any
one particular locality, so that Hoelemann is also in error,
inasmuch as, though he interprets the eagles as representing
the *Messiah and His angel-hosts*, he nevertheless understands
the carcase to mean Jerusalem as intended to form the
central scene of the advent. It is no less mistaken to
explain the latter of " the corpses of *Judaism* " (Hilgenfeld),
on the ground that, as Keim also supposes, Christ means to
represent Himself " as *Him who is to win the spoils amid the
physical and moral ruins of Israel.*" According to Cremer,
the carcase denotes the *anti-Messianic agitation* previously
described, which is destined to be suppressed and punished
by the *imperial power* (the eagles). This view is erroneous ;

for, according to ver. 27, the συναχθ. οἱ ἀετοί can only represent the παρουσία τ. υἱοῦ τ. ἀνθρ. Fritzsche and Fleck, p. 384: "ubi *Messias*, ibi *homines, qui ejus potestatis futuri sint*" (οἱ ἐκλεκτοί, ver. 31). Similarly such early expositors as Chrysostom (who thinks the angels and martyrs are intended to be included), Jerome, Theophylact (ὥσπερ ἐπὶ νεκρὸν σῶμα συνάγονται ὀξέως οἱ ἀετοὶ, οὕτω καὶ ἔνθα ἂν εἴη ὁ Χριστός, ἐλεύσονται πάντες οἱ ἅγιοι), Euthymius Zigabenus, Münster, Luther, Erasmus ("non deerunt capiti sua membra"), Beza, Calvin, Clarius, Zeger, Calovius, Jansen. But how inappropriate and incongruous it would be to compare the Messiah (who is conceived of as τροφὴ πνευματική, Euthymius Zigabenus) to the *carcase;* which is all the more offensive when, with Jerome, πτῶμα is supposed to contain a reference to the *death* of Jesus—a view which Calvin rejected. Wittichen in the *Jahrb. f. D. Theol.* 1862, p. 337, reverses the subjects of comparison, and takes the carcase as representing the Israelitish ἐκλεκτοί, and the eagles as representing the Messiah. But this interpretation is likewise forbidden by the incongruity that would result from the similitude of the carcase so suggestive of the domain of death, as well as by that universal character of the advent to which the context bears testimony. With astonishing disregard of the context, Kaeuffer observes: "μὴ πιστεύσητε, sc. illis, nam ubi materies ad praedandum, ibi praedatores avidi, h. e. nam in fraudem vestram erit." On the question as to whether πτῶμα without a qualifying genitive be good Greek, see Lobeck, *ad Phryn.* p. 375. — οἱ ἀετοί] are the *carrion-kites* (vultur percnopterus, Linnaeus) which the ancients regarded as belonging to the eagle species. See Plin. *N. H.* x. 3 ; Aristot. ix. 22. For the similitude, comp. Job xxxix. 30 ; Hos. viii. 1 ; Hab. viii. 1 ; Prov. xxx. 17 ; Ezek. xxxix. 17.

Ver. 29. Here follows the *second portion* of the reply of Jesus, in which He intimates what events, following at once on the destruction of Jerusalem, are *immediately to precede* His second coming (vv. 29–33); mentioning at the same time, that however near and certain this latter may be, yet the day and hour of its occurrence cannot be determined, and

that it will break unexpectedly upon the world (vv. 34–41);
this should certainly awaken men to watchfulness and preparedness (vv. 42–51), to which end the two parables, xxv.
1–30, are intended to contribute. The discourse then concludes with a description of the final judgment over which
the coming one is to preside (xxv. 31–46). — εὐθέως δὲ μετὰ
τ. θλίψιν τῶν ἡμερ. ἐκ.] *but immediately after the distress of
those days,* immediately after the last (τὸ τέλος) of the series
of Messianic woes described from ver. 15 onwards, and the
first of which is to be coincident with the destruction of
the temple. For τῶν ἡμερ. ἐκείνων, comp. vv. 19, 22; and
for θλίψιν, ver. 21. Ebrard's explanation of this passage
falls to the ground with his erroneous interpretation of vv.
23, 24, that explanation being as follows: *immediately after
the unhappy condition of the church* (vv. 23–28), *a condition
which is to continue after the destruction of Jerusalem,* — it
being assumed that the εὐθέως involves the meaning: "*nullis
aliis intercedentibus indiciis.*" It may be observed generally,
that a whole host of strange and fanciful interpretations have
been given here, in consequence of its having been assumed
that Jesus could not possibly have intended to say that His
second advent was to follow immediately upon the destruction of Jerusalem. This assumption, however, is contrary to
all exegetical rule, considering that Jesus repeatedly makes
reference elsewhere (see also ver. 34) to His second coming as
an event that is near at hand. Among those interpretations
may also be classed that of Schott (following such earlier
expositors as Hammond and others, who had already taken
εὐθέως in the sense of *suddenly*), who says that Matthew had
written פִּתְאֹם, *subito,* but that the translator (like the Sept.
in the case of Job v. 3) had rendered the expression "minus
accurate" by εὐθέως. This is certainly a wonderful supposition, for the simple reason that the פתאם itself would be a
wonderful expression to use if an interval of a thousand years
was to intervene. Bengel has contributed to promote this
view by his observation that: "Nondum erat tempus revelandi
totam seriem rerum futurarum a vastatione Hieros. usque ad
consummationem seculi," and by his paraphrase of the passage:

"De iis, quae *post pressuram dierum illorum*, delendae urbis Jerusalem, evenient *proximum*, quod in praesenti pro mea conditione commemorandum et pro vestra capacitate expectandum venit, hoc est, *quod sol obscurabitur*," etc. Many *others*, as Wetstein, for example, have been enabled to dispense with gratuitous assumptions of this sort by understanding ver. 29 ff. to refer to the *destruction of Jerusalem*, which is supposed to be described therein in the language of prophetic imagery (Kuinoel), and they so understand the verse in spite of the destruction already introduced at ver. 15. In this, however, they escape Scylla only to be drawn into Charybdis, and are compelled to have recourse to expedients of a still more hazardous kind in order to explain away the literal advent,[1] which is depicted in language as clear as it is sublime. And yet E. J. Meyer again interprets vv. 29–34 of the destruction of Jerusalem, and in such a way as to make it appear that the prediction regarding the final advent is not introduced till ver. 35. But this view is at once precluded by the fact that in ver. 35 ὁ οὐρανὸς κ. ἡ γῆ παρελεύσεται cannot be regarded as the leading idea, the theme of what follows, but only as a subsidiary thought (v. 18) by way of background for the words οἱ δὲ λόγοι μου οὐ μὴ παρέλθ. immediately after (observe, Christ does not say οἱ γὰρ λόγοι, κ.τ.λ., but οἱ δὲ λόγοι, κ.τ.λ.). Hoelemann, Cremer, Auberlen are right in their interpretation of εὐθέως, but wrong in regarding *the time of the culmination of the heathen power* — an idea imported from Luke xxi. 24 — as antecedent to the period indicated by εὐθέως. Just as there are those who seek to dispose of the historical difficulty connected with εὐθέως by twisting the sense of *what precedes*, and by an importation from Luke xxi. 24, so Dorner seeks to dispose of it by twisting the sense of *what comes after.* — ὁ ἥλιος σκοτισθ., κ.τ.λ.] Description of the great catastrophe in the heavens which is to precede the

---

[1] Comp. the Old Testament prophecies respecting the day of the coming of Jehovah, Isa. xiii. 9 ff., xxxiv. 4, xxiv. 21; Jer. iv. 23 f.; Ezek. xxxii. 7 f.; Hag. ii. 6 f. ; Joel ii. 10, iii. 3 f., iv. 15; Zeph. i. 15; Hag. ii. 21; Zech. xiv. 6, etc., and the passages from Rabbinical writers in Bertholdt, *Christol.* § 12; Gfrörer, *Gesch. d. Urchrist.* I. 2, pp. 195 ff., 219 ff.

second advent of the Messiah.   According to Dorner, our passage is intended as a prophetical delineation of the *fall of
heathenism,* which would follow immediately upon the overthrow
of Judaism ; and, accordingly, he sees in the mention of the
sun, moon, and stars an allusion to the *nature-worship* of the
heathen world, an idea, however, which is refuted at once by
ver. 34; see E. J. Meyer, p. 125 ff.; Bleek, p. 356; Hofmann, p. 636; Gess, p. 136.   Ewald correctly interprets:
" While the whole world is being convulsed (ver. 29, after
Joel iii. 3 f.; Isa. xxxiv. 4, xxiv. 21), the heaven-sent
Messiah appears in His glory (according to Dan. vii. 13) to
judge," etc. — οἱ ἀστέρες πεσοῦνται, κ.τ.λ.] Comp. Isa.
xxxiv. 4.   To be understood *literally,* but not as illustrative
of sad times (Hengstenberg on the Revelation ; Gerlach, *letzte
Dinge,* p. 102); and yet not in the sense of *falling-stars*
(Fritzsche, Kuinoel), but as meaning : the *whole* of the stars
together.   Similarly in the passage in Isaiah just referred to,
in accordance with the ancient idea that heaven was a firma-
ment in which the stars were set for the purpose of giving
light to the earth (Gen. i. 14).   The *falling* of the stars
(which is not to be diluted, with Bengel, Paulus, Schott,
Olshausen, Baumgarten-Crusius, Cremer, following the Greek
Fathers, so as to mean a mere *obscuration*) to the earth—
which, in accordance with the cosmical views of the time, is
the plain and natural sense of εἰς τὴν γῆν (see Rev. vi. 13)—
is, no doubt, impossible as an actual fact, but it need not surprise us to see such an idea introduced into a prophetic picture
so grandly poetical as this is,—a picture which it is scarcely
fair to measure by the astronomical conceptions of our own
day. — αἱ δυνάμεις τῶν οὐρανῶν σαλευθ.] is usually
explained of the *starry hosts* (Isa. xxxiv. 4, xl. 26; Ps.
xxxiii. 6 ; Deut. iv. 19 ; 2 Kings xvii. 16, etc.), which,
coming as it does after οἱ ἀστέρες πεσοῦνται, would introduce a tautological feature into the picture.   The words
should therefore be taken in a *general* sense: *the powers of the
heavens* (the powers which uphold the heavens, which stretch
them out, and produce the phenomena which take place in
them, etc.) *will be so shaken* as to lose their usual stability.

Comp. Job xxvi. 11. The interpretation of Olshausen, who follows Jerome, Chrysostom, Euthymius Zigabenus, in supposing that the trembling *in the world of angels* is referred to (Luke ii. 13), is inconsistent not merely with σαλευθήσ., but also with the whole connection which refers to the domain of *physical* things. For the *plural* τῶν οὐρανῶν, comp. Ecclus. xvi. 16. — This convulsion in the *heavens*, previous to the Messiah's descent *therefrom*, is not as yet to be regarded as the *end of the world*, but only as a prelude to it; *the earth* is not destroyed as yet by the celestial commotion referred to (ver. 30). The poetical character of the *picture* does not justify us in regarding the *thing* so vividly depicted as also belonging merely to the domain of poetry, —all the less that, in the present case, it is not political revolutions (Isa. xiii. 10, xxxiv. 4; Ezek. xxxii. 7 f.; Joel iii. 3 f.) that are in view, but the new birth of the world, and the establishment of the Messiah's kingdom.

Ver. 30. **Καὶ τότε**] *and then*, when what is intimated at ver. 29 shall have arrived. — φανήσεται] universally, and so not visible merely to the elect (Cremer), which would not be in keeping with what follows. — τὸ σημεῖον τοῦ υἱοῦ τ. ἀνθρ.] accordingly the sign inquired about in ver. 3, that phenomenon, namely, which is immediately to precede the coming Messiah, the Son of man of Dan. vii. 13, and which is to indicate that His second advent is now on the point of taking place, which is to be the *signal* of this latter event. As Jesus does not say *what* this is to be, it should be left quite indefinite; only this much may be inferred from what is predicted at ver. 29 about the *darkening* of the heavenly bodies, that it must be of the nature of a *manifestation of light*, the dawning of the Messianic δόξα which is perhaps to go on increasing in brilliancy and splendour until the Messiah Himself steps forth from the midst of it in the fulness of His glory. There is no foundation for supposing, with Cyril, Hilary, Chrysostom, Augustine, Jerome, Erasmus, that the allusion is to a *cross* appearing in the heavens; with Hebart, that it is to the rending of heaven or the appearing of angels; with Fleck and Olshausen, that it is to the *star* of the Messiah (Num. xxiv. 17);

similarly Bleek, though rather more by way of conjecture. Following the older expositors, Fritzsche, Ewald, Hengstenberg, R. Hofmann understand the coming *Messiah Himself:* "miraculum, quod Jesus revertens Messias oculis objiciet" (accordingly, taking τοῦ υἱοῦ τ. ἀνθρ. as a genitive of *subject;* while Wolf, Storr, Weiss, *Bibl. Theol.* p. 56, ed. 2, assume it to be a genitive of *apposition*). This view is inconsistent not only with what follows, where the words καὶ ὄψονται τὸν υἱὸν, κ.τ.λ. evidently point to something still farther in the future, and which the σημεῖον serves to introduce, but also with the question of the disciples, ver. 3. R. Hofmann thinks that the reference is to that apparition in the form of a man which is alleged to have stood over the holy of holies for a whole night while the destruction of the capital was going on. A legendary story (chronicled by Ben-Gorion); and it may be added that what is said, vv. 29–31, certainly does not refer to the destruction of Jerusalem, *after* which event Hofmann supposes our evangelist to have written. Lastly, some (Schott, Kuinoel) are even of opinion that σημεῖον does not point to any new and special circumstance at all—to anything beyond *what is contained* in ver. 29 ; but the introduction of the *sequel* by τότε is decidedly against this view. — καὶ τότε] a new point brought forward : *and then,* when this σημεῖον has been displayed. — κόψονται] Comp. Zech. xii. 10 ; Rev. i. 7 ; with what a totally different order of things are they now on the point of being confronted, what a breaking up and subversion of all the previous relationships of life, what a separation of elements hitherto mingled together, and what a deciding of the final destinies of men at the judgment of the old and the ushering in of the new αἰών! *Hence,* being seized with terror and anguish, they will *mourn* (see on xi. 17). The *sorrow of repentance* (Dorner, Ewald) is not to be regarded as excluded from this mourning. There is no adequate reason to suppose, with Ewald, that, in the collection of our Lord's sayings (the λογία), ὄψονται probably occurred twice here, and that it was reserved for the last redactor of those sayings to make a play upon the word by substituting κόψονται. — ἐρχόμενον, κ.τ.λ.] as in Dan. vii. 13. — μετὰ δυνάμ. κ. δόξ.

πολλ.] This *great power and majesty* will also be displayed in the accompanying angel-hosts, ver. 31. The πᾶσαι αἱ φυλαὶ τῆς γῆς are not: *" omnes familiae Judaeorum "* (Kuinoel), as those who explain ver. 29 ff. of the destruction of Jerusalem must understand the words, but: *all the tribes of the earth.* Comp. Gen. xii. 3, xxviii. 14.

Ver. 31. Καὶ ἀποστελεῖ] *And He will send forth, i.e.* from the clouds of heaven, 1 Thess. iv. 16, 17. — τοὺς ἀγγέλους αὐτοῦ] the angels specially employed in His service. — μετὰ σάλπιγγος φωνῆς μεγάλ.] *with* (having as an accompaniment) *a trumpet of a loud sound.* The second genitive qualifies and is governed by the first ; see Buttmann, *Neut. Gr.* p. 295 [E. T. 343]. The idea is not that the individual angels blow trumpets, but what is meant (Isa. xxvii. 13) is the last trumpet (1 Cor. xv. 52), the trumpet of God (1 Thess. iv. 16), which is sounded while the Messiah is sending forth the angels. The resurrection of believers is also to be understood as taking place on the sound of this trumpet being heard (1 Cor. as above ; 1 Thess. as above). — ἐπισυνάξουσι] *gather together* (xxiii. 27 ; 2 Thess. ii. 1 ; 2 Macc. i. 27, ii. 18), namely, *toward* the place where He is in the act of appearing upon earth. This gathering together of the elect, which is to be a gathering from every *quarter* (comp. Rev. i. 7), and from the whole *compass* of the earth, is an *act* and *accompaniment* of the second advent (in answer to Cremer's distinction, see Hoelemann, p. 171). But the ἁρπάζεσθαι εἰς ἀέρα, to meet the Lord as He approaches (1 Thess. iv. 17), is to be regarded as taking place *after* this gathering together has been effected. — τοὺς ἐκλεκτ. αὐτοῦ] *the elect belonging to Him* (chosen by God for the Messianic kingdom, as in ver. 22). Comp. Rom. i. 6. — ἀπὸ ἄκρων οὐραν.] *ab extremitatibus coelorum usque ad extremitates eorum, i.e.* from one horizon to the other (for οὐρανῶν without the article, see Winer, p. 115 [E. T. 150]), therefore from the *whole earth* (ver. 14), on which the extremities of the sky seem to rest. Deut. iv. 32, xxx. 4 ; Ps. xix. 7.—As showing the exegetical abuses to which this grand passage has been subjected, take the following, Lightfoot : " emittet filius homines ministros suos cum tuba evan-

gelica," etc.; Kuinoel (comp. Wetstein) : " in tanta calamitate
Judaeis, adversariis religionis Christianae, infligenda, ubivis
locorum Christi sectatores per dei providentiam illaesi serva-
buntur," etc.; Olshausen : he will send out men armed with
the awakening power of the Spirit of God, for the purpose of
assembling believers at a place of safety.   This is substantially
the view of Tholuck also.—It may be observed, moreover, that
this passage forbids the view of Köstlin, p. 26, that our Gospel
does not contain a specifically *Christian*, but merely an *ethical*
universalism (as contrasted with Jewish obduracy).   See, on
the other hand, especially viii. 11, xxii. 9 f., xxv. 31 ff.,
xxviii. 19, etc.

Ver. 32 f. Cheering prospect for the disciples in the midst
of those final convulsions—a prospect depicted by means of
a pleasing scene taken from nature.   The understanding of
this passage depends on the correct interpretation (1) of τὸ
θέρος, (2) of πάντα ταῦτα, and also (3) on our taking care not
to supply anything we choose as the subject of ἐγγύς ἐστιν
ἐπὶ θύραις. — δέ is simply μεταβατικόν. — ἀπὸ τῆς συκῆς]
the article is *generic;* for ἀπό, comp. on xi. 29.   *From the
fig-tree, i.e.* in the case of the fig-tree, see the parable (τὴν
παρ.) that is intended for your instruction in the circumstances
referred to.   For the *article* conveys the idea of *your* similitude ; here, however, παραβολή means simply a *comparison,*
παράδειγμα.   Comp. on xiii. 3. — καὶ τὰ φύλλα ἐκφύῃ]
and puts forth the leaves (the subject being ὁ κλάδος).
Matthaei, Fritzsche, Lachmann, Bleek, on the authority of E F.
G H K M V Δ, Vulg. It., write ἐκφυῇ, taking it as an
aorist, *i.e. et folia edita fuerint* (see, in general, Kühner, I.
p. 930 f.).   But in that case what would be the meaning of
the allusion to the branches recovering their sap ?   Further,
it is only by taking κ. τ. φ. ἐκφύῃ as *present* that the *strictly
definite* element is brought out, namely : when the κλάδος *is
in the act of budding.* — τὸ θέρος] is usually taken in the
sense of *aestas,* after the Vulgate.   But, according to the correct interpretation of πάντα ταῦτα, summer would be *too late*
in the present instance, and too indefinite ; nor would it be
sufficiently near to accord with ἐγγύς ἐστιν ἐπὶ θύραις.   Hence

it is better to understand the *harvest* (equivalent to θερισμός, Photius, p. 86, 18) as referred to, as in Prov. xxvi. 1 ; Dem. 1253. 15, and frequently in classical writers ; Jacobs, *ad Anthol.* VIII. p. 357. Comp. also Ebrard, Keim.   It is not, however, the *fig-harvest* (which does not occur till August) that is meant, but the *fruit*-harvest, the formal commencement of which took place as early as the second day of the Passover season. — οὕτω κ. ὑμεῖς] so understand *ye also.* For the preceding *indicative*, γινώσκετε, expressed what was matter of *common* observation, and so, in a way corresponding to the observation referred to, should (γινώσκ. imperative) *the disciples also* on their part understand, etc. — ὅταν ἴδητε πάντα ταῦτα] *when ye will have seen all this.*   It is usual to seek for the reference of πάντα ταῦτα in the part of the passage *before* ver. 29, namely, in what Jesus has just foretold as to all the things that were to *precede* the second coming.   But arbitrary as this is, it is outdone by those who go the length of merely picking out a few from the phenomena in question, in order to restrict the reference of πάντα ταῦτα to them ; as, for example, the *incrementa malignitatis* (Ebrard), or the *cooling of love* among believers, *the preaching to the Gentiles,* and the *overthrow of Jerusalem* (Gess). If we are to take the words in their plain and obvious meaning (ver. 8), πάντα ταῦτα can only be understood to refer to what *immediately precedes,* therefore to what has been predicted, from that epoch-making *ver.* 29 *on to ver.* 31, respecting the σημεῖον *of the Son of man, and the phenomena that were to accompany the second coming itself.*   When they shall have seen all that has been announced, vv. 29–31, they are to understand from it, etc. — ὅτι ἐγγύς ἐστιν ἐπὶ θύραις] To *supply* a subject here is purely arbitrary ; the *Son of man* has been supposed by some to be understood (Fritzsche, de Wette, Hofmann, Bleek, Weiss, Gess) ; whereas the subject is τὸ θέρος, which, there being no reason to the contrary, may also be extended to ver. 33.   This θέρος is neither the *second coming* (Cremer), nor the *judgment* (Ebrard), nor the *kingdom of God* generally (Olshausen, Auberlen), nor even the *diffusion of Christianity* (Schott), but simply the *harvest,* understanding it, however, in the *higher Messianic* sense symbolized by the natural harvest (Gal. vi. 9 ; 2 Cor. ix. 6), namely, the reception in *the Messianic kingdom of that eternal reward* which awaits all true workers and patient sufferers. That is the joyful (Isa. ix. 2) and blessed *consummation* which the Lord encourages His disciples to expect immediately after the phenomena and convulsions that are to accompany His second advent. — On ἐπὶ θύραις without the article, see Bornemann, *ad Xen. Cyr.* i. 3. 2 ; and for the plural, see Kühner, II. 1, p. 17.

Ver. 34. Declaration to the effect that all this is to take place before the generation then living should pass away. The well-nigh absurd manner in which it has been attempted to force into the words ἡ γενεὰ αὕτη such meanings as : *the creation* (Maldonatus), or : *the human race* (Jerome), or : *the Jewish nation* (Jansen, Calovius, Wolf, Heumann, Storr, Dorner, Hebart, Auberlen ; see, on the other hand, on Mark xiii. 30), or : " the class of men consisting of *my believers* " (Origen, Chrysostom, Theophylact, Euthymius Zigabenus, Clarius, Paulus, Lange), resembles the unreasonable way in which Ebrard, following up his erroneous reference of πάντα ταῦτα (see on ver. 33), imports into the saying the idea : *inde ab ipsorum* (discipulorum) *aetate omnibus ecclesiae temporibus interfutura*, an imaginary view which passages like x. 23, xvi. 28, xxiii. 39, should have been sufficient to prevent. This also in opposition to the interpretation of Cremer : "*the generation of the elect* now in question," and that of Klostermann : " the (future) generation *which is to witness those events*," both of which are foreign to the sense. Comp. xxiii. 36. — The πάντα ταῦτα is the same as that of ver. 33, and therefore denoting neither the mere *prognostics* of the second advent, or, to be more definite, " *the taking away of the kingdom from Israel* " (Gess), nor specially the destruction of Jerusalem (Schott, E. J. Meyer, Hoelemann, Bäumlein in Klaiber's *Stud.* I. 3, p. 41 ff.). That the second advent itself is intended to be included, is likewise evident from ver. 36, in which the subject of the day and hour of the advent is introduced.

Ver. 35. With the preceding πάντα ταῦτα γένηται will

commence the passing away of the fabric of the world as it now exists (2 Pet. iii. 7, 8); but what I say (generally, though with special reference to the prophetic utterances before us) *will certainly not pass away, will abide as imperishable truth* (v. 18). The utterance which fails of its accomplishment is conceived of as something that *perishes* (Addit. Esth. vii. 2), that ceases to exist. Comp. ἐκπίπτειν, Rom. ix. 6.

Ver. 36. The affirmation of ver. 34, however, does not exclude the fact that no one knows the *day and hour* when the second advent, with its accompanying phenomena, is to take place. It is to occur during the *lifetime of the generation then existing*, but no one knows on what *day* or at what *hour* within the period thus indicated. Accordingly it is impossible to tell you anything more *precise* in regard to this than what is stated at ver. 34. — εἰ μὴ ὁ πατ. μου μόνος] This reservation on the part of the Father excludes even the incarnate *Son* (Mark xiii. 32). The limitation implied in our passage as regards the human side of our Lord's nature is to be viewed in the same light as that implied in xx. 23. See, besides, on Mark xiii. 32.

Vv. 37–39. But (δέ, introducing an analogous case from an early period in sacred history) as regards the ignorance as to the precise moment of its occurrence, it will be with the second coming as it was with the flood. — ἦσαν ... τρώγοντες] not for the imperfect, but to make the predicate more strongly prominent. Comp. on vii. 29. τρώγειν means simply *to eat* (John vi. 54–58, xiii. 18), not *devouring* like a beast (Beza, Grotius, Cremer), inasmuch as such an unfavourable construction is not warranted by any of the matters afterwards mentioned. — γαμοῦντες κ. ἐκγαμ.] *uxores in matrimonium ducentes et filias collocantes*, descriptive of a mode of life without concern, and without any foreboding of an impending catastrophe. — καὶ οὐκ ἔγνωσαν] The "it" (see Nägelsbach, *Iliad*, p. 120, ed. 3) to be understood after ἔγνωσαν is the flood that is so near at hand. Fritzsche's interpretation: "quod debebant intelligere" (namely, from seeing Noah build the ark), is arbitrary. The *time* within which it may be affirmed with certainty that the second advent will suddenly burst upon the world, cannot be supposed to refer to that which intervenes *between* the destruction of Jerusalem and the advent, a view precluded by the εὐθέως of ver. 29. That period of worldly unconcern comes in *just before* the final consummation, ver. 15 ff., whereupon the advent is immediately to follow (vv. 29–32). This last and most distressing time of all, coupled with the advent immediately following it, forms the *terminus ante quem*, and corresponds to the πρὸ τοῦ κατακλυσμοῦ of the Old Testament analogy. — ἐν ἡμέρᾳ ᾗ] without repeating the preposition before ᾗ (John iv. 54). Comp. Xen. *Anab.* v. 7. 17, and Kühner on the passage; Winer, p. 393 [E. T. 524 f.]; Stallbaum, *ad Plat. Apol.* p. 27 D. Comp. ver. 50.

Vv. 40, 41. Τότε] *then*, when the second advent will have thus suddenly taken place. — παραλαμβάνεται] *is taken away*, namely, by the angels who are gathering the elect together, ver. 31. The use of the *present* tense here pictures what is *future* as though it were already taking place. But had this referred to *the being caught up in the clouds*, mentioned 1 Thess. iv. 17 (Theophylact, Euthymius Zigabenus, Jansen), ἀναλαμβάνεται would have been used instead. — ἀφίεται] *is left*, expressing οὐ παραλαμβάνεται in its positive form. Comp. xxiii. 38, xv. 14; Soph. *O. R.* 599. It is tantamount to saying: *away! thou art not accepted.* To understand the terms as directly the opposite of each other in the following sense: the one is *taken captive*, the other *allowed to go free* (Wetstein, Kuinoel), is grammatically wrong (παραλαμβ. cannot, when standing alone, be taken as equivalent to *bello capere*, although it is used to denote the receiving of *places* into surrender, *in deditionem accipere*, Polyb. ii. 54. 12, iv. 63. 4, iv. 65. 6), and does violence to the context to suit the exigencies of the erroneous reference to the destruction of Jerusalem. Rather compare John xiv. 3. It is no doubt admissible to interpret the expression in the hostile sense: the one is *seized* (Polyb. iii. 69. 2; similarly Baumgarten-Crusius) or *carried off* (iv. 5, 8; Num. xxiii. 27; 1 Macc. iii. 37, iv. 1), namely, to be punished. But the ordinary explanation harmonizes better with the reference to ver.

31, as well as with the subsequent parable, ver. 45 ff., where the πιστὸς δοῦλος is *first* introduced.—δύο ἀλήθουσαι, κ.τ.λ.] *of two who grind at the mill, one will,* etc. For the construction, in which, by means of a μετάβασις ἀπὸ ὅλου εἰς μέρη, the plural-subject is broken up into two separate persons, comp. Hom. *Il.* vii. 306 f. : τὼ δὲ διακρινθέντε, ὁ μὲν μετὰ λαὸν Ἀχαιῶν ἤϊ, ὁ δ᾽ ἐς Τρώων ὅμαδον κίε. Plat. *Phaedr.* p. 248 A, *al.;* see Dissen, *ad Pind. Ol.* viii. 37 ; also *ad Dem. de cor.* p. 237 f. If we were to adopt the *usual* course of supplying ἔσονται from ver. 40, we would require to translate as follows : *two will be grinding at the mill.* But this supplying of ἔσονται is not at all necessary ; as may be gathered from the annexing of the participle, we have in this other case, ver. 41, just a *different* mode of presenting the matter. — ἀλήθουσαι] the hard work usually performed by the lower order of female slaves (Ex. xi. 5 ; Isa. xlvii. 2 ; Job xxxi. 10 ; Eccles. xii. 3), and such as is still performed in the East by *women,* either singly or by two working together (Rosenmüller, *Morgenl.* on Ex. xi. 5 ; and on the present passage, Robinson, *Paläst.* II. p. 405 f.). A similar practice prevailed in ancient Greece, Hermann, *Privatalterth.* § 24. 8. Hemsterhuis, *ad Lucian. Tim.* xxiii. On the unclassical ἀλήθειν (for ἀλεῖν), see Lobeck, *ad Phryn.* p. 151.— ἐν τῷ μύλῳ] which is not to be confounded (see the critical notes) with μύλωνι (a mill-house), is the *millstone* (xviii. 6) of the ordinary household hand-mill. It may denote the lower (Deut. xxiv. 6) as well as the upper stone (Isa. xlvii. 2), which latter would be more precisely designated by the term ἐπιμύλιον (Deut. as above). It is the upper that is intended in the present instance ; the women sit or kneel (Robinson as above), hold the handle of the upper millstone in their hands (hence ἐν τ. μ. : *with* the millstone), and turn it round upon the lower, which does not move.

Ver. 42. Moral inference from vv. 36–41. Comp. xxv. 13. —The following ὅτι κ.τ.λ. (*because ye,* etc.) is an emphatic epexegesis of οὖν. This exhortation is likewise based on the assumption that the second advent is to take place in the lifetime of the disciples, who are called upon to wait for it in an attitude of spiritual watchfulness (1 Cor. xvi. 13, 22). The idea of watchfulness, the opposite of security, coincides with that implied in the constant ἐτοιμασία τοῦ εὐαγγελίου (Eph. vi. 15). Comp. ver. 44. — ποίᾳ] *at what* (an early or a late). Comp. ver. 43 ; Rev. iii. 3 ; 1 Pet. i. 11 ; Eur. *Iph. A.* 815 ; Aesch. *Ag.* 278.

Ver. 43. *But* (that I may show you by means of a warning example how you may risk your salvation by allowing yourselves to be betrayed into a state of unpreparedness) *know this, that if,* etc. — ὁ οἰκοδεσπότης] the particular one whom the thief has anticipated. — εἰ ἤδει ... ἐγρηγόρησεν ἄν] *if he had been aware at what watch in the night the thief comes,* to break into his house, *he would have watched.* But as he does not know the hour which the thief chooses (it being different in different cases), he is found off his guard when the burglary is being committed. The rendering *vigilaret* (Luther, Kuinoel, Bleek, after the Vulg.) is incorrect. For the illustration of the thief, comp. 1 Thess. v. 2, 4 ; 2 Pet. iii. 10 ; Rev. iii. 3, xvi. 15.

Ver. 44. Διὰ τοῦτο] in order that, as regards your salvation, your case may not be similar to the householder in question, who ought to have watched, although he did not know the φυλακή of the thief. — καὶ ὑμεῖς] as the householder would have been had he watched. — ἕτοιμοι] spoken of their spiritual readiness for the second advent, which would take them by surprise (xxv. 10 ; Tit. iii. 1). This preparedness they were *to acquire for themselves* (γίνεσθε).

Ver. 45 f. Τίς ἄρα, κ.τ.λ.] *who therefore,* considering the necessity for preparedness thus indicated. The inference itself is presented in the form of an allegory, the δοῦλος representing the disciples whom the Lord has appointed to be the guides of His church, in which they are required to show themselves *faithful* (1 Cor. iv. 1 f.) and *prudent,* the *former* by a *disposition* habitually determining their whole behaviour and characterized by devotion to the will of the Lord, the *latter* by the *intelligent choice of ways and means, by taking proper advantage of circumstances,* etc. The τίς is not equivalent to εἰ τις (Castalio, Grotius), which it never can be ; but

ver. 45 asks: *who then is the faithful slave?* and ver. 46
contains the *answer;* the latter, however, being so framed that
instead of simply saying, in accordance with the terms of
the question, "*it is he,* whom his lord, on his return," etc.,
prominence is given to the *blessedness* of the servant here in
view. According to Bengel, Fritzsche, Fleck, de Wette, our
question touchingly conveys the idea of *seeking for : quis
tandem,* etc., " *hunc scire pervelim.*" To this, however, there is
the logical objection, that the relative clause of ver. 45 would
in that case have to be regarded as expressing the *characteristic feature* in the faithful and wise slave, whereas this
feature is first mentioned in the relative clause of ver. 46,
which clause therefore must contain the *answer* to the question, τίς ἄρα ἐστὶν ὁ πιστὸς δ. κ. φρ. — οἰκετεία, *domestic
servants,* Lucian, *Merc. cond.* 15 ; Strabo, xiv. p. 668. Comp.
οἰκετία, Symmachus, Job i. 3 ; Lobeck, *ad Phryn.* p. 505. —
οὕτως] *thus,* in accordance with duty assigned him in ver.
45 ; the principal emphasis being on this word, it is put at
the end of the sentence.

Ver. 47. He will assign him a far higher position, setting him not merely over his domestics, but, etc. The
συμβασιλεύειν in the Messiah's kingdom is represented as
being in accordance with that principle of gradation on which
faithfulness and prudence are usually rewarded in the case
of ordinary servants. Comp. xxv. 21 ff.; Luke xix. 17 ff.

Vv. 48-51. Ἐὰν δὲ, κ.τ.λ.] the emphasis is on ὁ κακός
as contrasting with ὁ πιστὸς κ. φρόνιμος, ver. 45, therefore
ὁ ἄπιστος κ. ἄφρων. — ἐκεῖνος] refers back to ὃν κατέστησεν,
κ.τ.λ., ver. 45, and represents the sum of its contents. Hence :
but suppose *the worthless servant who has been put in that
position* shall have said, etc. To assume that we have
here a blending of two cases (the servant is either faithful or wicked), the second of which we are to regard as
presupposed and pointed to by ἐκεῖνος (de Wette, Kaeuffer),
is to burden the passage with unnecessary confusion. —
ἄρξηται] *will have begun,* does not refer to the circumstance
that the lord surprises him in the midst of his misde-
meanours (Fritzsche), because in that case what follows would

also have to be regarded as depending on ἄρξηται, but on the contrary it brings out the *fearless wickedness* of the man abandoning himself to tyrannical behaviour and sensual gratifications. — ἐσθίῃ δὲ κ. π.] Before, we were told what his conduct was toward his fellow-slaves over whom he had been set; now, on the other hand, we are shown how he behaved himself apart from his relation to the οἰκετεία. — διχοτομήσει αὐτόν] *he will cut him in two* (Plat. *Polit.* p. 302 F ; Polyb. vi. 28. 2 ; x. 15. 5 ; Ex. xxix. 17), a form of punishment according to which the criminal was sawn asunder, 2 Sam. xii. 31 ; 1 Chron. xx. 3 ; Heb. xi. 37. Comp. Sueton. *Calig.* xvii.: " medios serra dissecuit." Herod. vii. 37. See, in general, Wetstein and Rosenmüller, *Morgenl.,* on our passage. There is no force in the usual objection that, in what follows, the slave is assumed to be still living; for, in the words καὶ τὸ μέρος αὐτοῦ, κ.τ.λ., which are immediately added, we have a statement of the *thing* itself, which the similitude of that terrible punishment was intended to *illustrate.* All other explanations are inconsistent with the text, such as: *he will tear him with the scourge* (Heumann, Paulus, Kuinoel, Schott, de Wette, Olshausen), or : *he will cut him off from his service* (Beza, Grotius, Jansen, Maldonatus ; comp. Jerome, Euthymius Zigabenus), or : he will *withdraw his spiritual gifts from him* (Basil, Theophylact), or generally : *he will punish him with the utmost severity* (Chrysostom). — καὶ τὸ μέρος αὐτοῦ, κ.τ.λ.] *and will assign him his proper place among the hypocrites, i.e.* he will condemn him to have his fitting portion in common with the hypocrites, that thenceforth he may share their fate. Comp. on John xiii. 8, and the classical phrase ἐν μέρει τινὸς τίθεσθαι. Rabbinical writers likewise regard Gehenna as the portion of hypocrites ; see Schoettgen. But the expression τῶν ὑποκριτ. is made use of here because the κακὸς δοῦλος *is* a hypocrite in the inmost depths of his moral nature, inasmuch as he acts under the impression χρονίζει μου ὁ κύριος, though he hopes that when his lord arrives he will be able to assume the appearance of one who is still faithfully discharging his duty, just as he must have pretended to be good at the time when he received the trust which had been committed to him; but now he is suddenly unmasked. — ἐκεῖ] namely, in hell, viii. 12, xiii. 42, 50, xxii. 13, xxv. 30.

REMARK 1.—It is exegetically certain that *from ver. 29 onward* Jesus announces His second advent, after having spoken, in what precedes that verse, of the destruction of Jerusalem, and of that, too, as an event that was to take place immediately before His second coming. All attempts to obtain, for the εὐθέως of ver. 29, a different *terminus a quo* (see on ver. 29), and therefore to find room enough before this εὐθέως for an interval, the limits of which cannot as yet be assigned, or to fix upon some different point in the discourse as that at which the subject of the second advent is introduced (Chrysostom: ver. 23; E. J. Meyer: ver. 35; Süsskind: ver. 36; Kuinoel: ver. 43; Lightfoot, Wetstein, Flatt: not till xxv. 31; Hoelemann: as early as xxiv. 19), are not the fruits of an objective interpretation of the text, but are based on the assumption that every trifling detail must find its fulfilment, and lead to interpretations in which the meaning is explained away and twisted in the most violent way possible. The attempts of Ebrard, Dorner, Cremer, Hoelemann, Gess, to show that the prediction of Jesus is in absolute harmony with the course of history, are refuted by the text itself, especially by ver. 29; above all is it impossible to explain vv. 15–28 of some event which is still in the womb of the future (in opposition to Hofmann, *Schriftbew.* II. p. 630 ff.); nor again, in ver. 34, can we narrow the scope of the πάντα ταῦτα, or extend that of the γενεὰ αὕτη, or make γίνηται denote merely the dawning of the events in question.

REMARK 2.—It is true that the predictions, ver. 5 ff., regarding the events that were to precede the destruction of Jerusalem were not fulfilled in so special and ample a way as to harmonize with the *synoptical representations of them;* still, that they were so in all essential respects, is proved by what we learn from history respecting the impostors and magicians that appeared, the wars that raged far and near, the numerous cases of famine and earthquake that occurred, the persecutions of the Christians that took place, the moral degeneracy that prevailed, and the way in which the gospel had been proclaimed throughout the world, and all shortly before the destruction of Jerusalem (after the Jews had begun to rise in rebellion against the Roman authority in the time of Gessius Florus, who became procurator of Judea in 64). This prophecy, though in every respect a genuine prediction, is not without its imaginative element, as may be seen from the poetical and pictorial form in which it is embodied. Compare on ver. 7, Remark. But it is just this mode of representation which shows that a *vaticinium post eventum* (see on ver. 1) is not to be thought of. Comp. Holtzmann, Weizsäcker, Pfleiderer.

REMARK 3. — With regard to the difficulty arising out of the fact that the second advent did not take place, as Jesus had predicted it would, immediately after the destruction of Jerusalem,—and as an explanation of which the assumption of a blending of type and antitype (Luther) is arbitrary in itself, and only leads to confusion,—let the following be remarked : (1) Jesus has spoken of His advent *in a threefold* sense ; for He described as His second coming (*a*) that outpouring of the Holy Spirit which was shortly to take place, and which was actually fulfilled ; see on John xiv. 18 f., xvi. 16, 20 ff., also on Eph. ii. 17 ; (*b*) that historical manifestation of His majesty and power which would be seen, immediately after His ascension to the Father, in the triumph of His cause upon the earth, of which Matt. xxvi. 64 furnishes an undoubted example; (*c*) His coming, in the strict eschatological sense, to raise the dead, to hold the last judgment, and to set up His kingdom, which is also distinctly intimated in such passages of John as vi. 40, 54, v. 28, xiv. 3 (Weizel in the *Stud. u. Krit.* 1836, p. 626 ff.), and in connection with which it is to be observed that in John the ἀναστήσω αὐτὸν ἐγὼ τῇ ἐσχάτῃ ἡμέρᾳ (vi. 39 f., 44, 54) does not imply any such nearness of the thing as is implied when the spiritual advent is in question ; but, on the contrary, presupposes generally that believers will have to undergo death. Again, in the parable contained in Matt. xxii. 1–14, the calling of the Gentiles is represented as coming after the destruction of Jerusalem; so that (comp. on xxi. 40 f.) in any case a longer interval is supposed to intervene between this latter event and the second coming than would seem to correspond with the εὐθέως of xxiv. 29. (2) But though Jesus Himself predicted His second coming as an event close at hand, without understanding it, however, in the literal sense of the words (see above, under *a* and *b*) ; though, in doing so, He availed Himself to some extent of such prophetical phraseology as had come to be the stereotyped language for describing the future establishment of the literal kingdom of the Messiah (xxvi. 64), and in this way made use of the notions connected with this literal kingdom for the purpose of embodying his conceptions of the ideal advent, —it is nevertheless highly conceivable that, in the minds of the disciples, the sign of Christ's *speedy* entrance into the world again came to be associated and ultimately identified with the expectation of a literal kingdom. This is all the more conceivable when we consider how difficult it was for them to realize anything so ideal as an invisible return, and how natural it was for them to apprehend *literally* the figurative language in which Jesus predicted *this return*, and how apt they were, in consequence, to take everything He said about His second coming, in the threefold sense above mentioned, as having reference to the one great object of eager expectation, viz. the glorious establishment of the Messiah's kingdom. The separating and sifting of the heterogeneous elements that were thus blended together in their imagination, Jesus appears to have left to the influence of future development, instead of undertaking this task Himself, by directly confuting and correcting the errors to which this confusion gave rise (Acts i. 7, 8), although we must not overlook the fact that any utterances of Jesus in this direction would be apt to be lost sight of—all the more, that they would not be likely to prove generally acceptable. It may likewise be observed, as bearing upon this matter, that the spiritual character of the Gospel of John—in which the idea of the advent, though not altogether absent, occupies a very secondary place as compared with the decided prominence given to that of the coming again in a spiritual sense—is a phenomenon which presupposes further teaching on the part of Jesus, differing materially from that recorded in the synoptic traditions. (3) After the idea of imminence had once got associated in the minds of the disciples with the expectation of the second advent and the establishment of the literal kingdom, the next step, now that the resurrection of Jesus had taken place, was to connect the hope of fulfilment with the promised baptism with the spirit which was understood to be near at hand (Acts i. 6); and they further expected that the fulfilment would take place, and that they would be witnesses of it before they left Judea,—an idea which is most distinctly reflected in Matt. x. 23. *Ex eventu* the horizon of this hope came to be gradually enlarged, without its extending, however, beyond *the lifetime of the existing generation.* It was during this interval that, according to Jesus, the destruction of Jerusalem was to take place. But if He at the same time saw, and in prophetic symbolism announced, what He could not fail to be aware of, viz. the connection that there would be between this catastrophe and the triumph of His ideal kingdom, then nothing was more natural than to expect that, with Jerusalem still standing (differently in Luke xxi. 24), and the duration of the existing generation drawing to a close, the second advent would take place *immediately after* the destruction of the capital,—an expectation which would be strengthened by the well-known descriptions furnished by the prophets of the triumphal entry of Jehovah and the disasters that were to precede it (Strauss, II. p. 348), as well as by that form of the doctrine of the *dolores Messiac* to which the Rabbis had given currency (Langen, *Judenth. in Paläst.* p. 494 f.). The form of the *expectation* involuntarily modified the form of the *promise ;* the *ideal* advent and establishment of the kingdom came to be identified with the *eschatological*, so that in men's minds and in the traditions alike the former gradually disappeared, while the latter alone remained as the object of earnest longing and expectation, surrounded not merely with the gorgeous colouring of prophetic delineation, but also placed in the same relation to the destruction of Jerusalem as that in which the *ideal* advent, announced in the language of prophetic imagery, had originally stood. Comp. Scherer in the *Strassb. Beitr.* II. 1851, p. 83 ff. ; Holtzmann, p. 409 f. ; Keim, III. p. 219 f.—Certain expositors have referred, in this connection, to the sentiment of the modern poet, who says : "*the world's history is the world's judgment*," and have represented the destruction of Jerusalem as the first act in this judgment, which is supposed to be immediately followed (ver. 29) by a renovation of the world through the medium of Christianity,—a renovation which is to go on until the last revelation from heaven takes place (Kern, Dorner, Olshausen). But this is only to commit the absurdity of importing into the passage a *poetical* judgment, such as is quite foreign to the *real* judgment of the New Testament. No less objectionable is Bengel's idea, revived by Hengstenberg and Olshausen (comp. also Kern, p. 56 ; Lange, II. p. 1258 ; Schmid, *Bibl. Theol.* I. p. 354), about the *perspective* nature of the prophetic vision,— an idea which could only have been vindicated from the reproach of imputing a *false* vision, *i.e.* an optical *delusion*, to Jesus if the latter had *failed* to specify a definite time by means of a statement so very precise as that contained in the εὐθέως of ver. 29, or had not added the solemn declaration of ver. 34. Dorner, Wittichen, rightly decide against this view. As a last shift, Olshausen has recourse to the idea that some condition or other is to be understood : "All those things will happen, *unless men avert the anger of God by sincere repentance*,"—a reservation which, in a prediction of so extremely definite a character, would most certainly have been expressly mentioned, even although no doubt can be said to exist as to the conditional nature of the Old Testament prophecies (Bertheau in the *Jahrb. f. D. Theol.* 1859, p. 335 ff.). If, as Olshausen thinks, it was the wish of the Lord that His second advent should always be looked upon as a possible, nay, as a probable thing, —and if it was *for this reason* that He spoke as Matthew represents Him to have done, then it would follow that He made use of false means for the purpose of attaining a moral end, —a thing even more inconceivable in His case than theoretical error, which latter Strauss does not hesitate to impute. According to this view, to which Wittichen also adheres, it is to the *ethical* side of the ministry of Jesus that the chief importance is to be attached. But it is precisely this ethical side that, in the case of Him who was the very depository of the intuitive truth of God, would necessarily be compromised by such an error as is here in view,—an error affecting a prediction so intimately connected with His whole work, and of so much importance in its moral consequences. Comp. John viii. 46.

REMARK 4.—The statement of ver. 29, to the effect that the second advent would take place immediately after the destruction of Jerusalem, and that of ver. 34, to the effect that it would occur during the lifetime of the generation then living, go to decide the date of the composition of our Greek Matthew, which must accordingly have been written at some time *previous* to the destruction of the capital. Baur, indeed (*Evangelien*, p. 605 ; *Neut. Theol.* p. 109), supposes the judgment that was immediately to precede the second advent to be represented by the Jewish war in the time of Hadrian, and detects the date of the composition of our Gospel (namely, 130–134) in the βδελ. τῆς ἐρημώσ. of ver. 15, which he explains of the statue of Jupiter which Hadrian had erected in the temple area (Dio Cass. lxix. 12). Such a view should have been felt to be already precluded by vv. 1–3, where, even according to Baur himself, it is only the first devastation under Titus that *can* be meant, as well as by the parallel passages of the other Synoptists; to say nothing, moreover, of the fact that a literal *destruction* of Jerusalem in the time of Hadrian, which is mentioned for the first time by Jerome in his comment on Ezek. v. 1, is, according to the older testimony of Justin, *Ap.* i. 47, and of Eusebius, iv. 6, highly questionable (Holtzmann, p. 405). But as regards the γενεά, in whose lifetime the destruction of the capital and the second advent were (ver. 34) to take place, Zeller (in the *Theol. Jahrb.* 1852, p. 299 f.), following Baur and Hilgenfeld, *üb. d. Ev. Justin's*, p. 367, has sought to make the duration of the period

in question extend over a *century* and more, therefore to somewhere about the year 130 and even later, although the common
notion of a γενεά was such that a century was understood to be
equal to something like three of them (Herod. ii. 142 ; Thuc.
i. 14. 1; Wesseling, *ad Diod.* i. 24). The above, however,
is an erroneous view, which its authors have been constrained
to adopt simply to meet the exigencies of the case. For, with
such passages before them as x. 23, xvi. 28, neither their critical
nor their dogmatical preconceptions should have allowed them
to doubt that anything else was meant than the ordinary lifetime of the existing generation, the generation living at the
time the discourse was being delivered (the γενεά ἡ κατὰ τὸν
παρόντα χρόνον, Dem. 1390, 25), and that, too, only the portion
of their lifetime that was still to run. Comp. Kahnis, *Dogm.*
I. p. 494; Holtzmann, p. 408; Keim, p. 206; also Köstlin, p:
114 ff.

CHAPTER XXV.

VER. 1.[1] ἀπάντησιν] Lachm. and Tisch. 8 : ὑπάντησιν, following B C
א, 1, Method. Had this been the original reading, it would also
have forced its way into ver. 6, in which latter, however, it is
found only in 157, Cyr. — Ver. 2. Lachm. and Tisch. 8 : πέντε
δὲ ἐξ αὐτῶν ἦσαν μωραὶ καὶ πέντε φρόνιμοι, following B C D L Z א, min.
and vss. (also Vulg. It.). Considering what a preponderance of
evidence is here, and seeing how ready the transcribers would
be to place the wise first in order, the reading of the Received
text must be regarded as a subsequent transposition. — Ver. 3.
For αἵτινες there are found the readings (glosses): αἱ δὲ in Z,
Vulg. codd. of the It. Lachm., and αἱ γάρ in B C L א, Tisch. 8 ;
likewise αἱ οὖν in D. — Ver. 4. In witnesses of importance αὐτῶν
is wanting after ἀγγείοις, so that, with Lachm. and Tisch. 8, it
is to be deleted as a common interpolation. — Ver. 6. ἔρχεται]
is wanting in such important witnesses (B C* D L Z א, 102,
Copt. Sahid. Ar[po]. Cant. Method. Ephr. Cyr.), and has so much
the look of a supplement, that, with Lachm. and Tisch. 8, it
should be erased. But the αὐτοῦ after ἀπάντ., which Tisch. 8
deletes, is wanting only in B א, 102, Meth. Cyr. — Ver. 7. For
αὐτῶν it is better, with Lachm. and Tisch., to read ἑαυτῶν, following
A B L Z א. The reflective force of the pronoun had never been
noticed, especially with ver. 4 preceding it, in which verse ἑαυτῶν
instead of αὐτῶν after λαμπ. (so Tisch. 8) is supported only by the
evidence of B א. — Ver. 9. For οὐκ, as in the Received text,
there is a preponderance of evidence in favour of reading οὐ μή,
which Griesb. has recommended, and which Lachm., Tisch. 7,
and also Scholz have adopted. The μή, which Fritzsche and
Tisch. 8 have discarded, was omitted from its force not being
understood. — δέ after πορεύεσθε (in Elz., Tisch. 7) would be just
as apt to be inserted as a connective particle, as it would
be ready to be omitted if πορεύεσθε, κ.τ.λ. was taken as the
apodosis. Accordingly, the matter must be decided by a

---

[1] The *Codex Alex.* (A) joins the list of critical authorities for the first time at
ch. xxv. It begins at ver. 6 with the word ἐξέρχισθι.

preponderance of evidence, and that is in favour of deleting
the δέ. — Ver. 11. καὶ αἱ] Lachm. has simply αἱ, but against
decisive evidence; and then think how readily καί might
be dropped out between ΤΑΙ and ΑΙ! — Ver. 13. After ὥραν
Elz. inserts ἐν ᾗ ὁ υἱὸς τοῦ ἀνθρώπου ἔρχεται, words which, in
accordance with a decided preponderance of evidence, are to be
regarded as a gloss (xxiv. 44). — Ver. 16. ἐποίησεν] A** B C
D L א** min.: ἐκέρδησεν. Recommended by Griesb. and Schulz,
adopted by Lachm.   Gloss derived from what follows. — The
omission of the second τάλαντα by Lachm. is without adequate
authority, nor had the transcribers any motive for inserting it;
comp. ver. 17. — Ver. 17. καὶ αὐτός] is wanting in important
witnesses, and is erased by Lachm. and Tisch. 8; but, owing
to the circumstance of ὡσαύτως καί having preceded, it may very
readily have been left out as superfluous and clumsy. — Ver. 18.
Lachm. inserts τάλαντον after ἕν, only on the authority of A, It.;
but ἔκρυψεν (Lachm. Tisch.) for ἀπέκρυψεν is supported by such
a preponderance of evidence that it is unnecessary to regard
it as taken from ver. 25. — Ver. 19. It is better, with Lachm.
and Tisch., to adopt in both cases the order πολὺν χρόνον and
λόγον μετ' αὐτῶν, in accordance with preponderating evidence.—
Ver. 20. ἐπ' αὐτοῖς] is omitted by Lachm. and Tisch. 8, both
here and in ver. 22, following B D L א, min. and vss., while
E G, min. read ἐν αὐτοῖς; but D, Vulg. It. Or. insert ἐπεκέρδησα
before the ἐπ' αὐτοῖς.   Later variants are interpretations of
the superfluous (and therefore sometimes omitted) ἐπ' αὐτοῖς
— Ver. 21. δέ, which Elz. inserts after ἔφη, has been deleted,
in accordance with preponderating evidence, as being an interpolation of the connective particle (so also Griesb., Scholz,
Fritzsche, Lachm., Tisch.). — Ver. 22. λαβών] is wanting in
A B C L Δ א, min. Syr.ᵘᵗʳ·; a few min. have εἰληφώς.   Deleted
by Lachm. and Tisch.   Correctly; a supplement. — Ver. 27.
For τὸ ἀργύρ. μου Tisch. 8 reads τὰ ἀργύριά μου, following B
א*, Syr.ᵖ·   Correctly; the plural would be apt to be replaced
by the singular (comp. Luke), because it is a question of one
talent, and because of the τὸ ἐμόν following. — Ver. 29. ἀπὸ δὲ
τοῦ] B D L א, min.: τοῦ δέ.   Approved by Griesb., adopted by
Fritzsche, Lachm., Tisch.; the ordinary reading is by way of
helping the construction. — Ver. 30. ἐκβάλετε for ἐκβάλλετε (in
Elz.) is confirmed by decisive evidence. — Ver. 31. Elz. Scholz
insert ἅγιοι before ἄγγελοι, in opposition to B D L Π* א, min. and
many vss. and Fathers.   An adjective borrowed from the ordinary
ecclesiastical phraseology, and which, though it might readily
enough be inserted, would scarcely be likely to be omitted.

Comp. Zech. xiv. 5. — Ver. 40. τῶν ἀδελφῶν μου] wanting only in B* and Fathers. Bracketed by Lachm. But comp. ver. 45. — Ver. 41. οἱ κατηραμ.] Tisch. 8 has deleted the article, in accordance with B L א, and that correctly ; it is taken from ver. 34.

Ver. 1 f. An additional exhortation to watchfulness in consequence of the day and hour of the advent being un-known, and embodied *in the parable of the ten virgins*, extend-ing to ver. 13, which parable is peculiar to Matthew (having been taken from the collection of our Lord's sayings) ; for it is not the echoes of *the present* narrative, but something essen-tially different, that we meet with in Mark xiii. 35–37 and Luke xii. 35–38. — τότε] *then, i.e.* on the day on which the master will return, and inflict condign punishment upon his worthless slave. Not : *after* inflicting this punishment (Fritzsche), for the parable is intended to portray the *coming* of the Messiah ; but neither, again, is it to be taken as point-ing back to ver. 37 and ver. 14 of the previous chapter (Cremer), which would be an arbitrary interruption of the regular sequence of the discourse as indicated by τότε. — ὁμοιωθήσεται] *will be made like*, actually so ; see on vii. 26. — ἡ βασιλ. τῶν οὐραν.] *the Messianic kingdom*, in respect, that is, of the principle of admission and exclusion that will be followed when that kingdom comes to be set up. — ἐξῆλθον εἰς ἀπάντ. τοῦ νυμφ.] Here the marriage is not represented as taking place in the house of the bridegroom, in accordance with the usual practice (Winer, *Realw.* I. p. 499; Keil, *Arch.* § 109), but in that of the bride (Judg. xiv. 10), from which the ten bridesmaids set out in the evening for the purpose of meeting the expected bridegroom. The *reason* why the parable transfers the scene of the marriage to the *home of the bride*, is to be found in the nature of the *thing* to be illus-trated, inasmuch as, at the time of His advent, Christ is to be understood as coming to the earth and as setting up His kingdom here below, and not in heaven. Comp. also the fol-lowing parable, ver. 14 ff. — ἐξῆλθον] *they went out*, namely, from the bride's house, which is self-evident from the context (εἰς ἀπάντησιν τοῦ νυμφίου). Bornemann in the *Stud. u. Krit.*

1843, p. 112 f.,—who, like the majority of expositors, supposes that what is here in view is the ordinary practice of
conducting the bride from her own house to that of the bridegroom (but see on ver. 10),—and Ewald understand ἐξῆλθον
of the setting out of the maids *from their own homes* to go
to the house of the bride, in order to start from the latter
for the purpose of meeting the bridegroom as he comes to
fetch home his bride.   But the meaning of the terms forbids
us to assume different starting - points for ἐξῆλθον and εἰς
ἀπάντησιν (Acts xxviii. 15); this is further precluded by
the supposition, in itself improbable, that the foolish virgins
could not have obtained a fresh supply of oil at the house
of the bride.—Whether *ten* was the *usual* number for bridesmaids cannot be determined; but generally " numero denario
(as the base of their numeral system) gavisa plurimum est
gens Judaica et in sacris et in civilibus," Lightfoot.   Comp.
Luke xix. 13.— φρόνιμοι] Comp. xxiv. 45, vii. 24, 26.
This second virtue belonging to a right ἑτοιμασία (see on
xxiv. 55), viz. *practical wisdom,* is here intended to be made
specially prominent.   The idea of a contrast between chastity
and its opposite (Cremer) is quite foreign to the context.
Comp. κοράσιον φρόνιμον, Tob. vi. 12.

Ver. 3. Αἵτινες μωραί] sc. ἦσαν, *quotquot erant stultae.* —
ἔλαβον] they *took,* on setting out; not for the pluperfect
(Erasmus, Vatablus). —μεθ᾽ ἑαυτῶν] with *themselves,* namely,
besides the oil that was burning in their *lamps.*

Vv. 5, 6. The virgins, who, ver. 1, have left the house of
the bride (in opposition to Cremer and Lange, who suppose
ἐξῆλθον to contain a prolepsis), and therefore are no longer
there, have betaken themselves to some house on the way
(ἐξέρχεσθε, observe), in order there to await the passing by of
the bridegroom.   The coming of the latter was delayed on till
midnight; the maids who sat waiting began to get wearied,
they *nodded* (aorist), and *slept* (imperfect).   Comp. Isa. v. 27;
Ps. xxi. 4.   Vulgate: " dormitaverunt omnes et dormierunt."
— ἰδοὺ ὁ νυμφίος (without ἔρχεται, see critical remarks):
behold the bridegroom !   The cry of the people who see him
coming a little way off.   They are made aware of his approach

from seeing the light of the torches or lamps carried by those who accompanied him in the procession.

Ver. 7 f. 'Εκόσμησαν] *they put in proper order*, namely, by trimming the wick and such like, they *dressed* them. — ἑαυτῶν (see critical remarks) : each one her own ; betokening the *individual* preparation that was now going on. — σβέννυνται] *are just on the point of going out*.

Ver. 9. Μήποτε . . . ὑμῖν] Since οὐ μή is the correct reading (see critical remarks), and seeing that the ἀρκέσῃ following cannot be regarded as dependent on μήποτε, but only on οὐ μή, the punctuation should be as follows : μήποτε· οὐ μὴ ἀρκέσῃ, κ.τ.λ. : *never* (shall we give you of our oil) : *there will certainly not be enough for us and you!* For the absolute negative μή, comp. xxvi. 5 ; Ex. x. 11 ; Matthiae, p. 1454 ; Kühner, II. 2, p. 1047. Correctly Bornemann, as above, p. 110 ; Bleek, Lange, Luthardt. Comp. Winer, p. 556 [E. T. 632]; Ellendt, *Lex. Soph.* II. p. 107.

Ver. 10 f. *While they were going away, came* (not: *advenerat*, Fritzsche). — εἰσῆλθον μετ' αὐτοῦ] namely, into the house of the bride, whither the bridegroom was on his way, and to which the maids were conducting him, with a view to the celebration of the marriage. The idea of the *bridegroom's house* being that referred to (see on ver. 1) is precluded by the correlation in which ἦλθεν ὁ νυμφίος and εἰσῆλθον μετ' αὐτοῦ stand to each other. — κύριε, κύριε] expressive of most urgent and anxious entreaty. Comp. vii. 21.

Ver. 12 f. Οὐκ οἶδα ὑμᾶς] because ye were not amongst the bridesmaids who welcomed me, ye are to me as entire strangers whom I do not know, and who, therefore, can have no part in the marriage! The knowledge of experience arising out of the intercourse of life (vii. 23 ; 1 Cor. viii. 3, xiii. 12 ; Gal. iv. 9) is the point intended to be thus *illustrated*. Besides, Jesus might also have said (in opposition to Cremer): οὐκ ἔγνων ὑμ. (I have not known you). — οὖν] because the foolish virgins were shut out, and because something corresponding to this would happen to you unless you watch.— According to ver. 13, *the teaching of the parable is: that the moral preparedness that continues to maintain itself up till the moment of the advent, the day and hour of which do not admit of being determined, will lead to participation in the Messianic kingdom, whereas those in whom this preparedness has not been maintained till the end will, when surprised by the sudden appearing of the Lord, experience in themselves the irreparable consequences of their foolish neglect, and be shut out from His kingdom.* This latter is a negative expression of *condemnation*, not, as Olshausen supposes notwithstanding the ἐκλείσθη ἡ θύρα, merely a way of designating such a salvation as is spoken of in 1 Cor. iii. 15. More specific interpretations—of the virgins, the lamps, the oil, the κραυγή, etc.—are to be found not only in Origen, Hilary, Cyrill, Chrysostom, Theophylact, Euthymius Zigabenus, Augustine, Jerome (see Cremer, p. 156 ff.), but also in Olshausen, von Meyer, Cremer, Lange, Auberlen. In those interpretations subjective opinion has, in most diverse and arbitrary fashion, exceeded the limits indicated by Jesus in ver. 13. Calvin well remarks: "Multum se torquent quidam in lucernis, in vasis, in oleo. Atqui simplex et genuina summa est, non sufficere alacre exigui temporis studium, nisi infatigabilis constantia simul accedat." Neither is the *falling asleep* of the virgins intended to be specially significant; for, as it happened in the case of the exemplary wise ones as well, it cannot represent any moral shortcoming.

Ver. 14. *The parable of the talents*, extending to ver. 30,[1] is introduced as an additional ground for the γρηγορεῖτε, and that by viewing it as a question of work and responsibility. The parable in Luke xix. 12 ff., which, notwithstanding the differences in regard to individual features, resembles the present in its leading thoughts and illustrations, is to be regarded as a modification, arising in the course of the Gospel tradition, of the more original and simpler one before us (in opposition to Calvin, Olshausen, Neander, Holtzmann, Volkmar), and which Luke also represents as having been spoken

---

[1] In connection with this parable, compare the following traditional sayings attributed to Christ : γίνεσθε τραπεζῖται δόκιμοι (*Hom. Clem.* ii. 51, iii. 50, xviii. 20, etc. ; Clement of Alexandria, Origen ; *Apostolical Constitutions*) ; and ἐν οἷς ἂν ὑμᾶς καταλάβω, ἐν τούτοις καὶ κρινῶ (Justin, *c. Tr.* 47). Eusebius gives a kindred parable from the Gospel of the Hebrews, and for which see Mai's *Nova patrum biblioth.* IV. p. 155.

at a different time; comp. Weizsäcker, p. 181. In this latter Gospel we have what was originally an independent parable (that of the rebellious subjects) blended with that of the talents (Strauss, I. p. 636 f.; Ewald, p. 419 f.; Bleek, Keim, Weiss, 1864, p. 128 ff.). If it be maintained, as Kern, Lange, Cremer, are disposed to do, that in Matthew and Luke we have two distinct parables, spoken by Jesus on two different occasions, then there is no alternative but either to accept the *unnatural* view that the simpler (Matthew's) is the later form, or to suppose, *in opposition to what is recorded*, that Jesus spoke the parable in Matthew, where, however, the connection is perfectly apposite, somewhat earlier than that in Luke (Schleiermacher, Neander). The one view as well as the other would be all the more questionable, that the interval during which Christ "intentionally employs the same parabolic materials for the purpose of illustrating different subjects" (Auberlen) would thus comprise only a few days. Mark xiii. 34 is extracted from what Matthew has taken from the collection of our Lord's sayings. — ὥσπερ, κ.τ.λ.] a case of *anantapodosis* similar to that of Mark xiii. 34, and doubtless reproducing what already appeared in the collection of sayings from which the passage is taken. Comp. Rom. v. 12. Fritzsche on ver. 30. At the outset of the discourse it would be the intention to connect the whole parable with ὥσπερ, and, at the conclusion, to annex an apodosis by means of οὕτως (probably οὕτω καὶ ὁ υἱὸς τ. ἀνθρώπου ποιήσει, or οὕτως ἔσται καὶ ἡ παρουσία τ. υἱοῦ τ. ἀνθρ.); but, considering the somewhat lengthened character of the parable, this had to be omitted. — ἀποδημ.] on the point of going abroad (xxi. 33). — τοὺς ἰδίους δούλους] not strangers, such as exchangers, but *his own servants*, of whom, therefore, he had a right to expect that they would do their best to lay out for his advantage the money entrusted to them.

Ver. 15. Κατὰ τὴν ἰδίαν δύναμιν] not arbitrarily, therefore, but *according to each one's peculiar capabilities* (" prudentia et peritia," Beza) *for doing business.* The different *charismatic* gifts are bestowed in a manner corresponding to the varying *natural* aptitudes of men. Those endowments are conferred according to an *individualizing* principle. " Nemo urgetur ultra quam potest," Bengel. — εὐθέως] *immediately*, therefore without making any further arrangements for disposing of the money. Fritzsche, Rinck, and Tisch. 8 agree with B and several codd. of the It. in connecting εὐθέως with what follows. In that case it would be necessary either to insert the δέ of ver. 16 before πορευθ. (א**), or, with Tisch., to delete it altogether (א*). However, the evidence in favour of this view is quite inadequate. And it is precisely in connection with ἀπεδήμησεν that εὐθέως is seen to have a peculiar significance, that, namely, of showing that absolute independence was allowed in regard to the way in which the money was to be employed by those to whom it had been entrusted, which is admirably in keeping with κατὰ τὴν ἰδίαν δύναμιν. — τάλαντα] see on xviii. 25.

Ver. 16. Εἰργάσατο] *traded with them* (ἐν αὐτοῖς, instrumental). Very common in classical writers (especially Demosthenes) with reference to commerce and matters of exchange, though usually with the *simple* dative of the instrument. — ἐποίησεν] *he acquired, gained;* as in German : er *machte* Geld (he *made* money). See instances in Wetstein and Kypke. So also the Latin *facere.*

Ver. 18. Ἀπελθών] *he went away*, removed to a distance. How entirely different in the case of the two first, ver. 16 ! They started upon a *journey* (πορευθ.). — ὤρυξεν ἐν τ. γῇ] *he digged*, i.e. he made a hole *in the earth.* The reading γῆν, which Tisch. adopts, following B L א (C*: τὴν γῆν), but from which the vss. deviate, would mean: he *dug up the earth* (Plat. *Euthyd.* p. 288 E). — τὸ ἀργύρ. τοῦ κυρ. αὐτ.] brings out emphatically the idea of responsibility and dereliction of duty.

Ver. 20 f. Ἐπ᾿ αὐτοῖς] *in addition to them;* comp. on Col. iii. 14. The ἴδε points the master to what had been gained ; the boldness of a good conscience. — εὖ] is generally taken *absolutely: excellent ! that is right !* But this would have required εὖγε (Plat. *Gorg.* p. 494 C ; *Lach.* p. 181 A ; Soph. *Phil.* 327), which reading (taken from Luke xix. 17, where εὖγε is the original one) Fritzsche actually adopts, following A*, Vulg. It. Or. (once). Consequently we should connect εὖ with ἦς πιστός : *Thou wast admirably (probe) faithful in regard to a little.* For εὖ when separated from the word to which it belongs, comp. Xen. *Cyr.* i. 6. 24 ; *Mem.* ii. 1. 33, and Kühner thereon. Ἀγαθέ and πιστέ represent the *genus* and *species* of an upright character. The opposite of this : ver. 26. — εἰς τὴν χαρὰν τοῦ κυρίου σου] χαρά is not to be understood of a *feast* (Clericus, Schoettgen, Wolf, Michelsen, Kuinoel, Schott), a sense in which the word is not used (LXX. Esth. ix. 17 is an inaccurate rendering), and which the context does not sanction any more than it countenances the idea of a *festival* in honour of the master's return (in opposition to de Wette and Lange); but what is meant is that the slave is invited to *participate in the happiness which his master is enjoying* (Chrysostom admirably : τὴν πᾶσαν μακαριότητα διὰ τοῦ ῥήματος τούτου δεικνύς), thus exhibiting the thought of Rom. viii. 17. The use of the expression εἴσελθε is, in that case, to be regarded as due to the nature of the *thing* which the parable is meant to illustrate (the Messianic kingdom).

Ver. 24 f. Ἔγνων σε, ὅτι] well-known attraction. Winer, p. 581 [E. T. 781]. The *aorist* is not used here in the sense of the *perfect, I know thee* (Kuinoel), but : *I knew thee, and hid.*—What follows characterizes, in proverbial language (by a figure taken from farming), a man *unconscionably* hard to please, and demanding more than is reasonable. — συνάγων ὅθεν οὐ διεσκόρπ.] *gathering* (corn into the ἀποθήκη) *from a place where you have not threshed* (with reference to the threshing-floor of another man's farm). διασκορπίζειν, *to scatter so as to separate from each other* (for the classical character of which expression see Lobeck, *ad Phryn.* p. 213), is *expressly* used in the present instance, because it forms a better contrast to συνάγων than λικμᾶν (xxi. 44). If it were to be taken as equivalent to σπείρειν, the result would be a *tautological* parallelism (in opposition to Erasmus, Beza, de Wette).—The entire excuse is a false pretext invented by moral indolence, —a pretext which is reduced *ad absurdum* in vv. 26, 27. —

φοβηθείς] namely, of losing the talent in business, or of not being able to satisfy thee. — τὸ σόν] self-righteous.

Ver. 26 f. The master chastises the worthless and indolent (Rom. xii. 11) servant with his own weapons. — ᾔδεις, κ.τ.λ.] *question of astonishment*, which is more spirited and more in keeping with the surprising nature of the excuse than to understand the words in a *conceding* sense (Kuinoel, de Wette), or as an independent hypothesis (Bernhardy, p. 385), in which case the οὖν of the apodosis would be deprived of its force (see Hartung, *Partikell.* II. p. 22 f.; Klotz, *ad Devar.* p. 718 f.). — βαλεῖν . . . τοῖς τραπεζ.] *flinging down upon the table of the money-changers*, represents the *indifference* of the proceeding. — ἐγώ] is emphatic as related to the preceding ἴδε, ἔχεις τὸ σόν, ver. 25. To it likewise corresponds τὸ ἐμόν, to which, however, σὺν τόκῳ is now added for sake of emphasis.

Vv. 28–30. Οὖν] because his conduct was so inexcusable. —Ver. 29. Justification of this mode of proceeding, by appealing to a principle founded on universal experience, and which was to find its verification in the case before us. Comp. xiii. 12.— τοῦ δὲ μὴ ἔχοντος] see critical remarks. The genitive, here placed first for sake of emphasis, might be regarded as dependent on ἀρθήσεται (Fritzsche), in accordance, that is, with the construction of verbs of depriving with τινός τι (Kühner, II. 1, p. 282). Inasmuch, however, as the ἀπ' αὐτοῦ which follows would thus be superfluous and clumsy, it is better to take the genitive as *absolute: as for him who has not* (the poor man); comp. Thuc. v. 18. 8, and Krüger thereon. We thus obtain "duobus membris factis ex uno *oppositio nervosior*" (Dissen, *ad Dem. de cor.* p. 272). For ὁ ἔχων, *the rich man*, comp. Isocr. vii. 55 and Benseler thereon. — For ver. 30, comp. viii. 12, xiii. 42, 50, xxii. 13, xxiv. 51. The verse is not here out of place, but acquires a certain solemnity from its resemblance to the conclusion of ch. xxiv. (in opposition to Weiss, 1864, p. 129).

Teaching of the parable.—By a faithful use, after my departure, of those varied endowments which I have bestowed on each of you according to his special capacity, you are to do your utmost to promote my cause. For when I return and reckon with you (ver. 19), then those who have exerted themselves in a dutiful manner will receive a distinguished reward in the kingdom of the Messiah; but those who have allowed their gifts, however small, to lie unused, will be deprived of that which has been entrusted to them, and be cast into Gehenna. For more minute and specific interpretations, all of them of a more or less arbitrary character, see Origen, Chrysostom, Theophylact. The reference to all *Christian endowments generally* (1 Cor. xii.), is to be regarded rather as an *application* of the parable in a more comprehensive sense.

Ver. 31 ff. It is unnecessary to suppose that this utterance *about the judgment*—an utterance taken, like the preceding, from the collection of our Lord's sayings (λόγια)—should be immediately connected with xxiv. 30 f. (Fritzsche, de Wette) or with xxiv. 51 (Ewald). The coming of the Messiah and His judicial dealing with His servants had been portrayed immediately before, and now the prophetic glance extends and takes in *the judgment of all nations*,—a judgment which is to be presided over by the Lord when He returns in His glory. This is the grand closing scene in which the eschatological predictions are all to be realized, and depicted too with a simplicity and beauty so original that there is but the less reason for imagining that this discourse about the judgment is the product of the apostolic period (Hilgenfeld, Volkmar, Scholten, Wittichen, Keim). — It is *usual* to understand *those who are being judged* as representing *men generally*, Christians and non-Christians alike (see, among modern expositors, Kuinoel, Fritzsche, de Wette, Lange, Weizel, as above, p. 603; Kaeuffer, *de ζωῆς αἰων. not.* p. 44; Hofmann, *Schriftbew.* p. 645), Bleek arbitrarily assuming that the evangelists have *extended* the application of what originally referred only to Christians. On the other hand, Keil (in the *Opusc., ed. Goldh.* p. 136 ff., and *Anal.* 1813, III. 177 ff.) and Olshausen, as well as Baumgarten-Crusius, Georgii in Zeller's *Jahrb.* 1845, p. 18 f.; Hilgenfeld, Weizsäcker, Volkmar, Keim, Wittichen, Auberlen, Cremer, understand all *who are not Christians* to be referred to, some of them, however, expressly excluding the Jews. But *non-*

Christians could not have been intended, because it would be improper to say that the Messianic kingdom has been prepared for such, to say nothing of the ἀπὸ καταβολῆς κόσμου, ver. 34, in which the idea of the ἐκλεκτοί is exclusively involved; further, because it would be no less improper to suppose, without more ado, that non-Christians are intended by the οἱ δίκαιοι of ver. 37, which latter we are not at liberty to understand in a generalized sense, but only as equivalent to the elect; again, because those things which Jesus represents (vv. 35, 36, 60) as manifestations of love toward Himself cannot possibly be conceived of as done by those who, nevertheless, continued to remain outside the Christian community; finally, because both sides of the assemblage use such language (vv. 37 ff., 44) as compels us to acknowledge their belief in the Judge before whom they now stand. Their language is the expression of a consciousness of their faith in the Messiah, towards whom, however, they have had no opportunity of displaying their love. If *the Messianic felicity* were here adjudged to pure *heathens* according to the way in which they may have acted toward Christians (Hilgenfeld), this would be to suppose a " remarkable toleration " (Keim) altogether at variance with the whole tenor of the New Testament, and such as even Rev. xxi. 24 (see Düsterdieck on that passage) does not countenance,—a humanity which does not *need* faith, because it *compensates for the want of it* by its love (Volkmar, p. 546). If, after all this, we cannot suppose that a judgment of *non-Christians* is here meant, we may even go still further, and say that non-Christians are not *included* at all, and so we must also reject the view *usually adopted*, since Chrysostom and Augustine, that what is here exhibited is a judgment of all men, believers and unbelievers alike. For, so far from the mention of the divine ἐκλογή, ver. 34, or the idea of the δίκαιοι, ver. 37, or what Jesus says at ver. 35, or the answer of those assembled before the Judge, vv. 37 and 44, or the entire omission generally of any distinction between belief and unbelief, harmonizing with the notion of a mixed body consisting of Christians *and* non-Christians, they *entirely* exclude the latter. We should therefore return to the very old view (Lactantius, *Instit.* vii. 20; Jerome, Euthymius Zigabenus), which, though it had been neglected in consequence of the prevalent eschatology, was preserved by Grotius, the view, namely, that what Jesus is here depicting is *the judgment of Christians:* περὶ τῶν Χριστιανῶν δὲ μόνων ὁ λόγος ἐνταῦθα, Euthymius Zigabenus, who proves this, above all, from vv. 35, 36. All the points previously adduced as arguments against the other explanations combine to favour this view. It is confirmed by the whole fundamental idea on which the Judge's sentence turns (the determining principle being the love manifested toward Jesus), by the figure of the shepherd and his sheep, and finally, and at the same time somewhat more definitely, by the fact that those who are being judged are called πάντα τὰ ἔθνη. For the latter words are not intended to limit the reference expressly to the Gentiles, but they are to be taken as assuming the realization of the *universality of Christianity* by the time of the advent when *all the nations* of the earth (ἔθνη, as expressing the idea of *nation*, does not exclude the Jews; comp. xxviii. 19, xxiv. 9, and see on John xi. 50) will have heard the gospel and (to a proportionable degree) received Christ (xxiv. 14; Rom. xi. 25). Jesus, then, is here describing the universal judgment of *those who have believed in Him*, in whom, as they will be gathered around His throne, His prophetic glance beholds all the nations of the world (xxviii. 19). Comp., for the judgment of *Christians*, 2 Cor. v. 10; Rom. xiv. 10. The judgment of unbelievers (1 Cor. xv. 23, vi. 2; comp. on xix. 28), who are not in question at present, forms a distinct scene in the universal assize; and hence in the preceding parable also the reference is to His servants, therefore to believers. Neither here nor in the passages from Paul do those different judgment scenes presuppose anything in the shape of chiliastic ideas. The Messianic judgment is one *act* consisting of two *scenes*, not two acts with a chiliastic interval coming in between. See, on the other hand, xiii. 37 ff. — πάντες οἱ ἄγγελοι] "omnes angeli, omnes nationes; quanta celebritas!" Bengel. — τὰ πρόβατα ἀπὸ τῶν ἐρίφων] *sheep* and *goats* (Ecclus. xlvii. 3;

Gen. xxxviii. 17) are here represented as *having been pastured together* (comp. Gen. xxx. 33 ff.). The *wicked* are conceived of under the figure of the ἔριφοι, not on account of the wantonness and stench of the latter (Grotius), or in consequence of their stubbornness (Lange), but generally because those animals were considered to be comparatively worthless (Luke xv. 29); and hence, in ver. 33, we have the diminutive τὰ ἐρίφια for the purpose of expressing contempt. — For the *significance* attached to the right and left side (Eccles. x. 2), see Schoettgen and Wetstein on our passage. Hermann, *Gottesd. Alterth.* § xxxviii. 9 f. Comp. Plat. *Rep.* p. 614 C; Virg. *Aen.* vi. 542 f.

Ver. 34. Ὁ βασιλεύς] because Christ is understood to have appeared ἐν τῇ βασιλείᾳ αὐτοῦ, xvi. 28, which fact is here self-evident from ver. 31. — οἱ εὐλογημένοι τοῦ πατρός μου] *the blessed of my Father* (for "in *Christo* electi sumus," Bengel), now actually so (see on Eph. i. 3) by being admitted into the Messianic kingdom that has been prepared for them. On the use of the participial substantive with a genitive, see Lobeck, *ad Aj.* 358; Winer, p. 178 [E. T. 236]. — ἡτοιμασμένην] not merely *destined*, but: *put in readiness;* comp. xx. 23; 1 Cor. ii. 9; John xiv. 2. Καὶ οὐκ εἶπε· λάβετε, ἀλλά· κληρονομήσατε, ὡς οἰκεῖα, ὡς πατρῷα, ὡς ὑμέτερα, ὡς ὑμῖν ἄνωθεν ὀφειλόμενα, Chrysostom. This κληρονομία is the fulfilment of the promise of v. 5, κληρονομήσουσι τὴν γῆν. Comp. xix. 29. — ἀπὸ καταβ. κ.] xiii. 35, not equivalent to πρὸ κ. κ., when *the election* took place (Eph. i. 4; 1 Pet. i. 20). For the order of the words, comp. Kühner, *ad Xen. Anab.* iv. 2. 18.

Ver. 35 f. Συνηγάγετέ με] *ye have taken me along with, introduced* me, that is, into your family circle along with the members of your family. *This* meaning, but not that of Fritzsche: "simul *convivio* adhibuistis," is involved in the idea of ξένος. For συνάγω, as used with reference to a *single* individual who is gathered in along with others, comp. Xen. *Cyrop.* v. 3. 11; LXX. Deut. xxii. 2; 2 Sam. xi. 27; Judg. xix. 18; Ecclus. xiii. 15. For instances of Rabbinical promises of *paradise* in return for hospitality, see Schoettgen and Wetstein.—γυμνός] " Qui male vestitum et pannosum violit, *nudum* se vidisse dicit," Seneca, *de benef.* v. 3 ; Jas. ii. 15!. Comp. on John xxi. 7 ; Acts xix. 16.

Ver. 37 ff. Not mere modesty (not even, according to Olshausen, unconscious modesty), but an actual *declining with humility*, on the ground that they have never rendered the loving services in question to *Christ Himself;* for they do not venture to estimate the moral value of those services according to the lofty principle of Christ's unity with His people, xviii. 5, x. 40. The Lord Himself then explains what He means, ver. 40. Hence it does not follow from this passage that these δίκαιοι " have not as yet been consciously leading the New Testament life " (Auberlen, Cremer). Bengel well remarks : " *Fideles* opera bona sua, impii mala ver. 44, non perinde aestimant ut judex."—πότε σὲ εἴδομεν] three times, earnestly, honestly.—ἐφ' ὅσον] *in quantum, inasmuch as;* see on Rom. xi. 13.—ἐποιήσατε] ye have done it, namely, the things previously mentioned.—ἑνὶ τούτων τῶν ἀδελφῶν μου τῶν ἐλαχίστων] *to a single one of these my brethren, and that of the most insignificant of them.* Those words, which are referred by Keil, Olshausen, Georgii, Hilgenfeld, Keim (see on ver. 31 f.), *to Christians in general ;* by Cremer, to the elect; by Luthardt, to the Christian church *in its distress ;* by Auberlen, to their poor miserable *fellow-men* (comp. de Wette, Ullmann in the *Stud. u. Krit.* 1847, p. 164 ff.),—do not admit of being also referred to the *apostles* (xxviii. 10 ; 1 Cor. iv. 13), to whom, as surrounding His judgment-throne, Christ is supposed to point; for the amount of love shown to the *apostles* cannot be taken as the universal standard of judgment; and though the apostles themselves, appearing here, as they do, in their relation to the rest of Christians, may well be called the *brethren* of Christ (xxviii. 10 ; John xx. 17) ; yet they would certainly not be described by Him as the *least* of such brethren. No; as during His earthly life Christ is always surrounded by the obscure and despised (the poor, the humble, publicans and sinners, and such like), who seek their salvation through Him ; so He also represents Himself as still surrounded by such as these on the occasion of the judgment (comp. Ewald, p. 420). In consequence of their longing after Him, and of their love for Him, and the eternal salvation to be found in Him (as ἠγαπηκότες τὴν ἐπιφάνειαν αὐτοῦ, 2 Tim. iv. 8), they here come crowding around the throne of His glory; and to *these* He now points. *They are* the πτωχοί, πενθοῦντες, πραεῖς, δεδιωγμένοι of the Sermon on the Mount, who are now on the point of receiving the promised bliss.

Ver. 41. Οἱ κατηραμένοι] opposite of οἱ εὐλογημένοι. This consigning to everlasting destruction is also a reality, and the *doing of God.* But the words τοῦ πατρός μου are omitted this time, because the idea of πατήρ accords only with the loving act of blessing. The divine κατάρα is the effect of holy wrath and the consequence of human guilt. — τὸ ἡτοιμασμένον] not this time ἀπὸ καταβολῆς κόσμου; this the hearer knew as matter of course. The Rabbins are not agreed as to whether Gehenna, any more than paradise and the heavenly temple, came into existence before or after the first day of creation. See the passages in Wetstein. From our passage nothing can be determined one way or another, especially as it is not the *aorist* participle that is made use of. Observe, however, that, in this instance, Jesus does not follow up ἡτοιμασμ. with ὑμῖν, as in ver. 34, but with τῷ διαβόλῳ, κ.τ.λ.; because the fall of the angels (Jude 6; 2 Pet. ii. 4), which Scripture everywhere presupposes in its doctrine of the devil and his kingdom (Hahn, *Theol. d. N. T.* I. p. 313 ff.), took place *previous* to the introduction of sin among men (John viii. 44; 2 Cor. xi. 3), so that it was for the former in the first instance that the everlasting fire was prepared; comp. viii. 29. But as men became partakers in the guilt of demons, so now are they also condemned to share in their punishment. For ἄγγελοι τοῦ διαβ., comp. 2 Cor. xii. 7; Rev. xii. 7.

Ver. 44. Self-justification, by repelling the accusation as unwarranted. — καὶ αὐτοί] *they too;* for their answer is in exact correspondence with that of the righteous. — πότε ... καὶ οὐ διηκονήσ. σοι] *when saw we Thee hungry,* etc., *without ministering to Thee?* What was the occasion on which,

according to Thy accusation, we saw Thee hungry, and did not
give Thee food ?   Such an occasion never occurred ; as we
have never seen Thee in such circumstances, so can we never
have refused Thee our good services.   In this self-justification
it is assumed that *if* they had seen Him, they would have
shown their love toward Him.

Ver. 46. Comp. Dan. xii. 2.   The absolute idea of *eternity*,
in regard to the punishment of hell (comp. ver. 41), is not to
be got rid of either by a popular toning down of the force of
αἰώνιος (Paulus), or by appealing (de Wette, Schleiermacher,
Oetinger) to the figurative character of the term *fire* and the
supposed incompatibility between the idea of eternity and
such a thing as evil and its punishment, any more than by
the theory that the whole representation is intended simply
by way of *warning* (according to which view it is not meant
thereby to throw light upon the eternal nature of things, but
only to portray the κρίσις, *i.e.* the cessation of the conflict
between good and evil by the extinction of the latter) ; but is
to be regarded as exegetically established in the present
passage (comp. iii. 12, xviii. 8) by the opposed ζωὴν αἰώνιον,
which denotes the everlasting Messianic life (Kacuffer, as
above, p. 21) ; comp. also Weizel in the *Stud. v. Krit.* 1836,
p. 605 ff. ; Schmid in the *Jahrb. f. D. Theol.* 1870, p. 136 ff.
— οἱ δὲ δίκαιοι] " hoc ipso judicio declarati," Bengel.
Comp. Rom. v. 19.

REMARK.—Because the judgment is a judgment of *Christians*
(see on ver. 31), *faith* is *presupposed* though not *formally
mentioned.*   The truth is, the Judge regulates His decision
according to the way in which faith has been *evidenced* by *love*
(1 Cor. xiii. 1 ff. ; John xiii. 35), without which as its necessary
fruit faith does not save (Gal. v. 6).   Comp. *Apol. Conf.* A,
p. 138.   The manifestations of love, as forming the principle of
the Christian's life, accordingly constitute the πρᾶξις by which
he is to be judged (xvi. 27 ; 2 Cor. v. 10).   Comp. v. 7.   But, in
so far as, according to this concrete view of the judgment, Jesus
bases His sentence upon the principle that love shown to or
withheld from the least of His brethren is the same as love
shown to or withheld from *Himself,* He does so in harmony
with the view contained in xviii. 5, x. 40.   Comp. John xiii. 20.

CHAPTER XXVI.

VER. 3. After ἀρχιερεῖς Elz. Scholz have καὶ οἱ γραμματεῖς, which, in accordance with A B D L ℵ, min. vss. Or. Aug., has been deleted as an interpolation from Mark xiv. 1, Luke xxii. 2.—Ver. 4. The order δόλῳ κρατήσωσι (reversed in Elz.) is supported by decisive evidence.—Ver. 7. βαρυτίμου] Lachm. and Tisch. 8 : πολυτίμου, which, though in accordance with A D L M Π ℵ, min., is, nevertheless, taken from John xii. 3. Comp. Mark xiv. 3. From this latter passage is derived the order ἔχουσα ἀλάβ. μύρου (Lachm. and Tisch. 8, following B D L ℵ, min.).— τὴν κεφαλήν] Lachm. and Tisch. 8 : τῆς κεφαλῆς, following B D M ℵ, min. Chrys. But the genitive would be suggested to the transcribers by a comparison with ver. 12, quite as readily as by Mark xiv. 3.—Ver. 8. αὐτοῦ] is, with Lachm. and Tisch., to be deleted, both here and in ver. 45, as being a common interpolation ; similarly with Tisch. after βλασφ., ver. 65.—Ver. 9. τοῦτο] Elz. inserts τὸ μύρον, against decisive evidence ; borrowed from Mark xiv. 5; John xii. 5.—The *article* before πτωχοῖς, which may as readily have been omitted, in accordance with John xii. 5, as inserted, in accordance with Mark xiv. 3, is, with Elz. and Tisch. 8, to be left out. There is a good deal of evidence on both sides ; but the insertion might easily take place out of regard to ver. 11.—Ver. 11. πάντοτε γὰρ τοὺς πτωχοὺς] E F H M Γ, min. Chrys. : τοὺς πτωχοὺς γὰρ πάντοτε. Recommended by Griesb., adopted by Fritzsche. As this reading may have been taken from John xii. 8 as readily as that of the Received text from Mark xiv. 7, the matter must be determined simply by the balance of evidence, and this is in favour of the Received text.—Ver. 17. ἑτοιμάσωμεν] The evidence of D K U, min. Or. in favour of the reading ἑτοιμάσομεν (Fritzsche) is inadequate.—Ver. 20. Lachm. and Tisch. read μαθητῶν after δώδεκα, on the authority of A L M Δ Π ℵ, min. vss. Chrys. Correctly ; the omission is due to Mark xiv. 17. — For ἕκαστος αὐτῶν, ver. 22, it is better, with Lachm. and Tisch., to adopt εἷς ἕκαστος, in accordance with weighty evidence. Had εἷς been derived from Mark xiv. 19, we should have had εἷς καθ' εἷς; αὐτῶν, again, was an interpolation of extremely common occurrence. — Ver. 26. εὐλογήσας] Scholz: εὐχαριστήσας, following A E F H K M S U V Γ Δ Π, min. vss. Fathers. Considering, however, the weight of evidence that still remains in favour of εὐλογ. (B C D L Z א), and having regard to the preponderating influence of Luke and Paul (1 Cor. xi. 23 ff.) rather than Mark, upon the ecclesiastical phraseology of the Lord's Supper, it is better to retain εὐλογ.—For this reason we should also retain τόν before ἄρτον, though deleted by Lachm. and Tisch. 8, and not found in B C D G L Z א, min. Chrys. Theophyl.—For ἐδίδου Lachm. reads δούς, omitting at the same time καί before εἶπε, in accordance with B D L Z א** min. Cant. Copt. Due to a desire to make the construction uniform with the preceding. Had δούς been changed to a tense in accordance with Mark and Luke, we should have had ἔδωκε. — Ver. 27. τὸ ποτήριον] The article, which is deleted by Tisch., and is wanting in B E F G L Z Δ א, min., is due to the ecclesiastical phraseology to which Luke and Paul have given currency. — Ver. 28. τὸ τῆς] Lachm. and Tisch. have simply τῆς, in accordance with B D L Z א, 33. τὸ is an exegetical addition. — καινῆς before διαθ. is wanting in B L Z א, 33, 102, Sahid. Cyr., and is a liturgical addition. Had it been originally written, this is just the place of all others where it would not have been omitted. — Ver. 31. διασκορπισθήσεται] A B C G H* I L M א, min. Or. (once): διασκορπισθήσονται. So Lachm. and Tisch. The reading of the Received text is a grammatical correction. — Ver. 33. Instead of εἰ καί of the Received text, there is decisive evidence for the simple εἰ. καί would be written in the margin from Mark xiv. 29, but would not be inserted in the text as in the case of Mark. — ἐγώ] The evidence in favour of inserting δέ (which is adopted by Griesb., Matth., Fritzsche) is inadequate. An addition for the purpose of giving prominence to the contrast. — Ver. 35. After ὁμοίως important witnesses read δέ, which has been adopted by Griesb., Matth., Scholz, Fritzsche. Taken from Mark xiv. 31. — Ver. 36. ἕως οὗ] Lachm.: ἕως οὗ ἄν; D K L Δ, min.: ἕως ἄν. The reading of Lachm., though resting only on the authority of A, is nevertheless to be regarded as the original one. οὗ ἄν would be omitted in conformity with Mark xiv. 32 (C M* א, min. have simply ἕως), and then there would come a restoration in some instances of οὗ only, and, in others, merely of ἄν.—Ver. 38. We should not follow Griesb., Matth., Fritzsche, Scholz, Tisch. 7, in adopting ὁ Ἰησοῦς after αὐτοῖς; a reading which, though attested by important witnesses, is nevertheless contradicted by a preponderance of evidence (A B C* D J L

א, and the majority of vss.), while, moreover, it would be inserted more readily and more frequently (in this instance probably in conformity with Mark xiv. 34) than it would be omitted. — Ver. 39. προσελθών] so B M π, It. Vulg. Hilar. Elz. Lachm. and Tisch. 7. The preponderance of evidence is in favour of προσελθών, which, indeed, has been adopted by Matth., Scholz, and Tisch. 8; but it is evidently a mechanical error on the part of the transcriber; προέρχεσθαι occurs nowhere else in Matth.— The μου after πάτερ (deleted by Tisch. 8) is suspected of being an addition from ver. 42; however, the evidence in favour of deleting it (A B C D א, etc.) is too weighty to admit of its being retained. — Ver. 42. τὸ ποτήριον] is wanting in A B C I L א, min. vss. and Fathers; in D it comes *before* τοῦτο (as in ver. 39); in 157, Arm., it comes before ἐάν, in which position it also occurs in Δ, though with a mark of erasure. Suspected by Griesb., deleted by Fritzsche, Lachm., and Tisch. A supplement from ver. 39. Further, the ἀπ᾽ ἐμοῦ following, though the evidence against it is not quite so strong (B D L א, however), and though it is defended by Fritzsche, and only bracketed by Lachm., is to be condemned (with Griesb., Rinck, Tisch.) as an interpolation from ver. 39. — Ver. 43. εὑρίσκει αὐτούς πάλιν] Lachm. and Tisch., with the approval of Griesb. also: πάλιν εὗρεν αὐτούς, following B C D I L א, min. and the majority of vss.; while other important witnesses (such as A K Δ) also read εὗρεν, but adhere to the order in the Received text. Accordingly, εὗρεν is decidedly to be adopted, while εὑρίσκει is to be regarded as derived from ver. 40; as for πάλιν, however, there is so much diversity among the authorities with reference to its connection, and consequently with reference to its position, that only the preponderance of evidence must decide, and that is favourable to Lachm. and Tisch. — In ver. 44, again, πάλιν is variously placed; but, with Lachm. and Tisch., it should be put before ἀπελθών, in accordance with B C D I L א, min. vss. ἐκ τρίτου, which Lachm. brackets, is, with Tisch., to be maintained on the strength of preponderating evidence. Had it been inserted in conformity with ver. 42, it would have been placed after πάλιν; had it been from Mark xiv. 41, again, we should have had τὸ τρίτον. The omission may have been readily occasioned by a fear lest it should be supposed that Jesus prayed τὸν αὐτὸν λόγον but *once* before.—After εἰπών Tisch. 8 repeats the πάλιν (B L א, min. Copt.), which may easily have been omitted as superfluous. However, the preponderance of evidence (especially that of the vss. also) is against adopting it, so that there is reason to regard it rather as a mechanical repetition. — Ver. 50. The reading ἐφ᾽ ὅ (instead of ἐφ᾽ ᾧ, as in Elz.) is attested by decisive evidence. — Ver. 52. ἀπολοῦνται] F H K M S U V Γ Δ, min. vss. and Fathers: ἀποθανοῦνται. Approved by Griesb. in opposition to the principal mss.; a gloss, for which Sahid. must have read πεσοῦνται. — Ver. 53. The placing of ἄρτι after παρασ. μοι, by Tisch. 8, is in opposition to a preponderance of evidence, and is of the nature of an emendation ; ὧδε is likewise inserted by some. — πλείους] Lachm. and Tisch.: πλείω, after B D אֶ*. Correctly ; the reading of the Received text is an unskilled emendation. For the same reason the following ἤ, which Lachm. brackets, should, with Tisch., be deleted, in accordance with B D L אֶ; though we should not follow Tisch. 8 in reading λεγιώνων (A C K L Δ Π* אֶ*) for λεγεῶνας, because the genitive is connected with the reading πλείους. — Ver. 55. πρὸς ὑμᾶς] is, with Tisch., following B L אֶ, 33, 102, Copt. Sahid. Cyr. Chrys., to be deleted as an interpolation from Mark xiv. 49. — Ver. 58. ἀπὸ μακρόθεν] ἀπό should be deleted, with Tisch., in accordance with important evidence. Taken from Mark xiv. 54. — Ver. 59. καὶ οἱ πρεσβύτεροι] is wanting, no doubt, in B D L אֶ, min. vss. and Fathers, but it was omitted in conformity with Mark xiv. 55. Suspected by Griesb., deleted by Lachm. and Tisch. 8. A desire to conform with Mark also serves to explain the fact that, in a few of the witnesses, ὅλον is placed *before* τὸ συνέδρ. — θανατώσωσιν] θανατώσουσιν, as read by Lachm. and Tisch., is supported by decisive evidence, and had been altered to the more usual subjunctive. αὐτόν should likewise be put *before* θανατ. (B C D L N אֶ, min. Vulg. It.). — Ver. 60. The reading of the Received text, which is attested by the important evidence of A C** E F G, etc., and likewise maintained by Fritzsche and Scholz, is : καὶ οὐχ εὗρον. Καὶ πολλῶν ψευδομαρτύρων προσελθόντων οὐχ εὗρον. Griesb. : καὶ οὐχ εὗρον πολλῶν ψευδ. προσελθ. Lachm. and Tisch. : καὶ οὐχ εὗρον πολλ. προσελθ. ψευδ., after which Lachm. gives the second οὐχ εὗρον in brackets. This second οὐχ εὗρον is wanting in A C* L N* אֶ, min. vss. and Fathers (Or. twice) ; while in A B L Θ.ʳ אֶ, min. Syr. Or. Cyr. the order of the words is : πολλ. προσελθ. ψευδ. Further, Syr. Arr. Pers.ᵖ Syr.ʲᵉʳ Slav., though omitting the second οὐχ εὗρον, have retained καί before πολλῶν; and this reading (accordingly: καὶ οὐχ εὗρον καὶ πολλῶν προσελθόντων ψευδομαρτύρων) I agree with Rinck, *Lucubr. crit.* p. 282 f., regarding as the original one. This καί, the force of which was missed from its not being followed by a verb, occasioned considerable embarrassment to the transcribers, who disposed of the difficulty by adding a second οὐχ εὗρον, while others got rid of the troublesome καί by simply omitting it. — διὸ ψευδομάρτ.] Tisch., following B L א, min. vss. (also Syr.) and Or. (once), reads merely δύο. Correctly; ψευδομάρτ. is an addition, which might seem all the more necessary since a saying of Christ's actually underlay the words. — Ver. 65. ὅτι] is wanting before ἐβλασφήμ. in such important witnesses, that Lachm. and Tisch. are justified in deleting it as a common interpolation. — Ver. 70. For αὐτῶν πάντων read, with Tisch. 8, following preponderating evidence, merely πάντων, to which αὐτῶν was added for sake of greater precision. — Ver. 71. For τοῖς ἐκεῖ, which Tisch. 8 has restored, Scholz and Tisch. 7 read αὐτοῖς ἐκεῖ. Both readings are strongly attested; but the latter is to be preferred, because the current τοῖς ἐκεῖ would involuntarily suggest itself and supersede the less definite expression αὐτοῖς ἐκεῖ.—Ver. 74. καταθεματίζειν] Elz., Fritzsche : καταναθεματίζειν, against decisive evidence. A correction.

Ver. 1 f.[1] For this form of transition, by which a marked pause is indicated at the close of a somewhat lengthened discourse, comp. vii. 28, xi. 1, xiii. 53, xix. 1. — πάντας] referring back, without any particular object in view (such as to call attention to the fact that our Lord's functions as a teacher were now ended, Wichelhaus and the earlier expositors), to the preceding discourse, consisting, as it does, of several sections (xxiv. 4–xxv. 46), not a parallel to LXX. Deut. xxxi. 1 (Delitzsch). — μετὰ δύο ἡμέρας] *after the lapse of two days,* i.e. *the day after next* the Passover commenced. It would therefore be Tuesday, if, as the Synoptists inform us (differently in John, see on John xviii. 28), the feast began on Thursday evening. — τὸ πάσχα] פֶּסַח, Aram. פַּסְחָא, the *passing over* (Ex. xii. 13), a Mosaic feast, in commemoration of the sparing of the first-born in Egypt, began after sunset on the 14th of Nisan, and lasted till the 21st. On its original meaning as a feast in connection with the consecration of the first-fruits of the spring harvest, see Ewald, *Alterth.* p. 466 f. ; Dillmann in Schenkel's *Lex.* IV. p. 387 f. — καὶ ὁ υἱός, κ.τ.λ.] a definite prediction of what was to happen to Him at the Pass-

---

[1] See on ch. xxvi. f. (Mark xiv., Luke xxii.); Wichelhaus, *ausführl. Kommentar über die Gesch. des Leidens J. Chr.,* Halle 1855 ; Steinmeyer, *d. Leidensgesch. d. Herrn in Bezug auf d. neueste Krit.,* Berl. 1868.

over, but represented as something already known to the disciples (from xx. 19), and which, though forming part of the contents of οἴδατε, is at the same time introduced by a *broken construction* (not as dependent on ὅτι), in accordance with the depth of His emotion.

Vv. 3–5. Τότε] *i.e.* at the time that Jesus was saying this to His disciples. Fatal coincidence. — εἰς τὴν αὐλὴν τοῦ ἀρχ.] It is usual to understand the *palace* of the high priest, in direct opposition to the use of αὐλή[1] in the New Testament (not excluding Luke xi. 21). We should rather interpret it of the *court* enclosed by the various buildings belonging to the house (see Winer, *Realw.* under the word *Häuser;* Friedlieb, *Archäol. d. Leidensgesch.* p. 7 f.), such courts having been regularly used as meeting-places. Comp. Vulg. (*atrium*), Erasmus, Castalio, Calvin, Maldonatus. This meeting is not to be regarded as one of the public sittings of the Sanhedrim (on the probable official meeting-place of this body at that time, the so-called *taverns*, see Wieseler, *Beitr.* p. 209 ff.), but as a *private conference* of its members. — τοῦ λεγομ. Καϊάφα] *who bore the name of Caiaphas.* Comp. ii. 23. This was a *surname;* the original name was Joseph (Joseph. *Antt.* xviii. 2. 2); but the surname having become his ordinary and official designation, it was used for the *name* itself; hence λεγομένου, not ἐπικαλουμένου or ἐπιλεγομένου. Caiaphas (either = כֵּיְפָא, *depressio*, or כֵּיפָא, *rock*) obtained his appointment through the procurator Valerius Gratus, and, after enjoying his dignity for seventeen years, was deposed by Vitellius, Joseph. *Antt.* xviii. 2. 2, 4. 3. — συνεβουλεύσαντο, ἵνα] *they consulted together, in order that they,* John xi. 53. — μὴ ἐν τῇ ἑορτῇ] namely: *let us arrest him, and put him to death!* For the absolute μή, comp. on Gal. v. 13. The reference is to the entire *period* over which the feast *extended*, not to the *place* where it was celebrated (Wieseler, *Chronol. Synops.* p. 367). It is true

---

[1] Of course αὐλή is used as equivalent to βασίλειον (see, for example, the passages from Polyb. in Schweighäuser's *Lex.* p. 101), not only by later Greek writers (Athen. *Deipn.* iv. p. 189 D; Herodian, i. 13. 16, frequently in the Apocr.) but also by Homer (see Duncan, *Lex.*, ed. Rost, p. 181), Pindar, and the nonlli[?] tr., etc. Never, however, is it so used in the New Testament. Even refus[?] tc.i. 15, αὐλὴ τοῦ ἀρχιερ. is undoubtedly the *court* of the house.

MAT

no scruple was felt, especially in urgent and important cases (comp. on Acts xii. 3 f.), about having executions (*Sanhedr.* f. 89. 1) during the feast days (although most probably never on the first of them, on which, according to *Mischna Jom tob* v. 2, the trial took place; comp. on John xviii. 28, and see, above all, Bleek's *Beitr.* p. 136 ff.), and that with a view to making the example more deterrent (Deut. xvii. 13). But the members of the Sanhedrim dreaded an uprising among the numerous sympathizers with Jesus both within and outside the capital (a very natural apprehension, considering that this was just the season when so many strangers, and especially Galilaeans, were assembled in the city; comp. Joseph. *Antt.* xvii. 9. 3; *Bell.* i. 4. 3), though, by and by, they overcame this fear, and gladly availed themselves of the opportunity which Judas afforded them (ver. 14). " Sic consilium divinum successit," Bengel.   To regard μὴ ἐν τῇ ἑορτῇ as meaning: *previous to the feast!* as though, during the feast itself, the execution were to be considered as already a thing of the past (Neander, p. 678; Hausrath), would be quite in keeping with John's statement as to the day on which the crucifixion took place (comp. on Mark xiv. 2); but it would not suit the connection as found in Matthew and Mark, because, according to them, the consultation among the members of the Sanhedrim had taken place so very shortly before the Passover (ver. 2) that the greater part of the multitude, whose rising was apprehended, must have been present by that time.

Ver. 6 ff. *This anointing*, which is also recorded in Mark xiv. 3 ff. (followed by Matthew), is not the same as that of Luke vii. 36 ff., but is so essentially different from it, not only as to the time, place, circumstances, and person, but as to the whole historical and ethical connection and import, that even the peculiar character of the incident is not sufficient to warrant the assumption that each case is but another version of one and the same story (in opposition to Chrysostom, Grotius, Schleiermacher, *Schr. d. Luk.* p. 110 ff.; Strauss, Weisse, Hug, Ewald, Bleek, Baur, Hilgenfeld, Schenkel, Keim). This, however, is not a different incident (in opposition to Origen, Chr. *Leidens-* Jerome, Theophylact, Euthymius Zigabenus, Osiander.

Wolf) from that recorded in John xii. 1 ff.[1] The deviations in John's account of the affair—to the effect that the anointing took place not two, but six days before the feast; that Martha was the entertainer, no mention being made of Simon; that it was not the head, but the feet of Jesus that were anointed; and that the carping about extravagance is specially ascribed to Judas—are not to be disposed of by arbitrarily assuming that the accounts of the different evangelists were intended to supplement each other (Ebrard, Wichelhaus, Lange), but are to be taken as justifying the inference that in John alone (not in Matthew and Mark) we have the narrative of an eye-witness. The incident, as given in Matthew and Mark, appears to be an episode taken from a tradition which had lost its freshness and purity, and inserted without exact historical connection, although, on the whole, in its right order, if with less regard to precision as to the time of its occurrence. Hence the loose place it occupies in the pragmatism of the passage, from which one might imagine it removed altogether, without the connection being injured in the slightest degree. The tradition on which the narrative of Matthew and Mark is based had evidently suffered in its purity from getting mixed up with certain disturbing elements from the first version of the story of the anointing in Luke vii., among which elements we may include the statement that the name of the entertainer was Simon.

Ver. 6. Γενομ. ἐν Βηθαν.] *i.e. having come* to Bethany, ?, Tim. i. 17; John vi. 25, and frequently in classical writers; c⸴ρ, κ.ϱn Phil. ii. 7. To remove this visit *back* to a point of ‑οin *previous* to that indicated at ver. 2, with the effect of simp‑ /destroying the sequence (Ebrard, Lange), is to do such

---

[1] On the controversy in which Faber Stapul. has been involved in consequence of his theory that Jesus had been anointed by *three different* Marys, see Graf in Niedner's *Z⸴tschr. f. histor. Theol.* 1852, I. p. 54 ff. This distinguishing of three Marys (which was also adopted by so early an expositor as Euthymius Zigaben ϐ, and by τινές, to whom Theophylact refers) is, in fact, rather too much at var⌐ 'ce with the tradition that the sister of Lazarus is identical with the woman who ᵉlᵢs a sinner, Luke vii., and was no other than Mary Magdalene. Yet in nonᵤlif the three accounts of anointing is this latter to be understood as the Mary ref⸦us 1 tc.

harmonistic violence to the order observed in Matthew and Mark as the τότε of ver. 14 should have been sufficient to avert. — Σίμωνος τοῦ λεπροῦ] In a way no less unwarrantable has the person here referred to (a person who had formerly been a leper, and who, after his healing, effected probably by Jesus, had continued to be known by this epithet) been associated with the family of Bethany ; he has been supposed to have been the deceased father of this family (Theophylact, Ewald, *Gesch. Chr.* p. 481), or some other relative or friend (Grotius, Kuinoel, Ebrard, Lange, Bleek), or the owner of the house. Of the person who, according to Matthew and Mark, provided this entertainment, nothing further is known ; whereas, according to John, the entertainment was given by the family of which Lazarus was a member; the latter is the correct view, the former is based upon the similar incident recorded in Luke vii.

Ver. 7. Γυνή] According to John, it was *Mary.* — ἀλάβαστρον] Among classical writers the *neuter* of this word does not occur except in the *plural ;* in the *singular* ἀλάβαστρος is masculine, as also in 2 Kings xxi. 13, and feminine. " Unguenta optime servantur in alabastris," Plin. *N. H.* iii. 3 ; Herod. iii. 20 ; Theocr. *Id.* xv. 114 ; *Anth. Pal.* ix. 153. 3 ; Jacobs, *ad Anthol.* XI. p. 92. — ἐπὶ τ. κ. αὐτοῦ] A divergence from John's account, not to be reconciled in the arbitrary manner in which Calvin and Ebrard have attempted, as though the oil had been so unsparingly poured on that it ran down and was used for the feet as well (comp. Morison). Matthew narrates an anointing of the *head ;* John, of *that t.* The practice of anointing the *heads* of guests by *not* of showing them respect is well known (comp. Pla, *Rep.* p. 398 A, and Stallbaum thereon). Seeing, however, that the anointing of the *feet* was *unusual* (in opposition to Ebrard), and betokened a special and extraordinary amount of respect (as is, in fact, apparent from Luke v. 46), our passage would have been all the less likely to " *omit* it (Lange), had it really formed part of the tradition. — ἀνακειμένου] *while He was reclining at table,* a circumstance qualifying the αὐτοῦ.

Ver. 8. The feature peculiar to John, and having an essential bearing upon the character of his narrative, to the effect that it was Judas who censured the proceeding, had come to be obliterated in the tradition represented by our present passage. Our narrative, then, is certainly not contradictory of that of John, but only *less precise*. Arbitrary attempts have been made to explain our passage by saying either that, in Matthew, the narrative is to be regarded as *sylleptical* (Jerome, Beza, Maldonatus), or that Judas simply *gave utterance* to an observation in which the others have innocently *concurred* (Augustine, Calvin, Grotius, Kuinoel, Paulus, Wichelhaus), or that *several of them* betrayed *symptoms* of murmuring (Lange). — ἡ ἀπώλεια αὕτη] *this loss*, in making such a use of an expensive oil. This word never occurs in the New Testament in a transitive sense (as in Polyb. vi. 59. 5).

Ver. 9. Πολλοῦ] put more precisely in Mark xiv. 5; John xii. 5. On the expensiveness of spikenard, a pound of which is alleged to have cost even upwards of 400 denarii, see Plin. *N. H.* xii. 26, xiii. 4. — καὶ δοθῆναι] the subject (the equivalent in money, had it been sold) may be inferred from the context (πραθῆναι πολλοῦ). See Kühner, II. 1, p. 30 f.

Ver. 10. Γνούς] Comp. xvi. 8. We may imagine what precedes to have been spoken among the disciples in a low murmuring tone. — κόπους παρέχειν, *to give trouble*, to cause annoyance. See Kypke, *Obss.* I. p. 130. Comp. πόνον παρέχειν (Herod. i. 177), and such like. — ἔργον γάρ, κ.τ.λ.] Justification of the disapproval implied in the foregoing question. καλόν, when used with ἔργον, is, according to ordinary usage, to be taken in an *ethical* sense; thus (comp. v. 16): an *excellent* deed, one that is *morally* beautiful, and not a piece of waste, as ye are niggardly enough to suppose. The disciples had allowed their estimate of the action to be determined by the principle of mere *utility*, and not by that of *moral propriety*, especially of love to Christ.

Ver. 11 f. Justification of the καλόν on the ground of the peculiar circumstances under which the anointing took place. Jesus was on the very threshold of death; they would always

have opportunities of showing kindness to the poor, but by
and by it would be no longer in their power to do a loving
service to Him in person upon earth!   Accordingly there is
a moral propriety in making the special manifestation of love,
which was possible only now, take precedence of that general
one which was always possible. — οὐ πάντοτε ἔχετε] a
sorrowful *litotes* involving the idea: *but I will soon be removed
by death*, to which idea the γάρ of ver. 12 refers. — βαλοῦσα]
inasmuch as she has poured . . . she has done it (this outpouring)
with the view (as though I were already a corpse) *of embalming
me* (Gen. l. 2).   The *aorist* participle represents the act as
finished *contemporaneously* with ἐποίησαν.   Comp. xxvii. 4;
Eph. i. 9, *al.*; Hermann, *ad Viger.* p. 774; Müller in the
Luther. Zeitschr. 1872, p. 631 ff.   For the rest, it may be said
that, under the influence of grateful emotion, Jesus *ascribes* a
special motive to the woman, though she herself simply meant
to testify her love and reverence.   Such feelings, intensified as
they were by the thought of the approaching death of the
beloved Master, and struggling to express themselves in this
particular form, could not but receive the highest consecration.

Ver. 13. Τὸ εὐαγγ. τοῦτο] comp. on xxiv. 14.   In
this instance, however, the emphasis is not on τοῦτο (as in
xxiv. 14), but on τὸ εὐαγγέλιον: this *message of redemption*,
where τοῦτο points to the subject of the message just hinted
at, vv. 11, 12, viz. the *death of Jesus*; and although the
allusion may be but slight, still it is an allusion in living
connection with the thoughts of death that filled His soul, and
one that naturally springs from the sorrowful emotion of His
heart.   The *thing* to which τοῦτο refers is, when put in *explicit*
terms, identical with τὸ εὐαγγ. τῆς χάριτος τ. θεοῦ (Acts xx.
24), τὸ εὐαγγ. τῆς σωτηρίας ὑμ. (Eph. i. 13), τὸ εὐαγγ. τῆς
εἰρήνης (Eph. vi. 15), ὁ λόγος τοῦ σταυροῦ (1 Cor. i. 18). —
ἐν ὅλῳ τῷ κόσμῳ] is not to be connected with λαληθ.
(Fritzsche, Kuinoel), but with κηρυχθῇ.   Comp. Mark xiv.
9; ὅπου denotes the locality in its *special*, ἐν ὅλῳ τῷ κόσμῳ in
its *most comprehensive* sense. — εἰς μνημόσ. αὐτ.] belongs to
λαληθ.   She has *actually* been remembered, and her memory
is *blessed*.

Vv. 14–16. On 'Ιούδας 'Ισκαρ., see on x. 4. — τότε]
after this repast, but not because he had been so much
offended, nay, embittered (Wichelhaus, Schenkel, following the
older expositors), by the reply of Jesus, ver. 10 ff. (comp.
John xii. 7 f.),—a view scarcely in keeping with the mournful
tenderness of that reply in which, moreover, according to
Matthew, the name of Judas was not once mentioned.
According to John xiii. 27, the devil, after selecting Judas
as his instrument (xiii. 2), impelled him to betray his
Master, *not, however, till the occasion of the last supper,*—a
divergence from the synoptical narrative which ought, with
Strauss, to be recognised, especially as it becomes very marked
when Luke xxii. 3 is compared with John xiii. 27. — εἰς τῶν
δώδεκα] *tragic* contrast; found in all the evangelists, even in
John xii. 4; Acts i. 17.—In ver. 15 the mark of interrogation
should not be inserted after δοῦναι (Lachmann), but allowed
to remain after παραδ. αὐτόν. Expressed syntactically, the
question would run : What will ye give me, *if I deliver Him to
you ?* In the eagerness of his haste the traitor falls into a
broken construction (Kühner, II. 2, p. 782 f.): What will ye
give me, *and* I will, etc. Here καί is the explicative *atque,*
meaning : *and so;* on ἐγώ, again, there is an *emphasis expressive
of boldness.* — ἔστησαν] *they weighed for him,* according to the
ancient custom, and comp. Zech. xi. 12. No doubt *coined*
shekels (Otto, *Spicil.* p. 60 ff.; Ewald in the *Nachr. v. d. Gesellsch.
d. Wiss.,* Gött. 1855, p. 109 ff.) were in circulation since the
time of Simon the Maccabee (143 B.C.), but *weighing* appears
to have been still practised, especially when considerable sums
were paid out of the temple treasury; it is, in any case, unwarrantable to understand the ἔστησαν merely in the sense of :
they paid. For ἵστημι, *to weigh,* see Wetstein on our passage;
Schleusner, *Thes.* III. p. 122 ; Valckenaer, *ad Eurip. Fragm.* p.
288. The interpretation of certain expositors : *they arranged
with him, they promised him* (Vulg. Theophylact, Castalio,
Grotius, Elsner, Fritzsche, Käuffer, Wichelhaus, Lange), is in
opposition not only to xxvii. 3, where the words τὰ ἀργύρια
refer back to the shekels *already paid,* but also to the terms of
the prophecy, Zech. xi. 12 (comp. Matt. xxvii. 9). — τριάκ. ἀργ.]

ἀργύρια, *shekels*, only in Matthew, not in the LXX., which, in Zech. xi. 12, has τριάκοντα ἀργυροῦς (*sc.* σίκλους); comp. Jer. xxxii. 9. They were *shekels of the sanctuary* (שֶׁקֶל הַקֹּדֶשׁ), which, as containing the standard weight, were heavier than the ordinary shekels; according to Joseph. *Antt.* iii. 8. 2, they were equivalent to four Attic drachmae, though, according to Jerome (on Mic. iii. 10), whose estimate, besides being more precise, is found to tally with existing specimens of this coin, they were equal to twenty oboli, or to $3\frac{1}{3}$ drachmae—*i.e.* to something like 26 to 27 silbergroschen (2s. 6d.). See Bertheau, *Gesch. d. Isr.* pp. 34, 39; Keil, *Arch.* II. p. 146. — ἐζήτει εὐκαιρίαν, ἵνα] *he sought a good opportunity* (Cic. *de off.* i. 40) *for the purpose of*, etc. Such a εὐκαιρία as he wanted would present itself whenever he saw that συλληφθέντος οὐκ ἔμελλε θόρυβος γενέσθαι, Euthymius Zigabenus; comp. ver. 5.

REMARK 1.—As the statement regarding the *thirty pieces of silver* is peculiar to Matthew, and as one so avaricious as Judas was would hardly have been contented with so moderate a sum, it is probable that, from its not being known exactly how much the traitor had received, the Gospel traditions came ultimately to fix upon such a definite amount as was suggested by Zech. xi. 12. Then, as tending further to impugn the historical accuracy of Matthew's statement, it is of importance to notice that it has been adopted neither by the earlier Gospel of Mark, nor the later one of Luke, nor by John. Comp. Strauss, Ewald, Scholten.

REMARK 2.—As regards the idea, that what prompted Judas to act as he did, was a desire to bring about a rising of the people at the time of the feast, and to constrain "the dilatory Messiah to establish His kingdom by means of popular violence" (Paulus, Goldhorn in *Tzschirn. Memor.* i. 2; Winer, Theile, Hase, Schollmeyer, *Jesus u. Judas*, 1836; Weisse, I. p. 450),—the traitor himself being now doubtful, according to Neander and Ewald, as to whether Jesus was the Messiah or not,—it may be affirmed that it has no foundation whatever in the Gospel record, although it may be excused as a well-meant effort to render a mysterious character somewhat more comprehensible, and to make so strange a choice on the part of Jesus a little less puzzling. According to John especially, the subjective motive which, in conjunction with Satanic agency (Luke xxii. 3; John xiii. 2, 27), led to the betrayal was simply *avarice*, not wounded *ambition* as well, see on ver. 14; nor *love of revenge* and such like (Schenkel); nor *shipwrecked faith* on the occasion of the anointing of Christ (Klostermann); nor *melancholy*, combined with irritation against Jesus because the kingdom He sought to establish was not a kingdom of this world (Lange). Naturally passionate at any rate (Pressensé), and destitute of clearness of head as well as force of character (in opposition to Weisse), he was now so carried away by his own dark and confused ideas, that though betraying Jesus he did not anticipate that he would be condemned to death (xxvii. 3), and only began to realize *what* he had done when the consequences of his act stared him in the face. Those, accordingly, go too far in combating the attempts that have been made to palliate the deed in question, who seek to trace it to *fierce anger against Jesus, and the profoundest wickedness* (Ebrard), and who represent Judas as having been from the first—even at the time he was chosen—the most consummate scoundrel to be found among men (Daub, *Judas Ischar.* 1816). That fundamental vice of Judas, πλεονεξία, became doubtless, in the abnormal development which his moral nature underwent through intercourse with Jesus, the power which completely darkened and overmastered his inner life, culminating at last in betrayal and suicide. Moreover, in considering the crime of Judas, Scripture requires us to keep in view the *divine teleology*, Peter already speaking of Jesus (Acts ii. 23) as τῇ ὡρισμένῃ βουλῇ καὶ προγνώσει τοῦ θεοῦ ἔκδοτον, in a way corresponding very much to the view taken of the conduct of Herod and Pilate in Acts iv. 28. Judas is thus the tragic instrument and organ of the divine εἱμαρμένη, though not in such a sense as to extenuate in the least the enormity and culpability of his offence, ver. 24. Comp. John xvii. 12; Acts i. 25; and see, further, on John vi. 70, Remark 1.

Ver. 17. *Τῇ δὲ πρώτῃ τῶν ἀζύμ.*] on the first day of the unleavened bread, i.e. on the first day *of the feast*, the day *on which the unleavened bread* (המצות) *is eaten.* The day referred to is the 14th of Nisan (Thursday, according to the synoptic evangelists), which, following the loose popular mode of reckoning, to which Josephus (*Antt.* ii. 15. 1) also conforms when he represents the feast as extending over *eight* days, was counted as one of the feast days, although the Passover did not begin till the evening of that day, Num. xxviii. 16; Ex. xii. 18 (Otto, *Spicil.* p. 70). — *ποῦ*] in what house. — σοι] "Jesus est ut paterfamilias inter discipulorum familiam," Bengel. — τὸ πάσχα] the *Passover lamb*, to be eaten on the evening of the 14th of Nisan. See on John xviii. 28. This lamb was slain (not by the priests) in the fore-court of the temple in the afternoon before sunset (בֵּין הָעַרְבָּיִם, see Hupfeld, *de primitiva festor. ap. Hebr. ratione*, I. p. 12). — It may seem strange that, at a season when the presence of such multitudes of strangers in the city was certain to create a scarcity of accommodation (Joseph. *Bell.* ii. 1. 3, vi. 9. 3 ; *Antt.* xvii. 9. 3), Jesus should have put off His arrangements for celebrating the feast till now. This, however, may be accounted for by the fact that He must have had certain friends in the town, such as the one referred to in ver. 18, whose houses were so much at His disposal at all times that it was unnecessary to make any earlier preparation.

REMARK.—According to John's account, the last meal of which Jesus partook was not that of the Passover ; while His death is represented as having taken place on the day before the feast, the day which Matthew here calls the πρώτη τῶν ἀζύμων. On this great and irreconcilable discrepancy, which even the most recent exhaustive inquiry, viz. that of Wieseler (*Beitr.* p. 230 ff.), has failed to dispose of, see on John xviii. 28.

Ver. 18. Εἰς τὴν πόλιν] *to Jerusalem*. According to ver. 6 ff., they were still at Bethany. — πρὸς τὸν δεῖνα] as we say when we either cannot or will not mention the name of the person intended : *to so and so*. See Wetstein and Hermann, *ad Vig.* p. 704. But it was not *Jesus Himself* who omitted to mention the name ("ut discipulus ex diuturna consuetudine notissimum," Fritzsche), for, after the question of the disciples, ver. 17, He could not assume that it was quite well understood who it was that He referred to ; but it has been omitted by the *evangelist* in his narrative (comp. even Augustine, *de cons. ev.* ii. 80), either because it had not been preserved as part of the tradition, or for some other reason, to us unknown. — ὁ διδάσκ.] the Teacher κατ' ἐξοχήν. Doubtless the unknown person here referred to was also a believer. Comp. xxi. 3. — ὁ καιρός μου] *i.e.* the time *of my death* (John xiii. 1), not : for my *observing the Passover* (Kuinoel), which would render

the words singularly meaningless; for *this* time was, in fact,
the same for all. There is nothing whatever to justify the
very old hypothesis, invented with a view to reconcile the
synoptic writers with John, that Jesus partook of His last
Passover meal a day earlier than that on which it was wont
to be eaten by the Jews. See on John xviii. 28. Further, this
preliminary preparation implies a *pious regard* for Jesus on the
part of the δεῖνα, who was thus singled out; this Passover observance, for which preparations are being made, was destined,
in fact, to be a *farewell* feast! According to Ewald, ὁ καιρός
μου denotes the time when the *Messianic phenomena would
appear in the heavens* (comp. xxiv. 34), which, however, is at
variance with the text, where the *death* of Jesus is the all-
pervading thought (see vv. 2, 4, 11 f., 21). Comp. ἐλήλυθεν
ἡ ὥρα, John xvii. 1. — ποιῶ] is not the *Attic future* (Fritzsche,
Bleek), but the *present*, representing what is future as now
going on, and suited to the idea of a *distinct* friendly arrangement beforehand : *at thy house I observe the Passover.* Comp.
Ex. xii. 48 ; Josh. v. 10 ; Deut. xv. 1 ; 3 Esdr. i. 6. Similarly
classical writers frequently use ποιεῖν in the sense of *to
observe a feast.* — Matthew's account presupposes nothing
miraculous here, as Theophylact and Calvin would have us
believe, but simply an arrangement, of which nothing further
is known, which Jesus had come to with the person in question, and in consequence of which this latter not only understood what was meant by the ὁ καιρός μου, but was also
keeping a room in reserve for Jesus in which to celebrate the
Passover. It is probable that Jesus, during His stay in
Jerusalem after the triumphal entry, had come to some understanding or other with him, so that all that now required to
be done was to complete the preparations. It was reserved
for the later tradition, embodied in Mark and Luke, to
ascribe a miraculous character to these preparations, in which
respect they seem to have shared the fate of the incident
mentioned at xxi. 2 f. This being the case, the claim of
originality must be decided in favour of what is still the very
simple narrative of Matthew (Strauss, Bleek, Keim), in preference to that of Mark and Luke (Schulz, Schleiermacher,

Weisse, Ewald, Weiss).   As represented, therefore, by Matthew
(who, according to Ebrard and Holtzmann, seems to have
regarded the circumstance about the man bearing a pitcher
of water as only "an unnecessary detail," and whose narrative here is, according to Ewald, "somewhat winnowed"),
this incident is a natural one, though the same cannot be
said of the account given by Mark and Luke (in opposition to
Olshausen and Neander).—*Who* that unknown person above
referred to might be, is a point which cannot be determined.

Ver. 20. Ἀνέκειτο] for the enactment (Ex. xii. 11)
requiring the Passover lamb to be eaten *standing*, staff in
hand, and in travelling attire, had been subsequently superseded by the necessity of reclining.   See *Hieros Pesachim*
f. 37. 2 : " Mos servorum est, ut edant stantes, at nunc come-
dant recumbentes, ut dignoscatur, exisse eos e servitute in liber-
tatem."   See Usteri, *Comment. Joh. ev. genuin. esse.* 1823, p. 26
ff.—It was considered desirable that no Passover party should
ever consist of fewer than *ten* guests (Joseph. *Bell.* vi. 9. 3),
for the lamb had to be entirely consumed (Ex. xii. 4, 43 ff.)

Ver. 21. Ἐσθιόντων αὐτῶν] *whilst they were eating*, but
previous to the institution of the supper, ver. 26, which is at
variance with Luke xxii. 21.   The correct version of the
matter is unquestionably that of Matthew, with whom John
also agrees in so far as he represents the announcement of the
betrayer as having taken place immediately after the feet-
washing and the accompanying discourse, xiii. 21 ff.

Ver. 22. Ἤρξαντο] portrays *the unfolding of one scene
after another* in the incident.   Jesus did not answer till this
question had been addressed to Him by all of them in turn. —
μήτι ἐγώ εἰμι] *surely it is not I ?* presupposes a reply in the
negative.   " Cum scelus exhorreant, cupiunt ab ejus suspicione
purgari ; bona tamen conscientia freti, libere testari volunt,
quam procul remoti sint a tanto scelere," Calvin.   The account
in John xiii. 22 ff. does not exclude, but supplements that
before us, particularly because it also mentions that Judas
had retired before the supper was instituted.

Ver. 23. Ὁ ἐμβάψας, κ.τ.λ.] *he who has dipped* (not : *is
dipping*, Luther, following the Vulgate).   We have here no such

definite allusion as John xiii. 26 represents Jesus to have made to *Judas.* For it is not probable that the dipping in question took place *subsequent* to the intimation by Jesus in ver. 21 and the commotion of ver. 22,—two circumstances calculated to interrupt for a little the progress of the meal,— but rather *before* them, when there may have been others besides Judas dipping into the dish from which Jesus was eating. The allusion can be said to point specially to Judas only in so far as, happening to recline near to Jesus, he must have been eating out of the same dish with Him (for there would be several of such dishes standing on the table). Comp. Grotius. The ἐμβαπτόμενος of Mark xiv. 20 (see on the passage) is not a substantial variation; neither has it been *misunderstood* by Matthew (in opposition to Weiss in the *Stud. u. Krit.* 1861, p. 53 f.), and *converted* by him into a special means of recognition (Holtzmann). The contents of the dish were the broth *charoset* (חרוסת), made out of dates, figs, etc., and of the colour of brick (to remind those who partook of it of the bricks of Egypt, Maimonides, *ad Pesach.* vii. 11). See Buxtorf, *Lex. Talm.* p. 831. — ἐν τῷ τρυβλίῳ] has dipped *in the dish*, into which he has put his hand, holding a piece of bread. Hom. *Od.* ix. 392; Aesch. *Prom.* 863; LXX. Deut. xxxiii. 24; Ruth ii. 14.

Ver. 24. Ὑπάγει] μεταβαίνει ἀπὸ τῆς ἐνταῦθα ζωῆς, Euthymius Zigabenus. Comp. οἴχεσθαι, ἀπέρχεσθαι, הָלַךְ. Jesus is conscious that His death will be a going away to the *Father* (John vii. 33, viii. 22). — καλὸν, κ.τ.λ.] *well would it have been for him,* etc.; for in that case he would not have existed at all, and so would not have been exposed to the severe punishment (of Gehenna) which now awaits him. Comp. Ecclus. xxiii. 14; Job iii. 1 ff.; Jer. xx. 14 ff., and the passages from Rabbinical writers in Wetstein. The expression is a *popular* one, and not to be urged with logical rigour, which it will not admit of. The fundamental idea embodied in it is: "multo melius est non subsistere quam male subsistere," Jerome. Observe, further, the *tragic emphasis* with which ὁ ἄνθρωπος ἐκεῖνος is repeated; but for καλὸν ἦν without ἄν, see Buttmann, *Neut. Gr.* pp. 188, 195 [E. T. 217,

226]; and on οὐ as a negative, where there is only one idea contained in the negation, consult Kühner, II. 2, p. 748; Buttmann, p. 299 [E. T. 347]. Euthymius Zigabenus aptly observes: οὐ διότι προώριστο, διὰ τοῦτο παρέδωκεν· ἀλλὰ διότι παρέδωκε, διὰ τοῦτο προώριστο, τοῦ θεοῦ προειδότος τὸ πάντως ἀποβησόμενον· ἔμελλε γὰρ ὄντως ἀποβῆναι τοιοῦτος οὐ ἐκ φύσεως, ἀλλ᾽ ἐκ προαιρέσεως.

Ver. 25. This final *direct intimation* regarding the betrayer (ὁ παραδιδούς), and addressed to this latter himself, is at variance with John xiii. 26 ff., where ver. 29 presupposes that it had *not* been given. Ver. 25 is an outgrowth of tradition, the absence of which from the older narrative of Mark is unquestionably correct. — σὺ εἶπας] a *Rabbinical* formula by which an emphatic affirmation is made, as in ver. 64. See Schoettgen. There is no such usage in the Old Testament or among classical writers. *At this point* in the narrative of Matthew, just after this declaration on the part of Jesus, we must suppose the *withdrawal* (mentioned at John xiii. 30) of Judas (who, notwithstanding the statement at Luke xxii. 21, was not present at the celebration of the last supper; see on John xiii. 38, Remark) to have taken place. Matthew likewise, at ver. 47, presupposes the withdrawal of the betrayer, though he does not expressly mention it; so that his account of the matter is less precise. The objection, that it was not allowable to leave before the Passover lamb was eaten, is sufficiently disposed of by the *extraordinary* nature of the circumstances in which Judas found himself; but see on ver. 26.

Ver. 26.[1] The meal—having been, naturally enough, interrupted by the discussion regarding Judas—would now be resumed; hence the repetition of the ἐσθιόντων αὐτῶν of ver. 21 with the continuative δέ, which latter is so often used in a similar way after parentheses and other digressions, especially

---

[1] On ver. 26 ff. and the parallel passages, see Ebrard (*Dogma vom heil. Abendm.* I. p. 97 ff.), who also (II. p. 751 ff.) mentions the earlier literature of the subject; see besides, the controversy between Ströbel and Rodatz in the *Luther. Zeitschr.* 1842 ff.; Rückert, *d. Abendm.*, Lpz. 1856, p. 58 ff.; Keim in the *Jahrb. f. D. Theol.* 1859, p. 63 ff.; of modern dogmatic writers, consult, in particular, Kahnis and Philippi. Comp. on Mark xiv. 22 f.; Luke xxii. 19 f.; 1 Cor. xi. 24 f.

in cases where previous expressions are repeated; comp. on
2 Cor. v. 8; Eph. ii. 4. — λαβὼν ὁ 'Ιησ. τ. ἄρτον] According to the Rabbis, the order of the Passover meal was as
follows (see Tr. *Pesach.* c. 10; Otho, *Lex. Rabb.* p. 448 ff.;
Lightfoot, p. 474 ff.; Lund, *Jüd. Heiligth.*, ed. Wolf, p. 1125
ff.; Wichelhaus, p. 248 ff.; Vaihinger in Herzog's *Encykl.* XI.
p. 141 ff.):—(1) It began with drinking wine, before partaking of which, however, the head of the family offered up thanks
for the wine and the return of that sacred day (according
to the school of Sammai, for the day and for the wine).
"Poculum ebibit, et postea benedicit de lotione manuum, et
lavat," Maimonides. (2) Then bitter herbs (מרורים, intended
to represent the bitter life of their forefathers in Egypt) were
put upon the table, some of which being dipped in a sour or
brinish liquid, were eaten amid thanksgivings. (3) The unleavened bread, the broth *charoset* (see on ver. 23), the lamb
and the flesh of the *chagiga* (see on John xviii. 28), were now
presented. (4) Thereupon the head of the family, after a
"*Benedictus, qui creavit fructum terrae*," took as much of the
bitter herbs as might be equal to the size of an olive, dipped
it in the broth *charoset*, and then ate it, all the other guests
following his example. (5) The *second* cup of wine was now
mixed, and at this stage the father, at the request of his son,
or whether requested by him or not, was expected to explain
to him the peculiarities of the several parts of this meal.
(6) This did not take place till the Passover viands had been
put a second time upon the table; then came the singing of
the first part of the *Hallel* (Ps. cxiii., cxiv.), another short
thanksgiving by the father, and the drinking of the second
cup. (7) The father then washed his hands, took two pieces
of bread, broke one of them, laid the broken pieces upon that
which remained whole, repeated the "*Benedictus sit ille, qui
producit panem e terra*," rolled a piece of the broken bread in
bitter herbs, dipped this into the broth *charoset*, and ate, after
having given thanks; he then took some of the *chagiga*, after
another thanksgiving, and so also with regard to the lamb.
(8) The feast was now continued by the guests partaking as
they felt inclined, concluding, however, with the father eating

the last bit of the lamb, which was not to be less than an olive in size, after which no one was at liberty to eat anything more.   The father now washed his hands, and, praise having been offered, the *third* cup (כסא הברכה) was drunk.   Then came the singing of the second part of the *Hallel* (Ps. cxv.–cxviii.) and the drinking of the *fourth* cup, which was, in some instances, followed by a fifth, with the final singing of Ps. cxx.– cxxxvii. (Bartolocc. *Bibl. Rabb.* II. p. 736 ff.). — Seeing that, according to this order, the feasting, strictly speaking, did not begin till No. 8, for all that preceded had the character of a ceremonial introduction to it; seeing, further, that it is in itself improbable that Jesus would interrupt or alter the peculiarly ceremonial part of the feast by an act or utterance in any way foreign to it; and considering, in the last place, that when Judas retired, which he did immediately after he was announced as the betrayer, and therefore previous to the institution of the last supper,—the Passover meal had already extended pretty far on into the night (John xiii. 30),—we must assume that the ἐσθιόντων αὐτῶν of ver. 21, as well as the similar expression in ver. 26, should come in after No. 7, and that the eating under No. 8 is the stage at which the Lord's supper was instituted ; so that the bread which Jesus took and brake would not be that mentioned under No. 7 (Fritzsche), but *the* ἄρτον (with the article, see the critical remarks), the *particular* bread *with which, as they all knew, He had just instituted the supper.*   He would have violated the Passover itself if He had proclaimed any new and peculiar symbolism in connection with the bread before conforming, in the first place, to the popular ceremonial observed at this feast, and before the less formal and peculiarly festive part of the proceedings was reached.   Again, had the breaking and distributing of the bread been that referred to under No. 7, one cannot see why he should not have availed Himself of the bitter herbs as well, furnishing, as they would have done, so appropriate a symbol of the suffering inseparable from His death. — καὶ εὐλογήσας] *after having repeated a blessing*—whether the "*Benedictus ille, qui producit panem e terra*" (comp. No. 7 above), or some other more appropriate to the particular act about to be performed, it is impossible to say. The latter, however, is the more probable, as it would be more in accordance with the very special nature of Christ's feelings and intention on this occasion. Now that the meal was drawing to a close (before the second part of the *Hallel* was sung, ver. 30), He felt a desire to introduce at the end a special repast of significance so profound as never to be forgotten. The idea that His εὐλογεῖν, as being the expression of His omnipotent will (Philippi, p. 467 ff.), possessed *creative* power, so that the body and blood became *realized* in the giving of bread and wine, may no doubt accord with the orthodox view of the sacrament, but can be as little justified, on exegetical grounds, as that orthodox view itself; even in 1 Cor. x. 16 nothing more is implied than a eucharistical *consecration prayer* for the purpose of setting apart bread and wine to a sacred use. — It is, further, impossible to determine whether by καὶ ἐδίδου τοῖς μαθητ. we are to understand the handing of the bread piece by piece, or simply the presenting of it all at once upon a plate. Considering, however, that the guests were *reclining*, the latter is the more probable view, and is quite in keeping with the λάβετε. This λάβετε denotes simply a taking with the hand, which then conveys to the mouth the thing so taken, not also a taking in a *spiritual* sense (Ebrard). Further, it must not be inferred from the words before us, nor from our Lord's interpretation (*my body*) of the bread which He presents, that He *Himself* had not eaten of it. See on ver. 29. He must, however, be regarded as having done so before handing it to the disciples, and before uttering the following words. — τοῦτό ἐστι τὸ σῶμά μου] There can be no doubt that τοῦτο is the subject, and (avoiding the Lutheran synecdoche) can only refer to *the bread that was being handed to them*, and not to the living body of Christ (Carlstadt), nor to the predicate which first follows (Ströbel), while it is equally certain that no emphasis of any kind is to be laid upon the enclitic μου (in opposition to Olshausen and Stier). But seeing, moreover, that the body of Jesus was still unbroken (still living), and that, as yet, His blood had not been shed, none of the guests can have supposed what, on the occasion of the first celebration of the supper, was, accordingly, a plain impossibility, viz., that they were *in reality* eating and drinking the *very* body and blood of the Lord,[1] and seeing also that, for the reason just stated, Jesus Himself could not have intended His simple words to be understood in a sense which they did not then admit of,—for to suppose any essential difference between the first and every subsequent observance of the supper (Schmid, *Bibl. Theol.* I. p. 341 ; Thomasius, *Chr. Pers. u. Werk*, III. 2, p. 62 ; Stier ; Gess, I. p. 167) is to have recourse to an expedient that is not only unwarrantable, but extremely questionable (see, on the other hand, Tholuck in the *Stud. u. Krit.* 1869, p. 126 f.), and because, so long as the idea of the κρέας is not taken into account, any substantial partaking of the σῶμα alone and by itself, without the αἷμα, appears utterly inconceivable ;[2] for here, again, the idea of a *spiritual* body, which it is supposed Jesus might even *then* have communicated (Olshausen ; Rodatz in the *Luther. Zeitschr.* 1843, 3, p. 56 ; Kahnis, *Abendm.* p. 453 ; Hofmann ; Schoeberlein, *üb. d. heil. Abendm.* 1869, p. 66), belongs entirely to the region of non-exegetical and docetic fancies, for which even the transfiguration furnishes no support whatever (see on 1 Cor. x. 16), and is inconsistent with the αἷμα (1 Cor. xv. 50 ; Phil. iii. 21):

---

[1] Wetstein well observes : "Non quaerebant utrum panis, quem videbant, panis esset, vel utrum aliud corpus inconspicuum in interstitiis, panis delitesceret, sed *quid haec actio significaret, cujus rei esset repraesentatio aut memoriale.*" Thomasius, however, as above, p. 61, finds no other way of disposing of the *simple impossibility* referred to, but by maintaining that this giving of Himself on the part of the Lord was of the nature of a *miracle.* Comp. Hofmann, *Schriftbew.* II. 2, p. 215, also Philippi, p. 433 f., who is at the same time disposed to assume that the Spirit illuminated the minds of the disciples as with lightning flash. The supposition of a miracle is certainly the *last* resort, and this on exegetical grounds is wholly unjustifiable in a case in which neither the narrative itself nor the thing narrated implies a miracle.

[2] In reply to the question why Jesus distributes the body and blood *separately,* Thomasius, p. 68, has no answer but this : "I do not know." We are accordingly met on the one hand with the assertion of a *miracle,* on the other with a *non liquet.* This is the way difficulties are supposed to be got over, but they remain, and continue to assert themselves all the same. There ought to be no hesitation in conceding that the *separate* participation, namely, of the body *without* the blood, and then of the blood by *itself,* is not to be understood as an actual eating and drinking of them, but as due to the symbolism based upon the circumstance of the body being put to death and the blood shed.

it follows that ἐστί is neither more nor less than the *copula of the symbolic statement:*[1] " *This*, which ye are to take and eat, this broken bread,[2] *is*, symbolically speaking, *my body*," —the body, namely, which is on the point of being put to death as a λύτρον ἀντὶ πολλῶν (xx. 28). The symbolical interpretation has also been correctly adhered to by David Schulz, de Wette, Julius Müller, Bleek, Rückert, Keim, Weizsäcker ; comp. Ewald, Morison, Weiss on *Mark*, and others. According to Matthew, as also according to Paul (1 Cor. xi. 24, where κλώμενον is spurious), Jesus omits entirely the *tertium comparationis*, — an omission, however, which in itself is more in keeping with the vivid symbolism of the passage and the deep emotion of our Lord. The symbolical *act* of *breaking*, which cannot possibly have anything to do with the *glorified* body, but which refers solely to that which was about to be put to death, was sufficient to enable us to perceive in this *breaking* what the point of comparison was ; for the breaking of the bread and the putting to death of the body resemble each other in so

[1] In the case of Luke and Paul, the necessity of adopting the symbolical interpretation of ἐστί shows itself above all (1) in the words used with reference to the cup (ἡ καινὴ διαθήκη). The new covenant has been made in and through the *actual* blood of Christ. This blood, inasmuch as it has been *shed*, is the essential objective *causa effectiva* of the covenant. It is so in virtue of the *historical fact of the shedding*, while it is this same fact that justifies its being designated a new covenant (John xi. 25). The wine poured into the cup can be said to be the blood of Christ as it *actually* was after being shed on the cross, only *in so far* as it *represents* that real covenant-blood as it was *previous* to its being shed, and with the *near* prospect of its shedding fully in view ; it *is* this blood, but only in the sense warranted by a profound vivid *symbolism*. (2) It is on the strength of this symbolical interpretation that Luke and Paul would appear to have added the expression εἰς τ. ἐμὴν ἀνάμνησιν to the words of the institution. See on Luke xxii. 19 f. The ἀνάμνησις denotes *a realizing of that as present* which is *no longer so* in bodily form.

[2] Not : that which I here hand to you *in the form* of bread (the *Catholic* view), nor : that which I here hand to you *in*, *with*, *and under the covenant* (the synecdoche of *Lutheran* orthodoxy). The doctrine of the *omnipresence* of Christ's body is inconsistent with the essential idea of a body, as was pointed out as early as the time of the Fathers, especially by Augustine : "Cavendum enim est, ne ita divinitatem adstruamus hominis, ut veritatem corporis auferamus," Augustine, *ep.* 57, *ad Dardan.* ; they understood the body of Christ to be in heaven, where it always remained.

far as the connection of the whole is violently destroyed, so
that the bread in fragments can no longer be said to be
the bread, nor the body when put to death to be any
longer a living being.[1] The *eating* (and the *drinking*),
on the other hand, is a symbol of the reception and
appropriation, in saving faith (John vi. 51 ff.), of the
atoning and redeeming virtue inherent in the death of the
body (Paul as above : τὸ ὑπὲρ ὑμῶν) and in the shedding of
the blood of Jesus ; so that the act of receiving the elements
in the consciousness of this, establishes a κοινωνία with the
body and blood that is *spiritually* living and active, and
therefore, in all ethical respects, genuine and real (see on
1 Cor. x. 16),—a fellowship in which the believing communicant realizes in his inward experience that the divine-human
life of the crucified Redeemer is being imparted to him with
saving efficacy, and in which he acquires a full assurance of
eternal life. With regard to the divers views that have
prevailed upon this point in the church, and of which the
two held by Protestants do not admit of being harmonized
without sacrificing their distinctive peculiarities (in opposition
to Ebrard, Lange), it may be said that those of the Catholics
and Lutherans are *exegetically* at one in so far as their interpretation of the ἐστί is concerned, for they agree in regarding
it as the *copula of actual being ;* it is only when they attempt
a more precise *dogmatic* definition of the *mode* of this actual
being that the divergence begins to show itself. Similarly,
there is no difference of an *exegetical* nature (Rodatz in Rudel-
bach's *Zeitschr.* 1843, 4, p. 11) between the interpretation
of Zwingli (and Oecolampadius) and that of Calvin ("externum
signum dicitur id esse, quod figurat," Calvin). On the rela-

---

[1] Philippi, p. 422 ff., is wrong in refusing to admit that the point of comparison lies in the breaking. The ἔκλασε is the circumstance above all which
the whole four evangelists agree in recording, making it appear, too, from
the terms they employ, that it was regarded as a special act. Moreover, the
fact that at a very early period the spurious κλώμενον of 1 Cor. xi. 24 had
come to be extensively adopted, may be regarded as affording evidence in
favour of the correctness of the church's interpretation of this symbolical
act. The same view is implied in the reading θρυπτόμενον ; comp. *Constitt.
Ap.* viii. 12. 16.

tion of Luther's doctrine to that of Calvin, see Julius Müller's
dogmat. Abh. p. 404 ff. For ἐστί (which, however, Jesus
would not express in Aramaic, His words probably being
הָא נִשְׂמִי) as a copula of symbolical or allegorical being, comp.
xiii. 38 f.; Luke xii. 1; John x. 6, xiv. 6; Gal. iv. 24; Heb.
x. 20; Rev. i. 20.—That Jesus might also have used σάρξ
instead of σῶμα (comp. John vi.) is clear; in that case prominence would have been given to the material of which the
σῶμα is composed (comp. Col. i. 22). Comp. Rückert, p. 69.
But it would not have been proper to use κρέας (dead flesh,
the flesh of what has been slain, Rom. xiv. 21; 1 Cor. viii.
13; see Schulz, *Abendm.* p. 94).

Ver. 27. Matthew says indefinitely: a cup, for τό before
ποτήρ. is spurious. Luke and Paul are somewhat more
precise, inasmuch as they speak of the cup as having been the
one which was presented μετὰ τὸ δειπνῆσαι. Accordingly, the
cup in question here is usually understood to have been the
poculum benedictionis, referred to above under No. 8, the *third*
cup. But in that case what becomes of the *fourth* one, over
which the second part of the *Hallel* was sung? As it is
not likely that this latter would be omitted; as it is no less
improbable that Jesus, after investing the cup now under consideration with the symbolism of His blood, would have sent
round another after it with which no such symbolical significance was associated; as ver. 29 expressly forbids the supposition of another cup having followed; and as, in the last
place, mention is made of the *Hallel* (the second portion of it)
as coming immediately after the drinking of this one,—we are
bound to suppose that it is the *fourth* cup that is here meant,
and in regard to which Maimonides (as quoted by Lightfoot)
observes: "*Deinde miscet poculum quartum, et super illud
perficit Hallel, additque insuper benedictionem cantici* (ברכת השיר),
quod est: Laudent te, Domine, omnia opera tua, etc., *et dicit:
Benedictus sit, qui creavit fructum vitis,—et postea non quic-
quam gustat ista nocte.*" Paul, no doubt, expressly calls the cup
used at the supper τὸ ποτήριον τῆς εὐλογίας (1 Cor. x. 16),
which corresponds with the name of the *third* cup (see on
ver. 26); but, as the epexegetical ὃ εὐλογοῦμεν shows, this

designation is not a *terminus technicus taken from the Jewish
ritual*, but it is to be traced to the *Christian* standpoint, in
fact, to the Christian act of *consecration*. See on 1 Cor. x.
16. — For the size of the Passover cups, and what is said
about the wine being red and mixed with water, consult
Grotius and Lightfoot. In the *Constitt. Ap.* viii. 12. 16,
Christ Himself is even spoken of as τὸ ποτήριον κεράσας ἐξ
οἴνου καὶ ὕδατος. — εὐχαριστ.] is substantially the same as
εὐλογ., ver. 26, which latter has reference to the *phraseology* of
the prayer (*benedictus*, etc.), comp. xiv. 19 ; Luke xxiv. 30 ;
Acts xxvii. 35 ; 1 Tim. iv. 3 f. ; Matt. xv. 36. The ברכה was
a thanksgiving prayer. Comp. on 1 Cor. xiv. 16.

Ver. 28. The death-symbolism is now applied to that which
contains the life (Gen. ix. 4 ff., and comp. on Acts xv.), viz.
the blood, which is described as *sacrificial blood* that is to
be shed in order to make atonement. Neither here nor anywhere else in the New Testament (Heb. xii. 24 not excepted)
can there be any question of the *glorified* blood of Christ.
Comp. on ver. 26, and on 1 Cor. x. 16. According to New
Testament ideas, *glorified* blood is as much a *contradictio in
adjecto* as glorified flesh. This also in opposition to Hofmann,
p. 220. — τοῦτο] *this*, which ye are about to drink, the wine
which is in this cup. Although this wine was red, it must not
be supposed that the point of the symbolism lay in the *colour*
(Wetstein, Paulus), but in the circumstance of *its being poured out*
(see below : τὸ π. πολλ. ἐκχυνόμ.) into the cup ; the outpouring
is the symbolical correlative to the breaking in the case of the
bread. — γάρ] *justifies* the πίετε . . . πάντες, on the ground
of the *interpretation* given to that which is about to be drunk.
— ἐστί] as in ver. 26. — τὸ αἷμά μου τῆς διαθήκης] This
is the preferable reading ; see the critical remarks. " *This is my
blood of the covenant*," my covenant blood (דַּם הַבְּרִית, Ex. xxiv. 8),
my blood which serves to ratify the covenant with God. This
is conceived of as *sacrificial* blood (in opposition to Hofmann).
See Delitzsch on Heb. ix. 20. In a similar way Moses ratified
the covenant with God by means of the sacrificial blood of an
animal, Ex. xxiv. 6 ff. On the double genitive with only one
noun, see Fritzsche, *Quaest. Luc.* p. 111 f. ; Lobeck, *ad Aj.* 309 ;

Winer, p. 180 [E. T. 239]. For the arrangement of the words, comp. Thuc. iv. 85. 2 : τῇ τε ἀποκλήσει μου τῶν πυλῶν. The connecting of the μου with αἷμα corresponds to the τὸ σῶμά μου of ver. 26, as well as to the amplified form of our Lord's words as given by Luke and Paul ; consequently we must not, with Rückert, connect the pronoun with τ. διαθήκης (the blood of my covenant). The covenant which Jesus has in view is that of *grace*, in accordance with Jer. xxxi. 31 ff., hence called the *new* one (by Paul and Luke) in contradistinction to the old one under the *law*. See on 1 Cor. xi. 26. — τὸ περὶ πολλῶν ἐκχυν. εἰς ἄφεσιν ἁμαρτιῶν] Epexegesis of τὸ αἷμά μου τῆς διαθήκης, by way of indicating who are to participate in the covenant (περὶ πολλῶν), the divine benefit conferred upon them (εἰς ἄφεσ. ἁμαρτ.), and the means by which the covenant is ratified (ἐκχυνόμ.) : *which is shed* (expressing as present what, though future, is near and certain) *for the benefit of many*, inasmuch as it becomes *instrumental* in procuring the *forgiveness of sins*. The last part of this statement, and consequently what is implied in it, viz. the *atoning* purpose contemplated by the shedding of blood (comp. Lev. xvii. 11), is to be understood as setting forth more precisely the idea expressed by περί. It must not be supposed, however, that ὑπέρ, which is used by Luke instead of περί, is essentially different from the latter; but is to be distinguished from it only in respect of the different moral basis on which the idea contained in it rests (like the German *um* and *über*), so that both the prepositions are often interchanged in cases where they have exactly one and the same reference, as in Demosthenes especially. See generally, on Gal. i. 4 ; 1 Cor. i. 13, xv. 3. — The shedding of the blood is the *objective medium* of the forgiveness of sins ; the *subjective* medium, viz. *faith*, is contained *by implication* in the use made in this instance, as in xx. 28 (see on the passage), of πολλῶν, as well as in the symbolic reference of the πίετε. — It is to be observed, further, that the *genuineness* of the words εἰς ἄφεσ. ἁμαρτ. is put beyond all suspicion by the unexceptionable evidence in their favour (in opposition to David Schulz), although, from their being omitted in every other record of the

institution of the supper (also in Justin, *Ap*. i. 66, *c. Tr*. 70),
they should not be regarded as having been originally spoken
by Christ, but as an explanatory addition introduced into the
tradition, and put into the mouth of Jesus.

REMARK 1.—That Jesus meant to institute a regular ordinance
to be similarly observed by His church in all time coming, is not
apparent certainly from the narrative in Matthew and Mark;
but it is doubtless to be inferred from 1 Cor. xi. 24–26, no less
than from the practice of the apostolic church, that the apostles
were convinced that such was the intention of our Lord, so
much so, that to the words of the institution themselves was
added that express injunction to repeat the observance εἰς τ.
ἐμὴν ἀνάμνησιν which Paul and Luke have recorded.   As bearing
upon this matter, Paul's declaration: παρέλαβον ἀπὸ τοῦ κυρίου, ver.
23, is of such decisive importance that there can no longer be
any doubt (Rückert, p. 124 ff.) as to whether Jesus intended to
institute an ordinance for future observance.   We cannot, therefore, endorse the view that the repetition of the observance was
due to the impression made upon the minds of the grateful
disciples by the first celebration of the supper (Paulus, comp.
also Weisse, *Evangelienfr.* p. 195).

REMARK 2.—The two most recent and exhaustive Protestant
monographs treating of the Lord's supper on the lines of the Confessions, but also discussing the subject exegetically, are : Ebrard,
das Dogma vom heil. Abendm., Frankf. 1845 f., as representing the
Reformed view, and Kahnis, *d. Lehre vom Abendm.*, Lpz. 1851,
as representing the *Lutheran.*   Rückert, on the other hand, *d.
Abendm., s. Wesen u. s. Gesch.* (Lpz. 1856), ignores the Confessions
altogether, and proceeds on purely exegetical principles.   The
result at which Ebrard arrives, p. 110 (comp. what he says,
Olshausen's *Leidensgesch.* 1862, p. 103), is as follows: " The
breaking of the bread is a memorial of the death of Jesus; the
eating of the bread thus broken is a symbolical act denoting
that this death is appropriated by the believer through his
fellowship with the life of Christ.   But inasmuch as Jesus
gives the bread to be eaten and the wine to be drunk, and
inasmuch as He declares those substances to be pledges of the
new covenant in His blood, the bread and the wine are, therefore, *not mere symbols*, but they assume that he who partakes
of them is an actual *sharer* in the atonement brought about
by the death of Christ.   And since such a fellowship with
Christ's death cannot exist apart from fellowship with His life ;

since, in other words," the new covenant "consists in an *actual connection and union*,—it follows that partaking of the Lord's supper involves as its result a true, personal central union and fellowship of life with Christ." The result at which Kahnis arrives in his above-cited work published in 1851 [1] is the orthodox Lutheran view, and is as follows : " The body which Christ gives us to feed upon in the supper is the same that was broken for us on the cross,—just as *its* substratum, the bread, was broken,—with a view to its being eaten. The blood which Christ gives us to drink in the supper is the same that was shed for us on the cross,—just as its substratum, the wine, was poured out,—with a view to its being drunk " (p. 104). He comes back to Luther's *synecdoche* in regard to τοῦτο, which latter he takes as representing the concrete union of two substances, the one of which, viz. the bread, constitutes the embodiment and medium of the other (the body); the former he understands to be, logically speaking, only *accidental* in its nature, the *essential* substance being brought out in the predicate. As for the second element, he considers that it expresses the identity of the communion blood with the blood of the atoning sacrifice, and that not in respect of the function, but of the thing itself (for he regards it as an arbitrary distinction to say that the former blood ratifies, and that the latter

---

[1] In his *Dogmatik*, however (1861), I. pp. 516, 616 ff., II. p. 657 ff., Kahnis candidly acknowledges the shortcomings of the Lutheran view, and the necessity of correcting them, and manifests, at the same time, a decided leaning in the direction of the Reformed doctrine. The supper, he says, "*is the medium of imparting to the believing communicant, in bread and wine, the atoning efficacy of the body and blood of Christ that have been sacrificed for us, which atoning efficacy places him to whom it is imparted in mysterious fellowship with the body of Christ.*" Kahnis now rejects, in particular, the Lutheran *synecdoche*, and approves of the symbolical interpretation in so far as bread and wine, being symbols of Christ's body and blood, constitute, in virtue of the act of institution, that sacramental word concerning our Lord's body and blood which when emitted by Christ has the effect of conveying the benefits of His death. He expresses himself more clearly in II. p. 557, where he says: "The Lord's supper is the sacrament of the altar which, in the form of bread and wine, the symbols of the body and blood of Christ, which have been sacrificed for us, imparts to the believing communicant the sin-forgiving efficacy of Christ's death." Those divinely-appointed symbols he regards as the *visible word* concerning Christ's body and blood, which word, as the terms of the institution indicate, is the medium through which the atoning power of His death, *i.e.* the forgiveness of sins, is communicated. From the bread and wine Christ is supposed to create a eucharistic corporeality, which He employs as the medium for the communication of Himself.

propitiates); and that, accordingly, the reality in point of efficacy which, in the words of the institution, is ascribed to the
latter necessarily implies a corresponding efficacy in regard to
the former.—By adopting the *kind* of exegesis that has been
employed in establishing the strictly *Lutheran* view, it would
not be difficult to make out a case in favour of that doctrine of
transubstantiation and the *mass* which is still keenly but
awkwardly maintained by Schegg, and which finds an abler
but no less arbitrary and mistaken advocate in Döllinger
(*Christenth. u. Kirche*, pp. 37 ff., 248 ff., ed. 2), because in both
cases the results are based upon the application of the exegetical method to *dogmatic* premises. — Then, in the last place,
Rückert arrives at the conclusion that, as far as Matthew and
Mark are concerned, the whole stress is intended to be laid
upon the *actions*, that these are to be understood *symbolically*,
and that the *words* spoken serve only as hints to enable us to
interpret the actions aright. He thinks that the idea of an
actual eating of the body or drinking of the blood never crossed
the mind either of Jesus or of the disciples ; that it was Paul
who, in speculating as to the meaning of the *material substances*,
began to attach to them a higher importance, and to entertain
the view that in the supper worthy and unworthy alike were
partakers of the *body and blood of Christ* in the *supersensual*
and *heavenly* form in which he conceived them to exist subsequent to the Lord's ascension. In this way, according to
Rückert, Paul entered upon a line of interpretation for which
sufficient justification cannot be found either in what was done
or in what was spoken by our Lord, so that his view has furnished the germs of a version of the matter which, so far at least
as its beneficial results are concerned, does not tell in his favour
(p. 242). In answer to Rückert in reference to Paul, see on
1 Cor. x. 16.

REMARK 3.—As for the *different versions of the words of the
institution* that are to be met with in the four evangelists, that
of Mark is the most concise (Matthew's coming next), and, considering the situation (for when the mind is full and deeply
moved the words are few) and the connection of this evangelist
with Peter, it is to be regarded as the most original. Yet the
supplementary statements furnished by the others are ser-
viceable in the way of exposition, for they let us see what
view was taken of the nature of the Lord's supper in the
apostolic age, as is pre-eminently the case with regard to the
τοῦτο ποιεῖτε εἰς τ. ἐμὴν ἀνάμνησιν of Paul and Luke. Comp. on Luke
xxii. 19. According to Gess, I. p. 147, the variations in question

are to be accounted for by supposing that, while the elements
were circulating, Jesus Himself made use of a variety of expressions. But there can be no doubt that on an occasion of such
painful emotion He would utter the few thoughtful words He
made use of only *once for all.* This is the only view that can
be said to be in keeping with the sad and sacred nature of the
situation, especially as the texts do not lead us to suppose that
there was any further speaking; comp., in particular, Mark
xiv. 23, 24.

Ver. 29. The certainty and nearness of His death, which
had just been expressed in the symbolism of the wine, impel
Jesus to add a sorrowful but yet comforting assurance
(introducing it with the continuative *autem*). — ὅτι οὐ μὴ
πίω] *that I will certainly not drink.* According to the
synoptic conception of the meal as being the one in connection
with the Passover, this presupposes that the cup mentioned at
ver. 27 f. was the last one of the meal (the fourth), and not
the one before the last. For it may be held as certain that,
at this feast above all, and considering His present frame of
mind, He would take care not to give offence by omitting the
fourth Passover-cup ; and what reason, it may be asked, would
He have had for doing so ? The cup in question was the
concluding one, during the drinking of which the second portion
of the *Hallel* was sung (ver. 30). — ἀπάρτι] *from this present
occasion,* on which I have just drunk of it. To suppose that
Jesus Himself did not also partake of the cup (Olshausen, de
Wette, Rückert, Weiss) is a gratuitous assumption, incompatible with the ordinary Passover usage. We are to understand the drinking on the part of Jesus as having taken place
after the εὐχαριστήσας, ver. 27, before He handed the cup to
the disciples, and announced to them the symbolical significance that was to be attached to it. Comp. Chrysostom.
Matthew does not mention this circumstance, because he did
not regard it as forming part of the *symbolism* here in view.
Euthymius Zigabenus correctly observes : εἰ δὲ τοῦ ποτηρίου
μετέσχε, μετέλαβεν ἄρα καὶ τοῦ ἄρτου. Comp. on ver. 26. —
ἐκ τούτου τοῦ γεννήμ. τ. ἀμπ.] *τούτου* is emphatic, and
points to the *Passover* - wine. Mark and Luke are less

precise, not having τούτου. From this it must not be
assumed that Jesus never drank any wine after His resurrection. Acts x. 41 ; Ignat. *Smyrn.* 3. For γέννημα as used
by later Greek writers (likewise the LXX.) in the sense of
καρπός, see Lobeck, *ad Phryn.* p. 286. For the reasons for
rejecting the reading γενήματος (Lachmann, Tischendorf), notwithstanding the far greater number of testimonies in its
favour, see Fritzsche on *Mark*, p. 619 f. The use of this term
instead of οἶνος has something *solemn* about it, containing,
as it does, an allusion to the form of thanksgiving for the
Passover wine : " benedictus sit, qui creavit *fructum vitis.*"
Comp. Lightfoot on ver. 27. — καινόν] *novum,* different
in respect of quality ; " novitatem dicit plane singularem,"
Bengel ; not *recens, νέον.* This conception of the new Passover
wine, which is to be the product of the coming aeon and of the
glorified κτίσις, is connected with the idea of the renewal of
the world in view of the Messianic kingdom. Luke xxii. 16,
comp. ver. 30. To understand the new celebration of the
Passover in the perfected kingdom only in a figurative sense,
corresponding somewhat to the feasts of the patriarchs, alluded
to at viii. 11 (" vos aliquando mecum in coelo summa laetitia
et felicitate perfruemini," Kuinoel, Neander), would, in presence
of such a characteristic allusion to the Passover, be as arbitrary
on the one hand as the referring of the expression (Chrysostom, Euthymius Zigabenus, Münster, Clarius) *to the period
subsequent to the resurrection of Jesus* (Acts x. 41) would be
erroneous on the other, and that on account of the τούτου and
the words ἐν τῇ βασιλ. τ. π. μ., which can only be intended
to designate *the kingdom of Messiah.* It is wrong to take
καινόν, as Kuinoel and Fritzsche have done, in the sense of
iterum, for it is a characteristic predicate of the *wine* that it is
here in question ; besides, had it been otherwise, we should
have had *anew*: ἐκ καινῆς, Thuc. iii. 92. 5, or the ordinary
πάλιν of the New Testament.

Ver. 30. Ὑμνήσαντες] namely, the second portion of the
Hallel (Ps. cxv.–cxviii.). See Buxtorf, *Lex. Talm.* p. 613 f.
Jesus also took part in the singing. Comp. Justin, *c. Tr.* 106.
— ἐξῆλθον, κ.τ.λ.] The regulation (comp. Ex. xii. 22), which

required that this night should be spent in the city (Lightfoot, p. 564), appears not to have been universally complied with. See *Tosapht in Pesach.* 8 in Lightfoot, *minister. templi*, p. 727. Ver. 31. Τότε] whilst they were going out, ver. 36. — πάντες] put first so as to be highly emphatic. — σκανδαλ.] Comp. on xi. 6. In this instance it means : instead of standing faithfully by me till the last, ye will be cowardly enough to run away and leave me to my fate, and thus show that your faith has not been able to bear the brunt of the struggle. Comp. John xvi. 32. See ver. 56. With what painful astonishment these words must have filled the disciples, sincerely conscious as they were of their faithful devotion to their Master! Accordingly this announcement is followed up with quoting the prediction in which the tragic event is foretold. The passage here introduced with γέγρ. γάρ is from Zech. xiii. 7 (quoted with great freedom). In the shepherd who, according to this passage, is to be smitten, Jesus sees a typical representation of *Himself* as devoted to death by God, so that the words cannot have had reference (Ewald, Hitzig) to the foolish shepherd (ch. xi. 15 ff.), but only to the one appointed by God Himself (Hofmann), whose antitype is Jesus, and His disciples the scattered sheep; comp. Hengstenberg, *Christol.* III. 1, p. 528.

Ver. 32 f. Προειπὼν τὰ λυπηρὰ, προλέγει καὶ τὰ παραμυθούμενα, Euthymius Zigabenus.—They were again to gather around Him in Galilee, the native scene of His ministry. Comp. xxviii. 10. The *authenticity* of these words in their present form may be called in question, in so far as Christ cannot have predicted His resurrection in such explicit terms. See on xvi. 21. The answer of Peter, given in the bold self-confidence of his love, savours somewhat of self-exaltation ; consequently the impression made upon him by the experience of his shortcomings was all the deeper.

Ver. 34 f. Πρὶν ἀλέκτορα φωνῆσαι] *before a cock crows*, therefore before the day begins to dawn. Cock-crowing occurs in the third of the four night watches (see on xiv. 24), which watch lasted from midnight till about three o'clock, and is called ἀλεκτοροφωνία in Mark xiii. 35. For the opposite

of the πρὶν ἀλ. φων., see Plat. *Symp.* p. 223 C : πρὸς ἡμέραν
ἤδη ἀλεκτρυόνων ᾀδόντων ; Lucian, *Ocyp.* 670 : ἐπεὶ δ᾽ ἀλέκτωρ
ἡμέραν ἐσάλπισεν ; Horace, *Sat.* i. 1. 10. For a later modification of the expression in conformity with the repeated
denials, see Mark xiv. 30. On the question as to whether
or not ἀλέκτωρ can be considered good Greek, consult Lobeck,
ad Phryn. p. 228 f. This prediction as to the time was subsequently confirmed *by the actual crowing of a cock*, ver. 74. —
ἀπαρνήσῃ με] *thou wilt deny me*, deny that I am thy
Lord and Master. Comp. Celsus in Origen, ii. 45 : οὔτε
συναπέθανον οὔτε ὑπεραπέθανον αὐτοῦ, οὐδὲ κολάσεων κατα-
φρονεῖν ἐπείσθησαν, ἀλλὰ καὶ ἠρνήσαντο εἶναι μαθηταί. For
σὺν σοὶ ἀποθ., comp. John xi. 16. — ἀπαρνήσομαι] The
future after οὐ μή (see Hartung, *Partikell.* p. 157 ; Winer,
p. 471 f. [E. T. 635]) is rather more expressive of a confident
assertion than the *subjunctive*, the reading of A E G, etc. —
ὁμοίως καὶ πάντες, κ.τ.λ.] Considering the sincere but as
yet untried love of each, this is not an improbable statement,
though it is found only in Matthew and Mark.

Ver. 36. Γεθσημανῆ or, according to a still better attested
form, Γεθσημανεί (Lachmann, Tischendorf), is most likely
the Greek equivalent of the Hebrew גַּת שֶׁמֶן, *an oil-press*. It
was a plot of ground (χωρίον, John iv. 5 ; Acts i. 18, iv.
34, v. 3, xxviii. 7), perhaps a small estate with a garden
(John xviii. 1) ; according to Keim, an olive-yard where
nobody lived. If the place was not public property, Jesus,
according to John xix. 2, must have been on friendly terms
with the owner. On the place (the present *Dschesmanije*),
which subsequent tradition has fixed upon as the site of the
ancient Gethsemane, see Robinson, *Pal.* I. p. 389 ; Tobler,
d. Siloahquelle u. d. Oelberg, 1852. — αὐτοῦ] *here ;* the only
other instances in the New Testament are found in Acts xv.
34, xviii. 19, xxi. 4 ; of frequent occurrence in classical
writers. — ἐκεῖ] pointing toward the place.

Ver. 37 f. Anticipating the inward struggle that awaited
Him, He retired farther into the garden, taking with Him none
(xvii. 1) but the three most intimate disciples. — ἤρξατο]
indicating the *first symptoms* of the condition in question. —

λυπεῖσθαι κ. ἀδημονεῖν] Climax. Suidas explains ἀδημον. as meaning: λίαν λυπεῖσθαι. See Buttmann, *Lexilog.* II. p. 135 f.; Ael. *V. H.* xiii. 3; Phil. ii. 26. — περίλυπος] *very sorrowful*, Ps. xliii. 5; 3 Esdr. viii. 71 f.; Isocr. p. 11 B; Aristot. *Eth.* iv. 3; Diog. L. vii. 97. The opposite of this is περιχαρής. — ἡ ψυχή μου] Comp. John xii. 27; Xen. *Hell.* iv. 4. 3: ἀδημονῆσαι τὰς ψυχάς. The soul, the intermediate element through which the spirit (τὸ πνεῦμα, ver. 41) is connected with the body in the unity of the individual (see Beck, *Bibl. Seelenl.* p. 11), is the seat of pleasure and pain. Comp. Stirm in the *Tüb. Zeitschr.* 1834, 3, p. 25 ff. — ἕως θανάτου] defining the extent of the περίλυπος : *unto death*, so as almost to cause death, so that I am nearly dead from very grief; Jonah iv. 9; Isa. xxxviii. 1; and see on Phil. ii. 27. The idea of the mors *infernalis* (Calovius), as though Christ had been experiencing the *pains of hell*, is here exegetically unwarrantable. Euthymius Zigabenus correctly observes : φανερώτερον ἐξαγορεύει τὴν ἀσθένειαν τῆς φύσεως ὡς ἄνθρωπος. — μείνατε . . . ἐμοῦ] "In magnis tentationibus juvat solitudo, sed tamen, ut in propinquo sint amici," Bengel.

Ver. 39. Μικρόν] belongs to προελθών : *after He had gone forward a short distance.* For μικρόν comp. Xen. *Cyrop.* iv. 2. 6 (μικρὸν πορευθέντες); *Hist. Gr.* vii. 2. 13 (μικρὸν δ' αὐτοὺς προπέμψαντες). — ἐπὶ πρόσωπον αὐτοῦ] The article was not necessary before πρόσωπ. (in opposition to Fritzsche, who takes αὐτοῦ as meaning *there*). Comp. xi. 10, xvii. 6, and elsewhere. Winer, p. 116 [E. T. 152]. Bengel appropriately observes : "*in faciem*, non modo in *genua ;* summa demissio." — εἰ δυνατόν ἐστι] ethical possibility according to the divine purpose. Similarly the popular expression πάντα δυνατά σοι is to be understood, according to the sense in which Jesus uses it, as implying the necessary condition of harmony with the divine will. — τὸ ποτήριον τοῦτο] *i.e.* this suffering and death immediately before me. Comp. xx. 22. — πλὴν οὐχ, κ.τ.λ.] The wish, to which in His human dread of suffering He gave utterance, that, if possible, He should not be called upon to endure it (ἔδειξε τὸ ἀνθρώπινον,

Chrysostom), at once gives place to absolute submission, John v. 30, vi. 38. The word to be understood after σύ (θέλεις) is not γενέσθω, but, as corresponding with the οὐχ (not μή, observe), γενήσεται, or ἔσται, in which the petitioner *expresses his final determination.* It may be observed further, that the broken utterance is in keeping with the deep emotion of our Lord. —For ὡς, which, so far as the essential meaning is concerned, is identical with the relative pronoun, comp. Hermann, *ad Hom. h. in Cer.* 172.

Ver. 40. The fact that the *disciples* slept, and that *these* disciples did so in circumstances such as the *present,* and that all *three* gave way, and that their sleep proved to be of so *overpowering* a character, is, notwithstanding Luke's explanation that it was ἀπὸ τῆς λύπης (xxii. 45), a psychological mystery, although, after utterances of Jesus so manifestly authentic as those of vv. 40 and 45, the statement that they did sleep is not to be regarded as *unhistorical,* but is to be taken as implying that Jesus had spent a considerable time in prayer, and that the disciples, in consequence of their deep mental exhaustion, found it impossible to keep awake. — καί] three times; the narrative is characterized by a simple pathos. — τῷ Πέτρῳ] to *him* He addressed words that were equally applicable to them *all ;* but then it was *he* who a little ago had surpassed all the others in so boldly declaring how much he was prepared to do for his Master, vv. 33, 35. — οὕτως] *siccine, thus,* uttered with painful surprise, is to be taken in connection with what follows, without inserting a separate mark of interrogation (in opposition to Euthymius Zigabenus and Beza). Comp. 1 Cor. vi. 5.

Ver. 41. Ἵνα] indicating, not the *object* of the προσεύχεσθε, but *purpose,* and that of the *watching and praying.* — εἰσέλθητε εἰς πειρασμόν] in order that ye may not be betrayed into circumstances in which ye might be led to show yourselves unfaithful to me (into the σκανδαλίζεσθαι of ver. 31). Comp. vi. 13. By watching and praying, as a means of maintaining clearness of judgment, freedom, and a determination to adhere to Christ, they were to avoid getting into such outward circumstances as might prove dangerous to their moral wellbeing.

The watching here is no doubt of a physical nature (ver. 40), but the προσεύχεσθαι has the effect of imparting to it the character and sacredness belonging to spiritual watchfulness (Col. iv. 2). — τὸ μὲν πνεῦμα, κ.τ.λ.] a *general* proposition (all the more telling that it is not introduced with a γάρ), intended to refer, by way of warning, to the circumstances in which the disciples were placed, as though it had been said : ye are no doubt, so far as the principle of your ethical life in its general aim and tendency is concerned, willing and ready to remain true to me ; but on the individual side of your nature, where the influence of sense is so strong, you are incapable of resisting the temptations to unfaithfulness by which you are beset. Comp. on John iii. 6. Euthymius Zigabenus : ἡ δὲ σάρξ, ἀσθενὴς οὖσα, ὑποστέλλεται καὶ οὐκ εὐτονεῖ. In order, therefore, to avoid getting into a predicament in which, owing to the weakness in question, you would not be able to withstand the overmastering power of influences fatal to your salvation without the special protection and help of God that are to be obtained through vigilance and prayerfulness, *watch* and *pray!*

Ver. 42 ff. Πάλιν ἐκ δευτέρου] a well-known pleonasm. John xxi. 15 ; Acts x. 15. Comp. δεύτερον πάλιν, Plat. *Polit.* p. 260 D, αὖθις πάλιν (p. 282 C), and such like. We sometimes find even a threefold form : αὖθις αὖ πάλιν, Soph. *Phil.* 940, *O. C.* 1421. — εἰ] not *quandoquidem* (Grotius), but : *if.* The actual feelings of Jesus are expressed in all their reality in the form of acquiescence in *that condition of impossibility* (οὐ δύναται) as regards the divine purpose which prevents the thing from being otherwise. — τοῦτο] without τὸ ποτήριον (see the critical remarks): *this*, which I am called upon to drink. — ἐὰν μὴ αὐτὸ πίω] *without my having drunk it ;* if it cannot pass from me unless it is drunk. —γενηθήτω τὸ θέλημά σου] this is the ὑπακοὴ μεχρὶ θανάτου σταυροῦ, Phil. ii. 8 ; Rom. v. 19. Observe in this second prayer the *climax of resignation* and submission ; His own will, as mentioned in ver. 39, is completely silenced. Mark's account is here less precise. — Ver. 43. ἦσαν γὰρ, κ.τ.λ.] *for their eyes* (see on viii. 3) *were heavy* (weighed down with drowsiness). Comp. Eur. *Alc.* 385.

— Ver. 44. ἐκ τρίτου] belongs to προσηύξ. Comp. 2 Cor.
xii. 8. — τ. αὐτ. λόγ.] as is given at ver. 42.

Ver. 45. The annoyance at finding the disciples asleep
(ver. 40 : οὕτως οὐκ ἰσχύσατε, κ.τ.λ.) now deepens into an in-
tensely *painful irony:* "*sleep* on now, and *have out your rest*"
(the emphasis is not on τὸ λοιπόν, but on καθεύδετε κ. ἀναπ.) !
He had previously addressed them with a γρηγορεῖτε, but to how
little purpose ! and, accordingly, He now turns to them with
the sadly ironical abandonment of one who has no further
hope, and tells them to do quite the reverse : *sleep on,* etc.
Comp. Euthymius Zigabenus, Beza, Münster, Erasmus, Calvin,
Er. Schmid, Maldonatus, Bengel, Jansen, Michaelis, Fritzsche,
Keim, Ewald.   On λοιπόν and τὸ λοιπόν, *for the rest of the time,*
in the sense of *jam* (Vulgate), *henceforward* (Plat. *Prot.* p. 321 C),
see Schaefer, *ad Long.* p. 400 ; Jacobs, *ad Philostr.* p. 663.
Comp. on Acts xxvii. 20.   To object, as is frequently done,
that the ironical view does not accord with the frame
of mind in which Jesus must have been, is to fail to
appreciate aright the nature of the situation.   Irony is not
inconsistent even with the deepest anguish of soul, especially
in cases where such anguish is also accompanied with such
clearness of judgment as we find in the present instance ;
and consider what it was for Jesus to see such an overpowering tendency to sleep on the part of His disciples, and
to find everything so different from what He needed, and
might reasonably have expected !   Winer, p. 292 [E. T. 391],
following Chrysostom, Theophylact (who, however, admits the
plausibility of the ironical view), and Grotius, excludes the
idea of irony, and interprets thus : "*sleep on, then, as you are
doing, and take your rest,*" which words are supposed to be
spoken *permissively* in accordance with the calm, mild, resigned
spirit produced by the prayers in which He had just been
engaged.   This is also substantially the view of Kuinoel,
de Wette, Morison, Weiss on *Mark ;* and see even Augustine,
who says : "verba *indulgentis* eis jam somnum." But the
idea that any such indulgence was seriously intended, would
be incompatible with the danger referred to at ver. 41, and
which He knew was threatening *even the disciples themselves.*

There are *others*, again, who are disposed to take the words interrogatively, thus: are ye *still* asleep? Such is the view of Henry Stephens, Heumann, Kypke, Krebs, in spite of the ordinary usage with regard to τὸ λοιπόν, to understand which in the sense of "*henceforth*" (Bleek, Volkmar) would be entirely out of keeping with the use of the *present* here. If, however, the mark of interrogation be inserted after καθεύδετε, and τὸ λοιπὸν καὶ ἀναπαύεσθε be then taken imperatively (Klostermann), in that case καί would have the intensive force of *even ;* but its logical position would have to be before τὸ λοιπόν, not before ἀναπαύεσθε, where it could be rendered admissible at all only by an artificial twisting of the sense ("now you may henceforth *rest on, even as long as you choose*").—While Jesus is in the act of uttering His καθεύδετε, κ.τ.λ., He observes the hostile band approaching; the painful irony changes to a painful earnestness, and He continues in abrupt and disjointed words: ἰδοὺ, ἤγγικεν, κ.τ.λ. The ἡ ὥρα should be taken *absolutely : hora fatalis*, John xvii. 1. The next clause describes in detail the character of that hour. — εἰς χεῖρας ἁμαρτ.] into *sinners' hands*. He refers to the *members of the Sanhedrim*, at whose disposal He would be placed by means of His *apprehension*, and not to the *Romans* (Maldonatus, Grotius, Hilgenfeld), nor to *both* of these together (Lange). The παραδιδούς is not God, but Judas, acting, however, in pursuance of the divine purpose, Acts ii. 23.

Ver. 46. Observe the air of *quick despatch* about the words ἐγείρεσθε, ἄγωμεν, ἰδού. — ἄγωμεν] is not a summons to take to *flight*, in consequence perhaps of a momentary return of the former shrinking from suffering (which would be inconsistent with the fact of the victory that had been achieved, and with the clear consciousness which He had that ὁ υἱὸς τ. ἀ. παραδίδοται, κ.τ.λ. ver. 45), but: *to go to meet the betrayer*, with a view to the fulfilling of the παραδίδοται of which He had just been speaking. Κἀντεῦθεν ἔδειξεν, ὅτι ἑκὼν ἀποθανεῖται, Euthymius Zigabenus.

REMARK.—On the *agony in the garden* (see, in general, Ullmann, *Sündlos.*, ed. 7, p. 127 ff.; Dettinger in the *Tüb. Zeitschr.* 1837, 4, 1838, 1; Hofmann, *Schriftbew.* II. 1, p. 306 ff.;

Keim, III. p. 306 ff.), the following points may be noted: (1)
As to the nature of it, we must not regard it simply as *bodily
suffering* (Thiess, Paulus), nor as consisting in sorrow on
account of the disciples and the Jews (Jerome), nor as pain
caused by seeing His hopes disappointed (*Wolfenbüttel Fragments*), nor as grief at the thought of parting from His friends
(Schuster in Eichhorn's *Bibl.* IX. p. 1012 ff.); but, as the prayer
vv. 39, 42 proves, *as consisting in fear and dread of the cruel
suffering and death that were so near at hand,* the prospect of
which affected Christ—whose sensibilities were purely human,
and not of the nature of a philosophical abstraction, like the
imperturbability of Socrates or the apathy of the Stoic
(Celsus, in *Origen,* ii. 24, charges Him with cowardice)—all the
more powerfully in proportion to the greater purity, and depth,
and genuineness of His feelings, and the increasing distinctness
with which He foresaw the approach of the painful and,
according to the counsel of the Father, inevitable issue. For
having been victorious hitherto over every hostile power,
because His hour had not yet come (John vii. 30, viii. 20), He
realized, now that it was come (ver. 45), the whole intensity of
horror implied in being thus inevitably abandoned, in pursuance
of God's redemptive purpose, to the disposal of such powers, with
the immediate prospect before Him of a most dreadful death,
a death in which He was expected, and in which He Himself
desired, to manifest His perfect obedience to the Father's will.
The momentary disturbing of the complete harmony of His
will with that of God, which took place in Gethsemane, is to
be ascribed to the human ἀσθένεια incidental to His state of
humiliation (comp. 2 Cor. xiii. 4; Heb. v. 7), and should be
regarded simply as a natural shrinking from suffering and
death, a shrinking entirely free from sin (comp. Dorner, *Jesu
sündlose Vollkommenh.* p. 6 f.). Neither was it in any way
due to the conviction, unwarrantably ascribed to Him by
Schenkel, that His death was not absolutely necessary for the
redemption of the world. That touch of human weakness
should not even be described as sin in embryo, sin not yet
developed (Keim), because the absolute resignation to the
Father's will which immediately manifests itself anew pre-
cludes the idea of any taint of sin whatever. To suppose,
however, that this agony must be regarded (Olshausen, Gess) as
an actual *abandonment by God. i.e.* as a withdrawing of the
presence of the higher powers from Jesus, is to contradict the
testimony of Heb. v. 7, and to suppose what is inconsistent
with the very idea of the Son of God (Strauss, II. p. 441); and

to explain it on the ground of the *vicarious* character of the suffering (Olshausen, Ebrard, Steinmeyer, following Luther, Melanchthon, Calvin, Beza, and the dogmatic writers of the orthodox school), as though it were to be regarded as "a concrete bearing of the whole concentrated force of a world's sin" (Ebrard), and of the wrath of God in all its fulness (comp. Thomasius, III. 1, p. 69 f.; Weber, *v. Zorne Gottes*, p. 266 ff.), is erroneously to take a materialistic and *quantitative* view of the ἱλαστήριον of Jesus; whereas Scripture estimates His atoning death according to its *qualitative* value,—that is to say, it regards the painful death to which the sinless Son of God subjected Himself in obedience to the Father's will as constituting the efficient cause of the atonement, and that not because He required to undergo such an *amount* of suffering as might be equivalent in quantity and intensity to the whole sum of the punishment due to mankind, but because the vicarious λύτρον on behalf of humanity consisted in the voluntary surrender of His own life. Comp. ver. 27 f., xx. 28; John i. 29; 1 John ii. 2, iii. 5; 1 Tim. ii. 6; 2 Cor. v. 21; Gal. iii. 13. But it would be unwarrantable, on the other hand, to ascribe the dread which Jesus felt *merely* to the thought of *death* as a divine *judgment*, and the agonies of which He was supposed to be already enduring by anticipation (Köstlin in the *Jahrb. f. D. Theol.* III. p. 125). Those who adopt this view lay great stress upon the sinlessness of our Lord as tending to intensify this painful anticipation of death (Dettinger, comp. Ullmann, Neander). (2) John, notwithstanding the fact that he was both an eye and ear witness of the agony in Gethsemane, makes no mention of it whatever, although he records something analogous to it as having taken place somewhat earlier, xii. 27. With the view of accounting for this silence, it is not enough to suppose that John had omitted this incident because it had been sufficiently recorded by the other evangelists, for a mere external reason such as this would accord neither with the spirit of his Gospel nor with the principle of selection according to which it was composed (in opposition to Lücke, Tholuck, Olshausen, Ebrard). We should rather seek the explanation of the matter in the greater freedom which characterizes the composition of this Gospel, and therefore in the peculiarities of style and form which are due to this work of John being an independent reproduction of our Lord's life. After the prayer of Jesus, which he records in ch. xvii., John felt that the agony could not well find a place in his Gospel, and that, after xii. 23 ff., there was no reason why it should be inserted any more than the cry of anguish on the cross. Comp. Ewald, *Gesch. Chr.* p. 557 f. In John, too, ch. xviii., the transition from acting to suffering is somewhat abrupt (in opposition to Hofmann); but after the high-priestly prayer, the suffering appears as one series of victories culminating in the triumphant issue of xix. 30; in fact, when Jesus offered up that prayer, He did so *as though* He were already victorious (xvi. 33). It is quite unfair to make use of John's silence either for the purpose of throwing discredit upon the *synoptic* narrative (Goldhorn in Tzschirner's *Magaz. f. chr. Pred.* 1, 2, p. 1 ff.; Schleiermacher, *L. J.* p. 422 f.), or as telling against *John* (Bretschneider, *Probab.* p. 33 ff.; Weisse, II. p. 268; Baur, Keim; likewise Theile in Winer's *Journ.* II. p. 353 ff., comp. however, his *Biogr. Jesu*, p. 62), or with a view to impugn the *historical* character of *both* narratives (Strauss, Bruno Bauer). The accounts of the two earliest evangelists bear the impress of living reality to such an extent that their character is the very reverse of that which one expects to find in a legend (in opposition to Gfrörer, *Heil. Sage*, p. 337; Usteri in the *Stud. u. Krit.* 1829, p. 465); nor is there any reason why, even after the high-priestly prayer, such an agony as that in question should not find a place in the Gospel narrative; for who shall presume to say what *changes* of feeling, what elevation and depression of spirit, may not have taken place on the eve of such a catastrophe in a heart so noble, so susceptible, and so full of the healthiest sensibilities, and that not in consequence of any moral weakness, but owing to the struggle that had to be waged with the natural human will (comp. Gess, p. 175; Weizsäcker, p. 563)? Comp. John, remark after ch. xvii. (3) The report of Jesus' prayer should not be (unpsychologically) supposed to have been communicated by the Lord Himself to His disciples, but ought rather to be regarded as derived from the testimony of those who, before sleep had overpowered them, were still in a position to hear at least the first words of it.

Ver. 47. Εἰς τῶν δώδεκα] precisely as in ver. 14, and repeated on both occasions in all three evangelists. In the oral and written tradition this *tragic* designation (κατηγορία, Euthymius Zigabenus) *had come to be so stereotyped* that it would be unconsciously inserted without there being any further occasion for doing so. The same holds true with regard to ὁ παραδιδοὺς αὐτόν, ver. 48, xxvii. 3. — ὄχλος πολύς] Matthew makes no reference to the Roman cohort, John

xviii. 3; his account, however, does not, at the same time, exclude it, as it is simply less precise. Luke xxii. 52 likewise represents the high priests and elders as appearing at this early stage among the throng; but this is an unwarrantable amplification of the tradition; see on Luke. — ξύλων] *cudgels, fustibus* (Vulgate). Herod. ii. 63, iv. 180; Polyb. vi. 36. 3. Wetstein on the passage. — ἀπὸ τῶν, κ.τ.λ.] belongs to ἦλθε; see on Gal. ii. 12.

Ver. 48. It is usual, though unwarrantable (see on John xviii. 24), to take ἔδωκεν in the sense of the *pluperfect* (comp. Mark xiv. 44), in which case it is necessary, with Ewald, to make ver. 48 a parenthesis. The Vulgate correctly renders by: *dedit*. He *communicated* the signal to them *while they were on the way.* — ὃν ἂν φιλήσω, κ.τ.λ.] Fritzsche inserts a colon after φιλήσω, and supposes the following words to be understood: *est vobis comprehendendus.* It may be given more simply thus: *Whomsoever I shall have kissed, He it is* (just He, no other is the one in question)! This αὐτός serves to single out the person intended, from those about Him. Hermann, *ad Viger.* p. 733.

Ver. 49. Εὐθέως] is not to be taken with εἶπε (Fritzsche), but with προσελθών: *immediately*, as soon as he had given them this signal, *he stepped up*, etc. No sooner said than done. — κατεφίλησεν] *embraced and kissed Him*, kissed Him most endearingly. Xen. *Mem.* ii. 6. 33 : ὡς τοὺς μὲν καλοὺς φιλήσαντός μου, τοὺς δ᾽ ἀγαθοὺς καταφιλήσαντος; Tob. vii. 6; Ecclus. xxix. 5; 3 Macc. v. 49; *Test. XII. patr.* p. 730. It is not the case, as de Wette imagines (see Luke vii. 38, 45; Acts xx. 37), that in the New Testament (and the LXX.) the compound has lost the force here ascribed to it; but it is to be insisted on in our present passage as much as in classical Greek. The signal, as arranged, was to be simply a *kiss;* the signal actually given was *kissing accompanied with embraces*, which was entirely in keeping with the excitement of Judas, and the desire he felt that there should be *no mistake* as to the person intended.

Ver. 50. Ἑταῖρε] as in xx. 13. — ἐφ᾽ ὃ πάρει] As the relative ὅς is *never* used in a direct (see Lobeck, *ad Phryn.* p.

57), but only in an indirect question (Kühner, II. 2, p. 942 ; Ellendt, *Lex. Soph.* II. p. 372), it follows that the ordinary *interrogative* interpretation must be wrong; and that to suppose (Winer, p. 157 [E. T. 207 f.]) that we have here one of those corrupt usages peculiar to the Greek of a less classical age, is, so far as ὅς is concerned, without any foundation whatever. Fritzsche, followed by Buttmann, *Neut. Gr.* p. 217 [E. T. 253], understands the expression as an *exclamation :* " ad qualem rem perpetrandam ades !" But even then, Greek usage would have required that it should have been put in an interrogative form and expressed by τί, or failing this we might have had the words ἐφ' οἷον instead (Ellendt, as above, p. 300 f.). The language, as might be expected from the urgent nature of the situation, is somewhat abrupt in its character : *Friend, mind what you are here for ! attend to that.* With these words He spurns the kisses with which the traitor was overwhelming Him. This suits the connection better than the supplying of εἰπέ (Morison). Instead of this hypocritical kissing, Jesus would prefer that Judas should at once proceed with the dark deed he had in view, and deliver Him to the catchpolls.—John xviii. 3 ff., it is true, makes no mention whatever of the kissing ; but this is not to be taken as indicating the legendary character of the incident, especially as there is nothing to prevent us from supposing that it may have taken place just before the question τίνα ζητεῖτε, John xviii. 4 ; see on this latter passage.

Ver. 51. It is strange that the Synoptists have not mentioned the name of Peter here (John xviii. 10, where the name of the high priest's servant is also given). It may be that, with a view to prevent the apostle from getting into trouble with the authorities, his name was suppressed from the very first, and that, accordingly, the incident came to be incorporated in the primitive gospel traditions without any names being mentioned, it having been reserved for John ultimately to supply this omission. — αὐτοῦ τὸ ὠτίον] *his ear* (see on viii. 3). On ὠτίον, see Lobeck, *ad Phryn.* p. 211. He missed the *head* at which the stroke was *aimed*.

Ver. 52. *Put back thy sword into its place* (θήκην, John xviii. 11 ; κολεόν, 1 Chron. xxi. 27). A pictorial representation ;

the sword *was uplifted.* — πάντες γὰρ, κ.τ.λ.] *All, who have taken a sword, will perish by the sword,*—an ordinary axiom in law (Rev. xiii. 10) adduced for the purpose of enforcing His disapproval of the unwarrantable conduct *of Peter,* not a προφητεία τῆς διαφθορᾶς τῶν ἐπελθόντων αὐτῷ Ἰουδαίων (Euthymius Zigabenus, comp. Grotius), nor " an *ideal sentence of death* " (Lange) pronounced upon *Peter*—all such interpretations being *foreign* to our passage. Luther, however, fitly observes : " Those take the sword who use it *without proper authority.*"

Ver. 53. Ἤ] *or,* in case this should not be sufficient to induce thee to thrust back thy sword. — ἄρτι] *this instant.* See on Gal. i. 10.—The *interrogation* does not extend merely as far as μου, in which case it would lose much of its significance, while the language would be rendered too abrupt, but on to ἀγγέλων ; yet not as though καί (for *that,* ὅτι) introduced a broken construction, but thus : Thinkest thou *that I am not able* . . . *and He will* (not) *place at my side,* etc. ? so that I can thus dispense entirely with thy protection ! The force of the negative runs through the whole sentence. — πλείω δώδεκα λεγεώνας ἀγγέλων (see the critical remarks) is a genuine Attic usage, according to which it is permissible to have the neuter πλεῖον or πλείω without a change of construction, or even without inserting ἤ. Lobeck, *ad Phryn.* p. 410 f. ; Stallbaum, *ad Plat. Apol.* p. 17 D ; Kühner, II. 2, p. 847. The number *twelve* corresponds to the number of the apostles, because of these only one had shown a disposition to defend him.

Ver. 54. Πῶς οὖν] *How, in that case, could it be,* if, that is, I were to be defended by thee or angel hosts, *how could it be* possible *that,* etc. In his comment on οὖν, Euthymius Zigabenus aptly analyses it as follows : εἰ μὴ οὕτως ἀναιρεθῶ. For πῶς, comp. on xxiii. 33. — ὅτι] states the *purport* of the γραφαί, so that to complete the sense a λέγουσαι or γράφουσαι may be understood (Fritzsche, *Quaest. Luc.* p. 58 f. ; Maetzner, *ad Antiph.* p. 215): *how shall the Scriptures be fulfilled* which say *that it must happen thus,* and not otherwise? Jesus here alludes to the fact of His *arrest,* which, according to Scripture, is a necessary part of the destiny assigned Him ; comp. Acts iv. 28 ; Luke xxiv. 25 f. We must not expect to find what is here referred to in any passages of Scripture *in particular ;* suffice it to know, that *all* the predictions relating to the sufferings of the Messiah find their necessary fulfilment in the historical events of our Lord's life, the arrest itself *not excluded.* Comp. ver. 31.—The healing of the wounded servant is peculiar to Luke xxii. 51. It probably came to be engrafted upon the tradition at a later period ; for this act of healing, in virtue of the peculiarity of its alleged occasion and character, as well as in virtue of its being the last which Jesus performed, would otherwise scarcely have been omitted by all the other evangelists ; see also on Luke as above.

Ver. 55. Ἐν ἐκείνῃ τῇ ὥρᾳ] *in that hour,* in which that was going on which is recorded between ver. 47 and the present passage, subsequently, however, to the scene with Peter, and while the arrest was taking place. Comp. xviii. 1, x. 19. — τοῖς ὄχλοις] not to the high priests, etc., as Luke xxii. 52 would have us suppose. What is meant is the crowds of which the ὄχλος πολύς of ver. 47 was composed.

Ver. 56. Τοῦτο . . . προφητῶν] It is still *Jesus* who speaks, and who with these words closes His address. Comp. also Mark xiv. 19. In Luke xxii. 53 we find a somewhat different conclusion given. Erasmus, Jansen, Bengel, Fritzsche, de Wette, Schegg, Bleek, Weiss, Holtzmann, Hilgenfeld, regard the words in question as a remark by the *evangelist* (comp. i. 22, xxi. 4) ; but if that were so, we should have expected some specific quotation instead of such a general expression as αἱ γραφαὶ τ. πρ., and what is more, our Lord's words would thus be deprived of their proper conclusion, of that which contains the very point of His remarks. For the gist of the whole matter lay in this avowal of His conviction as the God-man that all that was now taking place was a carrying out of the divine purpose with regard to the fulfilling of the Scriptures, and— thus the mystery of ver. 55 is solved. — τότε οἱ μαθηταὶ, κ.τ.λ.] Observe the πάντες. *Not one* of them stood his ground. Here was the verification of the words of Jesus, ver. 31 ; comp. John xvi. 32.

Ver. 57 f. The Synoptists make no mention of the judicial examination before Annas (John xviii. 13); their narrative is for this reason incomplete, though it does not exclude such examination (Luke xxii. 66). As for the trial before the members of the Sanhedrim, which took place at the house of Caiaphas, John merely *alludes* to it, xviii. 24, where, however, ἀπέστειλεν is not to be taken as a pluperfect. — ἀπὸ᾽ μακρόθεν] a well-known pleonasm : in later Greek the ἀπό is dropped. Lobeck, *ad Phryn.* p. 93. Bengel appropriately observes : " medius inter animositatem ver. 51 et timorem ver. 70." — τῆς αὐλῆς] not the *palace* but the *court*, as in ver. 3. — εἰσελθὼν ἔσω] see Lobeck, *ad Aj.* 741 ; *Paralip.* p. 538. — τὸ τέλος] *exitum rei ;* 3 Macc. iii. 14, common in classical writers. Luther renders admirably : " wo es hinaus wollte " (what the upshot would be).

Ver. 59 f. Καὶ τὸ συνέδριον ὅλον] and the whole Sanhedrim generally. This is a legitimate enough use of the words, even although certain individual members (Nicodemus and Joseph of Arimathea) did not concur in this proceeding. — ψευδομαρτυρίαν] so called from the *historian's* own point of view. Euthymius Zigabenus well remarks: ὡς μὲν ἐκείνοις ἐδόκει, μαρτυρίαν, ὡς δὲ τῇ ἀληθείᾳ, ψευδομαρτυρίαν. — ὅπως θανατ. αὐτ.] *with a view to putting Him to death,* which could only be effected by their pronouncing in the first instance a capital sentence, and then having it ratified by the authority of the imperial procurator. — καὶ οὐχ εὗρον καὶ πολλῶν προσελθόντων ψευδομαρτύρων (see the critical remarks): *and they found no means of doing so, even though many false witnesses had come forward.* There were *many* who presented themselves to bear witness against Jesus ; yet the Sanhedrim did not *find* what it *wanted* to find, doubtless because of the lack of that agreement between two of the witnesses at least which the law required (Num. xxxv. 30 ; Deut. xvii. 6, xix. 15). See what immediately follows : ὕστερον δὲ προσελθ. δύο, and comp. Mark xiv. 56. Though there was a show of *complying* with the ordinary forms of judicial process, they were nevertheless shamefully *violated* (in opposition to Salvador, Saalschutz), in that *exculpatory* evidence (John xviii. 20 f.) was never called for.

Ver. 61. The expression John ii. 19, which Jesus had made use of with reference to His *own body*, was not only misunderstood by those witnesses, but also misrepresented (John : λύσατε): whether wilfully or not, cannot be determined. But in any case the testimony was *objectively* false, and even in the case of the two who agreed it was in all probability *subjectively* so.   Comp. Acts vi. 13 f. — διὰ τριῶν ἡμερ.] not: *after* three days (Gal. ii. 1), but: *during* three days. The work of building was to extend over this short period, and would then be complete.   See on Gal. ii. 1.

Ver. 62. With the sublime calm of one who is conscious of his own superior worth, Jesus meekly abstains from uttering a single word before this contemptible tribunal in the way of self-vindication, εἰδὼς δὲ καὶ, ὅτι μάτην ἀποκρινεῖται παρὰ τοιούτοις, Euthymius Zigabenus ; whereas the high priest who finds, and that with considerable gratification, that the charge of being a Messianic pretender is now fully substantiated by the language of Jesus just deponed to (see ver. 63), quite forgets himself, and breaks out into a passion. — The breaking up of the following utterance into *two questions: answerest thou not ? what* (*i.e.* how heinous a matter) *do these witness against thee ?* is, so far as the latter question is concerned, neither feeble (de Wette) nor unnatural (Weiss), but entirely in keeping with the passionate haste of the speaker.   This being the case, the two clauses should not be run into one.   We should neither, on the one hand, following Erasmus, with Fritzsche, take τί in the sense of *cur*, or (*ad Marc.* p. 650) the whole sentence as equivalent to τί τοῦτό ἐστιν, ὃ οὗτοί σου καταμαρτυροῦσιν ; nor, on the other, with the Vulgate, Luther, de Wette, Ewald, Bleek, Keim, Weiss, should we adopt the rendering : " nihil respondes ad ea, quae isti adversum te testificantur ? " This latter, however, would not be inconsistent with the strict meaning of the terms employed, for it is quite permissible to use ἀποκρίνεσθαί τι in the sense of : *to reply to anything* (see Ast, *Lex. Plat.* I. p. 239), and to take τί as equivalent to ὅ,τι (Buttmann, *Neut. Gr.* p. 216 [E. T.

2ə1], who supposes "*hörend*" (hearing) to be understood before τί).

Ver. 63. The high priest *answers* this second refusal to speak by repeating a formal *oath*, in which Jesus is adjured to declare whether He be the *Messiah* or not. For *this* confession would determine how far they would be justified in pronouncing a capital sentence, and such as the Roman procurator would not fail to confirm. — ἐξορκίζω] means, like the earlier form ἐξορκόω: *I call upon thee to swear*, Dem. 1265, 6; Polyb. iii. 61. 10, vi. 21. 1, xvi. 31. 5. Comp. יִשְׁבַּעֲךָ, Gen. xxiv. 3, *al.* To give an affirmative answer to this formula was to take the full oath usually administered in any court of law. Michaelis, *Mos. R.* § 302 ; Matthaei, *doctr. Christi de jurejur.* 1847, p. 8 ; Keil, *Arch.* II. p. 256. The fact that Jesus took the oath has been denied, though without any reason whatever, by Wuttke, Döllinger, Steinmeyer. — κατὰ τοῦ θεοῦ, κ.τ.λ.] *by the living God.* Comp. 1 Kings iii. 24 ; Judith i. 12 ; common in Greek authors, see Kühner, I. 1, p. 434 ; also Heb. vi. 13, and Bleek thereon. The *living God* as such would not fail to *punish* the perjured, Heb. x. 31. It was the uniform practice in courts of law to swear by *God.* See Saalschütz, *M. R.* p. 614. — ὁ υἱὸς τοῦ θεοῦ] ordinary, recognised designation of the Messiah, into which, naturally enough, the metaphysical conception does not enter here, however much it may have been present to the mind of Christ Himself in making the affirmation which follows.

Ver. 64. Σὺ εἶπας] see on ver. 25. Mark xiv. 62 : ἐγώ εἰμι. A distinguished confession on the part of the Son in presence of the Father, and before the highest tribunal of the theocratic nation. — πλήν] not *profecto* (Olshausen), nor *quin* (Kuinoel), but: *however*, i.e. (comp. Klotz, *ad Devar.* p. 725) *apart* from what I have just affirmed, ye shall henceforward have reason to be satisfied, from actual observation, that I am the Messiah who was seen by Daniel in his vision (Dan. vii. 13). — ἀπάρτι] is not to be taken with λέγω ὑμῖν (Schulz in 3d ed. of Griesbach), but—since in any other connection it would lose its force—with ὄψεσθε ; nor is it to be understood in any other sense than that of *henceforth, i.c.*

from the time of my impending death, through which I am
to enter into my δόξα. But seeing that ἀπάρτι forbids us
to understand ὄψεσθε as denoting only a *single momentary*
glance (comp. on the contrary, John i. 51), we are bound
to suppose that Jesus used it somewhat *loosely* to express
the idea of *coming to perceive in the course of experience* (as
in the passage of John just referred to) the fact of His
being seated at the right hand of God (in allusion to Ps.
cx. 1), and that He did not intend ἐρχόμενον, κ.τ.λ. to refer to
the second advent, but (Beza, Neander, Holtzmann, Schenkel,
Gess, Weissenbach) to a coming in the *figurative* sense of
the word, namely, in the shape of those *mighty influences
which, from His place in heaven, He will shed upon the earth,*
—manifestations, all of them, of His sovereign sway. We
are shut up to this view by the fact that the *sitting*
cannot possibly be regarded as an object of actual sight, and
that ἀπάρτι ὄψεσθε can only be said of something that,
beginning now, is *continued* henceforth. — τῆς δυνάμ.] The
Mighty One is conceived of as *power* (the *abstract* for the *concrete*). Similarly in the Talmud הַגְּבוּרָה, Buxtorf, *Lex. Talm.*
p. 385. Such abstract terms (as for instance our : *majesty*)
have somewhat of an imposing character. Comp. 2 Pet. i.
17.

Ver. 65. As may be seen from 2 Kings xviii. 17, the rending
of the garments as an indication of unusual vexation was
indulged in above all on hearing any utterance of a blasphe-
mous nature. See Buxtorf, *Lex. Talm.* p. 2146 ; Schoettgen,
p. 234 ; Wetstein on our passage. Maimonides, quoted by
Buxtorf as above, thus describes the usual mode of proceeding
in such cases : " Laceratio fit stando, a collo anterius, non
posterius, non ad latus neque ad fimbrias inferiores vestis.
Longitudo rapturae palmus est. Laceratio non fit in interula
seu indusio linteo, nec in pallio exteriori : *in reliquis vestibus
corpori accommodatis omnibus fit, etiamsi decem fuerint.*" The
last-mentioned particular may serve to account for the use of
the plural τὰ ἱμάτια (1 Macc. ii. 14). That part of the law
which forbade the high priest to rend his garments (Lev. x. 6,
xxi. 10) had reference merely to ordinary mourning for the

dead. Comp. 1 Macc. xi. 71 ; Joseph. *Bell.* ii. 15. 4. —
ἐβλασφήμησε] in so far as by falsely pretending to be the
Messiah, the Son of God, and by further arrogating to Himself participation in *divine* honour and authority, ver. 64, He
had been guilty of insulting the majesty of God ; comp.
John v. 18, x. 33. The pain of the high priest no doubt
represented the genuine vexation of one who was most deeply
moved; but the judgment which he formed regarding Jesus
was based upon the gratuitous assumption that *He* was *not* the
Messiah, and indicates a predisposition to find Him guilty of
the *capital* charge (Lev. xxiv. 16). For τί ἔτι χρ. ἔχ. μαρτ.,
comp. Plat. *Rep.* p. 340 A.

Ver. 66. At this point the high priest, notwithstanding
the precipitancy with which the trial is being hurried through,
and notwithstanding the candid confession just made by the
accused, calls for a formal vote, the result of which is a verdict
of *guilty,* and that of an offence deserving to be punished by
death. The next thing that had to be considered was *the course
to be adopted with a view to the carrying out of the sentence.* It
was *this* that formed the subject of deliberation at that con-
clave to which reference is made at xxvii. 1.

Ver. 67. Those to whom Matthew here refers are the
members of the Sanhedrim (as are also the τινές of Mark xiv.
65). Μετὰ γὰρ τὴν ἄδικον καταδίκην ὡς ἄτιμόν τινα καὶ
τριωβολιμαῖον λάβοντες, κ.τ.λ., Euthymius Zigabenus. Coarse
outburst of passion on the verdict being announced. A
somewhat different form of the tradition is adopted by Luke
(xxii. 63), who, moreover, represents the maltreatment here
referred to as having taken place *before* the trial. The way
in which harmonists have cut and carved upon the individual
features of the narrative is altogether arbitrary. The account
in John xviii. 22 has no connection with that now before
us, but refers to an incident in the house of Annas, which
the Synoptists have entirely omitted. — ἐκολάφ.] *buffetings,
blows with the fist.* Comp. the Attic expression κόνδυλος. —
ἐρράπτ.] *slaps in the face* with the palm of the hand;
ῥαπισμὸς δὲ τὸ πταίειν κατὰ τοῦ προσώπου, Euthymius
Zigabenus; comp. v. 39; Hos. xi. 5; Isa. l. 6; Dem. 787,

23; Aristot. *Meteor.* ii. 8. 9; 3 Esdr. iv. 30; Lobeck, *ad Phryn.* p. 176; Becker, *Anecd.* p. 300. It is in this sense that the word is *usually* taken. But Beza, Bengel, Ewald, Bleek, Lange, maintain that it is a blow *with a rod* that is meant (Herod. viii. 59; Anacr. vii. 2; Plut. *Them.* xi.), the sense in which the word is commonly used by Greek authors, and which ought to be preferred here, because οἱ δέ (see on xxviii. 16) introduces the mention of a *different* kind of maltreatment, and because in Mark xiv. 65 the ῥαπίζειν is imputed to the *officers* of the Sanhedrim, which, however, would not warrant us in identifying with the latter the οἱ δέ of Matthew.

Ver. 68. Προφήτευσον ἡμῖν] Differently in Mark xiv. 65. But so far as the προφήτ., τίς ἐστιν, κ.τ.λ. is concerned, Luke xxii. 64 agrees with Matthew, although the favourite mode of accounting for this would seem to be that of tracing it to the obscuring influence of a later tradition; in no case, however, is this theory to be applied to the exposition of Matthew, for it would involve a point of *essential* consequence. According to Matthew, the sport lay in the demand that Jesus as Messiah, and consequently *as a prophet* (xxi. 11), *should tell* who it was that had struck Him, though He had no natural means of knowing. This conduct, of course, proceeds on the assumption that the Messiah possessed that higher knowledge which is derived from divine revelation; hence also the scoffing way in which they address Him by the title of Χριστός. Fritzsche thinks that the prominent idea here is that of *fore*telling, as being calculated, when thus conjoined with the preterite παίσας, to form an *acerba irrisio*. But that would be more likely to result in an *absurda* irrisio, unmarked by the slightest touch of humour.

Ver. 69. Ἔξω] with reference to the interior of the particular building in which the trial of Jesus had been conducted. In ver. 58 ἔσω is used because in that instance Peter went from the street into the court-yard. — μία παιδίσκη] μία is here used in view of the ἄλλη of ver. 71 below. Comp. on viii. 19. Both of them may have seen (ἦσθα, ἦν) Peter among the followers of Jesus somewhere in Jerusalem, and may have preserved a distinct recollection of his appearance. παιδίσκη, in the sense of a *female slave*, corresponds exactly to our (German) *Mädchen;* see Lobeck, *ad Phryn.* p. 239. — καὶ σὺ ἦσθα, κ.τ.λ.] categorical accusation, as in vv. 71, 73, and not a question (Klostermann). — τοῦ Γαλιλ.] which specific designation she may have heard applied to the Prisoner. The other slave (ver. 71) is still more specific, inasmuch as she calls Him ὁ Ναζωραῖος.

Ver. 70. Ἔμπροσθεν πάντων (see the critical remarks): *before all who were present.* — οὐκ οἶδα τί λέγεις] *evasive denial:* so little have I been with Him, that I am at a loss to know what is meant by this imputation of thine.

Ver. 71. Ἐξελθόντα] from the *court-yard* to the *porch,* which, passing through some part of the buildings that stood round the four sides of the former, conducted into the anterior court outside (προαύλιον; according to Mark xiv. 68, it was in this latter that the present denial took place). Comp. Hermann, *Privatalterth.* § 19. 9 ff. In spite of the plain meaning of πυλών, *door, doorway* (see Luke xvi. 20; Acts x. 17, xii. 13 f., xiv. 13; Rev. xxi.), it is usually supposed that it is the outer court in front of the house, the προαύλιον (see Poll. i. 77, ix. 16), that is meant. — αὐτοῖς ἐκεῖ] ἐκεῖ belongs to λέγει, while αὐτοῖς, in accordance with a loose usage of frequent occurrence (Winer, p. 137 f. [E. T. 181]), is meant to refer to the *people generally* whom she happened to meet with. It would be wrong to connect ἐκεῖ with καὶ οὗτος (Matthaei, Scholz), because in such a connection it would be meaningless.

Ver. 72. Observe the *climax* in the terms of the threefold denial. — μεθ᾽ ὅρκου] is peculiar to Matthew, and is *here* used in the sense of an oath. — τὸν ἄνθρωπον] *the man* (in question). Alas, such is the language, cold and distant, which Peter uses with reference to his Master! What a contrast to xvi. 16! "Ecce, columna firmissima ad unius aurae impulsum tota contremuit," Augustine.

Ver. 73. The answer of Peter given at ver. 72, and in the course of which his Galilaean dialect was recognised, gave occasion to those standing by (that they were exactly *Sanhedrim officers, apparitores,* Kuinoel, Paulus, does not necessarily follow from the use of ἑστῶτες) to step up to Peter after a little while, and to corroborate (ἀληθῶς) the assertion of the maid-servant. — ἐξ αὐτῶν] of those who were along with Jesus, ver. 71. — καὶ γάρ] *for even,* apart from circumstances by which thou hast been already identified. — ἡ λαλιά σου] *thy speech* (see on John viii. 43), namely, through the coarse provincial accent. The natives of Galilee were unable to distinguish especially the gutturals properly, pronounced the letter ע like a ה, etc. See Buxtorf, *Lex. Talm.* p. 435, 2417 ; Lightfoot, *Centur. Chorogr.* p. 151 ff.; Wetstein on our passage ; Keim, I. p. 310.

Ver. 74. Τότε ἤρξατο] for previously he had not resorted as yet to the καταθεματίζειν, but had contented himself with the simple ὀμνύειν (ver. 72, μεθ' ὅρκου). Whereas before he had only *sworn,* he now takes to *cursing* as well. "Nunc gubernaculum animae plane amisit," Bengel. The imprecations were intended to fall upon *himself* (should he be found, that is, to be telling an untruth). For the word καταθεματίζω, which was in all probability a vulgar corruption, comp. Rev. xxii. 3 ; Iren. *Haer.* i. 13. 2, 16. 3 ; Oecolampadius, *ad Act.* xxiii. 12. — ὅτι] *recitantis,* as in ver. 72. — ἀλέκτωρ] *a cock.* There are Rabbinical statements (see the passages in Wetstein) to the effect that it was *not allowable* to keep animals of this sort in Jerusalem; but as there are other Rabbinical passages again which assert the opposite of this (see Lightfoot, p. 483), it is unnecessary to have recourse (Reland, Wolf) to the supposition that the bird in question may have belonged to a *Gentile,* may even have been about Pilate's house, or some house outside the city.

Ver. 75. Ἐξελθ. ἔξω] namely, from the porch (ver. 71) in which the second and third denial had taken place. Finding he could no longer repress the feeling of sorrowful penitence that filled his heart, the apostle must go *outside* to be all *alone* with his remorse and shame. The fear of being detected (Chrysostom) had by this time undoubtedly become to him a very secondary consideration; he was now himself again. — εἰρηκότος αὐτῷ] *who had said to him* (ver. 34), in itself a superfluous

expression, and yet "grande participium," Bengel. — πικρῶς]
he wept *bitterly*. Comp. Isa. xxii. 4, and the passages in
Wetstein. How totally different was it with *Judas!* " Lacry-
marum physica amaritudo (comp. Hom. *Od.* iv. 153) aut
dulcedo (comp. γλυκύδακρυς, Meleag. 45), congruit cum affectu
animi," Bengel.

REMARK.—Seeing that the whole four evangelists concur in
representing *Peter as having denied Jesus three times*, we are
bound to regard the threefold repetition of the denial as one
of the *essential* features of the incident (in opposition to Paulus,
who, in the discrepancies that occur in the various accounts,
finds traces of no less than *eight* different denials). The information regarding this circumstance can only have been derived
from Peter himself; comp. also John xxi. 1 ff. As for the rest,
however, it must be acknowledged—(1) that John (and Luke
too, see on Luke xxii. 54 ff.) represents the three denials as
having taken place in a different locality altogether, namely, in
the court of the house in which *Annas* lived, and not in that of
Caiaphas; while to try to account for this by supposing that those
two persons occupied one and the same dwelling (Euthymius
Zigabenus, Ebrard, Lange, Lichtenstein, Riggenbach, Pressensé,
Steinmeyer, Keim), is a harmonistic expedient that is far from
according with the clear view of the matter presented in the
fourth Gospel; see on John xviii. 16, 25. (2) That the Synoptists agree neither with John nor with one another as to
certain points of detail connected with the three different scenes
in question, and more particularly with reference to the localities
in which they are alleged to have taken place, and the persons
by whom the apostle was interrogated as to his connection with
Jesus; while to say, in attempting to dispose of this, that
"Abnegatio ad plures plurium interrogationes facta *uno paro-
xysmo,* pro *una* numeratur" (Bengel), is to make a mere assertion,
against which all the accounts of this incident without exception enter, so to speak, an emphatic protest. (3) It is better,
on the whole, to allow the discrepancies to remain just as they
stand, and to look upon them as sufficiently accounted for by
the diverse forms which the primitive tradition assumed in
regard to details. This tradition has for its basis of fact the
threefold denial, not merely a denial *several times* repeated,
and, as Strauss alleges, reduced to the number three to agree
with the prediction of Jesus. It is to the narrative of John,
however, as being that of the only evangelist who was an

eye-witness, that we ought to trust for the most correct representation of this matter. Olshausen, however, gives to the synoptic narratives with the one hand so much of the merit in this respect as he takes from the Johannine with the other, and thus lays himself open to the charge of arbitrarily confounding them all.

CHAPTER XXVII.

VER. 2. αὐτόν] after παρέδ. has very important evidence both for and against it, being just as liable to be inserted as a very common supplement as to be omitted on account of its superfluous character, a character likely to be ascribed to it all the more that it is wanting also in Mark xv. 1. Deleted by Lachm. and Tisch. 8. — Ποντίῳ Πιλ.] B L א, 33, 102, vss. Or. have simply Πιλάτῳ; but the full form of the name is to be preferred all the more that the parallel passages have only Πιλάτ. — Ver. 3. παραδιδούς] Lachm.: παραδούς, following only B L 33, 259, vss. (?). The aorist would more readily occur to the transcribers, since the betrayal had already taken place. — Ver. 4. ἀθῷον] δίκαιον, although recommended by Griesb. and Schulz, has too little evidence in its favour, and should be regarded as an early exegetical correction with a view to render the expression more forcible; comp. xxiii. 35. — ὄψει] Scholz, Lachm., Tisch.: ὄψῃ, in accordance with decisive evidence. — Ver. 5. Instead of ἐν τῷ ναῷ, Tisch. 8 has εἰς τὸν ναόν. Exegetical emendation, against which there is a preponderance of evidence. — Ver. 9. Ἱερεμίου] The omission of the prophet's name in 33, 157, Syr. Pers. and Codd. in Aug., as well as the reading Ζαχαρίου in 22, Syr.ᴾ in the margin, is due to the fact that the quotation is not found in Jeremiah. — Ver. 11. ἔστη] B C L א, 1, 33, Or.: ἐστάθη. So Lachm. and Tisch. 8. Exegetical emendation with a view to greater precision. — Vv. 16, 17. Βαραββᾶν] Fritzsche: Ἰησοῦν Βαραββᾶν. So Origenᶦⁿᵗ several min. Aram. Syr.ʲᵉʳ, and early scholiasts. Advocated above all by Fritzsche in the *Litt. Blatt z. allgem. Kirchenzeit.* 1843, p. 538 f., in opposition to Lachm. *ed. maj.* p. xxxvii. f., with which latter critic Tisch. agrees. For my own part, I look upon the reading Ἰησοῦν Βαραββᾶν as the original one, for I am utterly at a loss to see how Ἰησοῦν should have found its way into the text (in answer to Holtzmann, who supposes that it was from Acts iv. 36 through a blunder of the transcriber, and in answer to Tisch. 8, who with Tregelles traces it to an abbreviation of the name Ἰησοῦν (Ι̅Ν̅), in which case it is supposed that ΥΜΙΝΙ̅Ν̅

came to be substituted for ΥΜΙΝ); and because to take away
the sacred name from the robber would seem very natural and
all the more justifiable that it is likewise omitted in vv. 20 f.,
26, and by the other evangelists, not to mention that, from a
similar feeling of reverence, it would seem to have been suppressed in the tradition current in the apostolic age. Comp.
also Rinck, *Lucubr. crit.* p. 285, de Wette, Ewald, Bleek, Keim,
Weizsäcker. The view that 'Ιησοῦν has been adopted from the
Gospel of the Hebrews (Tisch.) is a very questionable inference
from the statement of Jerome, that instead of Βαραββ. that
Gospel had substituted *filium magistri eorum.* It would be
just as warrantable to quote the same authority in favour of
the *originality* of the reading 'Ιησοῦν Βαραββ. — Ver. 22. αὐτῷ
(Elz., Scholz) after λέγουσι has been deleted in accordance
with preponderating evidence. — Ver. 24. The reading κατέναντι
(Lachm.) is supported only by the insufficient evidence of
B D; comp. xxi. 2. — τοῦ δικαίου τούτου] The words τοῦ
δικαίου are wanting in B D 102, Cant. Ver. Verc. Mm. Chrys.
Or.[int] They are placed after τούτου in A, while Δ reads τοῦ
τούτου δικαίου. Lachm. inserts them after τούτου, but in brackets ;
Tisch. deletes them, and that correctly. They are to be regarded as a gloss (suggested by the reading δίκαιον, ver. 4),
written on the margin at first, and afterwards, when incorporated in the text, conjoined in some instances with τοῦ αἵματος
(as in ver. 4) and in others with τούτου; hence so many
different ways of arranging the words. — Ver. 28. ἐκδύσαντες]
B D א** 157, Cant. Ver. Verc. Colb. Corb. 2, Lachm.: ἐνδύσαντες. Correctly ; ἐνδύσ. was not understood, and was accordingly altered.[1] Comp. on 2 Cor. v. 3. In what follows we
should, with Lachm. and Tisch., restore the arrangement χλαμ.
κοκκ. περιέθ. αὐτῷ, in accordance with important evidence. —
Ver. 29. ἐπὶ τὴν δεξιάν] As the reading ἐν τῇ δεξιᾷ (approved
by Griesb., adopted by Fritzsche, Lachm., Tisch.) has such
important evidence as that of A B D L N א, min. vss.
Fathers in its favour, and the one in the Received text might
so easily originate in a mechanical conforming with ἐπὶ τὴν κεφ.
(for which Tisch., in opposition to a preponderance of MS.
evidence, substitutes ἐπὶ τῆς κεφαλῆς), we cannot but regard ἐν
τῇ δεξιᾷ as having the best claim to originality. — Ver. 33. Elz.
has ὅς ἐστι λεγόμενος κρανίου τόπος. So also Scholz. There is a
multiplicity of readings here. Fritzsche, Rinck (comp. also

---

[1] Lachm. adopts the reading ἐνδύσαντες in accordance with his fundamental
principles of criticism, still he looks upon it as an error of early date. See his
Praef. ed. maj. II. p. 6.

Griesb.) have simply ὅ ἐστι κρανίου τόπος, while Lachm. and Tisch. read ὅ ἐστιν κρανίου τόπος λεγόμενος. The balance of evidence is decidedly in favour of regarding the neuter ὅ as genuine; it was changed to the masculine to suit τόπον and τόπος. Further, λεγόμενος is wanting only in D, min. Copt. Sahid. Arm. Vulg. It., where its omission may probably have been resorted to as a means of getting rid of a difficult construction, while the readings λεγόμενον, μεθερμηνευόμενος, μεθερμηνευόμενον (Mark xv. 22), καλούμενον (Luke xxiii. 33), are also to be regarded as exegetical variations. We ought therefore to retain the λεγόμενος, and in the order in which it is taken by Lachm. and Tisch., on the authority of B L ℵ, min. Ath. Its earlier position in Elz. is probably due to ἐστι λεγόμ. (comp. ἔστι μεθερμ., Mark xv. 22) being sometimes taken *together*. — Ver. 34. ὄξος] Lachm. and Tisch. 8: οἶνον, which is supported by evidence so important, viz. B D K L Π* ℵ, min. vss. and Fathers, that we must regard ὄξος as derived from Ps. lxviii. 22. The word οἶνον was allowed to remain in Mark xv. 23 because the *gall* did not happen to be mentioned there; and this being the case, the alteration, in conformity with Ps. lxviii. as above, would not so readily suggest itself. — Ver. 35. After κλῆρον Elz. inserts: ἵνα πληρωθῇ τὸ ῥηθὲν ὑπὸ τοῦ προφήτου· Διεμερίσαντο τὰ ἱμάτιά μου ἑαυτοῖς, καὶ ἐπὶ τὸν ἱματισμόν μου ἔλαβον κλῆρον. Against decisive evidence; supplement from John xix. 24. — Ver. 40. κατάβηθι] Lachm. and Tisch. 8: καὶ κατάβ., following A D ℵ, min. Syr.ᴶᵉʳ· Cant. Ver. Verc. Colp. Clar. Cyr. The καί has been added for the purpose of connecting the two clauses together. — Ver. 41. After πρεσβυτέρων, Matth., Fritzsche insert καὶ Φαρισαίων, for which there is important though not preponderant evidence. Those chief adversaries of Jesus were by way of gloss mentioned on the margin, but subsequently the words crept into the text, being sometimes found *along with*, and sometimes *substituted for*, πρεσβυτέρων (as in D, min. Cant. Ver. Verc. Colb. Clar. Corb. 2, Gat. Cassiod.). — Ver. 42. εἰ βασιλ.] Fritzsche and Tisch. read simply βασιλ., following B D L ℵ, 33, 102, Sahid. Correctly; εἰ is a supplementary addition from ver. 40, its insertion in D, min. vss. Eus. before πέποιθεν below being likewise traceable to the same source. — πιστεύσομεν] Lachm.: πιστεύομεν, only in accordance with A, Vulg. Ver. Verc. Colb. Or.ⁱⁿᵗ, but correctly notwithstanding. By way of gloss the present was replaced sometimes by the future (Elz.) and sometimes by the subjunctive πιστεύσωμεν. Tisch. 8 adopts the latter. — ἐπ' αὐτῷ] The witnesses are divided between αὐτῷ (Elz., Lachm.), ἐπ' αὐτῷ (Griesb., Tisch. 7), and ἐπ' αὐτόν (Fritzsche, Tisch. 8).

The reading ἐπ' αὐτῷ (E F G H K M S U V Δ Π, min.) should be preferred, inasmuch as this expression not only occurs nowhere else in Matthew, but is a somewhat rare one generally. — Ver. 44. For αὐτόν, Elz. has αὐτῷ, against decisive MS. authority. Emendation in conformity with the construction ὀνειδίζειν τινί τι. — Ver. 46. The MSS. present very considerable variety as regards the spelling of the Hebrew words. Lachm.: 'Ηλί ἠλί λημὰ σαβαχθανί. Tisch. 8: 'Ηλεί 'Ηλεί λιμὰ σαβαχθανί. The latter is the best attested. — Ver. 49. ἄλλος δὲ λαβὼν λόγχην ἔνυξεν αὐτοῦ τὴν πλευράν, καὶ ἐξῆλθεν ὕδωρ καὶ αἷμα, supported though it be by B C L U Γ ℵ, min. vss. Chrys., is clearly an irrelevant interpolation (after αὐτόν) borrowed from John xix. 34. Yet this interpolation occasioned the error condemned by Clem. v. 1311, that Christ's side was pierced before He expired. — Ver. 52. ἠγέρθη] B D G L ℵ, min. Or. Eus.: ἠγέρθησαν. So Fritzsche, Lachm., Tisch. But how readily would the whole surroundings of the passage suggest the plural to the mechanical transcribers ! — Ver. 54. γενόμενα] Lachm. and Tisch.: γίνομενα, following B D, min. Vulg. It. Or. (who, however, has γενόμενα as well). The aorist might have originated as readily in a failure to appreciate the difference of meaning as in a comparison of the present passage with Luke xxiii. 47 f. — Ver. 56. For 'Ιωσῆ, Tisch. 8 has 'Ιωσήφ, following D* L ℵ, vss. Or. Eus. Emendation suggested by the assumption that the mother of Jesus must have been intended (comp. on xiii. 55); hence ℵ* enumerates the three Marys thus: Μαρ. ἡ τοῦ 'Ιακώβου καὶ ἡ Μαρ. ἡ 'Ιωσήφ καὶ ἡ Μαρ. ἡ τῶν υἱῶν Ζεβ. — Ver. 57. ἐμαθήτευσε] Lachm. and Tisch. 8: ἐμαθητεύθη, following C D ℵ and two min. Altered in accordance with xiii. 52.— Ver. 64. Elz. inserts νύκτος after αὐτοῦ, against decisive evidence; borrowed from xxviii. 13. The δέ again, which Elz. has after ἔφη, ver. 65, is an interpolation for sake of connection, and is wanting in very important witnesses (not, however, in A C D ℵ).

Ver. 1. By the time the Sanhedrim met, as it now did, in *full* sederunt (πάντες, comp. xxvi. 59), for the purpose of consulting as to how they were now to *give effect to* the verdict of xxvi. 66, it was well on in the morning (after cock-crowing, xxvi. 74). — ὥστε] they consulted before going further (comp. on xxii. 15) as to what the consequence might be (comp. on xxiv. 24) if they carried out their *intention of putting Him to death*, in other words, if they were likewise to give *effect* to the verdict already agreed upon: ἔνοχος θανάτου ἐστί.

Ver. 2. $\varDelta\dot{\eta}\sigma a\nu\tau\epsilon\varsigma$] The shackles which had been put upon
Jesus at the time of His arrest (xxvi. 50, comp. with John
xviii. 12), and which He still wore when He was led away
from Annas to Caiaphas (John xviii. 24), would seem, from
what is here stated, to have been either wholly or partially
removed during the trial. With the view of His being
securely conducted to the residence of the procurator, they
take the precaution to put their prisoner in chains again. It
is not expressly affirmed, either by Matthew or Mark, that the
$\dot{a}\pi\dot{\eta}\gamma a\gamma o\nu$ was the work of the members of the Sanhedrim *in
pleno* (as generally supposed, Weiss and Keim also sharing in
the opinion); and, indeed, it is scarcely probable that they
would have so far incurred the risk of a popular tumult
(comp. xxvi. 5). The statement in Luke xxiii. 1 is unquestionably the product of a later tradition. As for Matthew
and Mark, they seem to assume that merely a *deputation*
accompanied the prisoner, though doubtless it would be large
enough to be in keeping with the importance of the occa-
sion. Comp. also on ver. 3. — $\pi a\rho\dot{\epsilon}\delta\omega\kappa a\nu$ $a\dot{v}\tau\dot{o}\nu$ $\Pi o\nu\tau\dot{\iota}\varphi$,
$\kappa.\tau.\lambda.$] For after Judaea became a Roman province (from
the time that King Archelaus was dethroned, 759 u.c.), the
Sanhedrim had lost the *jus gladii*. Comp. on John xviii.
31. On Pontius Pilate, the fifth procurator of Judaea, who
was successor to Valerius Gratus, and who, after holding
office for ten years (from A.D. 26 onwards), was summoned
to Rome at the instance of Vitellius, then governor of Syria,
to answer to certain charges made against him, and then
(according to Euseb. ii. 7) banished to Vienne, where he
is said to have committed suicide, see Ewald, *Gesch. Chr.* p.
87 ff.; Leyrer in Herzog's *Encykl.* XI. p. 663 ff.; Gerlach,
d. Röm. Statthalter in Syr. u. Jud. p. 53 ff.; Hausrath, *Zeit-
gesch.* I. p. 312 ff. For certain Christian legends regarding
His death, consult Tischendorf's *Evang. Apocr.* p. 426 ff.
Caesarea was the place where the procurators usually resided
(Acts xxiii. 23 f., xxiv. 27, xxv. 1); but, as it was the
Passover season, Pilate was in Jerusalem (to be ready, in fact,
to quell any disturbance that might arise, comp. on xxvi. 5),
where he lived in the praetorium (see on ver. 27). — $\tau\dot{\varphi}$

ἡγεμόνι] *principi.* The more precise designation would have been τῷ ἐπιτρόπῳ, *procuratori.* Comp. Joseph. *Antt.* xviii. 3. 1: Πιλάτος δὲ ὁ τῆς Ἰουδαίας ἡγεμών. On the comprehensive sense in which ἡγεμών is frequently used, see Krebs, *Obss.* p. 61 ff.

Ver. 3. Τότε] as Jesus was being led away to the procurator. From this Judas *saw* that his Master had been condemned (xxvi. 66), for otherwise He would not have been thus taken before Pilate. — ὁ παραδιδοὺς αὐτόν] *His betrayer,* xxvi. 25, 48. — μεταμεληθεὶς, κ.τ.λ.] cannot be said to favour the view that Judas was animated by a good intention (see on xxvi. 16, Remark 2), though it no doubt serves to show he neither contemplated nor expected so serious a result. It is possible that, looking to the innocence of Jesus, and remembering how often before He had succeeded in disarming His enemies, the traitor may have cherished the hope that the issue would prove harmless. *Now:* " vellet, si posset, factum infectum reddere," Bengel. *Such* was his repentance, but it was not of a *godly* nature (2 Cor. vii. 9 f.), for it led to *despair.* — ἀπέστρεψε] *he returned them* (xxvi. 52; Thuc. v. 75, viii. 108; Xen. *Anab.* ii. 6. 3, *al.*), i.e. *he took them back* (Gen. xliii. 21; Judg. xi. 13; Jer. xxviii. 3), Heb. הֵשִׁיב. — τοῖς ἀρχ. κ. τ. πρεσβ.] from which it is to be inferred that Matthew did not look upon this as a *full* meeting of the Sanhedrin (ver. 2).

Ver. 4. Ἥμαρτον παραδούς] see on xxvi. 12. — αἷμα ἀθῷον] εἰς τὸ χυθῆναι, Euthymius Zigabenus; comp. Deut. xxvii. 25; 1 Macc. i. 37; 2 Macc. i. 8; Phalar. *ep.* 40; Heliod. viii. 10. — τί πρὸς ἡμᾶς] sc. ἐστι; *what is it as regards us?* i.e. *what matters it to us?* we are in no way called upon to concern ourselves about what thou hast done. Comp. John xxi. 22 f.; the words are also frequently used in this sense by Greek authors. — σὺ ὄψῃ] *Thou wilt see to it thyself,* thou wilt have to consider for thyself what is now to be done by thee; comp. ver. 24; Acts xviii. 15; 1 Sam. xxv. 17; 4 Macc. ix. 1. "Impii in facto consortes, post factum deserunt," Bengel.

Ver. 5. Ἐν τῷ ναῷ] is to be taken neither in the sense

of *near the temple* (Kypke), nor as referring to the room, *Gasith*, in which the Sanhedrim held its sittings (Grotius), nor as equivalent to ἐν τῷ ἱερῷ (Fritzsche, Olshausen, Bleek); but, in accordance with the regular use of ναός (see on iv. 5) and the only possible meaning of ἐν, we must interpret thus: he flung down the money in the *temple proper*, i.e. *in the holy place* where the priests were to be found. Judas *in his despair* had ventured within that place which none but priests were permitted to enter. — ἀπήγξατο] *he strangled himself.* Hom. *Od.* xix. 230; Herod. vii. 232; Xen. *Cyrop.* iii. 1. 14; Hier. vii. 13; Aesch. *Suppl.* 400; Ael. *V. H.* v. 3. There is no reason why the statement in Acts i. 18 should compel us to take ἀπάγχομαι as denoting, in a *figurative* sense, an *awakening of the conscience* (Grotius, Perizonius, Hammond, Heinsius), for although ἄγχειν is sometimes so used by classical authors (Dem. 406, 5; and see the expositors, *ad Thom. Mag.* p. 8), such a meaning would be inadmissible here, where we have no qualifying term, and where the style is that of a plain *historical* narrative (comp. 2 Sam. xvii. 23; Tob. iii. 10). With a view to reconcile what is here said with Acts i. 18, it is *usual* to assume that the traitor *first hanged himself, and then fell down headlong*, Matthew being supposed to furnish the first, and Luke the second half of the statement (Kuinoel, Fritzsche, Olshausen, Kaeuffer, Paulus, Ebrard, Baumgarten - Crusius). But such a way of parcelling out this statement, besides being arbitrary in itself, is quite inadmissible, all the more so that it is by no means clear from Acts i. 18 that *suicide* had been committed. Now as suicide was regarded by the Jews with the utmost abhorrence, it would for that very reason have occupied a prominent place in the narrative instead of being passed over in silence. It has been attempted to account for the absence of any *express mention* of suicide, by supposing that the historian assumed his readers to be familiar with the fact. But if one thing forbids such an explanation more than another, it is the highly rhetorical character of the passage in the Acts just referred to, which, rhetorical though it be, records, for example, the circumstance of the *purchase of the field* with all the historical fidelity of Matthew himself, the only difference being

that Luke's mode of *representing* the matter is almost poetical
in its character (in opposition to Strauss, Zeller, de Wette,
Ewald, Bleek, Pressensé, Paret, Keim, all of whom concur
with Paulus in assuming, in opposition to Matthew, that
Judas bought the field himself). Comp. on Acts i. 18. In
Matt. xxvii. 5 and Acts i. 18, we have two *different* accounts
of the fate of the betrayer, from which nothing further is to
be gathered by way of historical fact than that he came to a
violent end. In the course of subsequent tradition, however,
this violent death came to be represented sometimes as suicide
by means of hanging (Matthew, Ignatius, *ad Philipp. interpol.* 4),
at a later stage again as a fall resulting in the bursting of the
bowels, or at a later period still as the consequence of his
having been crushed by a carriage when the body was in a
fearfully swollen condition (Papias as quoted by Oecumenius,
ad Act. l.c., and by Apollinaris in Routh's *reliquiae sacr.* p. 9,
23 ff.; also in Cramer's *Catena,* p. 231; Overbeck in Hilgenfeld's *Zeitschr.* 1867, p. 39 ff.; Anger, *Synops.* p. 233).
There is no other way of accounting for so many diverse
traditions regarding this matter, but by supposing that nothing
was known as to how the death actually took place. Be
this as it may, we cannot entertain the view that *Judas
sunk into obscurity,* and so disappeared from history, but that
meanwhile the Christian legends regarding him were elaborated out of certain predictions and typical characters (Strauss,
Keim, Scholten) found in Scripture (in such passages as Ps.
cix. 8, lxix. 25); such a view being inadmissible, because it
takes no account of what is common to all the New Testament
accounts, the fact, namely, that Judas died a *violent* death, and
that very soon after the betrayal; and further, because the supposed predictions (Ps. lxix., cix., xx.) and typical characters (such
as Ahithophel, 2 Sam. xv. 30 ff., xvii. 23; Antiochus, 2 Macc.
ix. 5 ff.) did not help to create such stories regarding the
traitor's death, but it would be nearer the truth to say that
they were subsequently taken advantage of by critics to
account for the stories after they had originated.

Ver. 6. Οὐκ ἔξεστι] "argumento ducto ex Deut. xxiii.
18, *Sanhedr.* f. 112," Wetstein. — τιμὴ αἵματος] *the price*

of blood, which is supposed to have been shed. — κορβ.] τὸν ἱερὸν θησαυρόν, καλεῖται δὲ κορβανᾶς, Josephus, *Bell.* ii. 9. 4.

Ver. 7 f. Ἠγόρασαν] It is not said that they did so *immediately;* but the purchase took place *shortly* after, according to Acts i. 18. — τὸν ἀγρὸν τοῦ κεραμ.] *the field of the potter,* the field which had previously belonged to some well-known potter. Whether the latter had used the field for the purpose of digging clay, it is impossible to determine. — εἰς ταφὴν τ. ξένοις] *as a burying-place for the strangers,* namely, such foreign Jews (proselytes included) as happened to die when on a visit to Jerusalem; not *Gentiles* (Paulus), who, had they been intended, would have been indicated more specifically. — διό] because it had been bought with the τιμὴ αἵματος above (ver. 6). — ἀγρὸς αἵματος] חֲקֵל דְמָא, Acts i. 18, where, however, the name is traced to a different origin. On the place which in accordance with tradition is still pointed out as the field here referred to, see Robinson, II. p. 178 ff.; Tobler, *Topogr.*

Ver. 9 f. Τότε] when they bought this field for the thirty pieces of money.—The passage here quoted is a very free adaptation of Zech. xi. 12, 13,[1] Ἰερεμίου being simply a slip of the memory (comp. Augustine, *de cons. ev.* iii. 8, and recently Keil himself, following Calvin and the Fathers), such, however, as might readily enough occur through a reminiscence of Jer. xviii. 2. Considering that in the original Hebrew the resemblance of this latter passage to Zechariah, as above, is sufficiently close to warrant the typical mode of interpretation (Credner, *Beitr.* II. p. 152 f.), it is arbitrary to maintain, in the somewhat uncritical fashion of Rupert, Lyra, Maldonatus,

---

[1] If the evangelist had *meant to combine* two different predictions (Hofmann, *Weissag. u. Erf.* II. p. 128 f.; Haupt, *alttest. Citate,* p. 286 ff.), then, according to the analogy of ii. 23, we should have expected the words διὰ τῶν προφητῶν to be used. But, in short, our quotation belongs so exclusively to Zechariah, that candour forbids the idea of a combination with Jer. xviii., as well as the view adopted by Hengstenberg (comp. Grotius), that Zechariah reproduces the prediction of Jeremiah. For a detailed enumeration of the various attempts that have been made to deal with the inaccurate use of Ἰερεμίου, consult Morison, who follows Clericus in holding that there must have been a *transcriber's error* in the very earliest copy of our Gospel.

Jansen, Clericus, Friedlieb, that Ἰερεμίου is spurious; or, on
the other hand, to resort, as Origen, Euthymius Zigabenus,
Kuinoel, Ewald have done, to the idea of some *lost production* of Jeremiah's, or of some *oral* utterance that had never
been committed to writing (see, above all, Calovius, who in
support of this view lays great stress on ῥηθέν). As for the
statement of Jerome, that he had seen the passage in a copy
of Jeremiah belonging to some person at Nazareth, there can
be no doubt that what he saw was an interpolation, for he
also is one of those who ascribe the citation in question to
Zechariah. No less arbitrary is the conjecture of Eusebius,
Dem. ev. x. 4, that the Jews may have deleted the passage
from Jeremiah; for though it reappears again in a certain
Arabic work (Bengel, *Appar. crit.* p. 142), and in a Sahidic
and a Coptic lectionary (see Michaelis, *Bibl.* IV. p. 208 ff.;
Briefwechs. III. pp. 63, 89; *Einleit.* I. p. 264), it does so simply
as an interpolation from our present passage. See Paulus,
exeget. Handb. III. p. 615 ff.—According to the historical
sense of Zechariah, as above, the prophet, acting in Jehovah's
name, resigns his office of shepherd over Ephraim to Ephraim's
own ruin; and having requested his wages, consisting of 30
shekels of silver, to be paid him, he casts the money, as being
God's property, into the *treasury of the temple.* "And they
weighed for my wages thirty pieces of silver. Then Jehovah
said to me: Cast it into the treasury, that handsome (ironi-
cally) sum of which they have thought me worthy! So I
took the thirty pieces of silver, and cast them into the treasury
that was in God's house," Ewald, *Proph.;* Bleek in the *Stud. u.
Krit.* 1852, p. 279 ff. For we ought to read אֶל־הַיּוֹצֵר, *into the
treasury* (equivalent, as Kimchi explains, to אל האוצר, and as is
actually the reading of two MSS. in Kennicott), and not אֶל־הַיּוֹצֵר,
to the potter, as Matthew, in fact, also read and understood the
words, though such a meaning is entirely foreign to the context in Zechariah. Comp. Hitzig, *kl. Proph.* p. 374. The
expositors of Zechariah, who take היוצר in the sense of *potter,*
have had recourse to many an unfounded and sometimes
singular hypothesis. For specimens of these, see also Hengstenberg's *Christol.* III. 1, p. 457 ff.; Hofmann, *Weissag. u. Erf.*

II. p. 128 f.; Lange, *L. J.* II. p. 1494 f.; Steinmeyer, p. 105 f.; Haupt, *alttest. Citate*, p. 272 ff. — ἔλαβον] in Zechariah and LXX. is the *first* person singular, here it is the *third* person plural. The liberty thus used with the terms of the quotation may be supposed to be warranted by the concluding words : καθὰ συνέταξέ μοι ὁ κύριος. Neither the original Hebrew nor the LXX. countenances the supposition that the evangelist *erroneously* took ἔλαβον to be third person plural, like ἔδωκαν immediately following (in opposition to Hilgenfeld). — τὰ τριάκοντα ἀργύρ.] meaning, according to the typical reference in Matthew, the thirty shekels *brought back by Judas.* — τὴν τιμὴν, κ.τ.λ.] In apposition with τὰ τριάκ. ἀργ. The words correspond more with the Hebrew than with the LXX., though in this instance too a slight liberty is taken with them, inasmuch as for אֲשֶׁר יָקַרְתִּי we have once more (comp. on ἔλαβον) the third person plural ὃν ἐτιμήσαντο, and for מֵעֲלֵיהֶם the explanatory rendering ἀπὸ υἱῶν Ἰσραήλ. The passage then is to be rendered as follows : *And they took the thirty pieces of silver—the value of the highly valued One, on whom they put their own price* (middle, ἐτιμήσαντο) *at the instance of sons of Israel,* i.e. *the price of the priceless One, whose market value they fixed for themselves upon an occasion furnished by sons of Israel.* The expression υἱῶν Ἰσραήλ is the plural of category (ii. 20), and is regarded as finding its historical antitype in *Judas,* who, xxvi. 14 f., undertakes and carries through the shameful transaction there referred to,—he a son of Israel negotiates the sale of the Messiah of the people of Israel. In addition to what has just been observed, we would direct attention to the following details :—(1) τοῦ τετιμημένου is intended to represent the Hebrew word הַיְקָר (*pretii*) ; but the evangelist has evidently read הַיָּקָר (*cari, aestumati*), which he refers to *Jesus* as being the highly valued One κατ' ἐξοχήν; nor must we fail to notice here the remarkable collocation : *pretium pretiosi,* i.e. τὴν ὠνὴν τοῦ παντίμου Χριστοῦ, Euthymius Zigabenus ; comp. Theophylact, also Ewald. That distinguished personage, whose worth as such cannot in fact be estimated by any mere money standard (τιμή), they have actually valued (ἐτιμήσαντο) at thirty shekels ! To take the τοῦ τετιμημ.

merely in the sense of ὃν ἐτιμήσ. (*of the valued one*, him whom they have valued), as the majority of expositors do (including even yet de Wette, Lange, and Hofmann, *Weissag. u. Erf.* II. p. 130), instead of expressing the idea in a more forcible manner, would simply produce, especially after τ. τιμήν, a tautological redundancy. (2) The subject of ἐτιμήσαντο is the same as that of ἔλαβον, namely, the *high priests*; nor is the verb to be taken in the *sense* of estimating highly, as in the case of τετίμημ., but in that of *valuing, putting a price upon*, the sense in which it is used in Isa. lv. 2, and very frequently by classical writers, and in which the Hebrew יָקְרְתִּי is intended to be understood. (3) ἀπὸ υἱῶν Ἰσρ., which is a more definite rendering of the מעליהם of the original, must necessarily be connected, like its corresponding Hebrew expression, with ἐτιμήσαντο, and not with ἔλαβον (Fritzsche, Hilgenfeld), nor with τοῦ τετίμημ. (which de Wette considers possible), and be understood as denoting *origin, i.e.* as denoting, in our present passage, the *occasion* brought about by some one (comp. also Bleek) in connection with which the ἐτιμήσαντο took place; " ἀπό de eo ponitur, quod praebet occasionem vel opportunitatem, ut aliquid fieri possit," Stallbaum, *ad Plat. Rep.* p. 549 A; comp. Kühner, II. 1, p. 396; similarly xi. 19; see also Ellendt, *Lex. Soph.* I. p. 194. They were indebted to the sons of Israel (Judas, see above) for that which suggested and led to the ἐτιμήσαντο. We cannot approve of the course which some adopt of supplying τινές: equivalent to οἱ Ἰσραηλῖται (Euthymius Zigabenus), or "*qui sunt* ex filiis Israel" (Beza, Grotius, Maldonatus, Paulus, Kuinoel, Ewald, de Wette, Grimm, Anger), thus making ἀπὸ υἱῶν Ἰσρ. the subject of ἐτιμήσ. In that case, the ordinary ἐκ (comp. Buttmann, *Neut. Gr.* p. 138 [E. T. 158]) would have been used (as in xxiii. 34; John xvi. 17, *al.*), and instead of υἱῶν we should have had τῶν υἱῶν, inasmuch as the whole community would be intended to which the τινές are supposed to belong. Comp. also 1 Macc. vii. 33, 3 Macc. i. 8, where, though ἀπό is the preposition used, the article is conjoined with the substantive following. The absence of the article here is likewise unfavourable to the views of Hofmann, *Weissag. u. Erf.* II. p.

131, who, taking ἀπό to mean *on the part of*, interprets thus:
"What Caiaphas and Judas did (ἐτιμήσαντο), was done
indirectly *by the whole nation.*" To explain ἀπό as *others* have
done, by assuming the idea of *purchase* in connection with it
(Castalio: "quem licitati *emerunt* ab Israelitis," comp. Erasmus, Luther, Vatablus, Jansen, Lange), is not only arbitrary,
inasmuch as the idea involved in ἐτιμήσαντο does not justify
the supposed pregnant force of ἀπό (Buttmann, p. 276 [E. T.
322]), but is incompatible with the מֵעַל of the original. No
less inconsistent with the original is the explanation of Baumgarten-Crusius: "whom they had valued *from among the
children of Israel,*" that is to say, "which they had
fixed as the price of one of the children of Israel." In that
case, again, we should have required the article along with
υἱῶν; and, besides, what a poor designation of the Messiah
would be the result of such an interpretation! With an
equal disregard of the terms of the passage, Linder maintains, in the *Stud. u. Krit.* 1859, p. 513, that ἀπό is equivalent to τινὰ ἐκ: *as an Israelite* (whom they treated like a
slave); and to the same effect is the explanation of Steinmeyer,
p. 107: whom they have valued *in the name of the nation.*
Neither the simple ἀπό nor the anarthrous υἱῶν Ἰσρ. admits
of being so understood, although Hilgenfeld is also of opinion
that our passage meant to describe the betrayal as *an act
for which the whole body of the Jewish people was to be held
responsible.* Ver. 10. Καὶ ἔδωκαν αὐτὰ εἰς τὸν ἀγρὸν
τοῦ κεραμ.] Zech., as above, וָיַשְׁלִיךְ אֹתוֹ בֵּית יְהֹוָה אֶל הַיּוֹצֵר.
But, inasmuch as the important matter here was the
purchase of the potter's field, Matthew leaves בֵּית יהוה
entirely out of view, takes יוֹצֵר in the sense of *potter* (see,
on the other hand, on ver. 9 above), and, in order that
אֶל הַיּוֹצֵר may fully harmonize with a typical and prophetic
view of the passage, he paraphrases the words thus: εἰς τὸν
ἀγρὸν τοῦ κεραμέως, where εἰς is intended to express the
destined object of the thing: for the purpose of acquiring
the field belonging to the potter. — καθὰ συνέταξέ μοι
κύριος] corresponds to Zechariah's וַיֹּאמֶר יְהֹוָה אֵלַי, ver. 13, the
words employed by the *prophet* when he asserts that in

casting the shekels into the treasury of the temple he did so in obedience to the command of God. In accordance with the typical reference ascribed to the passage by Matthew, the words "*according to that which the Lord commanded me*" are so applied as to express the idea that the using of the traitor's reward for the purpose of buying the potter's field was simply giving effect to the decree of Him from whom the prophet had received the command in question. That which God had commissioned the prophet (μοι) to do with the thirty pieces of silver is done in the antitypical fulfilment of the prophecy by the high priests, who thus carry out the divine decree above referred to. Καθά, *just as* (Xen. *Mem.* iv. 6. 5; Polyb. iii. 107. 10; Lucian, *Cont.* 24; Diod. Sic. i. 36; in classical Greek καθάπερ is usually employed), occurs nowhere else in the New Testament. It is quite possible that the words used in the Hebrew original of Matthew were כַּאֲשֶׁר דִּבֶּר or כַּאֲשֶׁר צִוָּה, which in the LXX. are likewise rendered by καθὰ συνέταξε, Ex. ix. 12, xl. 25; Num. viii. 3.

Ver. 11 f. Continuation, after the episode in vv. 3–10, of the narrative introduced at ver. 2. The accusation preferred by the Jews, though not expressly mentioned, may readily be inferred from the procurator's question. See Luke xxiii. 2. In appearing before Pilate, they craftily give prominence to the *political* aspect of the Messianic pretensions of Jesus. — σὺ λέγεις] There is nothing ambiguous in such a reply (which was not so framed that it might be taken either as an affirmative *or* as equivalent to ἐγὼ μὲν τοῦτο οὐ λέγω, σὺ δὲ λέγεις, Theophylact), but such a *decided affirmative* as the terms of the question: *Art thou*, etc., were calculated to elicit, John xviii. 37. Comp. xxvi. 64. — οὐδὲν ἀπεκρ.] Comp. on xxvi. 62. The calm and dignified silence of the true king.

Ver. 14. Πρὸς οὐδὲ ἐν ῥῆμα] intensifying the force of the expression: *to not even a single word, i.e.* to not even a single inquisitorial interrogative. The silence mentioned in vv. 12, 14 comes in after the examination reported in John xviii. 37. — ὥστε θαυμάζειν] convinced as he was of the innocence of Jesus, he was all the more at a loss to understand the forbearance with which He maintained such sublime silence. .

Ver. 15. Κατὰ ἑορτήν] *on the occasion of the feast,* i.e. during the feast-time (Kühner, II. 1, p. 412; Winer, p. 374 [E. T. 500]); that the *Passover* is here meant is evident from the *context.* — As there is no allusion to this custom anywhere else (for an account of which, however, see Bynaeus, *de morte Chr.* III. p. 97 ff.), nothing whatever is known as to when it originated. But whether we date the custom back to the Maccabaean age or to an earlier period still (Ewald, *Gesch. Chr.* p. 570), or regard it as having been introduced[1] for the first time by the Romans (Grotius, Schleiermacher, Friedlieb) for the purpose of conciliating the Jews, we cannot fail to see in it a reference to that which is intended to be set forth by the Passover (*sparing mercy*), and applicable most probably to the 14th of Nisan (comp. on John xviii. 24, 39).

Ver. 16. Εἶχον] The subject is to be found in ὁ ἡγεμών, ver. 15, that is to say : *the procurator and his soldiers;* for, like Jesus, Barabbas had also to be examined before Pilate before his case could be finally disposed of. He was lying in the prison in the praetorium awaiting execution, after having received sentence of death. — Concerning this robber and murderer Jesus Barabbas (see the critical remarks), nothing further is known. The name Barabbas occurs very frequently even in the Talmud; Lightfoot, p. 489. There is the less reason, therefore, for thinking, with Olshausen, that the characteristic significance of the name בַּר אַבָּא, father's *son (i.e.* probably the *son of a Rabbi,* xxiii. 9), in close proximity with the person of Jesus, is an illustration of the saying : " *Ludit in humanis divina potentia rebus.*" Still it is possible

_____

[1] It may be mentioned as tending to favour this supposition, that while no trace of such a custom is met with in the Talmud, there is something to a certain modified extent analogous to it in the practice observed by the Romans at the feast of the *lectisternia* (Liv. v. 14). Schoettgen detects an allusion to some such origin in *Pesachim* f. 91, 1, though this is very doubtful. Then, as for the statement of Josephus, *Antt.* xx. 9. 3, which is quoted by Keim, it cannot be said to imply the existence of any practice, and it refers besides to a case in which ten persons were liberated.

that the accidental similarity in the name *Jesus* (see the critical remarks) may have helped to suggest to Pilate the release of *Barabbas* as an alternative, though, after all, the circumstance that the latter was a *most notorious* criminal undoubtedly swayed him most. For the baser the criminal, the less would Pilate expect them to demand his release. " But they would sooner have asked the devil himself to be liberated," Luther's gloss.

Ver. 17. Οὖν] In accordance with the custom referred to, and as it so happened that at that moment there lay under sentence of death (vv. 15, 16) a noted criminal called Jesus Barabbas, Pilate got the multitude that was collected outside gathered together, and then asked them to choose between Jesus *Barabbas* and Jesus who was called the *Messiah.* — αὐτῶν] refers not to the members of the Sanhedrim, but to the ὄχλος, ver. 15. See ver. 20.

Ver. 18. Γάρ] Had he not been aware, etc., he would not have thus attempted to effect the release of Jesus. — παρέδωκαν] The subject of the verb is, of course, the *members of the Sanhedrim* (ver. 2), whose dominant selfishness was too conspicuous in itself, as well as from the *animus* that characterized their behaviour, to escape his notice. They were *jealous* of the importance and influence of Jesus; διά denotes the *motive* which animated them : *because of envy;* see Winer, p. 372 [E. T. 497]. This was the *causa remotior.*

Ver. 19. Before, Pilate had submitted the question of ver. 17 to the consideration of the people by way of sounding them. Now, he seats himself upon the tribunal (upon the λιθόστρωτον, John xix. 13) for the purpose of hearing the decision of the multitude, and of thereafter pronouncing sentence. But while he is sitting on the tribunal, and before he had time again to address his question to the multitude, his wife sends, etc. This particular is peculiar to *Matthew;* whereas the sending to Herod, and that *before* the proposal about the release, occurs only in *Luke* (xxiii. 6 ff.) ; and as for *John,* he omits both those circumstances altogether, though, on the whole, his account of the trial before Pilate is much more *detailed* than the *concise* narrative of Matthew, and that without any want of harmony being found between the two evangelists. — ἡ γυνὴ αὐτοῦ] for since the time of Augustus it was customary for Roman governors to take their wives with them into the provinces. Tacit. *Ann.* iii. 33 f. According to tradition, the name of Pilate's wife was Procla, or Claudia Procula (see *Evang. Nicod.* ii., and thereon Thilo, p. 522 ff.). In the Greek church she has been canonised. — λέγουσα] through her messengers, xxii. 16, xi. 2. — μηδέν σοι κ. τ. δικ. ἐκ.] comp. viii. 29 ; John ii. 4. She was afraid that a judgment from the gods would be the consequence if he had anything to do with the death of Jesus. — πολλὰ γὰρ ἔπαθον, κ.τ.λ.] This alarming dream is to be accounted for on the understanding that the governor's wife, who in the *Evang. Nicod.* is described, and it may be correctly, as θεοσεβής and ἰουδαΐζουσα (see Tischendorf, *Pilati circa Christum judic. etc. ex actis Pilat.* 1855, p. 16 f.), may have heard of Jesus, may even have seen Him and felt a lively interest in Him, and may have been informed of His arrest as well as of the jeopardy in which His life was placed. There is nothing to show that Matthew intended us to regard this incident as a special *divine* interposition. There is the less reason for relegating it to the domain of *legend* (Strauss, Ewald, Scholten, Volkmar, Keim). — σήμερον] during the part of the night belonging to the current day. — κατ' ὄναρ] see on i. 20. It was a terrible *morning-dream*.

Ver. 20. The question of ver. 17 is still under the consideration of the assembled crowd ; and while Pilate, who had mounted the tribunal for the purpose of hearing their decision, is occupied with the messengers from his wife, the members of the Sanhedrim take advantage of this interruption to persuade the people, etc. — ἵνα] *purpose* of ἔπεισαν. Ὅπως is likewise used with πείθειν by Greek authors. See Schoem. *ad Plut. Cleom.* p. 192.

Ver. 21. Ἀποκριθεὶς δὲ, κ.τ.λ.] The governor, having from his tribunal overheard this parleying of the members of the Sanhedrim with the people, now *replies* to it by once more demanding of the latter, with a view to a final decision :

which of the two, etc. He thus puts a stop to the officious
conduct of the hierarchs, and resumes his attitude of waiting
for the answer of the crowd.

Ver. 22. *Τί οὖν ποιήσω Ἰησοῦν;*] *What, then* (if Barabbas is to be released), *am I to do with Jesus,* how shall I
dispose of him ?   On this use of the double accusative with
ποιεῖν, in the sense of doing good or evil to any one, comp.
Kühner, II. 1, p. 277; Wunder, *ad Soph. Phil.* 684. —
σταυρωθήτω] οὐ λέγουσι· φονευθήτω, ἀλλὰ σταυρωθήτω, ἵνα
καὶ τὸ εἶδος τοῦ θανάτου κακοῦργον (as a rebel) ἀπελέγχῃ
αὐτόν, Euthymius Zigabenus.   Doubtless it was also at the
instigation of the hierarchs that they demanded this particular form of punishment.

Ver. 23. *Τί γάρ*] does not presuppose a " *non faciam,*" or
some such phrase (Grotius, Maldonatus, Fritzsche), but γάρ
denotes an *inference* from the existing state of matters, and
throws the whole emphasis upon τί: *quid ergo.*   See on
John ix. 30 and 1 Cor. xi. 22. — Chrysostom appropriately
points out how ἀνάνδρως καὶ σφόδρα μαλακῶς Pilate behaved.

Ver. 24. The circumstance of Pilate's washing his hands,
which Strauss and Keim regard as legendary, is also peculiar
to Matthew. — ὅτι οὐδὲν ὠφελεῖ] *that it was all of no
avail,* John xii. 19.   "Desperatum est hoc praejudicium
practicum," Bengel. — ἀλλὰ μᾶλλον θόρυβος γίνεται] *that
the tumult is only aggravated thereby.* — ἀπενίψατο τὰς
χεῖρας] *he washed his hands,* to show that he was no
party to the execution thus insisted upon.   This ceremony
was a piece of *Jewish* symbolism (Deut. xxi. 6 f.; Joseph.
Antt. iv. 8. 16 ; *Sota* viii. 6); and as Pilate understood its
significance, he would hope by having recourse to it to make
himself the more intelligible to Jews.   It is possible that
what led the governor to conform to this Jewish custom
was the analogy between it and similar practices observed by
Gentiles *after* a murder has been committed (Herod. i. 35 ;
Virg. *Aen.* ii. 719 f.; Soph. *Aj.* 654, and Schneidewin
thereon ; Wetstein on our passage), more particularly as it was
also customary for Gentile judges before pronouncing sentence to protest, and that " πρὸς τὸν ἥλιον " (*Constitt. Ap.* ii.

52. 1 ; *Evang. Nicod.* ix.), that they were innocent of the blood of the person about to be condemned ; see Thilo, *ad Cod. Apocr.* I. p. 573 f.; Heberle in the *Stud. u. Krit.* 1856, p. 859 ff. — ἀπὸ τοῦ αἵματος] a Greek author would have used the genitive merely (Maetzner, *ad Lycurg.* 79). The construction with ἀπό is a Hebraism (מדם נקי, 2 Sam. iii. 27), founded on the idea of removing to a distance. Comp. Hist. Susann. 46, and καθαρὸς ἀπό, Acts xx. 26. — ὑμεῖς ὄψ.] See on ver. 4.

Ver. 25. Ἐφ' ἡμᾶς, κ.τ.λ.] Defiant and vindictive cry, in the hurry of which (τοιαύτη γὰρ ἡ ὁρμὴ κ. ἡ πονηρὰ ἐπιθυμία, Chrysostom) the verb is left to be understood (xxiii. 35). Comp. 2 Sam. i. 16, and see on Acts xviii. 6. From what we know of such wild outbursts of popular fanaticism, there is no ground for supposing (Strauss ; comp. also Keim, Scholten, Volkmar) that the language only represents the matter as seen from the standpoint of *Christians,* by whom the destruction of the Jews had come to be regarded as a judgment for putting Jesus to death. And as for their wicked imprecations on their own heads, they were only in accordance with the decrees of the divine nemesis, and therefore are to be regarded in the light of unconscious prophecy.

Ver. 26. Φραγελλώσας] a late word adopted from the Latin, and used for μαστιγοῦν. Comp. John ii. 15 ; see Wetstein. It was the practice among the Romans to *scourge* the culprit (with cords or thongs of leather) before crucifying him (Liv. xxxiii. 36 ; Curt. vii. 11. 28 ; Valer. Max. i. 7 ; Joseph. *Bell.* v. 11. 1, *al. ;* Heyne, *Opusc.* III. p. 184 f. ; Keim, III. p. 390 f.). According to the more detailed narrative of John xix. 1 ff., Pilate, after this scourging was over, and while the soldiers were mocking Him, made a final attempt to have Jesus set at liberty. According to Luke xxiii. 16, the governor contemplated ultimate scourging immediately after the examination before Herod,—a circumstance which neither prevents us from supposing that he subsequently carried out his intention (in opposition to Strauss), nor justifies the interpretation of our passage given by Paulus : *whom He had previously scourged* (with a view to His being liberated). — παρέδωκεν] namely, to the Roman soldiers, ver. 27. These latter were entrusted with the task of seeing the execution carried out.

Ver. 27. Εἰς τὸ πραιτώριον] It would appear, then, that the scourging had taken place outside, in *front* of the praetorium, beside the tribunal. This coincides with Mark xv. 16, ἔσω τῆς αὐλῆς, which merely defines the locality *more precisely*. The πραιτώριον was the *official residence*, the palace of the governor, it being commonly supposed (so also Ewald, *Gesch. Chr.* p. 53, and Keim, III. p. 359 ff.) that Herod's palace, situated in the higher part of the city, was used for this purpose. But, inasmuch as this latter building would have to be reserved for the accommodation of Herod himself whenever he had occasion to go to Jerusalem, and with what is said at Luke xxiii. 7 before us, it is more likely that the palace in question was a different and special one connected with fort Antonia, in which the σπεῖρα (comp. Acts xxi. 31– 33) was quartered. Comp. also Weiss on *Mark* xv. 16. — οἱ στρατιῶται τοῦ ἡγεμ.] who were on duty as the procurator's orderlies. — ἐπ᾿ αὐτόν] *about Him ;* comp. Mark v. 21, not *adversus eum* (Fritzsche, de Wette); for they were merely to make sport of Him. — τὴν σπεῖραν] *the cohort*, which was quartered at Jerusalem in the garrison of the praetorium (in Caesarea there were five cohorts stationed). Comp. on John xviii. 3. The expression: the *whole* cohort, is to be understood in its popular, and not in a strictly literal sense; the στρατιῶ- ται, to whose charge Jesus had been committed, and who only formed part of the cohort, invited all their comrades to join them who happened to be in barracks at the time.

Ver. 28. Ἐνδύσαντες (see the critical remarks) is to be explained by the fact that previous to the scourging all His clothes had been pulled off (Acts xvi. 22; Dionys. Hal. ix. 596). They accordingly put on His under garments again, and instead of the upper robes (τὰ ἱμάτια, ver. 31) they arrayed Him in a red *sagum*, the ordinary *military cloak* (Plut. *Sert.* 14; *Philop.* 9, 11), for the purpose, however, of ridiculing His pretensions to the dignity of *king ;* for kings and emperors likewise wore the χλαμύς, the only difference being that in their case the garment was longer and of a finer texture. Plut. *Demetr.* 41 f.; *Mor.* p. 186 C, *al.* On this military cloak, which was first used by the Macedonians, see Hermann, *Privatalterth.* § xxi. 20; Friedlieb, p. 118. According to the other evangelists, the cloak made use of on this occasion was of a *purple* colour; but Matthew would intend *scarlet* (Heb. ix. 19; Rev. xvii. 3; Num. iv. 8; Plut. *Fab.* xv.) to be taken as at least conveying the *idea* of purple.

Ver. 29 f. 'Εξ ἀκανθῶν] belongs to πλέξαντες. What is meant is something made by twisting together young flexible thorns so as to represent the royal diadem. The object was not to produce suffering, but to excite ridicule; so that while we cannot altogether dissociate the idea of something painful from this crown of thorns, we must not conceive of it as covered with prickles which were intentionally thrust into the flesh. Michaelis adopts the rendering *Bärenklau* (ἄκανθος); but this is incompatible with the ἀκάνθινον of Mark xv. 17, which adjective is never used with reference to the plant just mentioned. Besides, this latter was a plant that was *highly prized* (for which reason it was often used for ornamental purposes in pieces of sculpture and on the capitals of Corinthian pillars), and therefore would be but ill suited for a caricature. It is impossible to determine what *species* of thorn it was (possibly the so-called *spina Christi?*; see Tobler, *Denkbl.* pp. 113, 179). — καὶ κάλαμον] ἔθηκαν being understood, the connection with ἐπέθηκαν is *zeugmatic.*—Observe the imperfects ἐνέπαιζον and ἔτυπτον as indicating the *continuous* character of the proceeding.

Ver. 31. Καὶ ἐνέδυσαν αὐτὸν τὰ ἱμάτ. αὐτοῦ] His upper garments, for which they had substituted the *sagum.* This is in no way at variance with ἐνδύσαντες, ver. 28.—We are to understand that as the crown of thorns had now served its purpose, it was also taken off at the same time.

Ver. 32. 'Εξερχόμενοι] because the law required that all executions should take place *outside the city.* Num. xv. 35 f.; 1 Kings xxi. 13; Acts vii. 58; Lightfoot and Grotius on our passage.—On the question as to whether this *Simon of Cyrene,* a place in Libya Pentapolitana, thickly peopled with Jews,

resided statedly in Jerusalem (Acts vi. 19), or was only there
on a visit (Acts ii. 10), see below.   It was usual to compel the
person who was to be executed to carry his *own* cross (see on
x. 38, and Keim, p. 397 f.);[1] to this the case of Jesus was no
exception, John xix. 17.   This statement of John does not
exclude what is here said with regard to Simon and the cross,
nor does it pretend to deny it (Keim), but it simply passes it
over in silence, recording merely the main point in question,
—the fact, namely, that Jesus had to carry His own cross
(though there is nothing to prevent the supposition that He
may have broken down under the burden before reaching the
scene of the crucifixion).—That with such a large crowd
following (Luke xxiii. 27) they should notwithstanding compel
a foreigner who happened to be going toward the city (Mark,
Luke) to carry the cross the rest of the way, is a circumstance

[1] That is to say, the *post*, the *upright beam* of the cross, to which the trans-
verse beam was not attached till the scene of the execution was reached, where
the instrument of torture was duly put together and then set up with the criminal nailed to it.   Hence (because σταυρός originally meant a *post*) we find Greek
authors making use of such expressions as σταυρὸν φέρειν, ἐπιφέρειν, βαστάζειν,
λαμβάνειν, αἴρειν, comp. σταυροφορεῖν; Latin writers, however, with rather more
regard for precision, distinguish between the *upright beam* which the criminal
was called upon to *carry*, and the *crux* as it appeared when completed and *set
up* at the place of execution.   The *upright beam* which the cruciarius was
compelled to drag after him was called *patibulum;* hence we never meet with
the phrase *crucem ferre*, but always *patibulum* (the upright post) *ferre*, which
patibulum was placed upon the poor criminal's back, and with his outstretched
hands securely tied to it, he had to balance it the best way he could upon his
neck and shoulders.   It is this distinction between *crux* and *patibulum* that
enables us adequately to explain the well-known passages of Plautus: " Patibulum ferat per urbem, deinde affigatur cruci " (*ap. Non. Marcell.* 221), and
" Dispensis manibus quom patibulum habebis" (*Mil. glor.* ii. 4. 7), and similarly with regard to expressions referring to the cross (as completed and set up):
in crucem *tollere*, in crucem *agere* (Cicero and others), etc. ; the comic expression
crucisalus (Plaut. *Bacch.* ii. 3. 128) ; as also the passage in Tacit. *Ann.* xiv.
33, where the different modes of punishing by death are enumerated, beginning
with those of a general nature and ending with the more specific: " Caedes, *pati-
bula* (beams for penal purposes generally), igues, *cruces.*"   From this it is manifest at once that it would be incorrect to suppose, with Keim, that all that Christ
had to carry was the *cross-beam.*   Such a view is at variance both with the language of our text: τὸν σταυρὸν αἴρειν, and with the Latin phrase : *patibulum* ferre.
So much is the *patibulum* regarded as the main portion of the cross, that in poetry
it is sometimes used as equivalent to *crux*, as in Prudent. *Peristeph.* ix. 641 :
" Crux illa nostra est, nos patibulum ascendimus."

sufficiently accounted for by the *infamy* that attached to that odious thing. Possibly Simon was a slave. To suppose that he was one of *Jesus' followers*, and that *for this reason* he had been pressed into the service (Grotius, Kuinoel), is altogether arbitrary, for, according to the text, the determining circumstance lies in the fact that he was ἄνθρωπον Κυρηναῖον. A foreigner coming from Cyrene would not be considered too respectable a person to be employed in such degrading work. That Simon, however, *became* a Christian, and that perhaps in consequence of his thus carrying the cross and being present at the crucifixion, is a legitimate inference from Mark xv. 21 compared with Rom. xvi. 13. — ἠγγάρ.] See on v. 41. ἵνα] mentions the *object* for which this was done.

Ver. 33. Γολγοθᾶ, Chald. גֻּלְגָּלְתָּא, Heb. גֻּלְגֹּלֶת, meaning a *skull*. Jerome and most other expositors (including Luther, Fritzsche, Strauss, Tholuck, Friedlieb) derive the name from the circumstance that, as this was a place for executing criminals, it abounded with skulls (which, however, are not to be conceived of as lying unburied); while Cyrill, Jerome, Calovius, Reland, Bengel, Paulus, Lücke, de Wette, Ewald, Bleek, Volkmar, Keim, Weiss, on the other hand, trace the name to the *shape* of the hill.[1] The latter view, which is also that of Thenius (in Ilgen's *Zeitschr. f. Theol.* 1842, 4, p. 1 ff.) and Furer (in Schenkel's *Lex.* II. p. 506), ought to be preferred, because the name means nothing *more* than simply a *skull* (not *hill* of skulls, *valley* of skulls, and such like, as though the *plural* (skulls) had been used). A similar practice of giving to places, according to their shape, such names, as *Kopf, Scheitel* (comp. the hills called Κεφαλαί in Strabo, xvii. 3, p. 835), *Stirn*, and the like, is not uncommon among ourselves—

---

[1] In trying to account for the origin of the name, the Fathers, from Tertullian and Origen down to Euthymius Zigabenus, make reference to the tradition that Adam was buried in the place of a skull. This Judaeo-Christian legend is very old and very widely diffused (see Dillmann, "zum christl. Adambuch," in Ewald's *Jahrb.* V. p. 142); but we are not warranted in confidently assuming that it was of pre-Christian origin (Dillmann) simply because Athanasius, Epiphanius, and others have characterized it as Jewish; it would naturally find much favour, as being well calculated to serve the interests of Christian typology (Augustine : "quia ibi erectus sit medicus, ubi jacebat aegrotus," etc.).

(Germans). — ὅ ἐστι κρανίου τόπος λεγόμενος] *which*, i.e. which Aramaic term *denotes* (ἐστί) *a so-called* (λεγόμ., Kühner, II. 1, p. 232) *place of a skull*, Lat.: *quod calvariae quem dicunt locum significat.* It was probably a *round, bare hill.* But where it stood it is utterly impossible to determine, although it may be regarded as certain (in opposition to Raumer, Schubert, Krafft, Lange, Furer) that it was *not* the place *within* the city (the so-called Mount Calvary), which subsequently to the time of Constantine had been excavated under the impression that it was so,—a point, however, which Ritter, *Erdk.* XVI. 1, p. 427 ff., leaves somewhat doubtful. See Robinson, *Paläst.* II. p. 270 ff., and his *neuere Forsch.* 1857, p. 332 ff. In answer to Robinson, consult Schaffter, *d. ächte Lage d. heil. Grabes,* 1849. But see in general, Tobler, *Golgatha, seine Kirchen und Klöster,* 1851; Fallmerayer in the *Abh. d. Baier. Akad.* 1852, VI. p. 641 ff.; Ewald, *Jahrb.* II. p. 118 ff., VI. p. 84 ff.; Arnold in Herzog's *Encykl.* V. p. 307 ff.; Keim, III. p. 404 ff.

Ver. 34. The Jews were in the habit of giving the criminal a stupefying drink before nailing him to the cross. *Sanhedr.* vi. See Wetstein, *ad Marc.* xv. 23; Doughtaeus, *Anal.* II. p. 42. This drink consisted of *wine* (see the critical remarks) mixed with *gall*, according to Matthew; with *myrrh*, according to Mark. χολή admits of no other meaning than that of *gall*, and ·on no account must it be made to bear the sense of myrrh or wormwood[1] (Beza, Grotius, Paulus, Langen, Steinmeyer, Keim). The tradition about the *gall*, which unquestionably belongs to a later period, originated in the LXX.

---

[1] No doubt the LXX. translate לַעֲנָה, *wormwood*, by χολή (Prov. v. 4; Lam. iii. 15); but in those passages they took it *as meaning* literal "gall," just as in the case of Ps. lxix. 22, which regulates the sense of our present passage, they also understood gall to be *meant*, although the word in the original is רֹאשׁ (*poison*). Comp. Jer. viii. 14; Deut. xxix. 17. A usage so entirely foreign to the Greek tongue certainly cannot be justified on the ground of one or two passages, like these from the Septuagint. Had "bitter spiced wine" (Steinmeyer) been what Matthew intended, he would have had no more difficulty in expressing this than Mark himself. But the idea he wished to convey was that of wine along with *gall*, in fact *mixed* with it, and this idea he *expresses* as plain as words can speak it. Comp. Barnab. 7: σταυρωθεὶς ἐποτίζετο ὄξει καὶ χολῇ.

rendering of Ps. lxix. 22 ; people wished to make out that there was *maltreatment* in the very drink that was offered. — γευσάμενος] According to Matthew, then, Jesus rejected the potion because the taste of gall made it undrinkable. A later view than that embodied in Mark xv. 23, from which passage it would appear that Jesus does not even taste the drink, but declines it altogether, because He has no desire to be stupefied before death.

Ver. 35. Σταυρώσαντες] The cross consisted of the upright post and the horizontal beam (called by Justin and Tertullian : *antenna*), the former usually projecting some distance beyond the latter (as was also the case, according to the tradition of the early church, with the cross of Jesus, see Friedlieb, p. 130 ff. ; Langen, p. 321 ff.). As a rule, it was first of all set up, and then the person to be crucified was hoisted on to it with his body resting upon a peg (πῆγμα) that passed between his legs (ἐφ' ᾧ ἐποχοῦνται οἱ σταυρούμενοι, Justin, c. *Tryph.* 91 ; Iren. *Haer.* ii. 24. 4), after which the hands were nailed to the cross-beam. Paulus (see his *Komment., exeg. Handb.,* and *Skizzen aus m. Bildungsgesch.* 1839, p. 146 ff.), following Clericus on John xx. 27 and Dathe on Ps. xxii. 7, firmly maintains that the *feet* were not *nailed as well ;*[1] an opinion which is likewise held more or less decidedly by Lücke, Fritzsche, Ammon, Baumgarten-Crusius, Winer, *de pedum in cruce affixione,* 1845 ; Schleiermacher, *L. J.* p. 447. In answer to Paulus, see Hug in the *Freib. Zeitschr.* III. p. 167 ff., and V. p. 102 ff., VII. p. 153 ff. ; *Gutacht.* II. p. 174 ; and especially Bähr in Heydenreich and Hüffell's *Zeitschr.* 1830, 2, p. 308 ff., and in Tholuck's *liter. Anz.* 1835, Nos. 1–6. For the history of this dispute, see Tholuck's *liter. Anz.* 1834, Nos. 53–55, and Langen, p. 312 ff. *That the feet were usually nailed, and that the case of Jesus was no exception to the general rule,* may be regarded as beyond doubt, and that for the following reasons : (1) Because nothing can be more evident than that Plautus,

[1] This question possesses an interest not merely antiquarian ; it is of essential importance in enabling us to judge of the view held by Dr. Paulus, that the death of Jesus was only apparent and not real.

Mostell. ii. 1. 13 (" ego dabo ei talentum, primus qui in crucem excucurrerit, sed ea lege, *ut offigantur bis pedes, bis brachia* "), presupposes that to nail the feet as well as the hands was the *ordinary practice*, and that he intends the *bis* to point to something of an *exceptional* character ; (2) because Justin, *c. Tryph.* 97, expressly maintains (comp. *Apol.* I. 35), and that in a polemical treatise, at a time when crucifixion was still in vogue, that the feet of Jesus were pierced with nails, and treats the circumstance as a fulfilment of Ps. xxii. 17, without the slightest hint that in this there was any departure from the usual custom ; (3) because Tertullian (*c. Marc.* iii. 19), in whose day also crucifixion was universally practised (Constantine having been the first to abolish it), agrees with Justin in seeing Ps. xxii. 17 verified in Christ, and would hardly have said, with reference to the piercing of our Lord's hands and feet : " *quae proprie atrocitas crucis est,*" unless it had been generally understood that the feet were nailed as well ; (4) because Lucian, *Prometh.* 2 (where, moreover, it is not *crucifying* in the proper sense of the word that is alluded to), and Lucan, *Phars.* vi. 547 (" insertum *manibus* chalybem "), furnish nothing but arguments *a silentio*, which have the less weight that these passages do not pretend to give a *full* account of the matter ; (5) because we nowhere find in ancient literature any distinct mention of a case in which the feet *hung loose* or were merely *tied* to the cross, for Xen. *Eph.* iv. 2 merely informs us that the *binding* of the hands and the feet was a practice peculiar to the *Egyptians ;* (6) and lastly, because in Luke xxiv. 39 f. itself the piercing of the feet is taken for granted, for only by means of the *pierced* hands and feet was Christ to be identified (His *corporeality* was also to be proved, but that was to be done by the handling which followed). It is probable that each foot was nailed separately.[1] The most plausible arguments

[1] This view is borne out not only by the simple fact that it would be somewhat impracticable to pierce *both* the feet *when lying one above the other* (as they usually appear in pictures, and as they are already represented by Nonnus, John xx. 19), because in order to secure the necessary firmness, the nail would require to be so long and thick that there would be a danger of dislocating, if

in addition to the above *against* the view that the feet
were nailed are : (1) what is said in John xx. 25 (see
Lücke, II. p. 798), where, however, the absence of any
mention of the feet on the part of Thomas entirely accord
with his natural sense of propriety. He assumes the Lord,
who had been seen by his fellow-disciples, to be *standing
before him ;* and so, with a view to identification, he wishes
to feel the prints of the nails in his hands and the wound in
His side, those being the marks that *could then be most con-
veniently got at ;* and that is enough. To have stooped down
to examine the feet as well would have been going *rather far*,
would have seemed somewhat *indecent*, somewhat *undignified*,
nay, we should say that the introduction of such a feature into
the narrative would have had an *apocryphal* air; (2) the
fact that while Socrates, *H. E.* i. 17, speaks of the Empress
Helena, who found the cross, as having also discovered τοὺς
ἥλους οἳ ταῖς χερσὶ τοῦ Χριστοῦ κατὰ τὸν σταυρὸν ἐνεπά-
γησαν, he makes no mention of the nails for the *feet*. But,
according to the context, the nails for the hands are to be
understood as forming merely a *part* of what was discovered
along with the cross, as forming a portion, that is, of what *the
empress gave as a present to her son.* This passage, however,
has all the less force as an argument against the supposition
that the feet were nailed, that Ambrose, *Or. de obitu Theodos.*
§ 47, while also stating that two nails belonging to the
cross that was discovered were presented to Constantine,
clearly indicates at the same time that they were the *nails for
the feet* (" ferro pedum "). It would appear, then, that *two*
nails were presented to Constantine, but opinion was divided
as to whether they were those for the feet or those for the
hands, there being also a third view, to the effect that the
two *pairs* were presented together (Rufinus, *H. E.* ii. 8 ;

not of shattering the feet, but it is still further confirmed by the ancient tradition respecting the two *pairs* of nails that were used to fasten Jesus to the cross.
See below under No. 2. And how is it possible to understand aright what Plautus
says about feet *twice*-nailed, if we are to conceive of them as lying one upon the
other ! Probably they were placed alongside of each other, and then nailed
with the soles flat upon the upright beam of the cross. A board for the feet
(*suppedaneum*) was not used, being unnecessary.

Theodoret, *H. E.* i. 17). This diversity of opinion bears, however, a united testimony, not *against*, but *in favour of* the practice of nailing the feet, and that a testimony belonging to a time when there were many still living who had a vivid recollection of the days when crucifixion was quite common. — διεμερίσαντο τὰ ἱμάτια αὐτοῦ] The criminal when affixed to the cross was absolutely *naked* (Artemid. ii. 58 ; Lipsius, *de cruce*, ii. 7), and his clothes fell, as a perquisite, to the executioners (Wetstein on our passage). The supposition that there was a cloth for *covering the loins* has at least no early testimony to support it. See Thilo, *ad Evang. Nicod.* x. p. 582 f. — βάλλοντες κλῆρον] more precisely in John xix. 23 f. Whether this was done by means of dice or by putting the lots into something or other (a helmet) and then shaking them out (comp. on Acts i. 26), it is impossible to say.

Ver. 37. Whether it was *customary* to have a tablet (σανίς) put over the cross containing a statement of the crime (τὴν αἰτίαν αὐτοῦ) for which the offender was being executed, we have no means of knowing. According to Dio Cass. liv. 8, it might be seen hanging round the neck of the criminal even when he was passing through the city to the place of execution. Comp. also Sueton. *Domit.* 10 ; *Calig.* 32 ; Euseb. v. 1. 19. — ἐπέθηκαν] It was undoubtedly affixed to the part of the cross that projected above the horizontal beam. But it is inadmissible, in deference to the hypothesis that the "title" (John xix. 19) was affixed to the cross *before* it was set up, either to transpose the verses in the text (vv. 33, 34, 37, 38, 35, 36, 39, so Wassenbergh in Valckenaer, *Schol.* II. p. 31), or to take ἐπέθηκαν (Kuinoel) in the sense of the *pluperfect*, or to assume some *inaccuracy* in the narrative, by supposing, for example, that the various details are not given in chronological order, and that the mention of the watch being set is introduced too soon, from a desire to include at once all that was done (de Wette, Bleek) by the soldiers (who, however, are understood to have nailed up the "title" as well!). According to Matthew's statement, it would appear that when the soldiers had finished

the work of crucifixion, and had cast lots for the clothes, and
had mounted guard over the body, they proceed, by way of
supplementing what had been already done, to affix the "title"
to the top of the cross. The terms of the inscription are
given with diplomatic precision in John xix. 20, though
others, including Keim, prefer the shortest version, being that
found in Mark.

Ver. 38. Τότε] *then*, after the crucifixion of Jesus was
thus disposed of. — σταυροῦνται] spoken with reference to
another band of soldiers which takes the place of καθήμενοι
ἐτήρουν αὐτὸν ἐκεῖ, ver. 36. The whole statement is merely
of a cursory and summary nature.

Ver. 39. Οἱ δὲ παραπορ.] That what is here said seems
to imply, what would ill accord with the synoptic statement
as to the day on which our Lord was crucified, that this
took place on a *working day* (Fritzsche, de Wette), is not to be
denied (comp. on John xviii. 28 ; Mark xv. 21), though it
cannot be assumed with certainty that such was the case.
But there can be no doubt that the place of execution was
close to a public thoroughfare. — κινοῦντες τὰς κεφ. αὐτ.]
The shaking of the head here is not to be regarded as that
which expresses *refusal* or *passion* (Hom. *Il.* xvii. 200, 442;
Od. v. 285, 376), but, according to Ps. xxii. 8, as indicating *a*
malicious jeering at the helplessness of one who had made
such lofty pretensions, ver. 40. Comp. Job xvi. 4 ; Ps. cix.
25 ; Lam. ii. 15 ; Isa. xxxvii. 22 ; Jer. xviii. 16 ; Buxt. *Lex.*
Talm. p. 2039 ; Justin, *Ap.* I. 38.

Ver. 40. Ἔλεγον δὲ τὰ τοιαῦτα κωμῳδοῦντες ὡς ψεύστην,
Euthymius Zigabenus. We should not fail to notice the
parallelism in both the clauses (in opposition to Fritzsche, who
puts a comma merely after σεαυτόν, and supposes that in *both*
instances the imperative is conditioned by εἰ υἱὸς εἶ τοῦ θεοῦ),
ὁ καταλύων, κ.τ.λ. being parallel to εἰ υἱὸς εἶ τ. θ., and σῶσον
σεαυτόν to κατάβηθι ἀπὸ τοῦ σταυροῦ. — ὁ καταλύων, κ.τ.λ.]
is an allusion to xxvi. 61. For the use of the *present* participle in a *characterizing* sense (*the destroyer*, etc.), comp.
xxiii. 37. The allegation of the witnesses, xxvi. 61, had come
to be a matter of *public* talk, which is scarcely to be wondered

at considering the extraordinary nature of it. — Observe, moreover, that *here* the emphasis is on υἱός (comp. iv. 3), while in
ver. 43 it is on θεοῦ.

Ver. 42. Parallelism similar to that of ver. 40. — καὶ
πιστεύομεν (see the critical remarks) ἐπ᾽ αὐτῷ: *and we
believe on Him* (at once), that is, as actually being the Messiah.
ἐπί with the *dative* (Luke xxiv. 25) conveys the idea that the
faith *would rest upon Him.* So also Rom. ix. 33, x. 11;
1 Tim. i. 16 ; 1 Pet. ii. 6.

Ver. 43. In the mouth of the *members of Sanhedrim,* who in
ver. 41 are introduced as joining in the blasphemies of the
passers-by, and who, ver. 42, have likewise the inscription
over the cross in view, the jeering assumes a *more impious*
character.   They now avail themselves even of the language
of holy *writ,* quoting from the 22d Psalm (which, moreover,
the Jews declared to be *non-*Messianic), the 5th verse of
which is given somewhat loosely from the LXX. (ἤλπισεν
ἐπὶ κύριον, ῥυσάσθω αὐτόν, σωσάτω αὐτόν, ὅτι θέλει αὐτόν). —
θέλει αὐτόν] is the rendering of the Heb. בּוֹ חָפֵץ, and is to
be interpreted in accordance with the Septuagint usage of
θέλειν (see Schleusner, *Thes.* II. p. 51, and comp. on Rom.
vii. 21): if He is the object of his desire, *i.e. if he likes
Him ;* comp. Tob. xiii. 6 ; Ps. xviii. 19, xli. 11.   In other
instances the LXX. give the preposition as well, rendering the Hebrew (1 Sam. xviii. 22, *al.*) by θέλειν ἔν τινι.
Fritzsche supplies ῥύσασθαι ; but in that case we should have
had merely εἰ θέλει without αὐτόν ; comp. Col. ii. 18. — ὅτι
θεοῦ εἰμι υἱός] The emphasis is on θεοῦ, as conveying the idea:
I am not the son of a man, but of *God,* who in consequence
will be certain to deliver me.—Comp. Wisd. ii. 18.—Observe
further the short bounding sentences in which their malicious
jeering, ver. 42 f., finds vent.

Ver. 44. Τὸ δ᾽ αὐτό] not: *after the same manner* (as
generally interpreted), but expressing the *object itself* (comp.
Soph. *Oed. Col.* 1006 : τοσαῦτ᾽ ὀνειδίζεις με ; Plat. *Phaedr.*
p. 241 : ὅσα τὸν ἕτερον λελοιδορήκαμεν), for, as is well known,
such verbs as denote a *particular mode* of speaking or acting
are often construed like λέγειν τινά τι or ποιεῖν τινά τι.

Krüger, § xlvi. 12; Kühner, II. 1, p. 276. Comp. on Phil. ii. 18. — οἱ λῃσταί] different from Luke xxiii. 39; the *generic* interpretation of the plural (Augustine, *de cons. ev.* iii. 16; Ebrard, Krafft) is precluded by the necessary reference to ver. 38. The harmonists (Origen, Cyrill, Chrysostom, Theophylact, Euthymius Zigabenus, Zeger, Lange) resorted to the expedient of supposing that *at first* both of them may have reviled Him, but that *subsequently* only *one* was found to do so, because the other had in the meantime been converted. Luke does not base his account upon a later tradition (Ewald, Schenkel, Keim), but upon materials of a more accurate and copious character drawn from a different circle of traditions.

Ver. 45. Ἀπὸ δὲ ἕκτης ὥρας] counting from the *third* (nine o'clock in the morning), the hour at which He had been nailed to the cross, Mark xv. 25. Respecting the difficulty of reconciling the statements of Matthew and Mark as to the hour in question with what is mentioned by John at xix. 14, and the preference that must necessarily be given to the latter, see on *John,* xix. 14. — σκότος] An ordinary *eclipse of the sun* was not possible during full moon (Origen); for which reason the eclipse of the 202d Olympiad, recorded by Phlegon in Syncellus, *Chronogr.* I. p. 614, ed. Bonn, and already referred to by Eusebius, is equally out of the question (Wieseler, *chronol. Synops.* p. 387 f.). But as little must we suppose that the reference is to that *darkness in the air* which precedes an ordinary earthquake (Paulus, Kuinoel, de Wette, Schleiermacher, *L. J.* p. 448, Weisse), for it is not an earthquake in the *ordinary sense* that is described in ver. 51 ff.; in fact, Mark and Luke, though recording the darkness and the rending of the veil, say nothing about the earthquake. The darkness upon this occasion was of an *unusual*, a *supernatural* character, being as it were the voice of God making itself heard through nature, the gloom over which made it appear as though the whole earth were bewailing the ignominious death which the Son of God was dying. The prodigies, to all appearance similar, that are alleged to have accompanied the death of certain heroes of antiquity (see Wetstein), and those solar

obscurations alluded to in Rabbinical literature, were different
in kind fro n that now before us (ordinary eclipses of the
sun, such ·s that which took place after the death of
Caes·r, Ser˂ *ad. Virg. G. I.* 466), and, even apart from this,
would not j˕˚˓˓˟˘ us in relegating what is matter of history,
John's omis˘˓˓˓ ˘˕ it ˚otwithstanding, to the region of myth
(in opposi˕˓˓˚ ˕˚ St˓auss, Keim, Scholten), especially when
we consider that the death in this instance was not that of a
mere human hero, that there were those still living who could
corroborate the evangelic narrative, and that the darkness here
in question was associated with the extremely peculiar σημεῖον
of the rending of the veil of the temple. — ἐπὶ πᾶσαν τὴν
γῆν] Keeping in view the supernatural character of the event
as well as the usage elsewhere with regard to the somewhat
indefinite phraseology πᾶσα or ὅλη ἡ γῆ (Luke xxi. 35, xxiii.
44; Rom. ix. 17, x. 18; Rev. xiii. 3), it is clear that the only
rendering in keeping with the tone of the narrative is: *over
the whole earth* (κοσμικὸν δὲ ἦν τὸ σκότος, οὐ μερικόν, Theophylact, comp. Chrysostom, Euthymius Zigabenus), not merely:
over the whole land (Origen, Erasmus, Luther, Maldonatus,
Kuinoel, Paulus, Olshausen, Ebrard, Lange, Steinmeyer),
though at the same time we are not called upon to construe
the words in accordance with the laws of physical geography;
they are simply to be regarded as expressing the popular idea
of the matter.

Ver. 46. Ἀνεβόησεν] *He cried aloud.* See Winer, *de
verbor. cum praepos. compos. usu*, 1838, III. p. 6 f.; comp. Luke
ix. 38; LXX. and Apocr., Herod., Plato.—The circumstance of
the following exclamation being given in *Hebrew* is sufficiently
and naturally enough accounted for by the jeering language of
ver. 47, which language is understood to be suggested by the
sound of the *Hebrew* words recorded in our present passage.
— σαβαχθανί] Chald.: שְׁבַקְתַּנִי = the Heb. עֲזַבְתָּנִי. Jesus
gives vent to His feelings in the opening words of the twenty-
second Psalm. We have here, however, the purely human
feeling that arises from *a natural but momentary quailing
before the agonies of death*, and which was in every respect
similar to that which had been experienced by the author of

the psalm. The combination of profound mental anguish, in consequence of entire *abandonment* by men, with the well-nigh intolerable *pangs of dissolution*, was all the more natural and inevitable in the case of One whose feelings were so deep, tender, and real, whose moral consciousness was so pure, and whose love was so intense. In ἐγκατέλιπες Jesus expressed, of course, what He felt, for His *ordinary conviction* that He was in fellowship God had for the moment given way under the pressure of extreme bodily and mental suffering, and a mere passing *feeling* as though He were no longer sustained by the power of the divine life had taken its place (comp. Gess, p. 196); but this subjective feeling must not be confounded with actual *objective desertion on the part of God* (in opposition to Olshausen and earlier expositors), which in the case of Jesus would have been a metaphysical and moral impossibility. The *dividing of the exclamation into different parts*, so as to correspond to the different elements in Christ's nature, merely gives rise to arbitrary and fanciful views (Lange, Ebrard), similar to those which have been based on the metaphysical deduction from the idea of necessity (Ebrard). To assume, as the theologians have done, that in the distressful cry of abandonment we have the *vicarious enduring of the wrath of God* (" ira Dei adversus nostra peccata effunditur in ipsum, et sic satisfit justitiae Dei," Melanchthon, comp. Luther on Ps. xxii., Calvin, Quenstedt), or the *infliction of divine punishment* (Köstlin in the *Jahrb. f. D. Theol.* III. 1, p. 125, and Weiss himself), is, as in the case of the agony in Gethsemane, to go farther than we are warranted in doing by the New Testament view of the atoning death of Christ, the vicarious character of which is not to be regarded as consisting in an objective and actual equivalent. Comp. Remarks after xxvi. 46. *Others*, again, have assumed that Jesus, though quoting only the opening words of Ps. xxii., had the *whole* psalm in view, including, therefore, the comforting words with which it concludes (Paulus, Gratz, de Wette, Bleek; comp. Schleiermacher, *Glaubensl.* II. p. 141, ed. 4, and *L. J.* p. 457). This, however, besides being somewhat arbitrary, gives rise to the incongruity of introducing the element of reflection where only pure feeling

prevailed, as we see exemplified by Hofmann, *Schriftbew.* II. 1,
p. 309, who, in accordance with his view that Jesus was
abandoned to the mercies of an ungodly world, substitutes a
secondary thought ("request for the so long delayed deliverance through death") for the plain and direct sense of the
words.   The *authenticity* of our Lord's exclamation, which the
author of the *Wolfenbüttel Fragments* has singularly miscon-
strued (in describing it as the cry of despair over a lost cause),
is denied by Strauss (who speaks of Ps. xxii. as having served
the purpose of a programme of Christ's passion), while it is
strongly questioned by Keim, partly on account of Ps. xxii.
and partly because he thinks that the subsequent accompanying narrative is clearly (?) of the nature of a fictitious legend.
But legend would hardly have put the language of despair
into the mouth of the dying Redeemer, and certainly there
is nothing in the witticisms that follow to warrant the idea
that we have here one legend upon another. — ἱνατί] the
momentary but agonizing feeling that He is abandoned by
God, impels Him to ask what the *divine object* of this may
be.   He doubtless *knew* this already, but the pangs of death
had *overpowered* Him (2 Cor. xiii. 4),—a passing anomaly
as regards the spirit that uniformly characterized the prayers
of Jesus. — ἐγκαταλείπω] means: to abandon any one to
utter helplessness.   Comp. 2 Cor. iv. 9; Acts ii. 27; Heb.
xiii. 5; Plat. *Conv.* p. 179 A; Dem. p. 158, 10, *al. ;* Ecclus.
iii. 16, vii. 30, ix. 10.

Ver. 47. A heartless Jewish *witticism* founded upon a silly
malicious perversion of the words ἠλί, ἠλί, and not a *misunderstanding* of their meaning on the part of the Roman
soldiers (Euthymius Zigabenus), or illiterate Jews (Theophylact, Erasmus, Olshausen, Lange), or Hellenists (Grotius), for
the whole context introduces us to one scene after another
of envenomed *mockery ;* see ver. 49. — οὗτος] *that one
there !* pointing *Him* out among the three who were being
crucified.

Ver. 48 f. A touch of sympathy on the part of some one
who had been moved by the painful cry of Jesus, and who
would fain relieve Him by reaching Him a cordial.   What

a contrast to this in ver. 49 ! According to John xix. 28, Jesus expressly intimated that He was thirsty. Mark xv. 36 makes it appear that the person who reached the drink to Jesus was also one of those who were mocking Him, a discrepancy which we should make no attempt to reconcile, and in which we can have no difficulty in detecting traces of a more corrupt tradition. Luke omits this incident altogether, though in xxiii. 36 he states that by way of mocking our Lord the soldiers *offered* Him the *posca* just *before* the darkness came on. Strauss takes advantage of these discrepancies so as to make it appear that they are but different applications of the prediction contained in Ps. lxix., without, however, disputing the fact that drink had been given to Jesus on two different occasions. — ὄξους] *poscae*, sour wine, the ordinary drink of the Roman soldiers. Comp. ver. 34 and Wetstein thereon. — ἄφες] *stop! don't give him anything to drink!* we want to see whether Elias whom he is invoking as his deliverer will come to his help, which help you would render unnecessary by giving him drink. — ἔρχεται] placed first for sake of emphasis: whether he *is coming, does not fail coming!*

Ver. 50. Πάλιν] refers to ver. 46. *What* did Jesus cry in this instance ? See John xix. 30, from which Luke xxiii. 46 diverges somewhat, containing, in fact, an explanatory addition to the account of the great closing scene, that is evidently borrowed from Ps. xxxi. 6. — ἀφῆκε τὸ πνεῦμα] *i.e. He died.* See Herod. iv. 190 ; Eur. *Hec.* 571 : ἀφῆκε πνεῦμα θανασίμῳ σφαγῇ ; Kypke, I. p. 140 ; Gen. xxxv. 18 ; Ecclus. xxxviii. 23 ; Wisd. xvi. 14. There is no question here of a separating of the πνεῦμα from the ψυχή. See in answer to Ströbel, Delitzsch, *Psych.* p. 400 f. The theory of a *merely apparent death* (Bahrdt, Venturini, Paulus) is so decidedly at variance with the predictions of Jesus Himself regarding His end, as well as with the whole testimony of the Gospel, is so utterly destructive of the fundamental idea of the resurrection, undermines so completely the whole groundwork of the redemption brought about by Christ, is so inconsistent with the accumulated testimony of centuries as furnished by the very existence of the church itself, which is based upon the facts of the death and the resurrection of Jesus, and requires such a remarkable series of other theories and assumptions of an extraordinary and supernatural character in order to explain duly authenticated facts regarding Christ's appearance and actings after His resurrection,—that, with friends and foes alike testifying to the actual death of Jesus, we are bound at once to dismiss it as an utterly abortive attempt to get rid of the physiological mystery (but see on Luke, Remarks after xxiv. 51) of the resurrection. It is true that though those modern critics (Strauss, Weisse, Ewald, Schweizer, Schenkel, Volkmar, Scholten, Keim) who deny the literal resurrection of Christ's body, and who suggest various ways of accounting for His alleged reappearing again on several occasions, do not dispute the reality of His death, their view is nevertheless as much at variance with the whole of the New Testament evidence in favour of the resurrection as is the one just adverted to. Comp. xxviii. 10, Rem., and Luke xxiv. 51, Rem.

Ver. 51 f. Not an ordinary earthquake, but a *supernatural* phenomenon, as was that of the darkness in ver. 45. — $\kappa\alpha\grave{\iota}$ $\grave{\iota}\delta o\acute{v}$] "Hie wendet sich's und wird gar ein neues Wesen " [at this point the history enters upon a fresh stage, and something entirely new appears], Luther. The style of the narrative here is characterized by a simple *solemnity*, among other indications of which we have the frequent recurrence of $\kappa\alpha\acute{\iota}$. — $\tau\grave{o}$ $\kappa\alpha\tau\alpha\pi\acute{e}\tau\alpha\sigma\mu\alpha$] הַפָּרֹכֶת, the veil suspended before the holy of holies, Ex. xxvi. 31; Lev. xxi. 23; 1 Macc. i. 22; Ecclus. xxx. 5; Heb. vi. 19, ix. 3, x. 20. *The rending in two* (for $\epsilon\grave{\iota}\varsigma$ $\delta\acute{v}o$, comp. Lucian, *Tox.* 54; *Lapith.* 44), of which mention is also made by Mark and Luke, was not the effect of the convulsion in nature (which was a subsequent occurrence), but a divine $\sigma\eta\mu\epsilon\hat{\iota}o\nu$, accompanying the moment of decease, for the purpose of indicating that in this atoning death of Jesus the old dispensation of sacrifices was being done away, and free access to the gracious presence of God at the same time restored. Comp. Heb. vi. 19 f., ix. 6 ff., x. 19 f. To treat what is thus a matter of divine symbolism as though it were symbolical legend (Schleiermacher, Strauss, Scholten, Keim) is all the more unwarrantable that neither in Old Testament prophecy nor in the popular beliefs of the Jews do we find anything calculated to suggest the formation of any such legend. The influence of legend has operated rather in the way of transforming the rending of the veil into an incident of a more imposing and startling nature: " *superliminare* (the lintel) *templi* infinitae magnitudinis fractum esse atque divisum," *Evang. sec. Hebr.* quoted by Jerome. See Hilgenfeld, *N. T. extr. can.* IV. p. 17. The idea underlying this legend was that of the *destruction* of the temple.—What follows is peculiar to Matthew. *The rocks* in question were those in the immediate neighbourhood, and so also with regard to τὰ μνημεῖα. The *opening of the graves* is in like manner to be regarded as divine symbolism, according to which the death of Jesus is to be understood as preparing the way for the future resurrection of believers to the eternal life of the Messianic kingdom (John iii. 14 f., vi. 54). The *thing thus signified* by the divine sign—a sign sufficiently intelligible, and possessing all the characteristics of a genuine symbol (in opposition to Steinmeyer, p. 226)—was so moulded and amplified in the course of tradition that it became ultimately transformed into an *historical incident :* πολλὰ σώματα τῶν κεκοιμ. ἁγίων ἠγέρθη, κ.τ.λ. For a specimen of still further and more extravagant amplification of the material in question—material to which Ignatius likewise briefly alludes, *ad Magnes.* 9, and which he expressly mentions, *ad Trall. interpol.* 9—see *Evang. Nicod.* 17 ff. This legend respecting the rising of the Old Testament saints (ἁγίων) is based upon the assumption of the *descensus Christi ad inferos,* in the course of which Jesus was understood not only to have visitsd them, but also to have secured their resurrection (comp. *Ev. Nicod.;* Ignatius, *ad Trall. l.c.*). But it is quite arbitrary to assume that in those who are thus alleged to have risen from their graves we have mere " *apparitions* assuring us of the continued existence of the departed " (Michaelis, Paulus, Kuinoel, Hug, Krabbe, p. 505 ; Steudel, *Glaubensl.* p. 455 ; Bleek). Besides,

the legend regarding the rising of the saints on this occasion
is, in itself considered, no more incompatible with the idea
of Christ being the ἀπαρχὴ τῶν κεκοιμ. (1 Cor. xv. 20 ;
Col. i. 18) than the raising of Lazarus and certain others.
See on 1 Cor. xv. 20. It is true that, according to Epiphanius, Origen, Ambrose, Luther, Calovius (comp. also
Delitzsch, *Psych.* p. 414), the dead now in question came forth
in spiritual bodies and ascended to heaven along with Christ ;
but with Jerome it is at the same time assumed, in opposition
to the terms of our passage, that : " *Non antea resurrexerunt,
quam Dominus resurgeret, ut esset primogenitus resurrectionis
ex mortuis ;* " comp. also Calvin, and Hofmann, *Schriftbew.* II.
1, p. 492. In the *Acta Pilati* as found in Thilo, p. 810,
Abraham, Isaac, Jacob, the twelve patriarchs, and Noah, are
expressly mentioned as being among the number of those who
rose from the dead. The names are given somewhat differently
in the *Evang. Nicod.*

Ver. 53. Μετὰ τὴν ἔγερσιν αὐτοῦ] is to be taken in
an *active* sense (Ps. cxxxix. 2 ; Plat. *Tim.* p. 70 C ; comp.
ἐξέγερσις, Polyb. ix. 15. 4 ; ἀνέγερσις, Plut. *Mor.* p. 156 B),
yet not as though αὐτοῦ were a genitive of the *subject* (" post-
quam eos Jesus in vitam restituerat," Fritzsche, which would
be to make the addition of αὐτοῦ something like superfluous),
but a genitive of the *object,* in which case it is unnecessary to
say *who* it was that raised up Christ. The words are not to
be *connected* with ἐξελθόντες (de Wette, following the majority
of the earlier expositors), which would involve the absurd idea
that those here referred to had been lying in their graves
alive awaiting the coming of the third day ; but, as Heinsius,
with εἰσῆλθον. After life was restored they left their
graves, but only after the resurrection of Jesus did they
enter the holy city. Up till then they had kept themselves
concealed. And this is by no means difficult to understand ;
for it was only after the resurrection of Jesus that their
appearing could be of service in the way of bearing testimony
in favour of Him in whose death the power of Hades was
supposed to have been vanquished, and hence it was only then
that their rising found its *appropriate* explanation. — ἁγίαν

πόλιν] is in keeping with the solemnity of the entire narrative ; comp. iv. 5.

Ver. 54. Ὁ δὲ ἑκατόνταρχος] " Centurio supplicio praepositus," Seneca, de ira, i. 16. He belonged to the σπεῖρα, ver. 27. — οἱ μετ᾽ αὐτοῦ τηροῦντες τ. Ἰησ.] is to be taken as one expression ; see ver. 35 f. — καὶ τὰ γινόμενα] καί, as in xxvi. 59, and numerous instances besides, serves to conjoin the general with the particular : and what was taking place (generally, that is), viz. the various incidents accompanying the death of Jesus (ver. 46 ff.). The present participle (see the critical remarks) is used with reference to things they have been witnessing up till the present moment ; see Kühner, II. 1, pp. 117, 163. — ἐφοβήθησαν] they were seized with terror, under the impression that all that was happening was a manifestation of the wrath of the gods. — θεοῦ υἱός] in the mouth of heathens can only denote a son of God in the heathen sense of the words (hero, demi-god), the sense in which they certainly understood them to be used when they heard Jesus accused and mocked. — ἦν] during His life.

Ver. 55 f. Ἠκολούθησαν] Here, as in ver. 60 and often elsewhere, we have the aorist in the relative clause instead of the usual pluperfect. — ἡ Μαγδαληνή] from Magdala (see on xv. 39), comp. Luke viii. 2 ; she is not identical with the Mary of John xii. 1 ff., who again has been confounded with the sinner of Luke vii. 36. Comp. on xxvi. 6 ff. The מגדלינא is likewise mentioned in Rabbinical literature (Eisenmenger, entdeckt. Judenth. I. p. 277), though this must not be confounded with מגדלא, a plaiter of hair, which the Talmud alleges the mother of Jesus to have been (Lightfoot, p. 498). — ἡ τοῦ Ἰακώβου, κ.τ.λ.] the wife of Alphaeus. See on xiii. 55 ; John xix. 25. The mother of Joses is not a different Mary from the mother of James (Ewald, Gesch. Chr. p. 401), otherwise we should have had καὶ ἡ τοῦ Ἰωσῆ μήτηρ. See also Mark xv. 47, Remark. — ἡ μήτηρ τῶν υἱῶν Ζεβεδ.] Salome. Comp. on xx. 20. In John xix. 25 she is designated : ἡ ἀδελφὴ τῆς μητρὸς αὐτοῦ. The mother of Jesus, whose presence on this occasion is attested by John, is not mentioned by the Synoptists, though at the same time they do not exclude her (in opposition to Schenkel, Keim), especially as Matthew and Mark make no express reference to any but the women who *ministered* to the Lord. For this reason alone we feel bound to reject the hypothesis of Chrysostom and Theophylact, revived by Fritzsche, but refuted so long ago by Euthymius Zigabenus,—the hypothesis, namely, that it is the mother of Jesus who is meant by Μαρία ἡ τοῦ Ἰακώβου καὶ Ἰωσῆ μήτηρ (xiii. 55). So also Hesychius of Jerusalem in Cramer's *Catena*, p. 256.

Ver. 57. Ὀψίας δὲ γενομ.] the so-called first or early evening, just before the close of the Jewish day. Deut. xxi. 22 f.; Joseph. *Bell.* iv. 5. 2. See also Lightfoot, p. 499. — ἀπὸ Ἀριμαθ.] belongs to ἄνθρωπος πλούσιος. Comp. μάγοι ἀπὸ ἀνατολῶν, ii. 1. The other evangelists describe him as a member of the Sanhedrim; an additional reason for supposing him to have resided in Jerusalem. — ἦλθεν] namely, *to the place of execution*, as the context shows, and not *to the praetorium* (de Wette, Bleek), to which latter ver. 58 represents him as going only *after* his return from the scene of the crucifixion. *Arimathia*, רָמָתַיִם with the article, 1 Sam. i. 1, the birthplace of Samuel (see Eusebius, *Onom.*, and Jerome, *Ep.* 86, *ad Eustoch. epitaph. Paul.* p. 673), and consequently identical with *Rama* (see on ii. 18); LXX.: Ἀρμαθαίμ. — καὶ αὐτός] *et ipse*, like those women and their sons, ver. 56. — μαθητεύειν τινί] *to be a disciple of any one;* see Kypke, II. p. 141 f. Comp. on xiii. 52. He was a *secret* follower of Jesus, John xix. 38.

Ver. 58. According to Roman usage, the bodies of criminals were left hanging upon the cross, where they were allowed to decompose and be devoured by birds of prey. Plaut. *mil. glor.* ii. 4. 9; Horace, *Ep.* i. 16. 48. However, should the relatives in any case ask the body for the purpose of burying, there was nothing to forbid their request being complied with. Ulpian, xlviii. 24. 1, *de cadav. punit. ;* Hug in the *Freyb. Zeitschr.* 5, p. 174 ff. — προσελθ.] therefore from the place of execution to the praetorium. — ἀποδοθῆναι τὸ σῶμα] τὸ σῶμα is due not merely to the simple style of the narrative, but in its threefold repetition expresses with involuntary emphasis the author's own painful sympathy. $\dot{a}\pi o\delta o\theta$. has the force of *reddi* (Vulg.), the thing asked being regarded as the petitioner's own peculiar property. Comp. xxii. 21.

Ver. 59. "Jam initia honoris," Bengel. — $\sigma\iota\nu\delta\acute{o}\nu\iota$ $\kappa a\theta a\rho\underline{a}$] *with pure* (unstained linen) *linen*, the dative of instrument. Keeping in view the ordinary practice on such occasions, it must not be supposed that the reference here is to a dress (Kuinoel, Fritzsche), but (comp. Herod. ii. 86) to *strips* or *bands* (John xix. 40), in which the body was swathed after being washed. Comp. Wetstein. Matthew makes no mention of *spices* (John xix. 40), but neither does he exclude their use, for he may have meant us to understand that, in conformity with the usual practice, they would be put in, as matter of course, when the body was wrapped up (in opposition to Strauss, de Wette, Keim). Mark xvi. 1 and Luke xxiii. 56 represent the putting in of the spices as something *intended* to be done *after* the burial. This, however, is in no way inconsistent with the statement of John, for there is no reason why the women may not have supplemented with a subsequent and more careful dressing of the body ($\dot{a}\lambda\epsilon\acute{\iota}\psi\omega\sigma\iota\nu$, Mark xvi. 1) what had been done imperfectly, because somewhat hurriedly, by Joseph and (see John xix. 39) Nicodemus.

Ver. 60. `Ο $\dot{\epsilon}\lambda a\tau\acute{o}\mu\eta\sigma\epsilon\nu$] Aorist, as in ver. 55.—The other evangelists say nothing about *the grave having belonged to Joseph*; John xix. 42 rather gives us to understand that, owing to the necessary despatch, it was made choice of from its being close at hand. We thus see that Matthew's account is unsupported by the earlier testimony of Mark on the one hand, and the later testimony of Luke and John on the other. This, however, only goes to confirm the view that in Matthew we have a later amplification of the tradition which was expunged again by Luke and John, for this latter at least would scarcely have left unnoticed the *devotion* evinced by Joseph in thus giving up *his own* tomb, and yet it is John who distinctly alleges a *different* reason altogether for the choice of the grave. The *ordinary* supposition, that Matthew's account is intended to *supplement* those of the other evangelists, fails to meet the exigencies of the case, especially in regard to John, on whom so tender a feature in connection with the burial would doubtless have made too deep an impression to admit of his passing it over in silence. —As a *new* grave was calculated to do honour to Jesus (comp. on John as above), the circumstance that this one had not been previously used may have gone far to determine the choice, so that there is no ground for supposing that what is said with reference to this has been added without historical warrant (Strauss, Scholten). — ἐν τῇ πέτρᾳ] The article is to be understood as indicating a rocky place *just at hand.* — τῇ θύρᾳ] Comp. Hom. *Od.* ix. 243 : πέτρην ἐπέθηκε θύρῃσιν. In Rabbinical phraseology the stone used for this purpose is called גֹּלֵל, a roller. See Paulus, *exeget. Handb.* III. p. 819. Such a mode of stopping up graves is met with even in the present day (Strauss, *Sinai u. Golgatha,* p. 205).

Ver. 61. Ἦν δὲ ἐκεῖ] present at the burial. — ἡ ἄλλη Μαρ.] see ver. 56. The article is wanting only in A D*, and should be maintained, Wieseler (*Chronol. Synops.* p. 427) notwithstanding. Its omission in the case of A may be traced to the reading ἡ Ἰωσήφ, which this MS. has at Mark xv. 47. Wieseler approves of this reading, and holds the Mary of our text to be the wife or daughter of Joseph of Arimathea. But see remark on Mark xv. 47. — καθήμεναι, κ.τ.λ.] unoccupied, absorbed in grief; comp. Nägelsbach on Hom. *Il.* i. 134.

Ver. 62. Ἥτις ἐστὶ μετὰ τὴν παρασκ.] *which follows the day of preparation,* i.e. *on Saturday.* For παρασκευή is used to designate the day that immediately precedes the Sabbath (as in the present instance) or any of the feast days. Comp. on John xix. 14. According to the Synoptists, the παρασκευή of the Sabbath happened to coincide this year with the first day of the feast, which might also properly enough be designated σάββατον (Lev. xxiii. 11, 15),—this latter circumstance being, according to Wieseler (*Synops.* p. 417), the reason why Matthew did not prefer the simpler and more obvious expression ἥτις ἐστὶ σάββατον ; an expression which, when used in connection with the days of the Passover week, was liable to be misunderstood. But Matthew had already spoken so definitely of the first day of the feast as that on which Jesus was crucified (see xxvi. 17–xxvii. 1), that he had no cause to apprehend any misunderstanding of his words had he chosen to write ἥτις ἐστὶ σάββατον. But as little does that precise statement regarding the day permit us to suppose that the expression in question has been made to turn on the divergent narrative of John (in opposition to de Wette). The most natural explanation of the peculiar phraseology: ἥτις ἐστὶ μετὰ τ. παρασκ., is to be found in that *Christian* usage according to which the παρασκευή (*i.e.* the προσάββατον, Mark xv. 42) has come to be the recognised designation for the Friday of the crucifixion. Michaelis, Paulus, Kuinoel suppose that it is the part of *Friday* after sunset that is intended, by which time, therefore, the Sabbath had begun. This, however, is distinctly precluded by τῇ ἐπαύριον.

Ver. 63. Ἐμνήσθημεν] *we have remembered*, it has just occurred to us, the sense being purely that of the aorist and not of the perfect (in opposition to de Wette). — ἐκεῖνος ὁ πλάνος] *that deceiver* (2 Cor. vi. 8), *impostor;* Justin, c. Tr. 69 : λαοπλάνος. Without once mentioning His name, they contemptuously allude to Him as one now *removed to a distance*, as got rid of by *death*. This is a sense in which ἐκεῖνος is frequently used by Greek authors (Schoem. *ad Is.* p. 177 ; Ellendt, *Lex. Soph.* I. p. 559). — ἐγείρομαι] *present ;* marking the confidence with which he affirmed it.

Ver. 64. Καὶ ἔσται] is more lively and natural when not taken as dependent on μήποτε. The Vulgate renders correctly : *et erit.* — ἡ ἐσχάτη πλάνη] *the last error* (see on Eph. iv. 14), that, namely, which would gain ground among the credulous masses, through those who might steal away the body of Jesus pretending that He had risen from the dead. — τῆς πρώτης] which found acceptance with the multitude through giving out and encouraging others to give out that He was the Messiah. — χείρων] *worse, i.e.* more *fatal* to public order and security, etc. For the use of this expression, comp. xii. 45 ; 2 Sam. xiii. 15.

Ver. 65 f. Pilate's reply is sharp and peremptory. — ἔχετε κουστωδίαν] with Luther, Vatablus, Wolf, Paulus, de Wette, Keim, Steinmeyer, ἔχετε is to be taken as an *imperative*, *habetote* (comp. Xen. *Cyrop.* viii. 7. 11 ; Mark ix. 50, xi. 22 ; Soph. *Phil.* 778) : *ye shall have a watch !* For if it be taken as an *indicative*, as is generally done in conformity with the Vulgate, we must not suppose that the reference is to *Roman* soldiers (Grotius, Fritzsche), for the Sanhedrim had not any such placed at their disposal, not even to *the detachment that guarded the cross* (Kuinoel), for its duties were now over, but simply to the ordinary *temple guards.* But it is evident from xxviii. 14 that it was *not* these latter who were set to watch the grave. This duty was assigned to a company of *Roman* soldiers, which company the *Acta Pil.* magnifies into a cohort. — ὡς οἴδατε] *as*, by such means as, *ye know how to prevent it*, *i.e.* in the best way you can. The idea : " vereor autem, ut satis communire illud possitis " (Fritzsche), is *foreign* to the text. — μετὰ τῆς κουστωδίας] belongs to ἠσφαλίσ. τ. τάφ. ; they secured the grave *by means of* (Stallbaum, *ad Plat. Rep.* p. 530 D) *the watch*, which they posted in front of it. The intervening σφραγίσ. τ. λίθ. is to be understood as having preceded the ἠσφαλ. τ. τ. μετὰ τ. κουστ. : *after they had sealed* the stone. To connect μετὰ τ. κουστωδ. with σφραγίσ. (Chrysostom) would result either in the feeble and somewhat inappropriate idea that the watch had helped them with the sealing (Bleek), or in the harsh and unnecessary assumption that our expression is an abbreviation for μετὰ τοῦ προσθεῖναι τὴν κουστωδίαν (Fritzsche). — σφραγίσ.] Comp. Dan. vi. 17. The sealing was effected by stretching a cord across the stone at the mouth of the sepulchre, and then fastening it to the rock at either end by means of sealing-clay (Paulsen, *Regier. d. Morgenl.* p. 298 ; Harmar, *Beobacht.* II. p. 467) ; or if the stone at the door happened to be fastened with a cross-beam, this latter was sealed to the rock (Strauss, *Sinai und Golgatha,* p. 205).

REMARK.—As it is certain that Jesus cannot have predicted His resurrection in any explicit or intelligible manner even to His own disciples ; as, moreover, it is impossible to suppose

that the women who visited the grave on the resurrection
morning could have contemplated embalming the body, or
would have concerned themselves merely about how the stone
was to be rolled away, if they had been aware that a watch had
been set, and that the grave had been sealed; and finally, as
the supposition that Pilate complied with the request for a
guard, or at all events, that the members of the Sanhedrim so
little understood their own interest as both to leave the body of
Jesus in the hands of His followers instead of taking possession
of it themselves, and to bribe the soldiers to give false testimony
instead of duly calling them to account, as they might have
done, for their culpable neglect, is in the highest degree improbable, just as much so as the idea that the procurator would
be likely to take no notice of a dereliction of duty on the part
of his own soldiers, who, by maintaining the truth of a very
stupid fabrication, would only be proclaiming how much they
themselves were to blame in the matter: it follows that the
story about the watching of the grave—a story which is further
disproved by the fact that nowhere in the discussions belonging
to the apostolic age do we find any reference *confirmatory* or
otherwise to the alleged stealing of the body—*must be referred
to the category of unhistorical legend.* And a clue to the *origin*
of this legend is furnished by the evangelist himself in mentioning the rumour about the stealing of the body,—a rumour
emanating to all appearance from a Jewish source, and circu-
lated with the hostile intention of disproving the resurrection of
Jesus (Paulus, *exeg. Handb.* III. p. 837 ff.; Strauss, II. p. 562 ff.;
Schleiermacher, *L. J.* p. 458 ff.; Weisse, Ewald, Hase, Bleek,
Keim, Scholten, Hilgenfeld). The arguments advanced by Hug
in the *Freyburg. Zeitschr.* 1831, 3, p. 184 ff.; 5, p. 80 ff.; Kuinoel,
Hofmann, Krabbe, Ebrard, Lange, Riggenbach, Steinmeyer,
against the supposition of a legend, resolve themselves into
arbitrary assumptions and foreign importations which simply
leave the matter as historically incomprehensible as ever. The
same thing may be said with regard to the emendation which
Olshausen takes the liberty of introducing, according to which
it is made to appear that the Sanhedrim did not act in their
corporate capacity, but that the affair was managed simply
on the authority of Caiaphas alone. Still the unhistorical
character of the story by no means justifies the assumption
of an interpolation (in opposition to Stroth in Eichhorn's
Repert. IX. p. 141),—an interpolation, too, that would have
had to be introduced into three different passages (xxvii. 62, 66,
xxviii. 4, 11 ff.); yet one can understand how this apocryphal

story should have most readily engrafted itself specially and *exclusively* upon the Gospel of Matthew, a Gospel originating in Judaeo-Christian circles, and having, by this time, the more developed form in which it has come down to us.   For a further amplification of the legend, see *Ev. Nicod.* 14.

CHAPTER XXVIII.

VER. 2. ἀπὸ τ. θύρας] is wanting in B D א, 60, 84, Vulg. It. Or. Dion. Deleted by Lachm. and Tisch. Exegetical addition, which many witnesses have supplemented still further by adding τοῦ μνημείου (Mark xvi. 3). — Ver. 6. ὁ κύριος] is wanting, no doubt, only in B א, 33, 102, Copt. Aeth. Arm. Ar.ᵖᵒˡ one Cod. of the It. Or.ⁱⁿᵗ Chrys.; but, with Tisch., it is to be condemned. This designation is foreign to Matth., while as "*gloriosa appellatio*" (Bengel) it was more liable to be inserted than omitted. — Ver. 8. ἐξελθ.] Tisch.: ἀπελθ., following B C L א, 33, 69, 124. Correctly; the more significant reading of the Received text is derived from Mark. — Ver. 9. Before καὶ ἰδού the Received text inserts: ὡς δὲ ἐπορεύοντο ἀπαγγεῖλαι τοῖς μαθηταῖς αὐτοῦ. No such clause is found in B D א, min. Syr. Ar.ᵖᵒˡ Perss. Copt. Arm. Vulg. Sax. It. Or. Eus. Jer. Aug. Defended by Griesb. Matth. Fritzsche, Scholz, Bornem. (*Schol. in Luc.* p. xxxix.); condemned by Mill, Bengel, Gersd., Schulz, Rinck, Lachm., Tisch. There would be nothing feeble or awkward about the words if thus inserted, on the contrary, the effect would be somewhat solemn (see Bornem.); but seeing that they are wanting in witnesses so ancient and so important, and seeing that ὡς is not found in this sense anywhere else in Matth. (other grammatical grounds mentioned by Gersd. are untenable), there is reason to suspect that they are an early addition for the sake of greater precision. — Ver. 11. For ἀπήγγ. read, with Tisch. 8, ἀνήγγ., though only in accordance with D א, Or. Chrys. The Received reading is taken from ver. 10, while ἀναγγέλλειν occurs nowhere else in Matthew. — Ver. 14. ἐπὶ τοῦ ἡγ.] Lachm.: ὑπὸ τοῦ ἡγ., following B D, 59, Vulg. It. But this is an explanatory correction in consequence of not catching the sense. — Ver. 15. Lachm. inserts ἡμέρας after σήμερον, in accordance with B D L. Correctly; as Matth. does not add ἡμέρ. in any other instance (xi. 23, xxvii. 8), it was more natural for the transcriber to omit than to insert it. — Ver. 17. αὐτῷ] is wanting in B D א, 33, 102, Vulg. It. Chrys. Aug. Deleted by Lachm. and Tisch. 8. A somewhat common addition, for which other MSS. (min.) have αὐτόν. — Ver. 19. After πορευθ. Elz. inserts οὖν, which is bracketed by Lachm. and deleted by Matth. and Tisch. Added as a connecting particle, but wanting in very important witnesses, while other and less important ones have νῦν.

Ver. 1. On the various ways of viewing and interpreting the *story of the resurrection*, see, as regards their critical aspect, Keim, III. p. 527 ff. ; and on the apologetic side, consult Steinmeyer, *Apolog. Beitr.* III. 1871. — ὀψὲ δὲ σαββάτων] *but late on the Sabbath*, means neither . . . *after the close of the Sabbath* (Olshausen, de Wette, Baumgarten-Crusius, Ewald, Bleek), nor: *after the close of the week* (Severus of Antioch, Euthymius Zigabenus, Grotius, Wieseler, p. 425); for ὀψέ, *sero*, with a defining genitive (without which it occurs nowhere else in the New Testament) always denotes the lateness of *the period thus specified and still current* (τὰ τελευταῖα τούτων, Euthymius Zigabenus). Comp. in general, Krüger, § xlvii. 10. 4; Kühner, II. 1, p. 292. Take the following as examples of this usage from classical authors: Xen. *Hist.* ii. 1. 14; Thuc. iv. 93. 1: τῆς ἡμέρας ὀψέ; Dem. p. 541, *ult.*: ὀψὲ τῆς ὥρας ἐγίγνετο; Luc. *Dem. enc.* 14, and *de morte Peregr.* 21: ὀψὲ τῆς ἡλικίας. Hence by: *late on the Sabbath*, we are not to suppose Saturday evening to be intended,—any such misunderstanding being precluded both by the nature of the expression made use of, an expression by no means synonymous with the usual ὀψίας γενομένης (in opposition to Keim), and by what is still further specified immediately after,—but *far on in the Saturday night*, after midnight, *toward daybreak on Sunday*, in conformity with the civil mode of reckoning, according to which the ordinary day was understood to extend from sunrise till sunrise again. Lightfoot, comparing the Rabbinical expression בפיקי שובא, aptly observes: " ὀψέ *totam noctem denotat.*" Comp. so early a writer as Augustine, *de cons. ev.* 24. Consequently the point of time mentioned here is substantially identical with that given in Luke xxiv. 1: τῇ μιᾷ τῶν σαββάτων ὄρθρου βαθέος, and in John xx. 1: τῇ μιᾷ τῶν σαββ. πρωῒ σκοτίας ἔτι οὔσης; while, on the other hand, Mark xvi. 2 represents the sun as already risen. For ὀψέ, comp. Ammonius: ἑσπέρα μὲν γάρ ἐστιν ἡ μετὰ τὴν δύσιν τοῦ

ἡλίου ὥρα· ὀψέ δὲ ἡ μετὰ πολὺ τῆς δύσεως. — τῇ ἐπιφωσκ.
εἰς μίαν σαββάτων] *when it was dawning toward Sunday,*
i.e. as the light was beginning to appear on the morning of
Sunday. Understand ἡμέρα after ἐπιφωσκ.; and for ἐπιφώσκει
ἡ ἡμέρα, comp. Herod. iii. 86 : ἁμ᾽ ἡμέρῃ διαφωσκούσῃ, also
ix. 45. The participial expression without the ἡμέρα is
similar to ἡ ἐπιοῦσα, and the like (Kühner, II. 1, p. 228).
Keim supposes the *evening* to be intended, since, according to
the Jewish mode of reckoning, the day began with the rising
of the stars or the lighting of lamps, so that the meaning of
our passage would be as follows : " *In the evening after six
o'clock, just when the stars were beginning to twinkle.*" [1] But to
say nothing of the startling discrepancy that would thus arise
between Matthew and the other evangelists, we would be
under the necessity, according to Luke xxiii. 54 (see on the
passage), of understanding the words immediately following as
simply equivalent to : τῇ μίᾳ σαββάτων ἐπιφωσκούσῃ ; comp.
σαββάτου ἐπιφώσκει, *Ev. Nicod.* 12, p. 600, Thilo's edition.
Nor, if we adopt Keim's interpretation, is it at all clear what
substantive should be understood along with τῇ ἐπιφωσκ.
Ewald, *Apost. Zeit.* p. 82, unwarrantably supplies ἑσπέρᾳ, and,
like Keim, supposes the reference to be to the *evening* lighting
of the lamps, though he is inclined to think that Matthew intended *summarily to include* in his statement what the women
did on Saturday evening and early on Sunday, a view which
finds no support whatever in the text ; as for the intention to
embalm the body, there is *no trace* of such a thing in Matthew.
Lastly, to suppose that in framing his statement as to the
time here in question, the author of our revised Gospel has
had recourse to a *combination of* Mark xvi. 1 *and* 2 (Weiss),
is to give him but little credit for literary skill ; for instead
of taking the trouble to form any such combination, he had
only to take Mark's two statements and place the one after
the other, thus : διαγενομένου τοῦ σαββάτου, λίαν πρωΐ τῆς

[1] This idea of Keim's about the *twinkling of the stars* is an importation; for
the expression ἐπιφώσκει, as applied to the evening, has reference only to the
ordinary domestic lighting of the lamps. See in particular, Lightfoot on Luke
xxiii. 54.

μιᾶς σαββάτων. But so far from that, he has proceeded in entire independence of Mark. — The expression μία σαββάτων corresponds exactly to the Rabbinical mode of designating the days of the week: אחד בשבת, Sunday; שני בשבת, Monday; שלישי בשבת, Tuesday, and so on. See Lightfoot, p. 500. Observe that σάββατα denotes, in the first instance, *Sabbath*, and then *week ;* and similarly, that the ἡμέρᾳ to be understood with ἐπιφωσκ. is to be taken in the sense of day *light* (John ix. 4, xi. 9 ; Rom. xiii. 12 ; 1 Thess. v. 5). — ἡ ἄλλη Μαρία] as in xxvii. 56. — In John xx. 1 only Mary Magdalene is mentioned, whereas in the Synoptists we have an amplified version of the tradition as regards the number of the women, Matthew mentioning two, Mark three (Salome), while Luke (xxiv. 10) gives us to understand that, in addition to the two Marys and Joanna, whom he specially names, there were several others. In dealing with such discrepancies in the tradition we should beware of seeking to coerce the different narratives into harmony with one another, which can never be done without prejudice to their respective authors. We see an illustration of this in the supposition that Mary Magdalene came *first of all* to the grave, and then hastened back to the city to inform Peter of what had taken place, and that during her absence Mary the mother of James, Joanna, Salome, and the other women arrived (Olshausen, Ebrard). Comp. on John xx. 1. The same thing is exemplified by the other view, that Mary Magdalene went to the grave *along with* the rest of the women, but that on the way back she outran the others, etc. For the various attempts to harmonize the divergent narratives, see Griesbach, *Opusc.* II. p. 241 ff.; Strauss, II. p. 570 ff.; Wieseler, p. 425 ff. — θεωρῆσαι τὸν τάφον] to *look at the grave ;* according to Mark and Luke, to anoint the body. This latter statement is the *more original* and *more correct* of the two, though Matthew could not consistently adopt it after what he had said about the sealing and watching of the grave.

Ver. 2. It is wrong to take the *aorists* in a *pluperfect* sense (Castalio, Kuinoel, Kern, Ebrard), or to conceive of the action of the ἦλθε as not yet completed (de Wette). Matthew represents what is here recorded as taking place *in presence of the women* (ἦλθε ... θεωρῆσαι ... καὶ ἰδού), whose attention, however, had been so much occupied with the accompanying phenomena, that they did not observe (vv. 5, 6) the circumstance itself of our Lord's emerging from the grave (which, besides, must have been invisible to the outward eye owing to the nature of the body He had now assumed, comp. on ver. 17). The other evangelists make no mention of this (legendary) supernatural and visible rolling away of the stone; and, though differing as to the number of the angels, they agree in representing them as having appeared *inside* the grave. *Here*, if anywhere, however, amid so much that is supernatural, must we be prepared to expect divergent accounts of what took place, above all in regard to the angelic manifestations, which are matters depending on individual observation and experience (comp. on John xx. 12), and not the objective perceptions of impartial and disinterested spectators. — γάρ] assigning the reason for the violent earthquake which, as a divine σημεῖον, formed an appropriate accompaniment to this miraculous angelic manifestation. — κ. ἐκαθήτο, κ.τ.λ.] as the heaven-sent guardian and interpreter of the *empty* tomb.

Ver. 3 f. Ἡ ἰδέα αὐτοῦ] *his appearance*, his outward aspect, found nowhere else in the New Testament, though occurring in Dan. i. 15, 2 Macc. iii. 16, and frequently in classical authors. On the relation of this term to εἶδος, see Stallbaum, *ad Plat. Rep.* p. 596 A, and *Parmen.* p. 128 E; and comp. Ameis on Hom. *Od.* ix. 508, Appendix. The appearance of the *countenance* is meant; see what follows. Comp. xvii. 2. — ὡς ἀστραπή] not: as having the *form*, but as shining with the *brightness* of lightning. Comp. Plat. *Phaedr.* p. 254 B: εἶδον τὴν ὄψιν ἀστράπτουσαν. For the *white* raiment, comp. 2 Macc. xi. 8; Acts i. 10. The sentinels were convulsed (ἐσείσθησαν, 3 Esdr. iv. 36) with error at the sight of the angel (αὐτοῦ), and became as powerless as though they had been dead. The circumstance of these latter being mentioned again at this point is in strict keeping with the connection of Matthew's narrative.

Ver. 5 f. Ἀποκριθείς] said in view of the terrifying effect

which he saw was being produced upon the women by what
was taking place.   Comp. on xi. 25. — μὴ φοβεῖσθε ὑμεῖς].
ὑμεῖς is neither to be understood as a vocative (o vos !), nor to
be referred to what follows (both of which Fritzsche has suggested) ; but, as the simplicity of the address and a due regard
to the sense require, is to be taken thus : *ye should not be
afraid,* ὑμεῖς being thus regarded as forming a contrast to the
sentinels, who are paralyzed with terror.   To say that no particular emphasis ever rests upon the personal pronoun (de
Wette) is to say what, as regards the whole of the New Testament, is simply not the case (instance also Mark xiii. 9 ;
Acts viii. 24). — οἶδα γὰρ, κ.τ.λ.] *Ground* of the reassuring
terms in which the angel addresses them ; he *knows the loving
purpose* for which they are come, *and what joyful news he
has to tell them !*
    Ver. 7. Προάγει] he is in the act of going before you to
Galilee ; ὅτι is recitative.   Bengel correctly observes : " Verba
discipulis dicenda se porrigunt usque ad *videbitis.*"   Accordingly ὑμᾶς and ὄψεσθε refer to the *disciples* (comp. xxvi. 32),
not to the *women* as well, who, in fact, *saw Jesus forth-
with;* and see ver. 10.   For the meeting itself, which is
here promised, see ver. 16 ff. — ἐκεῖ] therefore not previously
in Jerusalem or anywhere else in Judaea.   Between what is
here stated and the narratives of Luke and John there is a
manifest and irreconcilable difference.   In the *Stud. u. Krit.*
1869, p. 532 ff., Graf still tries in vain to make out a case in
favour of assuming, as matter of course, the expiry of the
festival period before the προάγει and ὄψ.   Observe, moreover,
the ὄψεσθε ; on no earlier occasion than that of their meeting
in Galilee were they to *be favoured with a sight of Him.* — εἶπον
ὑμῖν] *I have told you it,* in the sense of : *take this as my
intimation of the fact* (see on John vi. 36), thus conjoining
with the announcement a hint carefully to note how certainly
it will be verified by the result.   It is wrong, therefore, to
suppose that for εἶπον we should read εἶπεν, after Mark xvi. 7
(Maldonatus, Michaelis), in which case some assume an error
in translation (Bolten, Eichhorn, Buslav, *de ling. orig. ev. M.*
p. 67) ; others, an error on the part of the transcriber (Schol-

ten); and others, again, an erroneous use of Mark (Schnecken-burger, Holtzmann). The ἰδού, εἶπον ὑμῖν is here *peculiar* to Matthew.

Ver. 8. Μετὰ φόβου, ἐφ᾽ οἷς εἶδον παραδόξοις· μετὰ χαρᾶς δὲ, ἐφ᾽ οἷς ἤκουσαν εὐαγγελίοις, Euthymius Zigabenus.— μεγάλης] applying to *both* substantives. For similar in-stances of the mingling of *fear with joy* (Virg. *Aen.* i. 514, xi. 807, *al.*), consult Wetstein ; Köster in the *Stud. u. Krit.* 1862, p. 351.

Ver. 9. On seeing the strange and superhuman appearance presented by the risen Lord, the women are so filled with consternation (μὴ φοβεῖσθε, ver. 10) that they take hold of His feet in a suppliant attitude (ἐκράτ. αὐτοῦ τ. πόδας), and testify their submission and reverence by the act of προσκύνη-σις. Bengel says correctly : " Jesum *ante* passionem alii potius alieniores adorarunt quam *discipuli.*"

Ver. 10. Μὴ φοβεῖσθε· ὑπάγετε, ἀπαγγ.] Asyndeton, the matter being pressing, urgent. — τοῖς ἀδελφοῖς μου] He thus designates His *disciples* (comp. on John xx. 17 ; Justin, *c. Tr.* 106), not πρὸς τιμὴν αὐτῶν (Euthymius Zigabenus), for which there was no occasion, but in view of that conception of Him as a *superhuman being* which had so profoundly im-pressed the women prostrate at His feet.—ἵνα] does not state the purport of the order involved in ἀπαγγ. (de Wette ; there is nothing whatever of the nature of an order about ἀπαγ.), but the idea is : *take word to my brethren* (namely, about my resurrection, about your having seen me, about my having spoken to you, and what I said), *in order that* (as soon as they receive these tidings from you) *they* may proceed to Galilee, xxvi. 32. — κἀκεῖ με ὄψονται] is not to be regarded as dependent on ἵνα, but : *and there they shall see me.* This repetition of the directions about going to Galilee (ver. 7), to which latter our evangelist gives con-siderable prominence as the scene of the new reunion (ver. 16 ff.), cannot be characterized as *superfluous* (de Wette, Bruno Bauer), or even as *poor and meaningless* (Keim), betraying the hand of a later editor, but is intended to be *express and emphatic ;* comp. Steinmeyer. With the exception

of John xxi., the other canonical Gospels, in which, however,
we cannot include the spurious conclusion of Mark, make no
mention of any appearance of the risen Lord in Galilee;
according to John xx., Jesus remained at least eight days
in Jerusalem, as did also His disciples, to whom He there
manifested Himself on two occasions, though it would appear
from John xxi. that the third manifestation took place in
Galilee, while Luke, on the other hand (xxiv. 49; Acts i. 4,
xiii. 31), *excludes* Galilee altogether, just as Matthew excludes
Judaea.   To harmonize these divergent accounts is impossible
(Strauss, II. p. 558 ff.; Holtzmann, p. 500 f.; Keim);
and, with regard to the account of *Matthew* in particular,
it may be observed that it is so far from assuming the
manifestations to the disciples in Judaea as having previously
occurred (in opposition to Augustine, Olshausen, Krabbe,
Ebrard, Lange), that it clearly intends the meeting with the
eleven, ver. 16 ff., as the *first* appearance to those latter, and
as the one that had been promised by the angel, ver. 7, and by
Jesus Himself, ver. 10.   From those divergent accounts, however, it may be fairly inferred that the tradition regarding the
appearances of the risen Lord to His disciples assumed a
threefold shape: (1) *the purely Galilaean*, which is that adopted
by Matthew; (2) *the purely Judaean*, which is that of Luke,
and also of John with the supplementary ch. xxi. *left out;*
(3) *the combined form* in which the appearances both in
Galilee *and* Judaea are embraced, which is that of John
with the supplementary chapter in question *included.*
That Jesus appeared to the disciples *both* in Jerusalem
and in Galilee *as well* might be already deduced *as a*
legitimate historical inference from the fact of a distinct
Judaean and Galilaean tradition having been current; but
the matter is placed beyond a doubt by John, if, as we
are entitled to assume, the apostle is to be regarded as the
author of ch. xxi.   The next step, of course, is to regard it
as an *ascertained historical fact* that the appearances in Judaea
preceded those in Galilee; though, at the same time, it should
not be forgotten *that Matthew's account* is not merely vague
and concise (Bleek), but that it, in fact, *ignores the appearances*

in Judaea altogether,[1] entirely *excludes* them as being unsuited to the connection; comp. Schleiermacher, *L. J.* p. 465 f. Now, as this is inconceivable in the case of Matthew the *apostle,* we are bound to infer from our narrative that this is another of those passages in our Gospel which show traces of other than apostolic authorship. See Introd. § 2.

REMARK.—It is evident from 1 Cor. xv. 5 ff. that, even taking the narratives of all the evangelists together, we would have but an *imperfect* enumeration of the appearances of Jesus subsequent to His resurrection, Matthew's account being the most deficient of any. With regard to the appearances themselves, modern criticism, discarding the idea that the death was only apparent (see on xxvii. 50), has treated them partly as *subjective creations,* either of the *intellect* (Strauss, Scholten), in its efforts to reconcile the Messianic prophecies and the belief in the Messiah with the fact of His death, or of ecstatic *vision* (Baur, Strauss, 1864; Holsten, Ewald), and therefore as mere mental phenomena which came to be embodied in certain objective incidents. There are those again who, attributing the appearances in question to some *objective* influence *emanating from Christ Himself,* have felt constrained to regard them as *real manifestations* of His *person* in the *glorified form* (Schenkel) in which it emerged from out of *death* (not from the grave),—a view in which Weisse, Keim, Schweizer substantially concur, inasmuch as Keim, in particular, lays stress on the necessity of "such a telegram from heaven" after the extinction of Christ's earthly nature, though he considers the question as to whether our Lord also communicated the form of the vision directly or only indirectly, as of but secondary consequence. But all these attempts to treat what has been recorded as an actual fact as

---

[1] Rud. Hofmann (*de Berg Galiläa,* 1856), following certain early expositors, has attempted to explain the discrepancies between the various narratives by maintaining that ἡ Γαλιλαία, Matt. xxviii., is not the *country,* but a *mountain* of this name, namely, the northmost of the three peaks of the Mount of Olives. But nowhere in the New Testament do we find such a designation applied to any locality but the well-known *province* of that name; nor, if we interpret fairly the passages quoted by Hofmann from Tertullian (*Apol.* 21), Lactantius (iv. 19), and Chrysostom, are we able to find in them any allusion to a *mountain* called Galilee; and surely it is not to be presumed that anything of a trustworthy nature can be learnt as to the existence of such a mountain from the confusions of a certain corrupt part of the text in the *Evang. Nicod.* 14; see already, Thilo, *ad Cod. Apocr.* I. p. 620 f.

though it were based merely on mental phenomena are in
opposition in general to the *explicit and unhesitating view* of all
the evangelists and apostles as well as in particular to the uniform
reference to the *empty grave*, and no less uniform use of the
expression *third day*, all classical testimonies which can never be
silenced.   If, in addition to all this, it be borne in mind that the
apostles found in the resurrection of their Lord a living and un-
failing source of courage and hope, and of that cheerfulness with
which they bore suffering and death,—that the apostolic church
generally saw in it the foundation on which its own existence
was based,—that Paul, in particular, insists upon it as incon-
trovertible evidence for, and as an ἀπαρχή of the resurrection of
the body (1 Cor. xv. 23; Rom viii. 11), and as constituting an
essential factor in man's justification (Rom. iv. 25; Phil. iii. 10),
though he is fond of speaking of being buried and raised up
with Christ as descriptive of what is essential to the moral
standing of the Christian (Rom. vi. 4; Col. ii. 12), and can only
conceive of the glorified body of the Lord, to which those of
believers will one day be conformed (Phil. iii. 21), as no other
than that which came forth from the grave and was taken up to
heaven,—if, we say, this be borne in mind, not the shadow of
an exegetical pretext will be left for construing the resurrection
from the grave of one whose body was exempted from corruption (Acts ii. 31, x. 41) into something or other which might
be more appropriately described as a resurrection *from the cross*,
and which would therefore require us to suppose that all the
apostles and the whole church from the very beginning had
been the victims of a delusion.   See, in answer to Keim,
Schmidt in the *Jahrb. f. D. Theol.* 1872, p. 413 ff.   If this
view of the resurrection were adopted, then, in opposition once
more to New Testament authority, we should have to identify it
with the ascension (comp. on Luke xxiv. 51, Remark); while,
on the other hand, it would be necessary to give up the *Descensus Christi ad inferos* as a second error arising out of that
which has just been referred to.

Ver. 11. *Πορευομ. δὲ αὐτ.*] *but while they were going away*,
to convey the intelligence to the disciples, ver. 10.   While,
therefore, the women are still on their way, the soldiers in
question repair to the city and report to the high priests what
had happened.

Ver. 12 ff. *Συναχθέντες*] Change of subject.   Winer, p.
586 [E. T. 787]. — *συμβούλ. τε λαβόντες*] *after consulting*

together, as in xii. 14, xxii. 15, xxvii. 1, 7. The conjunctive
particle τε has the same force as in xxvii. 48, and occurs nowhere else in Matthew; found so much the more frequently
in Luke's writings, especially in the Acts. — ἀργύρια] as in
xxvi. 15, xxvii. 3, 5, 9. *Silver pieces*, a sufficient number of
shekels. — εἴπατε, κ.τ.λ.] an *infelix astutia* (Augustine), seeing
that they could not possibly know what had taken place while
they were sleeping. — Ver. 14. ἐπὶ τοῦ ἡγεμόνος] *coram
procuratore*. ἀκούειν is not to be understood, with the majority
of expositors, merely in the sense of: *to come to the ears of*,
which is inadmissible on account of ἐπί (for in that case
Matthew would have simply written : καὶ ἐὰν ἀκούσῃ τοῦτο ὁ
ἡγ., or used the passive with the *dative*), but in the *judicial*
sense (John vii. 51 ; Xen. *Cyrop.* i. 2. 14, and frequently): *if
this comes to be inquired into, if an investigation into this matter
should take place* before the procurator. Erasmus : " si res apud
illum judicem agatur." Comp. Vatablus and Bleek.—ἡμεῖς]
with a self-important emphasis. Comp. ὑμᾶς in the next clause.
— πείσομεν αὐτόν] *we will persuade him*, i.e. satisfy, *appease
him* (see on Gal. i. 10), in order, that is, that he may not
punish you; see what follows. — ἀμερίμνους] *free from
all concern* (1 Cor. vii. 32), and, in the present instance, in
the objective sense : *free from danger and all unpleasant consequences* (Herodian, ii. 4. 3). — Ver. 15. ὡς ἐδιδάχθ.] *as
they had been instructed*, Herod. iii. 134. — ὁ λόγος οὗτος]
not: " the whole narrative " (Paulus), but, as the context
requires (ver. 13), *this story of the alleged stealing of the body.*
The industrious circulation of this falsehood is also mentioned
by Justin, *c. Tr.* xvii. 108. For an abominable expansion
of it, as quoted from the *Toledoth Jeschu*, see Eisenmenger's
entdeckt. Judenth. I. p. 190 ff. For ἡ σήμερον ἡμέρα, see
Lobeck, *Paral.* p. 534.

Ver. 16. The eleven disciples, in accordance with the
directions given them, ver. 10, proceeded to Galilee, to the
mountain, etc. — οὗ ἐτάξατο, κ.τ.λ.] an additional particular
as to the locality in question, which the women received, ver.
10, and had subsequently communicated to the disciples.
The οὗ, *ubi*, is to be regarded as also including the preceding

whither (to go and abide there), Luke x. 1, xxii. 10, xxiv. 28;
Winer, p. 439 f. [E. T. 592]; Kühner, II. 1, p. 473.

Ver. 17. Ἰδόντες, κ.τ.λ.] According to the account now
before us, evidently the *first* occasion of meeting again since
the resurrection, and the *first* impression produced by it—
corresponding to the ὄψεσθε of vv. 7, 10. See, besides, on
ver. 10.—οἱ δὲ ἐδίστασαν] It was previously said *in a*
general way that the eleven fell prostrate before Him, though
all did *not* do so: some *doubted* whether He, whom they saw
before them, could really be Jesus. This particular is added
by means of οἱ δέ, which, however, is not preceded by a
corresponding οἱ μέν before προσεκύνησαν, because this latter
applied to the majority, whereas the doubters, who did not
prostrate themselves, were only the exception. Had Matthew's
words been: οἱ μὲν προσεκύνησαν, οἱ δὲ ἐδίστασαν, he would
thus have represented the eleven as divided into two co-
ordinate parts, into as nearly as possible two halves, and so
have stated something different from what was intended.
This is a case precisely similar to that of the οἱ δὲ ἐρράπισαν
of xxvi. 67, where, in like manner, the preceding ἐκολάφισαν
αὐτόν (without οἱ μέν) represents what was done by *the*
majority. "Quibus in locis primum *universa res* ponitur,
deinde partitio nascitur, quae ostendit, priora quoque verba
non de universa causa jam accipi posse," Klotz, *ad Devar.* p.
358. Comp. Xen. *Hell.* i. 2. 14: ᾤχοντο ἐς Δεκέλειαν, οἱ δ᾽
ἐς Μέγαρα; *Cyrop.* iv. 5. 46: ὁρᾶτε ἵππους, ὅσοι ἡμῖν πάρεισιν.
οἱ δὲ προσάγονται, and the passages in Pflugk, *ad Eur. Hec.*
1160; Kühner, II. 2, p. 808. According to Fritzsche, a
preceding οἱ μὲν οὐκ ἐδίστασαν should be understood. This,
however, is purely arbitrary, for the ἐδίστασαν *has* its appropriate correlative *already* in the preceding προσεκύνησαν.
Again, as matter of course, we must not think of predicating
the προσεκύνησαν of the *doubters* as well, which would be
psychologically absurd (only after his doubts were *overcome*
did Thomas exclaim: ὁ κυριός μου κ. ὁ θεός μου!). Fritzsche
(comp. Theophylact, Grotius, and Markland in *Eur. Suppl.*
p. 326) attempts to obviate this objection by understanding
ἐδίστασαν in a *pluperfect* sense (they *had doubted* before they

saw Jesus); an expedient, however, of the same arbitrary nature as before (comp. on John xviii. 24), and such as no reader of our passage (with προσεκύνησαν before him) would have suspected to be at all necessary. *Others*, in spite of the plain and explicit statements of Matthew, and in order to free the *eleven* from the imputation of doubt, have here turned to account the *five hundred brethren*, 1 Cor. xv. 6 (Calovius, Michaelis, Ebrard, Lange), or the *seventy disciples* (Kuinoel), and attributed the ἐδίστασαν to *certain of these!* Others, again, have resorted to *conjecture;* Beza, for example, thinks that for οἱ δέ we might read οὐδέ; Bornemann, in the *Stud. u. Krit.* 1843, p. 126 (comp. Schleusner), suggests: οἱ δὲ διέστασαν (some fell prostrate, the others *started back from each other* with astonishment). *The doubting itself* on the part of the disciples (comp. Luke xxiv. 31, 37, 41; John xx. 19, 26) is not to be explained by the supposition of an already *glorified state of the body* (following the Fathers, Olshausen, Glöckler, Krabbe, Kühn, *wie ging Chr. durch d. Grabes Thür?* 1838; comp. Kinkel's unscriptural idea of a repeated ascension to heaven, in the *Stud. u. Krit.* 1841, p. 597 ff.), for after His resurrection Christ still retained His material bodily organism, as the evangelists are at some pains to remind us (Luke xxiv. 39–43; John xx. 20, 27, xxi. 5; comp. also Acts i. 21 f., x. 41). At the same time, it is not enough to appeal to the fact that "nothing that was subject to death any longer adhered to the living One" (Hase), but, in accordance with the evangelic accounts of the appearing and sudden vanishing of the risen Lord, and of the whole relation in which He stood to His disciples and His disciples to Him, we must assume some *change* in the bodily organism and outward aspect of Jesus, a mysterious transformation of His whole person, an *intermediate phase of existence* between *the* bodily nature as formerly existing and the glorified state into which He passed at the moment of the ascension,—a phase of existence, however, of which it is impossible for us to form any distinct conception, for this is a case where analogy and experience alike fail us. His body did not retain, as did those of Jairus' daughter, the young man of Nain, and Lazarus, exactly the same essential nature as belonged to it before death, but still it was not as yet the σῶμα τῆς δόξης αὐτοῦ (Phil. iii. 21), though it was certainly immortal, a fact which of itself would necessarily involve the very essential change which came over it; comp. also Bleek.

Ver. 18.[1] Προσελθών] From feelings of modesty and reverence, the eleven had not ventured to go quite close to Him. — ἐδόθη] with all the emphasis of the conviction that He was triumphant at last: *was given to me*, etc., was practically given, that is, when the Father awoke me out of death. Thereby His state of humiliation came to an end, and the resurrection was the turning-point at which Christ entered into the heavenly glory, in which He is to reign as κύριος πάντων till the time of the final surrender of His sway into the hands of the Father (1 Cor. xv. 28). It is true, no doubt, that when first sent forth by God He was invested with the ἐξουσία over all things (xi. 27; John xiii. 3); but in His state of κένωσις it would, of necessity, come to be limited by the conditions of that human life into which He had descended. With His resurrection, however, this limitation was removed, and His ἐξουσία fully and absolutely restored, so that He once more came into complete possession of His premundane δόξα (John xvii. 5; Luke xxiv. 26; Phil. ii. 9 f.; Rom. xiv. 9; Eph. i. 20 ff., iv. 10; 1 Cor. xv. 25 ff.), the δόξα in which He had existed as the λόγος ἄσαρκος, and to which He was again exalted as the glorified Son of man. Comp. on John i. 14.— πᾶσα ἐξουσία] *all authority*, nothing being excepted either in heaven or earth which can be referred to the category of ἐξουσία. Some, unwarrantably interpreting in a rationalistic sense, have understood this to mean the "potestas animis hominum per doctrinam imperandi" (Kuinoel),—or, as Keim expresses it, the handing over to Him of all spirits to be His instruments in carrying out His purposes in the world,—or absolute power to make all necessary arrangements for the establishment of the Messianic theocracy (Paulus), or power over the whole *world of humanity* with a view to its redemption (Volkmar), and such like. What is really meant, however, is the

_____
[1] Comp. for ver. 18 ff., Theod. Schott in the *Luther. Zeitschr.* 1871, p. 1 ff.

munus regium of Christ, *free from all limitation*, without, however, compromising in any way the absolute supremacy of the Father; John xiv. 28 ; 1 Cor. xv. 27, xi. 3.

Ver. 19. The οὖν of the Received text (see the critical remarks) is a gloss *correctly* representing the connection of the thoughts. The fact stated in ver. 18 is itself the *reason* why *all nations* should be *brought under His government*, and made subject to His sway by means of the μαθητεύειν, etc. — μαθη-τεύσατε] *make them my* μαθηταί (John iv. 1) ; comp. xiii. 52 ; Acts xiv. 21. This *transitive* use of the verb is not met with in classical Greek. Observe how here every one who becomes a believer is conceived of as standing to Christ in the personal relation of a μαθητής, in accordance with which view the term came to be applied to *Christians* generally. — πάντα τὰ ἔθνη] *all nations without exception*, xxv. 32, xxiv. 14, xxvi. 13. With these words—and this is the *new* feature in the present instructions—the previous prohibi-tion, x. 5, was cancelled, and the apostolic mission declared to be a mission to the *whole world*. On this occasion Jesus makes no mention of any particular *condition* on which *Gentiles* were to be admitted into the church, says nothing about whether it was or was not necessary that they should in the first instance become Jewish proselytes (Acts xv. 1 ; Gal. ii. 1), though He certainly meant that it was not neces-sary ; and hence, because of this omission, the difficulty which the apostles had at first about directly and unconditionally admitting the Gentiles. If this latter circumstance had been borne in mind, it could hardly have been asserted, as it has been, that the special revelation from heaven, for the purpose of removing the scruples in question, Acts x., tells against the authenticity of the commission recorded in our passage (in answer to Credner, *Einleit.* I. p. 203 ; Strauss, Keim). — βαπτίζοντες, κ.τ.λ.] in which the μαθητεύειν is to be *con-summated*, not something that must be done *after* the μαθητεύ-σατε (Hofmann, *Schriftbew.* II. 2, p. 164 ; comp. also, on the other hand, Theod. Schott, p. 18), as though our passage ran thus, μαθητεύσαντες . . . βαπτίζετε. Besides, that the phrase βαπτίζοντες κ.τ.λ. did not require in every case the *performance of the ceremony by the apostles themselves,* was distinctly manifest to them in the discharge of their functions even from the first (Acts ii. 41). Comp. also 1 Cor. i. 17.—βαπτίζειν εἰς] means *to baptize with reference to.* The particular object to which the baptism has reference is to be gathered from the context. See on Rom. vi. 3, and thereon Fritzsche, I. p. 359 ; comp. also on 1 Cor. x. 2. Here, where the βαπτίζειν εἰς τὸ ὄνομα is regarded as that through which the μαθητεύειν is operated, and through which, accordingly, the introduction into spiritual fellowship with, and ethical dependence upon Christ is brought about, it must be understood as denoting that by baptism the believer passes into that new phase of life in which he accepts the *name of the Father* (of Christ) *and of the Son and of the Holy Spirit as the sum of his creed and confession.* τὸ ὄνομα, · because it is precisely the *name* of him who is confessed that expresses his whole specific relation considered by itself, and with reference to him who confesses, and accordingly the three names, " Father, Son, and Spirit," are to be understood as expressing the *sum-total* of the distinctive confession which the individual to be baptized is to accept as his both now and for all time coming.[1] Consequently the Corinthians were not baptized εἰς τὸ ὄνομα Παύλου (1 Cor. i. 13), because it was not the name " *Paul,*" but the name " *Christ,*" that was to constitute the sum of their creed and their confession. For a similar reason, when the Samaritans circumcised, they did so לשם הר גריים (see Schöttgen on the passage), because the

---

[1] Had Jesus used the words τὰ ὀνόματα instead of τὸ ὄνομα, then, however much He may have intended the names of three distinct persons to be understood, He would still have been liable to be misapprehended, for it might have been supposed that the plural was meant to refer to the *various* names of *each separate person.* The *singular* points to the *specific name assigned in the text to each of the three respectively,* so that εἰς τὸ ὄνομα is, of course, *to be understood* both before τοῦ υἱοῦ and τοῦ ἁγίου πνεύματος ; comp. Rev. xiv. 1 : τὸ ὄνομα αὐτοῦ καὶ τὸ ὄνομα τοῦ πατρὸς αὐτοῦ. We must beware of making any such *dogmatic* use of the singular as to employ it as an argument either *for* (Basilides, Jerome, Theophylact) or *against* (the Sabellians) the orthodox doctrine of the Trinity. We should be equally on our guard against the view of Gess, who holds that Christ abstained from using the words " *of God* the Father," etc., because he considers the designation God to belong to the Son and the Holy Spirit as well. Such a dogmatic idea was not at all likely to be present to His

name " Gerizim " represented the specific point in their distin-
tive creed and confession (their *shibboleth*). *The dedication of
the believer* to the Father, etc., is of course to be regarded as
practically taking place in the course of the βαπτίζειν εἰς τὸ
ὄνομα κ.τ.λ.; for though this is not directly *intimated* by the
words themselves (in opposition to Hofmann, *Schriftbew.* II. 2,
p. 163 ; Thomasius, *Chr. Pers. u. Werk*, III. 2, p. 12), it is implied in the *act* of baptism, and could have been expressed by
the simple use of εἰς (without τὸ ὄνομα), as in 1 Cor. x. 2 ;
Rom. vi. 3 ; Gal. iii. 27. Further, εἰς τὸ ὄνομα is not to be
taken as equivalent to εἰς τὸ ὀνομάζειν (Francke in the *Sächs.
Stud.* 1846, p. 11 ff.), as though the meaning of the baptism
consisted merely in calling God the *Father*, Christ the *Son*,
and the Spirit the *Holy Spirit*. Such a view certainly could
not apply in the last-mentioned case, for, like Father and Son,
τὸ πνεῦμα ἅγιον must be understood to be a specifically Christian designation of the Spirit. τὸ ὄνομα is rather intended
to indicate the *essential nature* of the Persons or Beings to
whom the baptism has reference, that nature being revealed
in the gospel, then expressed in the name of each Person
respectively, and finally made the subject of the Christian's confession and creed. Finally, in opposition to the
utterly erroneous view of Bindseil (in the *Stud. u. Krit.*
1832, p. 410 ff.), that βαπτίζειν εἰς τὸ ὄνομα means: to
lead to the adoption of the name through baptism, *i.e.* to
get the person who is to be baptized to call himself *after the*

mind upon an occasion of leave-taking like the present, any more than was the
thing itself on which the idea is supposed to be based, for He was never known
to claim the name υἱός either for Himself or for the Holy Spirit. Still the New
Testament, *i.e.* the Subordinatian, view of the Trinity as constituting the summary
of the Christian creed and confession *lies at the root* of this whole phraseology.—
Observe, further, that the baptismal formula : "*in nomine*," and : " *in the
name*," rests entirely on a mistranslation on the part of the Itala and Vulgate,
so that there is accordingly no ground for the idea, adopted from the older
expositors, that the person who baptizes acts *as Christ's representative* (Sengel-
mann in the *Zeitschr. f. Protestantism.* 1856, p. 341 ff.), neither is this view
countenanced by Acts x. 48. Tertullian (*de bapt.* 13) gives the correct rendering *in nomen*, though as early as the time of Cyprian (*Ep.* lxxiii. 5) *in nomine*
is met with. The practice of dipping *three times* dates very far back (being
vouched for even by Tertullian), but cannot be traced to the apostolic age.

particular name or names in question, see Fritzsche as above.
But as for the view of Weisse (*Evangelienfr.* p. 186 f.) and of
Volkmar, p. 629, as well, that Christ's commission to baptize is
entirely unhistorical, it is only of a piece with their denial of
the actual bodily resurrection of Jesus.   Ewald, too (*Gesch. d.
Apost. Zeit.* p. 180), is disposed to trace the origin of the
commission to the inner world of a later apostolic consciousness.—It is a mistake to speak of our passage as the *formula
of baptism ;*[1] for Jesus is not to be understood as merely
repeating the *words* that were to be employed on baptismal
occasions (and accordingly no trace of any such use of the
words is found in the apostolic age ; comp. on the contrary,
the simple expression: βαπτίζειν εἰς Χριστόν, Rom. vi. 3 ;
Gal. iii. 27 ; βαπτίζειν εἰς τὸ ὄνομα X., Acts viii. 16, and
ἐπὶ τῷ ὀνόμ. X., Acts ii. 38), but as indicating the *particular
aim and meaning* of the act of baptism.   See Reiche, *de
baptism. orig.*, etc., 1816, p. 141 ff.   The *formula* of baptism
(for it was so *styled* as early as the time of Tertullian, *de bapt.*
13), which in its strictly literal sense has no bearing whatever upon the essence of the sacrament (Höfling, I. p. 40 ff.),
was *constructed* out of the words of the text at a subsequent
period (see already Justin, *Ap.* i. 61), as was also the case, at
a still later period, with regard to the baptismal *confession* of

---

[1] It is no less erroneous to suppose that our passage represents the first *institution* of baptism.   For long before this the disciples had been baptizing *in
obedience to the instructions of Jesus,* as may be seen from John iv. 1 f., where
baptism by the disciples is spoken of as tantamount to baptism by Jesus Himself,
and where again there is as little reason to suppose the mere continuation of the
baptism of *John* to be meant as there is in the case of our present passage (John
iii. 5).   In the passage before us we have the same commission as that just
referred to, only with this difference, that it is now *extended* so as to apply to *all
nations.*   This at once disposes of the question as to whether baptism should
not occupy merely a *secondary* place as a sacrament (Laufs in the *Stud. u. Krit.*
1858, p. 215 ff.).   Comp. also, on the other hand, 1 Cor. x. 1-3, where there is
an unmistakeable reference to baptism and the Lord's Supper as the two great
and equally important sacraments of the Christian church.   Of these two, however, it is clearly not the Lord's Supper, but baptism, on which the greatest stress
is laid as forming the divine constituent factor in the work of redemption, and
that above all in the Epistles of Paul, in which the only instance of anything
like a full treatment of the subject of the Lord's Supper is that of First Corinthians, and even then it is of a somewhat incidental character.

the three articles (see Köllner, *Symbol. d. Luth. K.* p. 14 ff.). There is therefore nothing here to justify those who question the *genuineness* of our passage (Teller, *Exc.* 2, *ad Burnet de fide et officiis Christianorum*, 1786, p. 262 ; see, on the other hand, Beckhaus, *Acchth. d. s. g. Taufformel*, 1794), or those who of late have doubted its *originality*, at least in the form in which it has come down to us (Strauss, Bruno Bauer, de Wette, Wittichen in the *Jahrb. f. D. Theol.* 1862, p. 336 ; Hilgenfeld, Volkmar, Scholten, Keim), and that because, forsooth, they have professed to see in it a ὕστερον πρότερον. Exception has been taken, again, partly to the πάντα τὰ ἔθνη, though it is just in these words that we find the broader and more comprehensive spirit that characterized, as might be expected, our Lord's farewell commission, and partly to the "studied summary" (de Wette) of the New Testament doctrine of the Trinity. But surely if there was one time more than another when careful reflection was called for, it was now, when, in the course of this calm and solemn address, the risen Redeemer was endeavouring to seize the whole essence of the Christian faith in its three great leading elements as represented by the three substantially co-equal persons of the Godhead with a view to its being adopted as a constant σημεῖον to be used by the disciples when they went forth to proclaim the gospel (Chrysostom : πᾶσαν σύντομον διδασκαλίαν ἐγχείρησας τὴν διὰ τοῦ βαπτίσματος). The conjecture put forward by Keim, III. p. 286 f., that Jesus instituted baptism—though without any specific reference to all nations—*on the night of the last supper*, to serve the purpose of a second visible sign of His continued fellowship with the church after His departure from the world, is inadmissible, because there is no trace of this in the text, and because, had such a contemporaneous institution of the two sacraments taken place, it would have made so deep an impression that it could never have been forgotten, to say nothing of the impossibility of reconciling such a view with John iv. 1 f.

Ver. 20. Διδάσκοντες αὐτούς, κ.τ.λ.] without being conjoined by καί, therefore not co-ordinate with, but *subordinate* to the βαπτίζοντες, intimating that a certain *ethical teaching*

must necessarily accompany in every case the administration
of baptism : *while ye teach them to observe everything*, etc.
This moral instruction must not be omitted[1] when you
baptize, but it must be regarded as an essential part of the
ordinance. That being the case, *infant* baptism cannot possibly have been contemplated in βαπτίζ., nor, of course, in
πάντα τ. ἔθνη either. — καὶ ἰδοὺ, κ.τ.λ.] Encouragement to
execute the commission entrusted to them, ver. 19. — ἐγώ]
with strong emphasis : *I* who am invested with that high
ἐξουσία to which I have just referred. — μεθ' ὑμῶν εἰμι]
namely, through the working of that power which has been
committed to me, ver. 18, and with which I will continue to protect, support, strengthen you, etc. Comp. Acts
xviii. 10 ; 2 Cor. xii. 9, 10. The ὑμεῖς are the *disciples* to
whom the Lord is speaking, not the *church ;* the *present* tense
(not ἔσομαι) points to the fact of His having now entered, and
that permanently, into His estate of exaltation. The promised
help itself, however, is that vouchsafed by the glorified
Redeemer in order to the carrying out of His own work (Phil.
iii. 21, iv. 13 ; Col. i. 29 ; 2 Cor. xii. 9), imparted through
the medium of the Spirit (John xiv.–xvi.), which is regarded
as the Spirit of Christ (see on Rom. viii. 9), and sometimes
manifesting itself also in signs and wonders (Mark xvi. 20 ;
Rom. xv. 19; 2 Cor. xii. 12; Heb. ii. 14), in visions and revela-
tions (2 Cor. xii. 1; Acts xxii. 17). But in connection with this
matter (comp. on xviii. 20) we must discard entirely the unscrip-

---

[1] Οὐκ ἀρκεῖ γὰρ τὸ βάπτισμα καὶ τὰ δόγματα πρὸς σωτηρίαν, εἰ μὴ καὶ πολιτεία
προσείη, Euthymius Zigabenus, who thus admirably points out that what is meant
by διδάσκοντες, κ.τ.λ., is not the teaching of the gospel with a view to conversion.
The ἀκοὴ πίστεως (Gal. iii. 2) and the πίστις ἐξ ἀκοῆς (Rom. x. 17) are understood,
as a matter of course, to have preceded the baptism. Comp. Theodor Schott,
who, however, without being justified by anything in the text, is disposed to
restrict the ὅσα ἐνετειλάμ. ὑμῖν, on the one hand, to the instructions contained in
the farewell addresses (from the night before the crucifixion on to the ascension),
and τηρεῖν, on the other, to a faithful observance on the part of the convert of
what he already knew. Comp., on the contrary, xix. 17 ; John xiv. 15, 21,
xv. 10 ; 1 Tim. vi. 14 ; 1 John ii. 3 f., iii. 22 f., v. 2 f.; Rev. xii. 17, xiv. 12 ;
Ecclus. xxix. 1, in all which passages τηρεῖν τὰς ἐντολάς means observe, *i.e.* to *obey*,
the commandments. Admirable, however, is the comment of Bengel : "Ut
baptizatis convenit, *fidei virtute.*"

tural idea of a substantial *ubiquity* (in opposition to Luther, Calovius, Philippi). Beza well observes : " Ut qui *corpore* est absens, *virtute* tamen sit totus praesentissimus." — πάσας τ. ἡμέρ.] *all the days* that were still to elapse ἕως τ. συντελ. τοῦ αἰῶνος, i.e. *until the close of the current age* (see on xxiv. 3), which would be coincident with the second advent, and after the gospel had been proclaimed throughout the whole world (xxiv. 14) ; " *continua* praesentia," Bengel.

REMARK 1.—According to John xxi. 14, the Lord's appearance at the sea of Tiberias, John xxi., which Matthew not only omits, but which he does not seem to have been aware of (see on ver. 10), must *have preceded* that referred to in our passage.

REMARK 2.—Matthew makes no mention of the return of Jesus and His disciples to Judaea, or of the ascension from the Mount of Olives ; he follows a tradition in which those two facts had not yet found a place, just as they appear to have been likewise omitted in the lost conclusion of Mark ; then it so happened that the apostolic λόγια terminated with our Lord's parting address, ver. 19 f. We must beware of imputing to the evangelist any subjective motive for making no mention of any other appearance but that which took place on the mountain in Galilee ; for had he omitted and recorded events in this arbitrary fashion, and merely as he thought fit, and that, too, when dealing with the sublimest and most marvellous portion of the gospel narrative, he would have been acting a most unjustifiable part, and only ruining his own credit for historical fidelity. By the apostles the *ascension*, the actual bodily mounting up into heaven, was regarded as a fact about which there could not be any possible doubt, and without which they would have felt the second advent to be simply inconceivable (Phil. ii. 9, iii. 20 ; Eph. iv. 10 ; 1 Pet. iii. 22 ; John xx. 17), and accordingly it is presupposed in the concluding words of our Gospel ; but the embodying of it in an outward incident, supposed to have occurred in presence of the apostles, is to be attributed to a tradition which Luke, it is true, has adopted (as regards the author of the appendix to Mark, see on Mark xvi. 19 f.), but which has been rejected by our evangelist and John, notwithstanding that in any case this latter would have been an eyewitness. But yet *the fact itself* that the Lord, shortly after His resurrection, ascended into heaven, and that not merely in spirit (which, and that in entire opposition to Scripture, would either exclude the *resurrection* of the actual body, or presuppose a second *death*), but in the body as perfectly transformed and glorified at the moment of the ascension, is one of the truths of which we are also fully convinced, confirmed as it is by the whole New Testament, and furnishing, as it does, an indispensable basis for anything like certainty in regard to Christian eschatology. On the ascension, see Luke xxiv. 51, Rem.

Lightning Source UK Ltd.
Milton Keynes UK
UKHW010642291222
414571UK00004B/290